D1370456

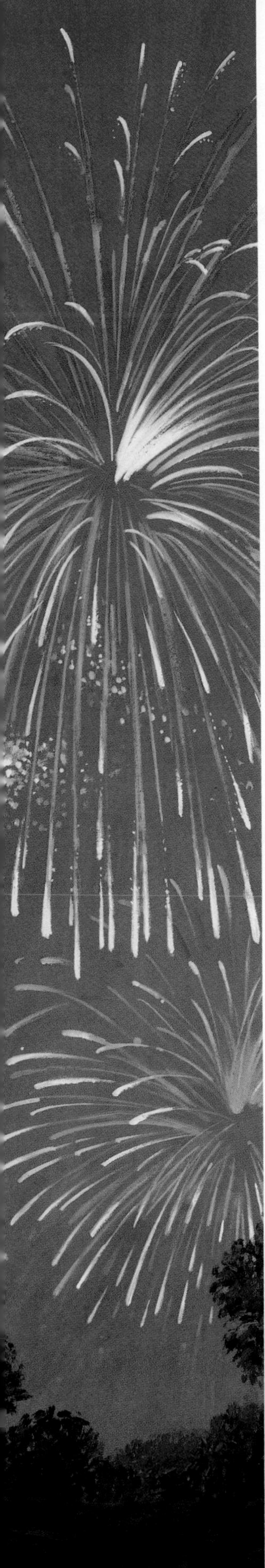

HBJ TREASURY OF LITERATURE

LIGHT UP THE SKY

SENIOR AUTHORS
ROGER C. FARR
DOROTHY S. STRICKLAND

AUTHORS
RICHARD F. ABRAHAMSON
ELLEN BOOTH CHURCH
BARBARA BOWEN COULTER
MARGARET A. GALLEGO
JUDITH L. IRVIN
KAREN KUTIPER
JUNKO YOKOTA LEWIS
DONNA M. OGLE
TIMOTHY SHANAHAN
PATRICIA SMITH

SENIOR CONSULTANTS
BERNICE E. CULLINAN
W. DORSEY HAMMOND
ASA G. HILLIARD III

CONSULTANTS
ALONZO A. CRIM
ROLANDO R. HINOJOSA-SMITH
LEE BENNETT HOPKINS
ROBERT J. STERNBERG

HARCOURT BRACE & COMPANY
Orlando Atlanta Austin Boston San Francisco Chicago Dallas New York
Toronto London

Printed in the United States of America

ISBN 0-15-300425-8

3 4 5 6 7 8 9 10 048 96 95 94 93

Acknowledgments continue on pages 590–591, which constitute an extension of this copyright page.

Acknowledgments

For permission to reprint copyrighted material, grateful acknowledgment is made to the following sources:

Alurista: "address" from *Floricanto en Aztlán* by Alurista. Copyright © 1971 by Aztlán Publications, UCLA.

Andrews & McMeel: Cover illustration by Michele Montez from *50 Simple Things Kids Can Do to Save the Earth* by The Earth Works Group. Illustration copyright © 1990 by John Javna.

Atheneum Publishers, an imprint of Macmillan Publishing Company: Cover illustration by Lloyd Bloom from *A Man Named Thoreau* by Robert Burleigh. Illustration copyright © 1985 by Lloyd Bloom. From pp. 114-123 in *Beetles, Lightly Toasted* (Retitled: "Who Won the Contest") by Phyllis Reynolds Naylor. Text copyright © 1987 by Phyllis Reynolds Naylor.

Avon Books: Cover illustration from *S. O. R. Losers* by Avi. Copyright © 1984 by Avi Wortis.

Bantam Books, a division of Bantam Doubleday Dell Publishing Group, Inc.: Cover illustration by Richard Williams from *Encyclopedia Brown and the Case of the Treasure Hunt* by Donald J. Sobol. Illustration copyright © 1989 by Richard Williams.

Bradbury Press, an Affiliate of Macmillan, Inc.: From *Hatchet* (Retitled: "Is There Anybody Listening?") by Gary Paulsen. Text copyright © 1985 by Gary Paulsen. From pp. 130-139 in *Mariah Keeps Cool* (Retitled: "In Rare Form") by Mildred Pitts Walter, cover illustration by Pat Cummings. Text copyright © 1990 by Mildred Pitts Walter; cover illustration copyright © 1990 by Pat Cummings.

Brandt & Brandt Literary Agents, Inc.: "Johnny Appleseed" from *A Book of Americans* by Rosemary and Stephen Vincent Benét. Text copyright 1933 by Rosemary and Stephen Vincent Benét; copyright renewed © 1961 by Rosemary Carr Benét.

Carolrhoda Books, Inc., Minneapolis, MN: Cover photograph from *Space Challenger: The Story of Guion Bluford* by Jim Haskins and Kathleen Benson. Cover illustration from *Song of the Chirimia* by Jane Anne Volkmer. Copyright © 1990 by Carolrhoda Books, Inc.

Cobblehill Books, an affiliate of Dutton Children's Books, a division of Penguin Books USA Inc.: Cover illustration by Elton C. Fax from *Take a Walk in Their Shoes* by Glennette Tilley Turner. Illustration copyright © 1989 by Elton C. Fax. Cover photograph from *Sea Otter Rescue* by Roland Smith. Copyright © 1990 by Roland Smith.

Delacorte Press: Cover illustration by Andrew Glass from *Rewind to Yesterday* by Susan Beth Pfeffer. Illustration copyright © 1988 by Andrew Glass. Cover illustration by Richard Lauter from *The War with Grandpa* by Robert Kimmel Smith. Illustration copyright © 1984 by Richard Lauter.

Dell Books, a division of Bantam Doubleday Dell Publishing Group, Inc.: From *Tornado! Poems* by Arnold Adoff, illustrated by Ronald Himler. Text copyright © 1976, 1977 by Arnold Adoff; illustrations copyright © 1977 by Ronald Himler. Cover illustration from *Fat Men From Space* by Daniel Manus Pinkwater. Copyright © 1977 by Manus Pinkwater.

The Dille Family Trust: "Tiger Men of Mars" Buck Rogers® cartoon from *The Collected Works of Buck Rogers in the 25th Century.* © 1929-1967, 1969, 1993 by The Dille Family Trust. Color added to original illustrations with permission.

Dover Publications, Inc.: Text and illustrations from *The American Revolution: A Picture Sourcebook* (Retitled: "A Look Back") by John Grafton. Copyright © 1975 by Dover Publications, Inc.

Farrar, Straus & Giroux, Inc.: Adapted from *The Green Book* (Retitled: "The Light of a New Sun") by Jill Paton Walsh, cover illustration by Peter Catalanotto. Text copyright © 1982 by Jill Paton Walsh; cover illustration copyright © 1986 by Peter Catalanotto. "seashell," "robins," "starfish," and "heron" from *Small Poems Again* by Valerie Worth, illustrated by Natalie Babbitt. Text copyright © 1975, 1986 by Valerie Worth; illustrations copyright © 1986 by Natalie Babbitt.

Greenwillow Books, a division of William Morrow & Company, Inc.: "The Sticks of Truth," "Fishing," and "The Cleverest Son" from *Stories to Solve: Folktales from Around the World* (Retitled: "Three Puzzlers") by George Shannon, illustrated by Peter Sis. Text copyright © 1985 by George W. B. Shannon; illustrations copyright © 1985 by Peter Sis.

Harcourt Brace Jovanovich, Inc.: From *In for Winter, Out for Spring* by Arnold Adoff, illustrated by Jerry Pinkney. Text copyright © 1991 by Arnold Adoff; illustrations copyright © 1991 by Jerry Pinkney. From *Lady for the Defense: A Biography of Belva Lockwood* (Retitled: "Teacher for the Day") by Mary Virginia Fox. Text copyright © 1975 by Mary Virginia Fox. Cover illustration by Paul Bacon from *Teammates* by Peter Golenbock. Illustration copyright © 1990 by Paul Bacon. From *The Bells of Christmas* (Retitled: "A Great Caravan on the National Road") by Virginia Hamilton, illustrated by Lambert Davis. Text copyright © 1989 by Virginia Hamilton; illustrations copyright © 1989 by Lambert Davis. From *The Riddle of Penncroft Farm* (Retitled: "The Battle of Brandywine") by Dorothea Jensen. Text copyright © 1989 by Dorothea G. Jensen. "Buffalo Dusk" from *Smoke and Steel* by Carl Sandburg. Text copyright 1920 by Harcourt Brace Jovanovich, Inc., renewed 1948 by Carl Sandburg. "See the Trees" from *The Complete Poems of Carl Sandburg* by Carl Sandburg. Text copyright 1950 by Carl Sandburg, renewed 1978 by Margaret Sandburg, Helga Sandburg Crile, and Janet Sandburg. "La Bamba" from *Baseball in April and Other Stories* by Gary Soto. Text copyright © 1990 by Gary Soto. Originally published in *Fiction Network.* Illustrations from *Many Moons* by James Thurber, illustrated by Marc Simont. Illustrations copyright © 1990 by Marc Simont. Cover illustration by Louis Slobodkin from *Many Moons* by James Thurber. Copyright 1943 by James Thurber, renewed 1971 by Helen Thurber. From *Pride of Puerto Rico: The Life of Roberto*

continued on pages 590 and 591

Dear Reader,

Five people sit in a space shuttle that will, in seconds, light up the sky. In the same way, the brilliance and warmth of the variety of people and cultures in these stories will light up your reading experiences. The literature in this anthology spotlights the richness of our cultural heritage and illuminates new paths for the future. Come in. See for yourself.

Come read brightly colored descriptions of the hottest day on record in the Sonoran Desert—a day that Bird Wing will survive only if she relies on her knowledge of nature. Be dazzled by a young baseball player, Roberto Clemente, who is determined to be the best in Barrio San Antón. Learn about brilliant African astronomers of ancient Egypt who charted the heavens. Blaze into the skies with Sally Ride and a space shuttle crew. In this literature, each of these people lights up the world like the fireflies described by Paul Fleischman:

> Fine artists in flight
> bright brush strokes
> Signing the June nights
> as if they were paintings

Come join us as we travel around the block and around the world. As you visit these exciting places with us, keep your eyes open for people with experiences and feelings just like your own. Keep your mind open as well, and watch the world through their eyes for just a moment. Let their experiences shed some light on your life and on your world. Join us now as we prepare to "light up the sky."

Sincerely,
The Authors

CONTENTS

UNIT ONE/CHALLENGES 16

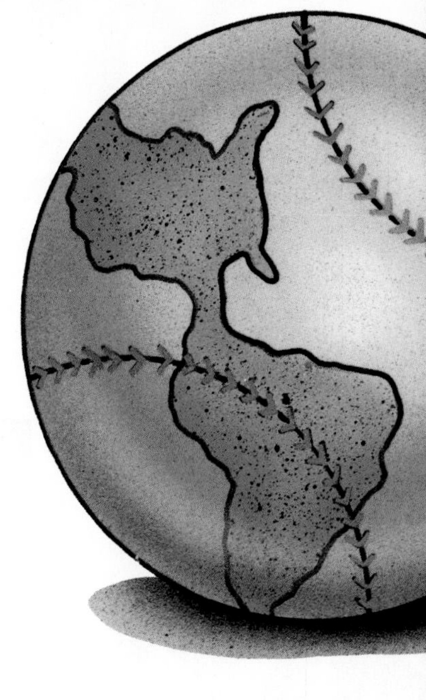

UNIT TWO/TRIALS 108

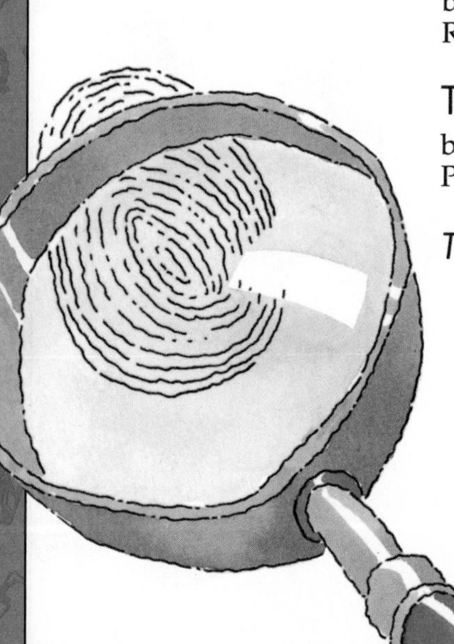

Washington
INN

UNIT
YESTERYEAR
THREE

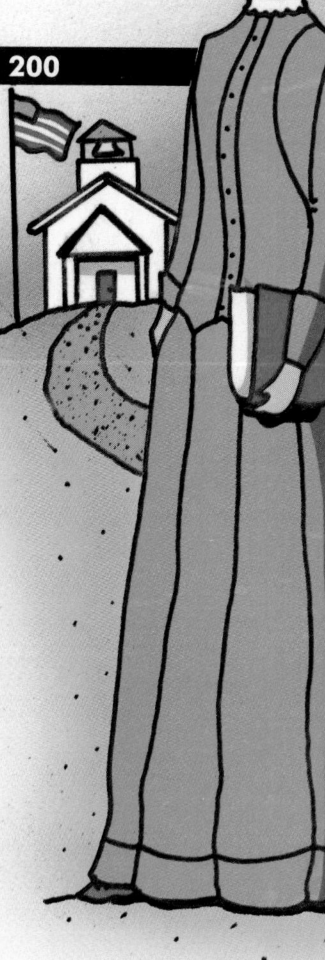

UNIT
SHENANIGANS
FOUR

UNIT
LIFELINES
FIVE

UNIT SIX/FLIGHTS 474

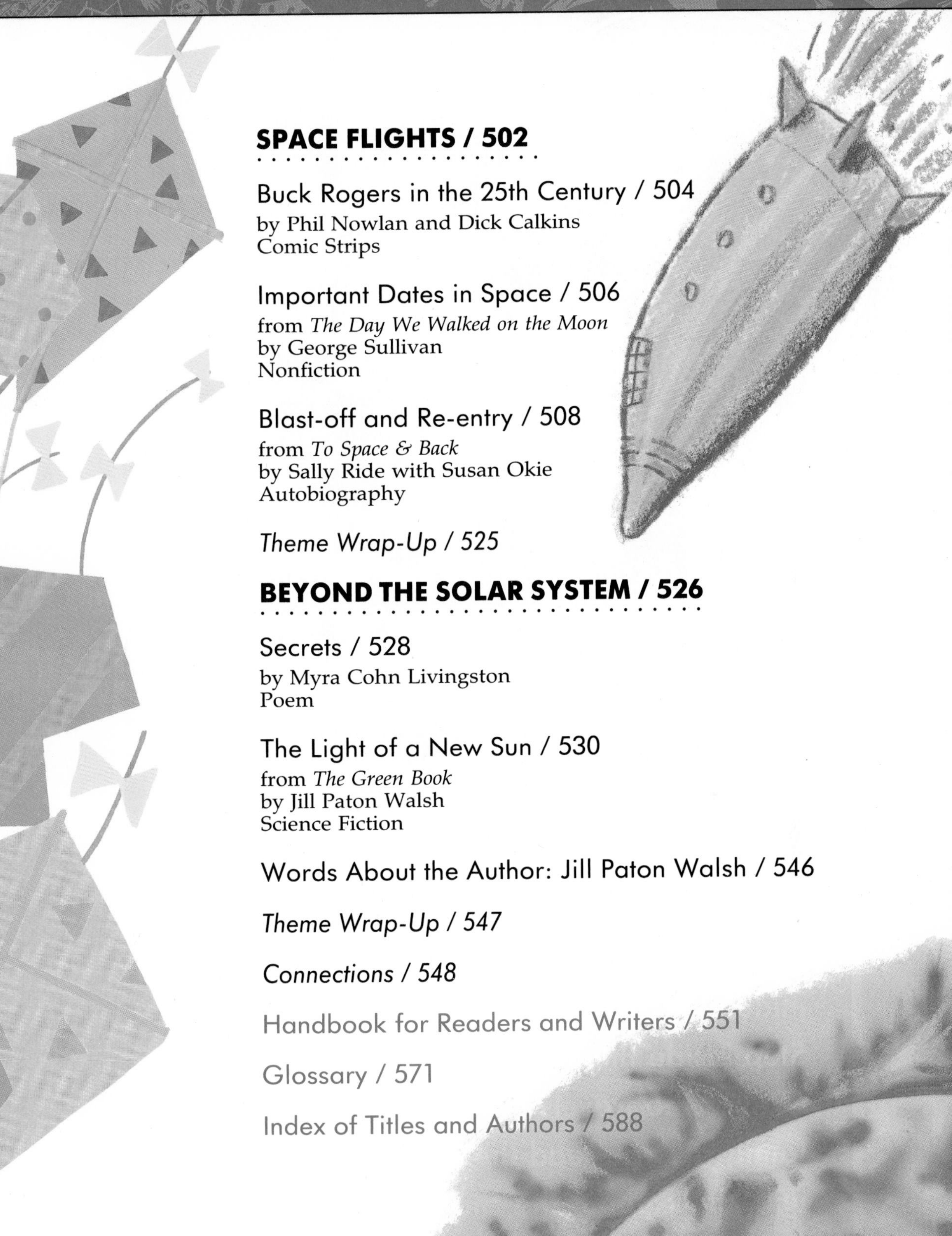

UNIT ONE CHALLENGES

How would you feel if you moved to a country where you didn't understand the language? What do you think it would be like to be in Spain, Mexico, or the Philippines and to play an unfamiliar sport such as jai alai for the very first time? These are the kinds of challenges that face some of the characters in this unit. Read about a young girl from China who finds herself in the middle of a strange game called *stickball.* Step inside the shoes of a woman from Maine who travels to Kansas to join a new family. As you read the selections in this unit, think about the challenges you face from day to day.

THEMES

BOOKSHELF

HAVE A HAPPY . . .

BY MILDRED PITTS WALTER

Chris is prepared for a holiday season with few presents or good times. Once he gets involved in the African American celebration of Kwanzaa, however, the season and Chris's life start to change.

HBJ LIBRARY BOOK

THE FACTS AND FICTIONS OF MINNA PRATT

BY PATRICIA MACLACHLAN

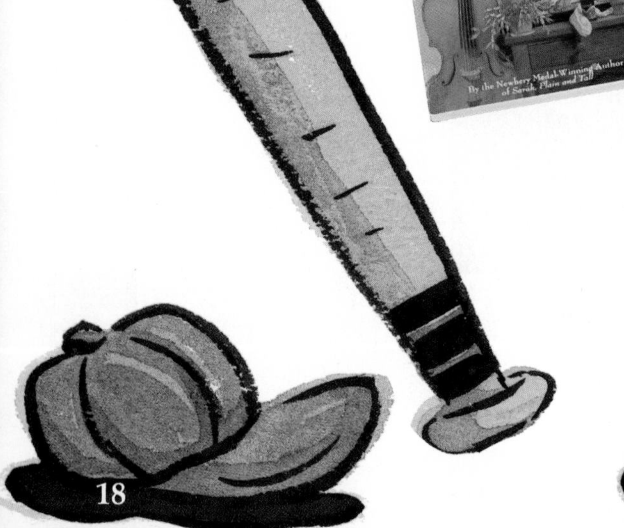

As she plays her many roles in life—the daughter, the sister, the friend, the musician—Minna Pratt struggles to sort out the facts from the fictions. ALA NOTABLE BOOK

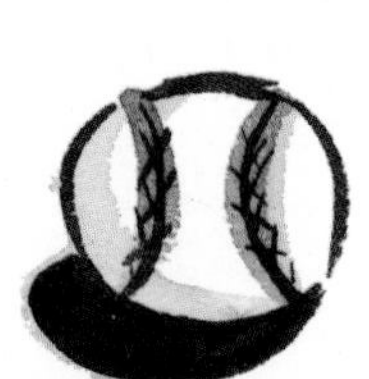

THE SECRET LANGUAGE OF THE SB

BY ELIZABETH SCARBORO

Adam's life is turned upside-down when his parents take in Susan, a foster child from Taiwan who doesn't even speak his language.

THE WAR WITH GRANDPA

BY ROBERT KIMMEL SMITH

When Peter is forced to give up his room to his grandfather, he decides to declare war. It is a decision that Peter soon comes to regret.

DO BANANAS CHEW GUM?

BY JAMIE GILSON

Sam Mott is great with numbers and has an amazing memory for facts. So why can't he spell even the simplest word?

DUE

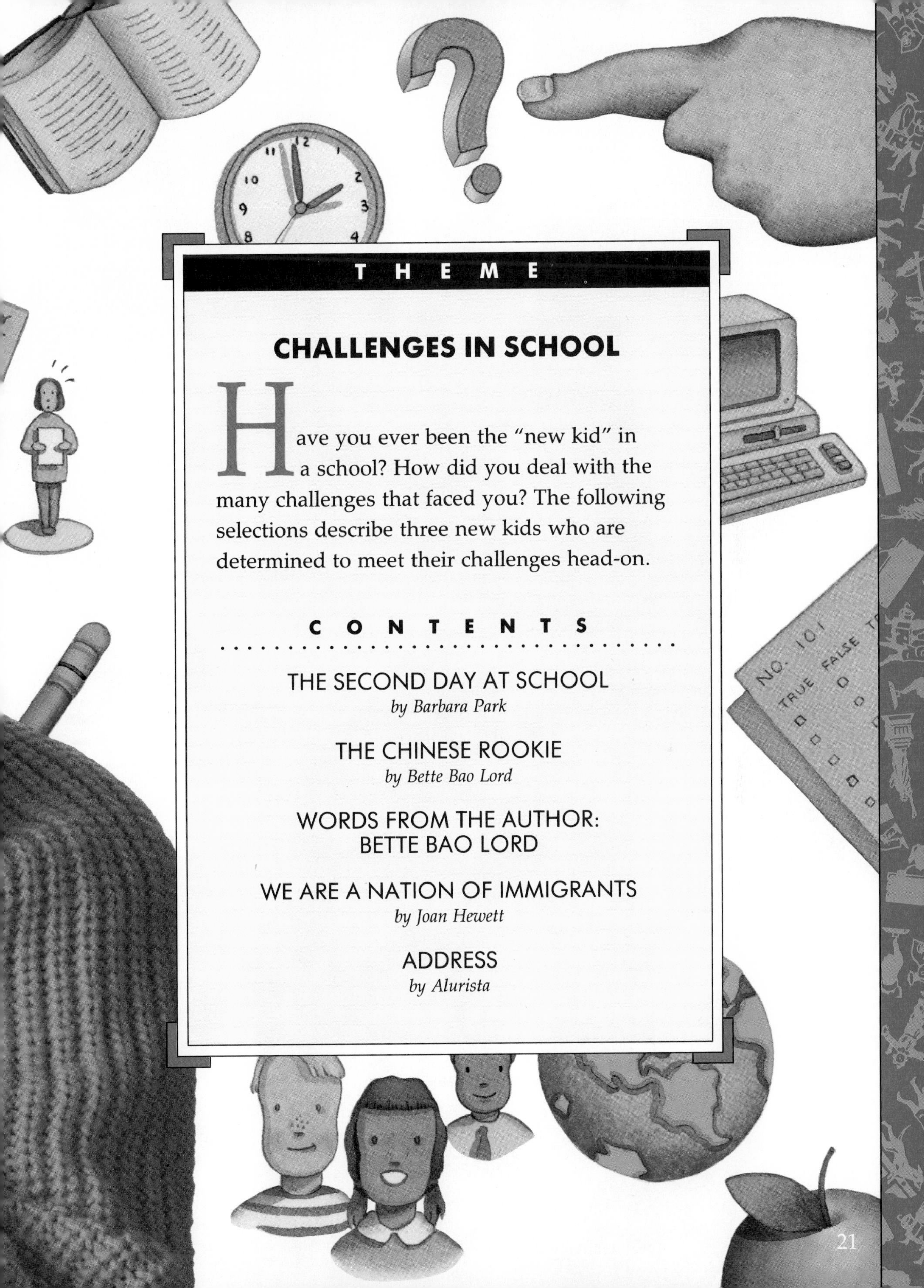

THEME

CHALLENGES IN SCHOOL

Have you ever been the "new kid" in a school? How did you deal with the many challenges that faced you? The following selections describe three new kids who are determined to meet their challenges head-on.

CONTENTS

Children's Choice
SLJ Best Books
of the Year

The Second Day at School

from *The Kid in the Red Jacket*

by Barbara Park

illustrated by Robert Chronister

When Howard's parents decide to move to Rosemont, Massachusetts, Howard is reluctant to go. He doesn't want to be a new kid, on a new block, in a new school.

As the school year begins, Howard is anxious to make friends. Unfortunately, the only person who befriends him is Molly Vera Thompson, his pesky six-year-old neighbor.

On my second day at school, believe it or not, I walked there with Molly Vera Thompson.

I was about halfway down the street when I first heard her.

"Hey! Hey, you! Howard Jeeper! Wait up! It's Molly Vera Thompson!"

I knew this was going to happen. I just knew it. But even though I had begged and begged for someone to drive me, both Mom and Dad had refused.

"One reason we bought this house was so that you could walk," my father informed me. "The exercise will be good for you."

"Hey, I said! Hold it!" she shouted again.

Two girls walking on the other side of the street started to laugh.

What was I supposed to do? If I didn't stop, she'd just keep shouting her head off. And if I ran, she'd run after me. Finally, I bent down, pretended to tie my shoe, and waited for her to catch up. The way I figured it, walking to school with a first-grader is bad enough, but being chased by one to school is even worse.

"That was close!" she yelled, running up behind me. "For a minute there I didn't think you heard me or something!"

Why was she still shouting? I was standing right next to her.

"Shhh!" I ordered. "Not so loud."

Molly's voice got quieter as she looked around us.

"Why? Is someone listening?"

"Only the whole world."

Molly just shrugged her shoulders and fell into step as I started walking again. We had only gone a couple of yards when she wrinkled up her nose and started to giggle.

"This is fun, isn't it, Howard Jeeper?"

I started walking a little faster.

"Hey! How's the weather up there?" she called, looking up at me. Then she started laughing like it was the funniest thing anyone had ever said.

I didn't answer. What was I supposed to say? Cloudy, with a chance of rain?

"Hey!" she persisted. "What's wrong? Cat got your tongue this morning?" Her legs hurried faster and faster, trying to keep up with me. "That's what my nonny says to me sometimes. 'Cat got your tongue, young lady?' she'll say. It means that you're being quiet."

"Yeah, right," I responded. I wasn't paying attention, of course. All I wanted to do was get to school before anyone saw the two of us together.

"Hey! Why are we walking so fast? Are we in a hurry?"

"Nope," I answered simply. "I always walk this fast. That's why you probably shouldn't walk with me. It's probably not good for a little kid like you."

"No. It's okay," she replied, huffing and puffing beside me. "I like to walk fast. It kind of bobs you up and down, doesn't it? See how fast my legs are going?"

Suddenly I started to run. I just didn't want to be with her anymore, that's all. I knew she couldn't catch me. And since I was getting closer to the playground, I couldn't risk the embarrassment of what she might do when we got there.

This time Molly didn't even try to keep up. As soon as I started to sprint, she stopped to watch me go.

I didn't feel guilty, either. Maybe I should have, but I didn't. Only a few more yards and I would be across the street, heading toward the gate of the playground. Alone. I was just about ready to breathe a sigh of relief when I heard it.

Still on the sidewalk where I left her, Molly had cupped her hands around her mouth like a megaphone and was shouting in the loudest voice I ever heard: *"Hey, Howard Jeeper! Why're you running? Do you have to go to the potty?"*

I wanted to die. I didn't stop running until I got inside the building. I know the whole playground must have heard. I tried not to look at anyone's face as I ran, but I could hear people laughing, so I'm sure they heard. They probably even heard on playgrounds in Russia.

The bell hadn't rung yet when I got to my classroom, but there were already three kids sitting down. One of them was the girl who sits in front of me. She didn't say hi or anything, but as it turned out, she was the first one in my class to talk to me. After I sat down, she turned around and asked if I would mind getting my big feet off the back of her chair.

"They're not big," I answered.

It wasn't much of a conversation, but when you're desperate, you appreciate almost anything.

At lunch, I sat by myself again. Only this time I picked a seat next to the wall so I could sort of blend in with the bricks.

As I started to eat I realized that a lot of the guys in my class were sitting at the next table. And since I was blending in with the wall pretty good, I could watch them without being too obvious. The guy I watched the most was this kid named Pete. I guess I was sort of scouting him out to see what kind of friend he'd make. Scouting is what they do in professional sports. It's a sporty word for spying.

I thought Pete might be someone I could like. I had noticed him on the soccer field. He was pretty athletic, you could tell that. And he wasn't a ball hog. Pete was the kid who had passed me the ball right before I took my big shot.

The other kid that I couldn't help noticing was this guy named Ollie. You could tell that he was the wise-guy type. He was real loud, and he talked a lot, and practically everything that came out of his mouth was a joke. He seemed like the kind of kid that grownups can't stand but kids sort of admire. The thing is, to be a wise guy in class takes guts. Kids admire guts. Adults don't. It's that simple.

When Ollie sat down, he took one look inside his lunch bag and held his nose. Then, without saying a word, he stood up and threw the whole thing into the garbage can. Back at the table, someone asked him what his mother had packed.

Ollie was still holding his nose. "Something dead and a cookie."

It really cracked me up. Something dead and a cookie. I was sitting all by myself, but I laughed out loud.

After that some kid threw Ollie an orange to eat. Instead of peeling it, he put the whole thing right into his mouth. It must have hurt his mouth to stretch it that far, but that's the great thing about wise guys. When it comes to acting stupid, they know no limit.

Anyway, when Ollie was standing there with that orange in his mouth, even Pete cracked up. You could tell by the expression on his face that he thought Ollie was acting like an idiot, but he still thought it was funny. Even quiet guys like Pete enjoy a good idiot once in a while.

It might sound dumb, but after lunch I felt like I knew the guys in my class a little better. I guess that's why at recess I hung around the group that was getting ready to play soccer. I was sure somebody would pick me. Maybe they'd pick me last, but I'd get picked. It's sort of this unwritten rule every kid knows. If you're standing there to play, somebody's got to pick you, even if you stink.

Just like the day before, Pete and this kid Joe were the captains. Pete picked me before Joe did. I didn't get chosen first or anything; but I wasn't last, either. A kid with his ankle in a cast was last. Still, it felt good when Pete chose me. All of a sudden he just looked over at me and said, "I'll take the kid in the red jacket."

It's funny. I used to think that being called something like that would really bother me. But the weird thing was, being called the kid in the red jacket hardly bothered me at all. Let's face it, after a couple of days of not being called anything, almost any name sounds good.

My father gave me some advice. He's tried this kind of thing before, but it's never worked out too well. The trouble is, most of the time his advice is about stuff he doesn't know how to do. Like during basketball season, he'll tell me how to shoot a lay-up. Then he'll shoot a lay-up and miss. It's hard to take advice like that.

"Horn in," he said one night at dinner. I was explaining how much I hated to eat lunch alone, and he looked right up from his pork chop and said, "Horn in."

"Er, horn in?" I repeated, confused. I guess it must be one of those old-time expressions they don't use much anymore.

"Sure. Be a little pushy. Stand up for yourself," he went on. "You can't wait for the whole world to beat a path to your door."

"Beat a path to my door?" I asked again. Another old-time expression, I think.

"That means you can't wait for everyone else to come to you, son," he explained. "Sometimes you've just got to take the bull by the horns."

"Oh geez. Not more horns," I groaned.

"Bull by the horns," repeated Dad. "Haven't you ever heard that before? It means you've got to get right in there and take charge. If you don't want to eat alone, then sit right down at the lunch table with the rest of them. Just walk up there tomorrow, put your lunch on the table, and say, 'Mind if I join you, fellas?' That's all there is to it."

I didn't say anything, but kids just don't go around talking like that. If a kid came up to a bunch of guys eating lunch and said, "Mind if I join you, fellas?" the whole table would fall on the floor laughing.

Still, I knew what Dad was getting at. I think it's something all new kids learn sooner or later. Even if you're the shy type, you have to get a little bold if you want to make any friends. You have to say hi and talk to people, even if it makes you nervous. Sometimes you even have to sit down at a lunch table without being invited. You don't have to say, "Mind if I join you, fellas?" though. I'm almost positive of that.

I have to admit that the "horning in" part worked out pretty well. The next day at lunch I took a deep breath, sat down at the table with the other guys, and started eating. That was that. No one seemed to mind, really. They hardly even stared.

After that it got easier. Once kids have seen you at their table, it's not as hard to accept you the next time. Then pretty soon they figure that you must belong, or you wouldn't be sitting there every day.

I'm not saying that after horning in I automatically started to love Rosemont, Massachusetts. All I mean is, the more days that passed, the less I felt like an outsider. I guess you'd say stuff started feeling more familiar. Like at school, if a stranger had asked me for directions, I could have steered him to all the water fountains and lavatories.

For some reason, knowing your lavatories sort of gives you a feeling of belonging.

I guess moving to a new school is like anything else you hate. Even though you can't stand the thought of it, and you plan to hate it for the rest of your life, after you've been doing it for a while, you start getting used to it. And after you start getting used to it, you forget to hate it as much as you'd planned. I think it's called adjusting. I've given this some thought, and I've decided that adjusting is one of those things that you can't control that much. It's like learning to like girls. It sort of makes you nauseous to think about it, but you know it's going to happen.

Think It Over

1. *What is Howard's problem in the story?*
2. *What does Howard's father tell him to do in order to make friends?*
3. *At what point does Howard begin to feel accepted by his classmates? How do you know?*
4. *What do you think is the worst experience Howard has? Explain your choice.*

Write

Do you think Howard goes about making friends in the right way? Write a friendly letter to Howard that gives him your advice on making friends.

Lord
In the Year of the Boar and Jackie Robinson
Bette Bao Lord
Author of SPRING MOON
In the Year of the Boar and Jackie Robinson
90000

THE CHINESE ROOKIE

FROM

IN THE YEAR OF THE BOAR AND JACKIE ROBINSON

by Bette Bao Lord

illustrated by Floyd Cooper

Leaving your homeland, China, and beginning school in the United States can be a very trying experience. In 1947, Shirley Temple Wong discovers a new friend, a love of baseball, and the excitement Americans were experiencing over a very special team—the Brooklyn Dodgers.

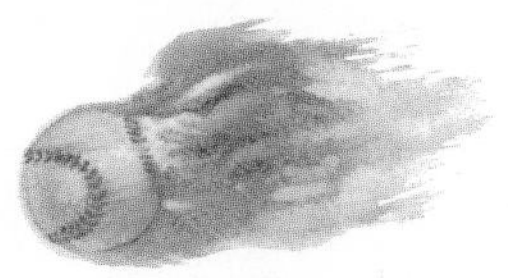

MAY

When the sides were chosen, Mabel pointed to a spot by the iron fence. "Shirley, you play right field. If a ball comes your way, catch it and throw it to me. I'll take care of the rest."

"Where you be?"

"I'm the pitcher."

"Picture?"

"Ah, forget it. Look for me, I'll be around."

Resisting the temptation to bow, Shirley headed for her spot.

Mabel's picture was something to see. First, hiding the ball, she gave the stick the evil eye. Then, twisting her torso and jiggling a leg, she whirled her arm around in a most impressive fashion, probably a ritual to shoo away any unfriendly spirits, before speeding the ball furiously into the hands of squatting Joseph.

After the change of sides, Mabel stood Shirley in place and told her she would be first to hit. Shirley would have preferred to study the problem some more, but was afraid to protest and lose face for her captain. Standing tall, with her feet together, stick on her shoulder, she waited bravely. Dog Breath had a ritual of his own to perform, but then, suddenly, the ball was coming her way. Her eyes squeezed shut.

"Ball one!" shouted the umpire.

"Good eye!" shouted Mabel.

Shirley sighed and started to leave, but was told to stay put.

Again the ball came. Again her eyes shut.

"Ball two!"

"Good eye!" shouted the team. "Two more of those and you're on."

Shirley grinned. How easy it was!

Sure enough, every time she shut her eyes, the ball went astray.

"Take your base," said the umpire.

Mabel came running over. "Stand on that red bookbag until someone hits the ball, then run like mad to touch the blue one. Got it?"

"I got."

Mabel then picked up the stick and with one try sent the ball flying. In no time, Shirley, despite her pigeon toes, had dashed to the blue bookbag. But something was wrong. Mabel was chasing her. "Go. Get going. Run."

Shirley, puzzled over which bookbag to run to next, took a chance and sped off. But Mabel was still chasing her. "Go home! Go home!"

Oh no! She had done the wrong thing. Now even her new friend was angry. "Go home," her teammates shouted. "Go home."

She was starting off the field when she saw Joseph waving. "Here! Over here!" And off she went for the green one. Just before she reached it, she stumbled, knocking over the opponent who stood in her way. He dropped the ball, and Shirley fell on top of the bag like a piece of ripe bean curd.

Her teammates shouted with happiness. Some helped her up. Others patted her back. Then they took up Mabel's chant.

"Hey, hey, you're just great
Jackie Robinson crossed the plate.
Hey, hey, you're a dream
Jackie Robinson's on our team."

Mabel's team won. The score was 10 to 2, and though the Chinese rookie never got on base again or caught even one ball, Shirley was confident that the next time . . . next time, she could. And yes, of course, naturally, stickball was now her favorite game.

JUNE

It was almost summer. An eager sun outshone the neon sign atop the factory even before the first bell beckoned students to their homerooms. Now alongside the empty milk crates at Mr. P's, brown paper bags with collars neatly rolled boasted plump strawberries, crimson cherries and bananas. The cloakroom stood empty. Gone, the sweaters, slickers and galoshes.

At the second bell, the fifth grade, as always, scrambled to their feet. As always, Tommy O'Brien giggled, and each girl checked her seat to see if she was his victim of the day. Susie Spencer, whose tardiness could set clocks, rushed in, her face long with excuses. Popping a last bubble, Maria Gonzales tucked her gum safely behind an ear while Joseph gave an extra stroke to his hair.

Finally Mrs. Rappaport cleared her throat, and the room was still. With hands over hearts, the class performed the ritual that ushered in another day at school.

Shirley's voice was lost in the chorus.

"Class, be seated," said Mrs. Rappaport, looking around to see if anyone was absent.

No one was.

"Any questions on the homework?"

All hands remained on or below the desks, etched with initials, new with splinters, brown with age.

"In that case, any questions on any subject at all?"

Irvie's hand shot up. It was quickly pulled down by Maria, who hated even the sound of the word "spider." Spiders were all Irvie ever asked about, talked about, dreamed about. How many eyes do spiders have? Do spiders eat three meals a day? Where are spiders' ears located?

By now, everyone in the fifth grade knew that spiders come with no, six or eight eyes. That spiders do not have to dine regularly and that some can thrive as long as two years without a bite. That spiders are earless.

Since Irvie was as scared of girls as Maria was of spiders, he sat on his hands, but just in case he changed his mind, Maria's hand went up.

"Yes, Maria?"

"Eh . . . eh, I had a question, but I forget."

"Was it something we discussed yesterday?"

"Yeah, yeah, that's it."

"Something about air currents or cloud formation, perhaps?"

"Yeah. How come I see lightning before I hear thunder?"

"Does anyone recall the answer?"

Tommy jumped in. "That's easy. 'Cause your eyes are in front, and your ears are off to the side." To prove his point, he wiggled his ears, which framed his disarming smile like the handles of a fancy soup bowl.

Laughter was his reward.

"The correct answer, Maria," said Mrs. Rappaport, trying not to smile too, "is that light waves travel faster than sound waves."

Shirley raised her hand.

"Yes?"

"Who's the girl Jackie Robinson?"

Laughter returned. This time Shirley did not understand the joke. Was the girl very, very bad? So bad that her name should not be uttered in the presence of a grown-up?

Putting a finger to her lips, Mrs. Rappaport quieted the class. "Shirley, you ask an excellent question. A most appropriate one. . . . "

The Chinese blushed, wishing her teacher would stop praising her, or at least not in front of the others. Already, they called her "teacher's dog" or "apple shiner."

"Jackie Robinson," Mrs. Rappaport continued, "is a man, the first Negro to play baseball in the major leagues."

"What is a Negro, Mrs. Rappaport?"

"A Negro is someone who is born with dark skin."

"Like Mabel?"

"Like Mabel and Joey and . . ."

"Maria?"

"No, Maria is not a Negro."

"But Maria is dark. Darker than Joey."

"I see what you mean. Let me try again. A Negro is someone whose ancestors originally came from Africa and who has dark skin."

"Then why I'm called Jackie Robinson?"

Mrs. Rappaport looked mystified. "Who calls you Jackie Robinson?"

"Everybody."

"Then I'll have to ask them. Mabel?"

"'Cause she's pigeon-toed and stole home."

The teacher nodded. "Well, Shirley, it seems you are not only a good student, but a good baseball player."

There, she'd done it again! The kids would surely call her "a shiner of apples for teacher's dog" next. Shirley's unhappiness must have been obvious, because Mrs. Rappaport evidently felt the need to explain further.

"It is a compliment, Shirley. Jackie Robinson is a big hero, especially in Brooklyn, because he plays for the Dodgers."

"Who is dodgers?" Shirley asked.

That question, like a wayward torch in a roomful of firecrackers, sparked answers from everyone.

"De Bums!"

"The best in the history of baseball!"

"Kings of Ebbets Field!"

"They'll kill the Giants!"

"They'll murder the Yankees!"

"The swellest guys in the world!"

"America's favorites!"

"Winners!"

Mrs. Rappaport clapped her hands for order. The girls quieted down first, followed reluctantly by the boys. "That's better. Participation is welcome, but one at a time. Let's do talk about baseball!"

"Yay!" shouted the class.

"And let's combine it with civics too!"

The class did not welcome this proposal as eagerly, but Mrs. Rappaport went ahead anyway.

"Mabel, tell us why baseball is America's favorite pastime."

Pursing her lips in disgust at so ridiculous a question, Mabel answered. "'Cause it's a great game. Everybody plays it, loves it and follows the games on the radio and nabs every chance to go and see it."

"True," said Mrs. Rappaport, nodding. "But what is it about baseball that is ideally suited to Americans?"

Mabel turned around, looking for an answer from someone else, but to no avail. There was nothing to do but throw the question back. "Whatta ya mean by 'suits'?"

"I mean, is there something special about baseball that fits the special kind of people we are and the special kind of country America is?" Mrs. Rappaport tilted her head to one side, inviting a response. When none came, she sighed a sigh so fraught with disappointment that it sounded as if her heart were breaking.

No one wished to be a party to such a sad event, so everybody found some urgent business to attend to like scratching, slumping, sniffing, scribbling, squinting, sucking teeth or removing dirt from underneath a fingernail. Joseph cracked his knuckles.

The ticking of the big clock became so loud that President Washington and President Lincoln, who occupied the wall space to either side of it, exchanged a look of shared displeasure.

But within the frail, birdlike body of Mrs. Rappaport was the spirit of a dragon capable of tackling the heavens and earth. With a quick toss of her red hair, she proceeded to answer her own question with such feeling that no one who heard could be so unkind as to ever forget. Least of all Shirley.

"Baseball is not just another sport. America is not just another country. . . ."

If Shirley did not understand every word, she took its meaning to heart. Unlike Grandfather's stories which quieted the warring spirits within her with the softness of moonlight or the lyric timbre of a lone flute, Mrs. Rappaport's speech thrilled her like sunlight and trumpets.

"In our national pastime, each player is a member of a team, but when he comes to bat, he stands alone. One man. Many opportunities. For no matter how far behind, how late in the game, he, by himself, can make a difference. He can change what has been. He can make it a new ball game.

"In the life of our nation, each man is a citizen of the United States, but he has the right to pursue his own happiness. For no matter what his race, religion or creed, be he pauper or president, he has the right to speak his mind, to live as he wishes within the law, to elect our officials and stand for office, to excel. To make a difference. To change what has been. To make a better America.

"And so can you! And so must you!"

Shirley felt as if the walls of the classroom had vanished. In their stead was a frontier of doors to which she held the keys.

"This year, Jackie Robinson is at bat. He stands for himself, for Americans of every hue, for an America that honors fair play.

"Jackie Robinson is the grandson of a slave, the son of a sharecropper, raised in poverty by a lone mother who took in ironing and washing. But a woman determined to achieve a better life for her son. And she did. For despite hostility and injustice, Jackie Robinson went to college, excelled in all sports, served his country in war. And now, Jackie Robinson is at bat in the big leagues. Jackie Robinson is making a difference. Jackie Robinson has changed what has been. And Jackie Robinson is making a better America.

"And so can you! And so must you!"

Suddenly Shirley understood why her father had brought her ten thousand miles to live among strangers. Here, she did not have to wait for gray hairs to be considered wise. Here, she could speak up, question even the conduct of the President. Here, Shirley Temple Wong was somebody. She felt as if she had the power of ten tigers, as if she had grown as tall as the Statue of Liberty.

Think It Over

1. *Many of our American words and customs seem strange to Shirley Temple Wong. What are some of the things that Shirley does not understand?*
2. *Why does Shirley want the teacher to stop praising her?*
3. *Why do you think Shirley is thrilled by Mrs. Rappaport's speech about America, baseball, and Jackie Robinson?*

Write

Imagine that you are about to spend a year in a school in China. Write a letter to Shirley Temple Wong. Ask her everything that you would want to know about her country and its schools.

Words from the Author:

Bette Bao Lord

Some of the parts of the story you read are true and others are made up, but the feelings Shirley Temple Wong has were very much my own.

I was eight when I came to America, and I didn't know a word of the language. As I say in *In the Year of the Boar and Jackie Robinson*, the conversation in the classroom sounded "like gargling water" to me. But one of the miracles of childhood is that you can do things that adults cannot. One of them is that you can learn languages easily. I learned English in a surprisingly short time. And I made friends and I learned about baseball. It was a very special year.

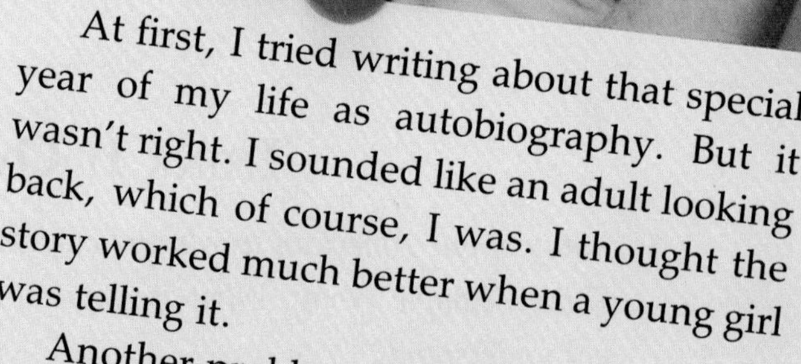

At first, I tried writing about that special year of my life as autobiography. But it wasn't right. I sounded like an adult looking back, which of course, I was. I thought the story worked much better when a young girl was telling it.

Another problem in writing the book for an adult audience was that adults don't believe much in the American Dream anymore. But I think children know that the American Dream of success is still possible. I know it. It happened to me. I came from China, and when I grew up, I married the American ambassador to China. And look at Jackie Robinson. He's still a symbol of the American Dream. That's why people remember him.

I've written a number of adult books, but *In the Year of the Boar and Jackie Robinson* is the book I enjoyed writing more than any other. After you write an adult book, you get letters about it for perhaps a year after it comes out. But hardly a week goes by when I do not get a letter about *In the Year of the Boar and Jackie Robinson.* One of the biggest thrills about writing a children's book is getting those letters. It's like a dividend.

I get many letters from immigrant children. It's interesting, because I think these children share the same experience I had. They are lonely in a new school, and it's difficult for them to make friends. They like the book because it's funny, but it speaks to them, too. One thing I'd like children to know is that their diversity enriches the group. I couldn't have written this book if I wasn't different! You can be different in any number of ways, but it is important to remember that those differences are what make you special.

AWARD-WINNING AUTHOR

Hector
LIVES IN
THE UNITED STATES NOW
The Story of a Mexican-American Child
By Joan Hewett – Photographs by Richard Hewe

We Are a Nation of Immigrants

from

Hector Lives in the United States Now

by Joan Hewett
photographs by Richard Hewett

Ten-year-old Hector Almaraz is a Mexican American. For as long as he can remember he has lived in Los Angeles—in this neighborhood, on this block.

Hector's parents are Leopoldo and Rosario Almaraz. He also has three brothers: nine-year-old Polo, and Miguel and Ernesto, who are seven and four.

Hector and Polo were born in Guadalajara, Mexico, and are Mexican citizens, like their parents. Their younger brothers, Miguel and Ernesto, were born in Los Angeles and are American citizens.

Hector did not speak English when he started kindergarten. It was a scary time. He was away from his mother and brothers. He understood only a few English words and did not know what was going on in class. In first grade Hector had trouble learning to read. But he was determined to learn English, and by the end of the second grade he was reading and writing as well as his classmates. School started to be fun.

Now Hector is a fifth grader, one of the big kids. In United States history, his class is reading about the different immigrant groups who helped settle the West. Their teacher says, "We are a nation of immigrants. Indians, also called Native Americans, have lived here for thousands of years. Everyone else has come to the continental United States from some other place." Then she smiles and says, "Let's find out about us."

The students in Hector's class are told to ask their parents about their ancestors and then write a brief history of their families. It is an exciting project. When they finish their reports, they will glue snapshots of themselves to their papers and hang them on the wall. But first they get to read them aloud.

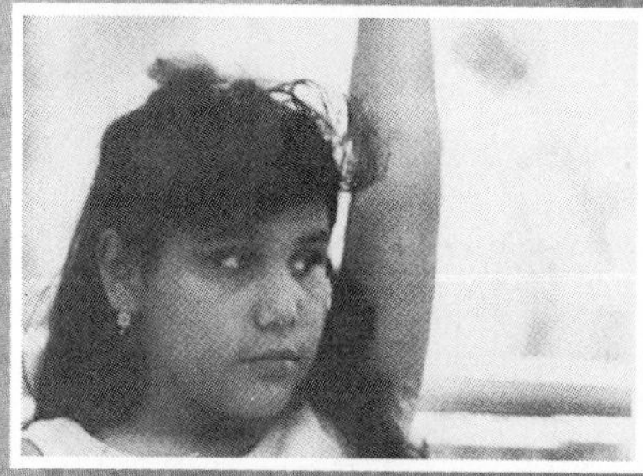

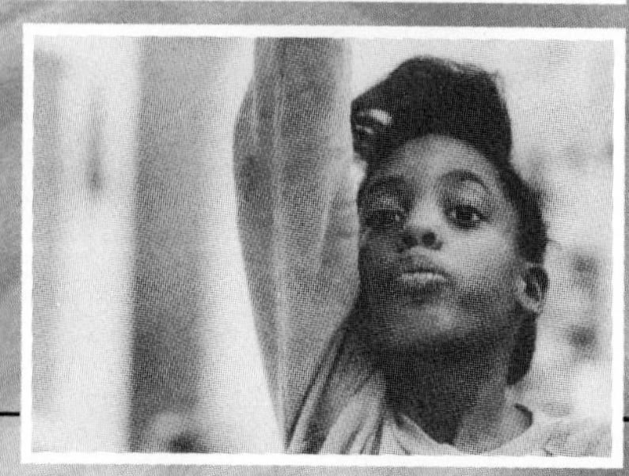

Philip traces his family back as far as his great-great-great-grandmother. His ancestors lived on a small Philippine island. Many of them were fishermen. Philip, his sister, and his parents are the only people in his family who have settled in the United States.

One side of Nicky's family came from Norway and Germany. His other ancestors came from Ireland and Sweden. All of them were farmers, and when they came to this country they homesteaded land, which means they farmed and built a house on uncultivated public land that then became theirs under a special homestead law.

Vanessa's great-great-grandmother was a Yaqui Indian from Sonora, Mexico. Her grandfather fought in the Mexican Revolution. Another one of her ancestors was French.

Erick is descended from Ukrainian, German, and Italian immigrants. His German grandfather and Ukrainian grandmother met in a prisoner-of-war camp. When they were released, they married and came to the United States by ship.

Julie is of French, Irish, and Spanish descent. Her Great-Great-Grandma Elm was born in Texas. When Elm was a child her family moved to California. They traveled by covered wagon.

Everyone is interested in Kyria's family history. One of her African ancestors was a soldier in the American Revolution. Another fought for the Confederacy in the Civil War. Other members of her family homesteaded in Oklahoma.

Hector tells the class about his Mexican ancestors. They were farmers and carpenters.

There are twelve other Mexican-American children in Hector's class, and some two hundred fifty thousand Mexican-American students in Los Angeles schools.

Before California became part of the United States, it belonged to Mexico. Some Mexican families have lived in California for hundreds of years, but most Mexican-American children are recent arrivals. Their numbers will keep increasing.

Compared to the United States, Mexico is not a prosperous country, and in the last few years Mexico's economy has declined sharply. More than half its workers cannot find jobs. So, many go north to look for jobs on the other side of the Mexican-American border, a 1,900-mile boundary that separates California, Arizona, New Mexico, and Texas from Mexico.

Some Mexicans are among the six hundred thousand immigrants from all over the world who are granted permanent residence in the United States each year.

Think It Over

1. *Describe how you would feel if you, like Hector, had to move to a new country and learn a new language.*
2. *What do you think Hector's teacher means when she says, "We are a nation of immigrants"?*

Write

Pretend that you are a member of Hector's class. Use the teacher's directions to write a few paragraphs giving a brief history of your own family or of one of your ancestors.

address

from *Floricanto en Aztlán*

by Alurista

illustrated by Buster O'Connor

address ______________________

occupation ______________________

age ______________________

marital status ______________________

perdone . . .
yo me llamo pedro

pardon . . .
my name is pedro

telephone ______________________

height ______________________

hobbies ______________________

previous employers ______________________

perdone . . .
yo me llamo pedro
pedro ortega

pardon . . .
my name is pedro
pedro ortega

zip code ______________________

i.d. number ______________________

classification ______________________

rank ______________________

perdone . . . mi padre era
el señor ortega
(a veces don josé)

pardon . . . my father was
señor ortega
(sometimes called don josé)

race ______________________

THEME WRAP-UP

CHALLENGES IN SCHOOL

How are the challenges faced by Howard, Shirley, and Hector alike? How are Shirley's and Hector's problems in school different from Howard's?

What do Howard's and Shirley's classmates do to help them fit into their new surroundings? How could you make Howard, Shirley, or Hector feel at home in your school?

WRITER'S WORKSHOP What experiences have you had that were similar to those described in the selections? Make a list of those experiences. Then choose the one that is the most similar, and write a short paragraph comparing your own experience with one of Howard's, Shirley's, or Hector's.

THEME

PLAYING TO WIN

What does it feel like to stand alone on a diving board, high above a hushed crowd? Or in a batter's box, in front of thousands of screaming fans? The people in these selections know!

CONTENTS

In Rare FORM

from *Mariah Keeps Cool*

by Mildred Pitts Walter

illustrated by Ian Watts

Mariah Metcalf and her friends, who call themselves the Friendly Five, have spent the summer training for the all-city swimming and diving competition. Their coaches, Brandon and Mr. Lyons, have confidence in the team and believe that the girls can win. Mariah, however, is nervous—especially when she thinks about diving against her main competitor, Lorobeth Dillon.

That night Mariah went to bed feeling both doubtful and confident. Would everything go well? One little something—a foot out of line, or a break in her rhythm—could mean the difference between a loss and a win. So much can go wrong, she thought. She smiled, thinking of the blue swim suits the team had chosen. Blue like the championship ribbons; and their sweats were yellow, the color of the winning gold. Her team had better win.

Now, as she did every night before she went to sleep, she imagined herself on the diving board doing one dive after another, smoothly entering the water.

Early in the morning, Mariah rode across town with the members of the team, quiet and subdued. She stared out of the window of the van, wondering why she had ever thought she and her friends could win against people who were in swim meets all the time. She and her friends had never swum in a meet. What was it like? she wondered. Would Lorobeth and her friends be there today?

When they arrived they had to stand in line at the registration table. There were so many teams wearing sweats of all colors. Mariah saw Lorobeth with her team dressed in royal purple.

Finally their turn came to register. All the officials smiled warmly and acted as if they had been waiting for them. Mariah and her friends signed the permission forms that had already been signed by their parents and Mr. Lyons.

Later Mariah sat and filled out her diving scoresheet. Brandon and Mr. Lyons did some last-minute coaching with the team during the warm-up. Other teams were getting last-minute instructions, too, showing off their best, trying to intimidate. Maybe we shouldn't have come, she thought.

The other Friendly Five members came through the preliminaries, qualifying for the finals in the competition for eleven- and twelve-year-olds. The joy of their staying in the competition helped Mariah in her diving. She felt at home in the large city pool.

"You're in rare form today," Brandon told her after she had completed her five required dives. "I believe you can walk away from here a winner."

Mariah didn't feel so confident. Besides Lorobeth, there were other good divers. But when all the divers had finished Mariah was among the eight listed in the finals. She had done well, and she and Lorobeth were top scorers, with Lorobeth leading Mariah by two points.

At the end of the preliminaries, the Friendly Five concluded they were in competition with Lorobeth and members of her team only. "If we come out ahead of them, I don't care if we don't beat anybody else," Trina declared.

That evening, for the finals, the grounds around the city pool were filled with families and friends of the swimmers. People brought picnic baskets; the city provided music and the atmosphere was festive. Mariah was glad that her family had come. They joined the families and friends of the Friendly Five.

At six o'clock the finals began. Mariah sat with her family to cheer their team. Mariah tried to restrain herself, but she forgot about saving her strength when the medley relay got underway. Jerri, with her fast reflexes, got a good start and moved ahead in the backstroke. At the touch, Mariah cheered as Nikki dove in for the breaststroke. And when Cynthia touched on the butterfly to give Trina a lead in the freestyle, Mariah lost control. They won the four hundred medley relay.

In their age group, they took first in the one hundred free, a second in the one hundred breast, and a third in the one hundred back. Cynthia was just touched out in butterfly for a second.

Then it was Mariah's turn. The officials announced the names of the eight divers, but Mariah was concerned with only two names: hers and Lorobeth's. "Lorobeth Dillon, first diver; Mariah Metcalf, fifth diver."

Mariah racked up scores with the three judges giving her sevens, eights, eights and one-halfs, and even a couple of nines. But Lorobeth's scores were right up there, too. When they had finished their required five dives and the first four optional ones, their scores were tied.

Mariah wished it were all over. If only she had chosen a more difficult program. But then she might be out of the competition: A tough dive not well-executed could be the kiss of death, bringing down the total score. Brandon and Mr. Lyons assured her she had done well and had a good chance to win.

Mariah paced back and forth, swinging her arms, breathing deeply, trying to relax. She heard the announcer call the final round. "Lorobeth Dillon will do a back dive with one somersault in the tuck position, degree of difficulty one point five."

"Oh, no," Mariah said. "That's my dive!"

Mariah's heart sank as she looked at Brandon. Brandon smiled. "Don't worry about that. You're lucky you come second. You have time to really concentrate and see yourself doing your dive."

Mariah didn't want to concentrate. She wanted to see her competitor. Lorobeth had style and grace. She stood tall and straight, motionless as she planned every move. Now, in the final dive, Mariah felt that Lorobeth stood forever before she slowly raised her arms preparing for the back takeoff. Finally, Lorobeth somersaulted backward in a tuck position. She misjudged her timing and straightened her body, opening her dive too soon. She landed on her stomach, and the crowd groaned.

At first Mariah was elated. Then she felt an added tension. She must not open up too soon like Lorobeth did, but she couldn't be too late either. Too late would put her on her back. Her timing had to be just right.

"Mariah Metcalf will now do a back dive with one somersault in the tuck position, degree of difficulty one point five," the official announced.

Mariah stepped up on the board and glanced at the judges. Then she slowly walked to the end of the board, turned around, and carefully balanced herself with her head held high, eyes straight ahead, body erect, and arms straight at her sides. She stood motionless, concentrating on the dive. She waited, feeling the expectant silence. All eyes were on her.

Just before she made her back press she breathed easily, seeing herself making a perfect dive. As she pressed back her arms reached up and she brought her knees to her chest. She felt herself turn. She opened right on time, ripping the dive and entering the water without a splash.

The roar of the crowd pushed through the water in her ears, and she knew she had won.

Think It Over

1. *What do you think is the most difficult part of the competition for Mariah?*
2. *What does Brandon mean when he tells Mariah that she is "in rare form"?*
3. *Why is it so important for Mariah to concentrate before her last dive?*
4. *How successful are the members of the Friendly Five in the six events of the finals?*

Write

Think of a competition or a test that was very challenging for you. Write a journal entry explaining how you prepared for it.

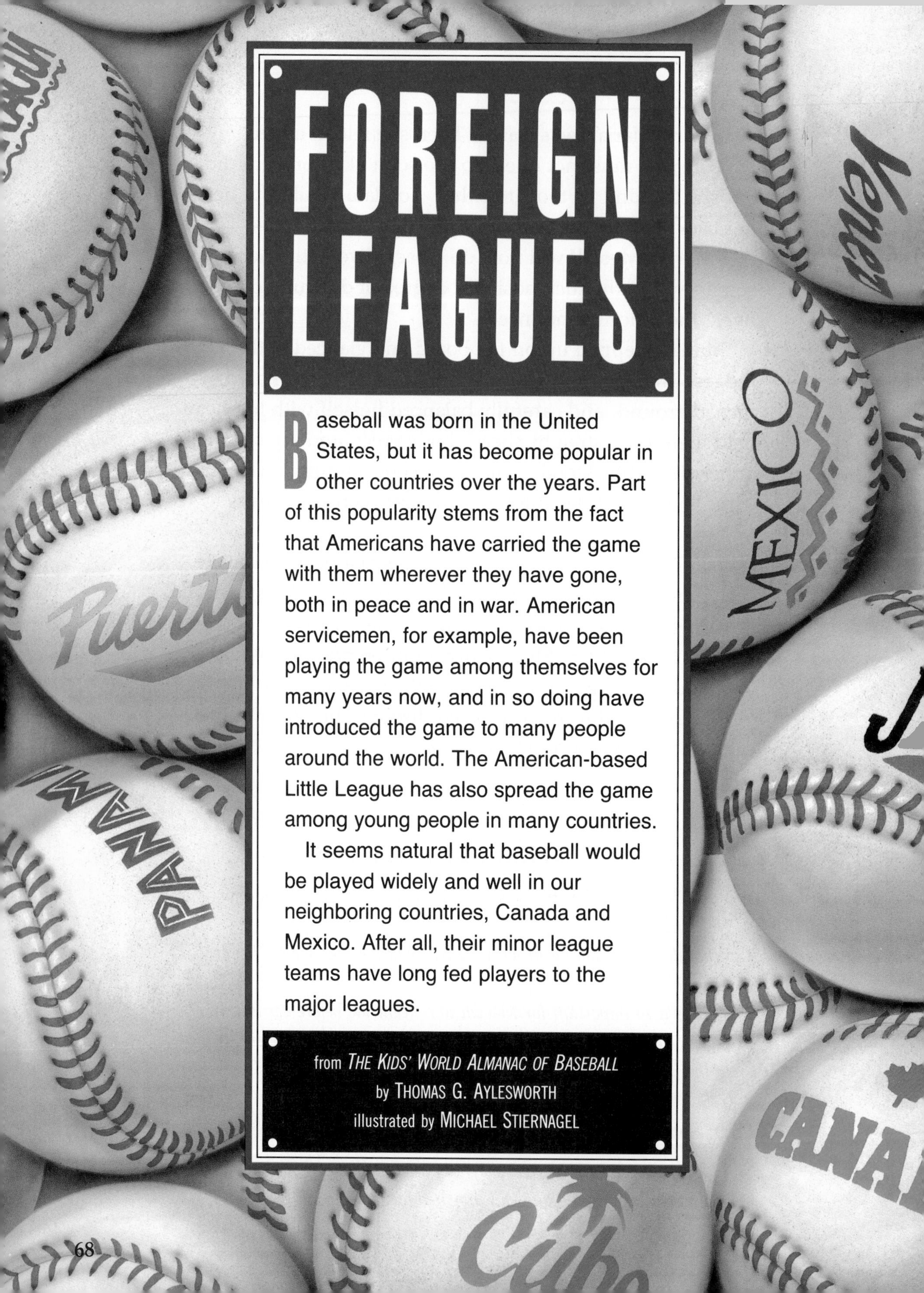

FOREIGN LEAGUES

Baseball was born in the United States, but it has become popular in other countries over the years. Part of this popularity stems from the fact that Americans have carried the game with them wherever they have gone, both in peace and in war. American servicemen, for example, have been playing the game among themselves for many years now, and in so doing have introduced the game to many people around the world. The American-based Little League has also spread the game among young people in many countries.

It seems natural that baseball would be played widely and well in our neighboring countries, Canada and Mexico. After all, their minor league teams have long fed players to the major leagues.

from *THE KIDS' WORLD ALMANAC OF BASEBALL*
by THOMAS G. AYLESWORTH
illustrated by MICHAEL STIERNAGEL

Baseball has been extremely popular throughout Latin America and the Caribbean Islands, and not only in places where the United States has had direct contacts, such as in Puerto Rico, Panama, and the Virgin Islands. Baseball is popular in Venezuela, Nicaragua, and the Dominican Republic, and there is a lengthening list of players from those countries who have moved up to become prominent players in the major leagues.

Cuba is a special case. Baseball was played there as early as 1878, and eventually Cuba supported a team, the Havana Cubans, which belonged to the Triple A International League. After Fidel Castro (who was good enough to have had a minor league contract offer to play baseball in the U.S.) took over as president, the United States severed diplomatic relations with Cuba in 1961, and thus cut off movement between the two countries. Now there are two independent leagues in Cuba, and baseball remains as popular as ever.

Baseball was introduced to Japan by Horace Wilson, an American teacher in Tokyo, in 1873. The sport caught on quickly and was supported by schools and universities, spurred on by occasional tours by American collegiate teams. Until the 1930s, baseball in Japan was an amateur sport, with the strongest teams coming out of the Japanese universities. To this day, the university teams remain as the "farm teams" for the professional leagues.

Then came the visit of an "all-star" team of American professionals in 1931 and the visit of Babe Ruth in 1934. Since then, the Japanese have embraced baseball. They now support two major leagues, the Pacific and the Central, each with six clubs that play 130-game seasons and play their own Japan Series.

Baseball has yet to catch on elsewhere around the world as it has in Japan and in Latin America, but it is played by semiprofessional teams in Italy, France, the Netherlands, Belgium, Spain, England, South Africa, Australia, Taiwan, and Tunisia. Baseball has truly become international.

THE WAY OF THE JIBARO

from

Pride of Puerto Rico

by Paul Robert Walker

illustrated by Harvey Chan

Roberto closed his eyes and imagined himself in the great stadium of San Juan. There were men on first and third with two outs in the bottom of the ninth. His team was losing, 5–3. A double would tie the game. A home run would win it. Everything depended on him.

He stepped confidently into the batter's box and took two level practice swings. Then he cocked his bat and waited for the pitch. The white ball came toward him in slow motion, its seams spinning clearly in the air. His bat was a blur as he whipped it around and smashed the ball over the left-field fence!

"Clemente!" cried a voice behind him. "Are you playing or dreaming?"

Roberto opened his eyes and stared seriously at the boy who had spoken. "I am playing," he said.

It was a warm tropical evening in Puerto Rico. Roberto Clemente was playing with a group of boys on a muddy field in Barrio San Antón. It was nothing at all like the great stadium in San Juan. There were bumps and puddles, and the outfield was full of trees. The bat in Roberto's hand was a thick stick cut from the branch of a guava tree. The bases were old coffee sacks. The ball was a tightly-knotted bunch of rags.

The boys on the field were black and white and many shades of brown. They shouted at each other in Spanish, encouraging their teammates, taunting their opponents. This was an important game between the boys of Barrio San Antón and a team from Barrio Martín Gonzalez.

Eight-year-old Roberto Clemente was one of the youngest and smallest boys on the field. As he stepped up to the plate, the thick guava stick felt very heavy in his hands. It was a great honor to represent his neighborhood. Everything depended on him.

Roberto looked over at third base, where his brother Andrés stood waiting to score. He looked at first, where another boy waited impatiently, hoping to score the tying run. Then he took a deep breath, cocked his bat and waited for the pitch.

The big ball of rags arched toward him as if it were in slow motion. Roberto swung with all his strength, but instead of sailing over the left-field fence, the ball rolled weakly back to the mound. The pitcher fielded it easily and threw to first for the final out. The game was over. San Antón had lost by a score of 5–3. Roberto stood alone while the other players left the field. He could feel tears trickling down his cheeks, and he was ashamed to cry in front of the older boys. His brother Andrés called to him from a few feet away. "Momen!" he said. "Are you going to stand there all night? It's time for supper."

"You go ahead," said Roberto. "I promised to meet Papá."

Roberto was the youngest of seven children in the Clemente family. There were six boys and one girl. When he was very little, Roberto's sister Rosa called him "Momen." It didn't mean anything in particular. It was just a made-up word, but to his family Roberto was always Momen.

Roberto's father, Don Melchor Clemente, worked as a foreman in the sugar fields. Sugar was the most important crop for the people of Puerto Rico. At harvest time, the sharp green stalks of sugar cane stood twice as tall as a man.

From sunrise to sunset, the men of Barrio San Antón worked in the fields, cutting the thick stalks of cane with their sharp machetes. It was hard, back-breaking work and the pay was $2.00 per week.

Don Clemente was more fortunate than most. As a foreman, he earned $4.00 a week. He and his wife, Doña Luisa, also ran a small store, selling meat and other goods to the workers on the sugar plantation. There was no money for luxuries like real baseballs and bats, but there was always plenty of rice and beans on the Clemente family table.

As he walked down the dirt road between the tall fields of sugar cane, Roberto thought about the game. He had failed his team. Perhaps he was not good enough to play with the bigger boys. Perhaps he would never be good enough. Once again he could feel the tears in his eyes.

It was late in the evening now, and the sun was setting over the fields like a great orange ball of fire. Roberto reached a high point in the road and looked for his father. Suddenly his tears disappeared. There, above the tall stalks of cane sat Don Melchor Clemente, riding slowly on his paso fino horse.

"Papá! Papá! Wait for me!"

Roberto ran through the cane field to where his father was riding. Don Melchor reached down and helped Roberto climb into the saddle behind him. Don Melchor Clemente was very proud to own such a fine horse. And Roberto was proud to ride behind his father.

"So, Momen," Don Melchor said as they rode home through the fields, "you come at last. I thought you had forgotten."

"Forgive me, Papá," said Roberto. "I was playing baseball."

"Ah, and how was the baseball?"

Roberto was silent for a moment. He thought again of the weak ground ball that ended the game for Barrio San Antón. He did not want to tell his father of his failure, but he knew that Don Melchor Clemente was a man who accepted only the truth. Finally he took a deep breath and spoke. "I lost the game, Papá."

"Hmmm," Don Melchor said. "That is very interesting." Father and son continued to ride in silence. Then Don Melchor spoke again. "I do not know very much about this baseball," he said. "But I know that there are many players on a team. I do not understand how one small boy can lose the game."

"But, Papá," said Roberto, "I was our only hope. I could have been the hero. Instead I was the last man out. The other boys will never ask me to play again."

They were out of the sugar fields now and riding slowly down the red dirt road that ran through Barrio San Antón. Don Melchor looked straight ahead as he guided his horse toward home. His words were strong and clear in the evening air.

"Momen," he said, "I want you to listen very carefully. Perhaps the other boys will ask you. Perhaps they will not. It does not matter. There are other boys and other teams, but there is only one life. I want you to be a good man. I want you to work hard. And I want you to be a serious person."

Don Melchor stopped his horse in the road. They were only a few hundred yards from home now, and Roberto could clearly see the wood and concrete house set in a grove of banana trees. Barrio San Antón lay on the outskirts of the city of Carolina. To the west was the capital city of San Juan. To the east were the cloud-covered slopes of El Yunque, barely visible in the fading light.

"Remember who you are," Don Melchor said. "Remember where you come from. You are a Jíbaro.[1] Like me. Like my

---

[1]hē′bä•rō′

father and my father's father. We are a proud people. Hundreds of years ago, we went into the mountains because we refused to serve the Spanish noblemen. In the wilderness, we learned to live off the land. Now, even in the sugar fields, we do not forget what we have learned.

"A man must be honest. He must work for what he needs. He must share with his brothers who have less. This is the way of the Jíbaro. This is the way of dignity." Don Melchor paused for a moment. It was dark now, and supper was waiting. "Do you understand, my son?" he asked.

Roberto thought carefully about his father's words. Then he spoke, quietly but firmly. "Yes, Papá," he said, "I understand."

Señora Cáceres stood behind her wooden desk and watched her new students file into the room. "You may choose your own seats," she said. "But remember, that will be your seat for the whole semester."

It was the first day of school at Vizcarrondo High School in the city of Carolina. Señora Cáceres waited until the students were settled into their seats before beginning the lesson.

"Today we will try to speak in English," she said. "I know that will be difficult for many of you, but the only way to improve is to practice. Now, who can tell me something about the history of Puerto Rico?"

Several students eagerly raised their hands. Señora Cáceres pointed to a pretty girl in the front row. The girl stood up and spoke in careful English.

"Puerto Rico was discovered by Christopher Columbus in 1493. He claim the island for Spain. The first governor was Ponce de León."

"Very good," said Señora Cáceres as the girl sat down. "And when did Puerto Rico become part of the United States?"

Again the same students raised their hands. Señora Cáceres looked around the room. Roberto sat in the very last row, his eyes staring at the floor. He had studied English in grammar school, but, like most of his friends, he could not really use it in conversation.

"Come now," said Señora Cáceres. "You'll never learn unless you try it."

Very slowly, Roberto raised his hand. Señora Cáceres smiled and pointed to the back row. As Roberto stood up and began to answer, he kept his eyes cast down toward the floor. His voice was very quiet. "We . . . become . . . United States . . . 1898," he said. "We are American . . . cities."

A few of the students laughed at Roberto's poor pronunciation. Señora Cáceres smiled and gently corrected him. "Citizens," she said. "We are American citizens."

As Roberto took his seat, Señora Cáceres noticed a group of girls giggling and whispering in the corner. "Yes," she thought, "this quiet one is a very handsome boy."

Señora Cáceres soon discovered that her quiet student was not so shy on the playing field. Roberto was the greatest athlete in the history of Vizcarrondo High School. He was not only a star on the baseball diamond; he also excelled in track and field. He could throw the javelin 190 feet, triple-jump 45 feet, and high-jump over 6 feet. Many people hoped that Roberto would represent Puerto Rico in the Olympic Games. But despite his success in track and field, baseball was his greatest love.

Bam! Bam! Bam!

Roberto stood on the muddy field in Barrio San Antón with a broomstick in his hands. Next to the boy on the pitcher's mound was a pile of old tin cans. Roberto and his friends were using the tin cans for batting practice. According to the rules, Roberto could bat until the pitcher struck him out. The rest of the boys had to wait in the field for their turn at bat.

Frowning in frustration, the pitcher reached down and picked up another tin can. Once again, he leaned back and tried to fire the can past Roberto at the plate. Bam! Once again, Roberto smashed the can into the outfield.

"Hey, Clemente!" yelled a boy at shortstop. "Why don't you give someone else a chance to bat?"

Roberto smiled seriously and shrugged his shoulders. "First you must strike me out," he said.

On the dirt road that ran along the field, Señor Roberto Marín leaned against his car and watched carefully. It was almost sunset, but he could still see the boys clearly in the twilight. Señor Marín was a man who loved baseball, and he was always looking for new talent. As part of his job with the Sello Rojo Rice Company, he was putting together an all-star softball team to represent the company in a big tournament in San Juan.

"*Caramba!*" said Señor Marín. "That boy can really hit those cans." Señor Marín walked across the field to Roberto. "Who are you?" he asked.

"I am Momen," Roberto replied.

"Well, I tell you, Momen. Why don't you come over to Carolina and try out for my softball team? I think we can use you."

The next day, Roberto rode his bicycle into Carolina to try out for the softball team. It was only a couple of miles from Barrio San Antón to the field in Carolina, but it was a big step for Roberto. He was only a freshman in high school. Most of the other players were much older.

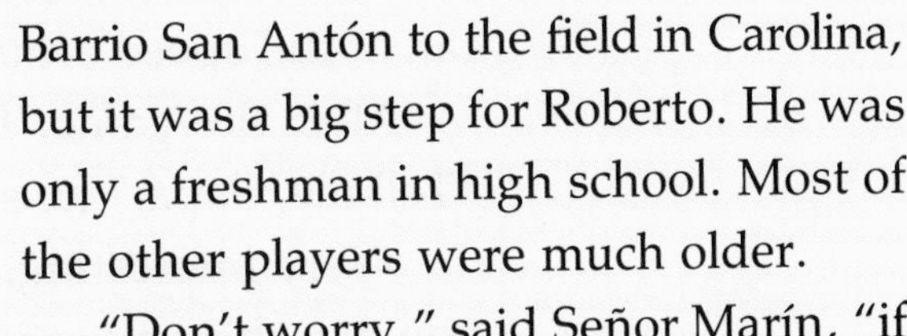

"Don't worry," said Señor Marín, "if you can hit a softball like you hit those tin cans, you'll do all right."

Roberto waited patiently at the plate as the softball sailed toward him in the evening air. At the last moment, he whipped his bat around and smashed the ball into right field. Señor Marín smiled with satisfaction. I know a ball-player when I see one, he thought.

For the next two years, Roberto played for the Sello Rojo softball team. At first he played shortstop, but Señor Marín decided he would be better in the outfield. Soon Roberto was entertaining the softball fans of Carolina and San Juan with his brilliant catches and powerful arm.

Although softball was his favorite game, Roberto also played hardball in the San Juan youth league. When he was sixteen, he played for the Ferdinand Juncos team in the Puerto Rican amateur league. Here the competition was stronger, and the quality of the players was similar to the Class-A minors in the professional leagues of the United States.

One day, Don Melchor came to watch his son. Roberto's father knew very little about baseball. Unfortunately, Roberto's teammates did not hit very well that day. Time after time, they struck out or grounded weakly to the infielders. But when Roberto came to bat, he smashed a long home run and ran at full speed around the bases.

After the game, Roberto approached his father proudly. "Tell me, Papá," he said, "how did you like the baseball?"

"Very interesting," Don Melchor replied. "But no wonder you are always tired! The other players just run to first base and walk back to the dugout. You run all the way around the bases!"

Don Melchor smiled slightly at his own joke. Then his face turned serious. "Momen," he said, "perhaps someday you will run to the major leagues."

Think It Over

1. *What special qualities did people see in young Roberto Clemente?*
2. *What did the boys in Barrio San Antón use as a bat and a ball?*
3. *Roberto was very upset that he had lost the baseball game. Why didn't his father seem to care about that at all?*

Write

The little boy called Momen went on to become a baseball star and national hero. Imagine that you could do the same. Create a baseball card for yourself that lists all the information a baseball fan might want to know about you, such as age, height, batting average, home runs, and so on.

THEME WRAP-UP

PLAYING TO WIN

Think about the selections you have read and your own knowledge of sports. In what ways are diving and baseball alike? In what ways are they different?

How does Mariah's experience at the diving competition differ from Momen's experience at the baseball game in Barrio San Antón?

WRITER'S WORKSHOP Imagine that you have been asked to explain the origins of baseball to a group of younger students. Take notes about the history of the sport from the selections, from an encyclopedia, or from other sources. Then use your notes to write an information paragraph describing where and how the sport originated.

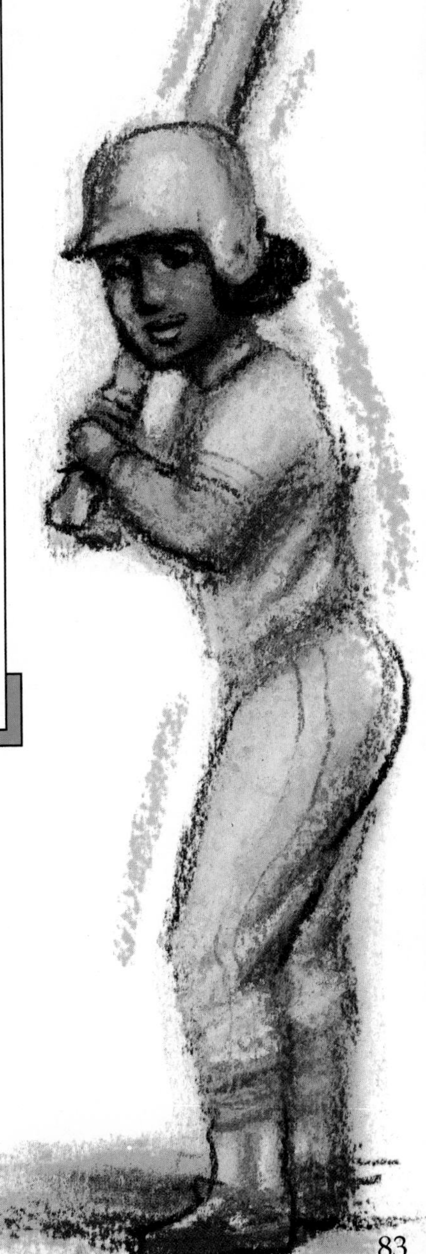

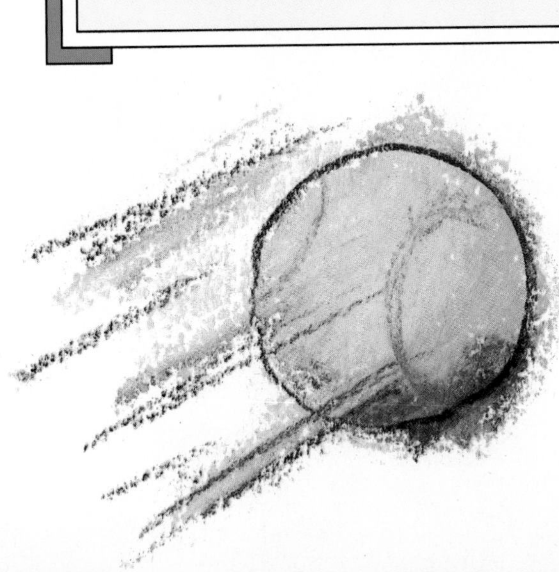

HBJ

UNDERSTANDING OTHERS

America is a huge country, with many types of land and people. Consider the seacoast of Maine and the prairie in Kansas. They are like two different worlds. What might happen when people from these two different worlds meet? Is it possible they could learn from each other?

CONTENTS

Tell Them I Sing

from

illustrated by Marcia Sewall

"Did Mama sing every day?" asked Caleb. "Every-single-day?" He sat close to the fire, his chin in his hand. It was dusk, and the dogs lay beside him on the warm hearthstones.

"Every-single-day," I told him for the second time this week. For the twentieth time this month. The hundredth time this year? And the past few years?

"And did Papa sing, too?"

"Yes. Papa sang, too. Don't get so close, Caleb. You'll heat up."

He pushed his chair back. It made a hollow scraping sound on the hearthstones, and the dogs stirred. Lottie, small and black, wagged her tail and lifted her head. Nick slept on.

I turned the bread dough over and over on the marble slab on the kitchen table.

"Well, Papa doesn't sing anymore," said Caleb very softly. A log broke apart and crackled in the fireplace. He looked up at me. "What did I look like when I was born?"

"You didn't have any clothes on," I told him.

"I know that," he said.

"You looked like this." I held the bread dough up in a round pale ball.

"I had hair," said Caleb seriously.

"Not enough to talk about," I said.

"And she named me Caleb," he went on, filling in the old familiar story.

"*I* would have named you Troublesome," I said, making Caleb smile.

"And Mama handed me to you in the yellow blanket and said . . ." He waited for me to finish the story. "And said . . . ?"

I sighed. "And Mama said, 'Isn't he beautiful, Anna?' "

"And I was," Caleb finished.

NEWBERY MEDAL
CHILDREN'S CHOICE
SLJ BEST BOOKS OF THE YEAR

Caleb thought the story was over, and I didn't tell him what I had really thought. He was homely and plain, and he had a terrible holler and a horrid smell. But these were not the worst of him. Mama died the next morning. That was the worst thing about Caleb.

"Isn't he beautiful, Anna?" Her last words to me. I had gone to bed thinking how wretched he looked. And I forgot to say good night.

I wiped my hands on my apron and went to the window. Outside, the prairie reached out and touched the places where the sky came down. Though winter was nearly over, there were patches of snow and ice everywhere. I looked at the long dirt road that crawled across the plains, remembering the morning that Mama had died, cruel and sunny. They had come for her in a wagon and taken her away to be buried. And then the cousins and aunts and uncles had come and tried to fill up the house. But they couldn't.

Slowly, one by one, they left. And then the days seemed long and dark like winter days, even though it wasn't winter. And Papa didn't sing.

Isn't he beautiful, Anna?

No, Mama.

It was hard to think of Caleb as beautiful. It took three whole days for me to love him, sitting in the chair by the fire, Papa washing up the supper dishes, Caleb's tiny hand brushing my cheek. And a smile. It was the smile, I know.

"Can you remember her songs?" asked Caleb. "Mama's songs?"

I turned from the window. "No. Only that she sang about flowers and birds. Sometimes about the moon at nighttime."

Caleb reached down and touched Lottie's head.

"Maybe," he said, his voice low, "if you remember the songs, then I might remember her, too."

My eyes widened and tears came. Then the door opened and wind blew in with Papa, and I went to stir the stew. Papa put his arms around me and put his nose in my hair.

"Nice soapy smell, that stew," he said.

I laughed. "That's my hair."

Caleb came over and threw his arms around Papa's neck and hung down as Papa swung him back and forth, and the dogs sat up.

"Cold in town," said Papa. "And Jack was feisty." Jack was Papa's horse that he'd raised from a colt. "Rascal," murmured Papa, smiling, because no matter what Jack did Papa loved him.

I spooned up the stew and lighted the oil lamp and we ate with the dogs crowding under the table, hoping for spills or handouts.

Papa might not have told us about Sarah that night if Caleb hadn't asked him the question. After the dishes were cleared and washed and Papa was filling the tin pail with ashes, Caleb spoke up. It wasn't a question, really.

"You don't sing anymore," he said. He said it harshly. Not because he meant to, but because he had been thinking of it for so long. "Why?" he asked more gently.

Slowly Papa straightened up. There was a long silence, and the dogs looked up, wondering at it.

"I've forgotten the old songs," said Papa quietly. He sat down. "But maybe there's a way to remember them." He looked up at us.

"How?" asked Caleb eagerly.

Papa leaned back in the chair. "I've placed an advertisement in the newspapers. For help."

"You mean a housekeeper?" I asked, surprised.

Caleb and I looked at each other and burst out laughing, remembering Hilly, our old housekeeper. She was round and slow and shuffling. She snored in a high whistle at night, like a tea-kettle, and let the fire go out.

"No," said Papa slowly. "Not a housekeeper." He paused. "A wife."

Caleb stared at Papa. "A wife? You mean a mother?"

Nick slid his face onto Papa's lap and Papa stroked his ears.

"That, too," said Papa. "Like Maggie."

Matthew, our neighbor to the south, had written to ask for a wife and mother for his children. And Maggie had come from Tennessee. Her hair was the color of turnips and she laughed.

Papa reached into his pocket and unfolded a letter written on white paper. "And I have received an answer." Papa read to us:

"Dear Mr. Jacob Witting,

"I am Sarah Wheaton from Maine as you will see from my letter. I am answering your advertisement. I have never been married, though I have been asked. I have lived with an older brother, William, who is about to be married. His wife-to-be is young and energetic.

"I have always loved to live by the sea, but at this time I feel a move is necessary. And the truth is, the sea is as far east as I can go. My choice, as you can see, is limited. This should not be taken as an insult. I am strong and I work hard and I am willing to travel. But I am not mild mannered. If you should still care to write, I would be interested in your children and about where you live. And you.

"Very truly yours,
"Sarah Elisabeth Wheaton

"P.S. Do you have opinions on cats? I have one."

No one spoke when Papa finished the letter. He kept looking at it in his hands, reading it over to himself. Finally I turned my head a bit to sneak a look at Caleb. He was smiling. I smiled, too.

"One thing," I said in the quiet of the room.

"What's that?" asked Papa, looking up.

I put my arm around Caleb.

"Ask her if she sings," I said.

Caleb and Papa and I wrote letters to Sarah, and before the ice and snow had melted from the fields, we all received answers. Mine came first.

Dear Anna,

Yes, I can braid hair and I can make stew and bake bread, though I prefer to build bookshelves and paint.

My favorite colors are the colors of the sea, blue and gray and green, depending on the weather. My brother William is a fisherman, and he tells me that when he is in the middle of a fogbound sea the water is a color for which there is no name. He catches flounder and sea bass and bluefish. Sometimes he sees whales. And birds, too, of course. I am enclosing a book of sea birds so you will see what William and I see every day.

Very truly yours,
Sarah Elisabeth Wheaton

Caleb read and read the letter so many times that the ink began to run and the folds tore. He read the book about sea birds over and over.

"Do you think she'll come?" asked Caleb. "And will she stay? What if she thinks we are loud and pesky?"

"You *are* loud and pesky," I told him. But I was worried, too. Sarah loved the sea, I could tell. Maybe she wouldn't leave there after all to come where there were fields and grass and sky and not much else.

"What if she comes and doesn't like our house?" Caleb asked. "I told her it was small. Maybe I shouldn't have told her it was small."

"Hush, Caleb. Hush."

Caleb's letter came soon after, with a picture of a cat drawn on the envelope.

Dear Caleb,

My cat's name is Seal because she is gray like the seals that swim offshore in Maine. She is glad that Lottie and Nick send their greetings. She likes dogs most of the time. She says their footprints are much larger than hers (which she is enclosing in return).

Your house sounds lovely, even though it is far out in the country with no close neighbors. My house is tall and the shingles are gray because of the salt from the sea. There are roses nearby.

Yes, I do like small rooms sometimes. Yes, I can keep a fire going at night. I do not know if I snore. Seal has never told me.

Very truly yours,
Sarah Elisabeth

"Did you really ask her about fires and snoring?" I asked, amazed.

"I wished to know," Caleb said.

He kept the letter with him, reading it in the barn and in the fields and by the cow pond. And always in bed at night.

One morning, early, Papa and Caleb and I were cleaning out the horse stalls and putting down new bedding. Papa stopped suddenly and leaned on his pitchfork.

"Sarah has said she will come for a month's time if we wish her to," he said, his voice loud in the dark barn. "To see how it is. Just to see."

Caleb stood by the stall door and folded his arms across his chest.

"I think," he began. Then, "I think," he said slowly, "that it would be good – to say yes," he finished in a rush.

Papa looked at me.

"I say yes," I told him, grinning.

"Yes," said Papa. "Then yes it is."

And the three of us, all smiling, went to work again.

The next day Papa went to town to mail his letter to Sarah. It was rainy for days, and the clouds followed. The house was cool and damp and quiet. Once I set four places at the table, then caught myself and put the extra plate away. Three lambs were born, one with a black face. And then Papa's letter came. It was very short.

Dear Jacob,

I will come by train. I will wear a yellow bonnet. I am plain and tall.

Sarah

"What's that?" asked Caleb excitedly, peering over Papa's shoulder. He pointed. "There, written at the bottom of the letter."

Papa read it to himself. Then he smiled, holding up the letter for us to see.

Tell them I sing was all it said.

Sarah came in the spring. She came through green grass fields that bloomed with Indian paintbrush, red and orange, and blue-eyed grass.

Papa got up early for the long day's trip to the train and back. He brushed his hair so slick and shiny that Caleb laughed. He wore a clean blue shirt, and a belt instead of suspenders.

He fed and watered the horses, talking to them as he hitched them up to the wagon. Old Bess, calm and kind; Jack, wild-eyed, reaching over to nip Bess on the neck.

"Clear day, Bess," said Papa, rubbing her nose.

"Settle down, Jack." He leaned his head on Jack.

And then Papa drove off along the dirt road to fetch Sarah. Papa's new wife. Maybe. Maybe our new mother.

Gophers ran back and forth across the road, stopping to stand up and watch the wagon. Far off in the field a woodchuck ate and listened. Ate and listened.

Caleb and I did our chores without talking. We shoveled out the stalls and laid down new hay. We fed the sheep. We swept and straightened and carried wood and water. And then our chores were done.

Caleb pulled on my shirt.

"Is my face clean?" he asked. "Can my face be *too* clean?" He looked alarmed.

"No, your face is clean but not too clean," I said.

Caleb slipped his hand into mine as we stood on the porch, watching the road. He was afraid.

"Will she be nice?" he asked. "Like Maggie?"

"Sarah will be nice," I told him.

"How far away is Maine?" he asked.

"You know how far. Far away, by the sea."

"Will Sarah bring some sea?" he asked.

"No, you cannot bring the sea."

The sheep ran in the field, and far off the cows moved slowly to the pond, like turtles.

"Will she like us?" asked Caleb very softly.

I watched a marsh hawk wheel down behind the barn.

He looked up at me.

"Of course she will like us." He answered his own question. "We are nice," he added, making me smile.

We waited and watched. I rocked on the porch and Caleb rolled a marble on the wood floor. Back and forth. Back and forth. The marble was blue.

We saw the dust from the wagon first, rising above the road, about the heads of Jack and Old Bess. Caleb climbed up onto the porch roof and shaded his eyes.

"A bonnet!" he cried. "I see a yellow bonnet!"

The dogs came out from under the porch, ears up, their eyes on the cloud of dust bringing Sarah. The wagon passed the fenced field, and the cows and sheep looked up, too. It rounded the windmill and the barn and the windbreak of Russian olive that Mama had planted long ago. Nick began to bark, then Lottie, and the wagon clattered into the yard and stopped by the steps.

"Hush," said Papa to the dogs.

And it was quiet.

Sarah stepped down from the wagon, a cloth bag in her hand. She reached up and took off her yellow bonnet, smoothing back her brown hair into a bun. She was plain and tall.

"Did you bring some sea?" cried Caleb beside me.

"Something from the sea," said Sarah, smiling. "And me." She turned and lifted a black case from the wagon. "And Seal, too."

Carefully she opened the case, and Seal, gray with white feet, stepped out. Lottie lay down, her head on her paws, staring. Nick leaned down to sniff. Then he lay down, too.

"The cat will be good in the barn," said Papa. "For mice."

Sarah smiled. "She will be good in the house, too."

Sarah took Caleb's hand, then mine. Her hands were large and rough. She gave Caleb a shell — a moon snail, she called it — that was curled and smelled of salt.

"The gulls fly high and drop the shells on the rocks below," she told Caleb. "When the shell is broken, they eat what is inside."

"That is very smart," said Caleb.

"For you, Anna," said Sarah, "a sea stone."

And she gave me the smoothest and whitest stone I had ever seen.

"The sea washes over and over and around the stone, rolling it until it is round and perfect."

"That is very smart, too," said Caleb. He looked up at Sarah. "We do not have the sea here."

Sarah turned and looked out over the plains. "No," she said. "There is no sea here. But the land rolls a little like the sea."

My father did not see her look, but I did. And I knew that Caleb had seen it, too. Sarah was not smiling. Sarah was already lonely. In a month's time the preacher might come to marry Sarah and Papa. And a month was a long time. Time enough for her to change her mind and leave us.

Papa took Sarah's bags inside, where her room was ready with a quilt on the bed and blue flax dried in a vase on the night table.

Seal stretched and made a small cat sound. I watched her circle the dogs and sniff the air. Caleb came out and stood beside me.

"When will we sing?" he whispered.

I shook my head, turning the white stone over and over in my hand. I wished everything was as perfect as the stone. I wished that Papa and Caleb and I were perfect for Sarah. I wished we had a sea of our own.

* * * * *

The dogs loved Sarah first. Lottie slept beside her bed, curled in a soft circle, and Nick leaned his face on the covers in the morning, watching for the first sign that Sarah was awake. No one knew where Seal slept. Seal was a roamer.

Sarah's collection of shells sat on the windowsill.

"A scallop," she told us, picking up the shells one by one, "a sea clam, an oyster, a razor clam. And a conch shell. If you put it to your ear you can hear the sea." She put it to Caleb's ear, then mine. Papa listened, too. Then Sarah listened once more, with a look so sad and far away that Caleb leaned against me.

"At least Sarah can hear the sea," he whispered.

Papa was quiet and shy with Sarah, and so was I. But Caleb talked to Sarah from morning until the light left the sky.

"Where are you going?" he asked. "To do what?"

"To pick flowers," said Sarah. "I'll hang some of them upside down and dry them so they'll keep some color. And we can have flowers all winter long."

"I'll come, too!" cried Caleb. "Sarah said winter," he said to me. "That means Sarah will stay."

Together we picked flowers, paintbrush and clover and prairie violets. There were buds on the wild roses that climbed up the paddock fence.

"The roses will bloom in early summer," I told Sarah. I looked to see if she knew what I was thinking. Summer was when the wedding would be. *Might* be. Sarah and Papa's wedding.

We hung the flowers from the ceiling in little bunches. "I've never seen this before," said Sarah. "What is it called?"

"Bride's bonnet," I told her.

Caleb smiled at the name.

"We don't have this by the sea," she said. "We have seaside goldenrod and wild asters and woolly ragwort."

"Woolly ragwort!" Caleb whooped. He made up a song.

"Woolly ragwort all around,
Woolly ragwort on the ground.
Woolly ragwort grows and grows,
Woolly ragwort in your nose."

Sarah and Papa laughed, and the dogs lifted their heads and thumped their tails against the wood floor. Seal sat on a kitchen chair and watched us with yellow eyes.

We ate Sarah's stew, the late light coming through the windows. Papa had baked bread that was still warm from the fire.

"The stew is fine," said Papa.

"Ayuh." Sarah nodded. "The bread, too."

"What does 'ayuh' mean?" asked Caleb.

"In Maine it means yes," said Sarah. "Do you want more stew?"

"Ayuh," said Caleb.

"Ayuh," echoed my father.

After dinner Sarah told us about William. "He has a gray-and-white boat named *Kittiwake*." She looked out the window. "That is a small gull found way off the shore where William fishes. There are three aunts who live near us. They wear silk dresses and no shoes. You would love them."

"Ayuh," said Caleb.

"Does your brother look like you?" I asked.

"Yes," said Sarah. "He is plain and tall."

At dusk Sarah cut Caleb's hair on the front steps, gathering his curls and scattering them on the fence and ground. Seal batted some hair around the porch as the dogs watched.

"Why?" asked Caleb.

"For the birds," said Sarah. "They will use it for their nests. Later we can look for nests of curls."

"Sarah said 'later,'" Caleb whispered to me as we spread his hair about. "Sarah will stay."

Sarah cut Papa's hair, too. No one else saw, but I found him behind the barn, tossing the pieces of hair into the wind for the birds.

Sarah brushed my hair and tied it up in back with a rose velvet ribbon she had brought from Maine. She brushed hers long and free and tied it back, too, and we stood side by side looking into the mirror. I looked taller, like Sarah, and fair and thin. And with my hair pulled back I looked a little like her daughter. Sarah's daughter.

And then it was time for singing.

Sarah sang us a song we had never heard before as we sat on the porch, insects buzzing in the dark, the rustle of cows in the grasses. It was called "Sumer Is Icumen in," and she taught it to us all, even Papa, who sang as if he had never stopped singing.

"Sumer is icumen in,
Lhude sing cuccu!"

"What is sumer?" asked Caleb. He said it "soomer," the way Sarah had said it.

"Summer," said Papa and Sarah at the same time. Caleb and I looked at each other. Summer was coming.

"Tomorrow," said Sarah, "I want to see the sheep. You know, I've never touched one."

"Never?" Caleb sat up.

"Never," said Sarah. She smiled and leaned back in her chair. "But I've touched seals. Real seals. They are cool and slippery and they slide through the water like fish. They can cry and sing. And sometimes they bark, a little like dogs."

Sarah barked like a seal. And Lottie and Nick came running from the barn to jump up on Sarah and lick her face and make her laugh. Sarah stroked them and scratched their ears and it was quiet again.

"I wish I could touch a seal right now," said Caleb, his voice soft in the night.

"So do I," said Sarah. She sighed, then she began to sing the summer song again. Far off in a field, a meadowlark sang, too.

Think It Over

1. *How does Sarah help the Witting family? How do the Wittings help Sarah?*
2. *Why is Anna afraid to see a look of loneliness on Sarah's face?*
3. *Sarah writes to Jacob Witting and his family several times. What things do Jacob and the children learn about Sarah from her letters?*
4. *What is the importance of singing in this story?*
5. *Would you enjoy living in Anna and Caleb's time and place? Explain why or why not.*

Write

Sarah first writes to Jacob to ask about his children and about the place where they live. Write a letter back to Sarah that describes the place where you live. Tell about the appearance, the weather, and the plants and animals that she might see.

A WORDS ABOUT THE AUTHOR:

PATRICIA MACLACHLAN

Descriptions of the prairie in *Sarah, Plain and Tall* are vivid, vibrant, and true because the author, Patricia MacLachlan, knows the prairie well. MacLachlan, who was born in Cheyenne, Wyoming, says that for her "the western landscape has always been a powerful force . . . fueling mind and imagination."

That lively imagination began in childhood when MacLachlan—an only child—invented characters she wished to be. Encouraged to read by her parents, who were teachers, she filled her world with characters from her books as well as from her imagination.

With such a vivid imagination and strong love of reading, writing stories should have followed naturally.

AWARD-WINNING AUTHOR

Yet the only story the author remembers writing as a child was a school assignment at age eight. The story was to be about a pet and had to have "a beginning, a middle, and an ending." Her teacher was not impressed with the story she turned in on a three-by-five card: *My cats have names and seem happy. Often they play. The end.* The young author was discouraged enough to write in her diary: "I shall try not to be a writer."

MacLachlan did indeed "try not to be a writer." Following in her parents' footsteps, she became an English teacher. But her powerful imagination and her love for books proved too strong a combination to resist. In her thirties, Patricia MacLachlan began to write novels with proper beginnings, middles, and endings. Now she shares her experiences in creative writing workshops that she conducts for adults and children.

While much of the action in *Sarah, Plain and Tall* comes from MacLachlan's imagination, the basic story idea is true. When Patricia was a child, her mother told her about "the real Sarah, who came from the coast of Maine to the prairie to become a wife and mother." Building on that fact, MacLachlan crafted a simple but fine story that expresses the importance of family—a theme that runs through many of her books. She has received several awards for *Sarah, Plain and Tall,* among them the 1986 Newbery Medal. The little girl who tried not to be a writer grew up to distinguish herself in that profession.

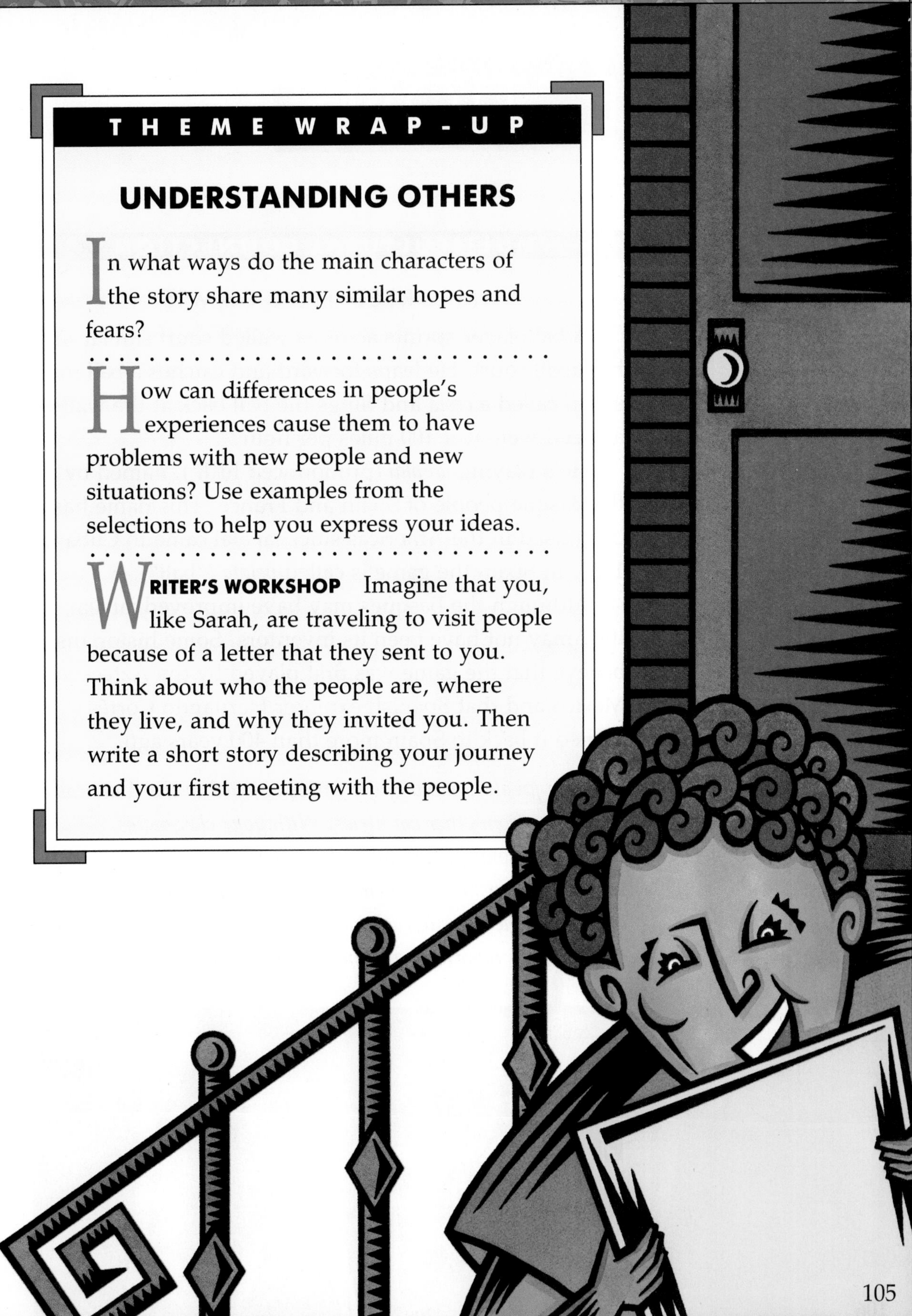

THEME WRAP-UP

UNDERSTANDING OTHERS

In what ways do the main characters of the story share many similar hopes and fears?

How can differences in people's experiences cause them to have problems with new people and new situations? Use examples from the selections to help you express your ideas.

WRITER'S WORKSHOP Imagine that you, like Sarah, are traveling to visit people because of a letter that they sent to you. Think about who the people are, where they live, and why they invited you. Then write a short story describing your journey and your first meeting with the people.

CONNECTIONS

MULTICULTURAL CONNECTION

IMPORTED BALL GAMES

A ballplayer sprints across a walled court similar to a handball court. He leaps forward and catches a ball in a scoop called a *cesta* and flings the ball back at the wall at a speed well over 100 miles per hour.

He's playing *jai alai* (pronounced hī′lī′), named by the Basque people of Spain and France. This name has been used in the Americas since jai alai came to Cuba in 1900. In Spain the game is called *pelota* ("ball").

Although the Basques may have improved jai alai, they may not have been its inventors. Some historians believe that the game was first played by the Aztecs in Mexico and that Spanish explorer Hernando Cortés carried it back to Spain more than 400 years ago.

■ *Like jai alai, many of the games enjoyed in the Americas have come from other countries. With your classmates, brainstorm some games you enjoy. Then, on your own, research one or more of them. Write a report that describes the origin and the rules of each game. You and your classmates can publish your reports in a games encyclopedia.*

SOCIAL STUDIES CONNECTION

GUARD THE CHIEF!

Games and sports have always helped young people prepare for life. Find out what games Native American children played to develop important survival skills. Teach one to your classmates. Then, with a group, create a bulletin board on Native American games.

Southern Ute schoolchildren play *Nia-Kup,* "The Hand Game"

HEALTH CONNECTION

FIT FOR LIVING

Sports and games generally make people healthier. Research how activity affects such physical functions as digestion, muscle tone, and circulation. Find out which physical activities are most beneficial and which are least beneficial. Share what you learn in a health newsletter.

You can present some of your findings in a chart like the one shown.

Name of Activity	Baseball	Hiking	Running
How it improves the body			
What it fails to do			
Overall rating as a physical fitness activity			

UNIT TWO

TRIALS

Trials can mean different things to different people. Long ago in India wise judges traveled with their "courtrooms" from town to town. Today trials can happen in front of hundreds of spectators or, as in trials held in many Native American nations, in front of only two participants and a judge. Maybe the most challenging trials are those that involve only one—a person standing alone while being tested by nature. As you read the selections in this unit, compare the many types of trials that people face. Which experiences have you shared? Which can you learn from?

THEMES

BOOKSHELF

ANNO'S HAT TRICKS

BY AKIHIRO NOZAKI AND MITSUMASA ANNO

If you like brainteasers, then hold on to your hat! Enter the world of the hatter. To solve his puzzles, you must learn how to think like a computer.

HBJ LIBRARY BOOK

REWIND TO YESTERDAY

BY SUSAN BETH PFEFFER

Kelly discovers that the rewind button on the new VCR not only rewinds tapes, it rewinds time! This fantasy story tells about the adventures that follow Kelly's amazing discovery.

SONG OF THE CHIRIMIA

BY JANE ANNE VOLKMER

Illustrations based on Mayan stone carvings accompany this colorful folktale from Guatemala, told in both Spanish and English.

THE SEARCH FOR GRISSI

BY MARY FRANCIS SHURA

Moving from Peoria to Brooklyn is lonely and frightening for Pete. Things start to improve, however, when he becomes involved in the search for a missing cat named Grissi.

ENCYCLOPEDIA BROWN AND THE CASE OF THE TREASURE HUNT

BY DONALD J. SOBOL

Match wits with the world's greatest fifth-grade detective in this collection of ten baffling cases.

T H E M E

NATURE'S FURY

Have you ever been frightened by lightning, pounded by hailstones, or snowed in by high drifts? If so, then you, like the people in these selections, know what it is like to face nature's fury.

C O N T E N T S

FROM

In for Winter, Out for Spring

by Arnold Adoff
illustrated by Jerry Pinkney

My Brother Aaron Runs Outside To Tell Us There Is A Severe
Thunder
Storm
Warning

Just Announced On The Radio While We Were Out
U n d e r

A Perfectly Blue Sky
We Know How Fast The Weather Can Change How
Fast Those Storms Can
Blow Across These Corn
Fields Every Spring

We Bring Our Books
And Toys Inside And
Listen To The Noon
News
Between The Soup
And Sandwiches
And
Try To Only Think
A b o u t
Our Lunch

Clouds Are Black
And
Dark Green This Afternoon
And They
Are Sitting Over Our Town
Just Rumb l i n g
A w a y

With Their Bragging
N o i s e

Who Ordered
The Thunder
Who Ordered That Flash Of Lightning
Flashing From The
West
Who Ordered The Rest Of This Dark Sky

Who Asked This S t o r m T o S t a y

Words from the Illustrator: Jerry Pinkney

People often think that an author and an illustrator work together on a book, but this is rarely the case. Usually, the author writes the book, and then the illustrator takes over. The situation with *In for Winter, Out for Spring* was a little different, though. I often run into Arnold Adoff, so for the first time I was working with an author I knew. While there was no discussion of how I would illustrate the book, Arnold did send me a tape of him reading the poems. That added a great deal to my interpretation.

After reading a manuscript, I draw small sketches called thumbnails. In these I sketch the situations that I think are the most interesting. Then I put together a dummy. This is a mock copy of the book showing the characters I plan to use. I send the dummy to the publisher, and if everyone agrees, I go ahead and hire the models for the characters.

With Arnold's poetry, I had a lot of images I could have chosen to illustrate. In the excerpt you read, for instance, I could have drawn more of the storm. But I had been looking for an opportunity to put the mother, the daughter, and the son in the same picture, and this seemed like a good place to do it. More than anything else, I wanted to emphasize the family aspect of this book.

STORMS
SEYMOUR SIMO
MORROW

THUNDERSTORMS

from *Storms*

by Seymour Simon

We live at the bottom of a blanket of air called the atmosphere. The atmosphere is always moving, sometimes slowly, other times quickly and violently. These changes in the atmosphere are called the weather. We call the violent changes storms.

Thunderstorms are the most powerful electrical storms in the atmosphere. In twenty minutes, a single thunderstorm can drop 125 million gallons of water and give off more electrical energy than is used in a large city during an entire week.

Lightning is an electrical discharge within a thunderstorm. As a thunderstorm develops, the clouds become charged with electricity. Scientists are still not sure exactly what causes this to happen. But they do know that as much as 100 million volts build up in the lower part of a thunderhead, and the temperature of a single bolt of lightning reaches 50,000 degrees F. within a few millionths of a second. That's almost five times greater than the temperature at the sun's surface.

Lightning flashes when the voltage becomes high enough for electricity to leap across the air from one place to another. Lightning can spark within the cloud, from one cloud to another, from ground to cloud, or from cloud to ground.

Thunder is the sound given off by the explosive expansion of air heated by a lightning stroke. When lightning is close, thunder sounds like a single, sharp crack. From farther away, thunder sounds like a growling or rumbling noise. Thunder usually can be heard easily from six or seven miles away, and even from twenty miles away on a quiet day.

Light is about a million times faster than sound, so you see a lightning bolt almost instantly, but the sound of thunder takes about five seconds to travel one mile. This makes it possible for you to judge the distance of a lightning stroke by timing how long it takes you to hear the thunder.

Count the number of seconds between the flash and the thunder. (You can count seconds by counting slowly in this way: and a one and a two and a three and a four and a five, and so on.) Divide the number of seconds by five. The number you get is the number of miles away the lightning struck.

Sometimes a thunderstorm gives birth to a tornado. The wind blows hard and trees bend. Heavy rains or hailstones fall. Lightning and thunder rip the dark sky, and a howling roar like hundreds of jet planes fills the air.

Spinning winds inside the thunderstorm begin forming a funnel-shaped cloud that reaches downward to the ground. When it contacts the earth, an explosion of flying dirt turns the tornado dark.

This remarkable series of photos shows the life of a tornado in hours, minutes, and seconds.

As the spinning winds pick up speed, the tornado grows larger and larger. The funnel skips across the ground, sometimes setting down, sometimes bouncing upward, and then touching down again, leaving semicircular marks on the ground like the hoofprints of giant horses. The funnel moves forward at speeds averaging thirty miles per hour, but some tornadoes travel at more than sixty miles per hour.

Like the hose of an enormous vacuum cleaner, the tornado picks up loose materials and whirls them aloft. In less than fifteen minutes, the funnel cloud becomes clogged with dirt and air and can no longer suck up any more. The cloud becomes lighter in color as less dirt is swept aloft. As the tornado begins to lag behind the parent thunderhead, it narrows and finally vanishes altogether.

15 28 17
15 31 34
15 37 59
15 39 50

The twisting winds of a tornado whirl around the funnel at speeds of 200 miles an hour or more. Houses may be knocked down and blown apart by the wind. Then the tornado picks up the pieces, along with chairs, tables, and beds, and carries them away.

If you know a tornado is coming, go indoors, but stay away from windows. In a house, the safest place is in the cellar. Get under a table or under the stairs. If there is no cellar, go to a closet or a small room in the middle of the house. Cover yourself with a blanket or heavy towels to protect against flying glass.

Tornadoes sometimes do strange things. Once a car with two people inside was lifted to a height of 100 feet, then deposited right side up without injuring the passengers. Another tornado lifted a train locomotive from one track, spun it around in midair, and then set it down on another track facing the opposite direction.

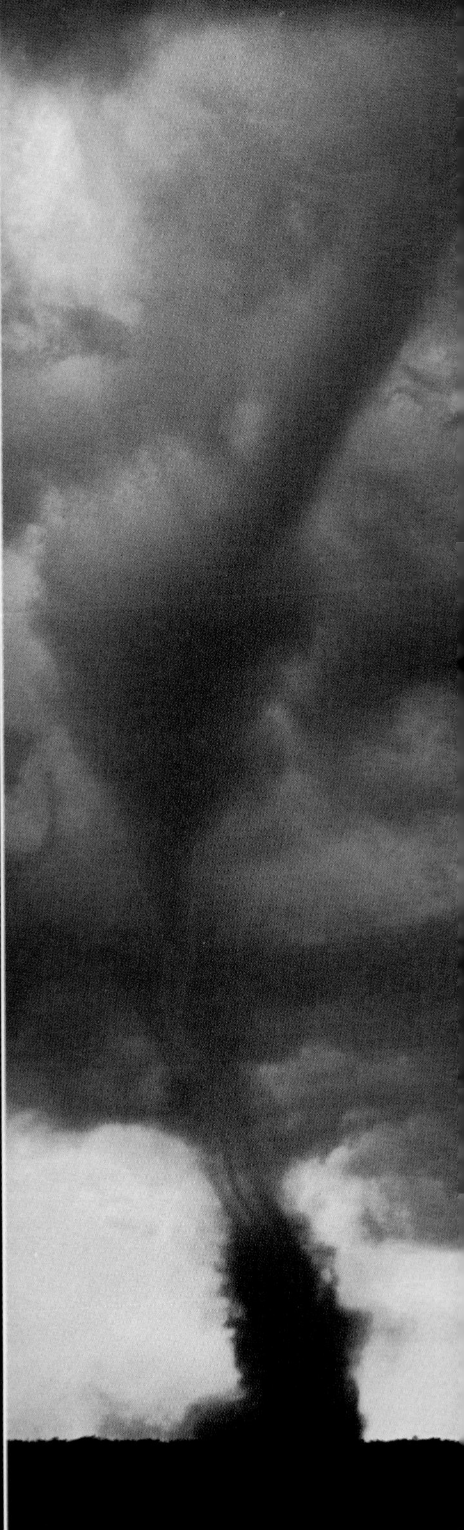

There are many ancient myths about storms. The early Norsemen believed that Thor was the god of thunderstorms. They thought that lightning struck when Thor threw his mighty hammer and thunder rumbled when his chariot struck storm clouds.

Nowadays, radar, satellites, and computers keep track of storms and help scientists forecast their behavior. But the more scientists learn about storms, the more complicated they find them to be. Storms still arouse our sense of awe and wonder.

Think It Over

1. *What are some of the dangerous things that can happen during a thunderstorm?*
2. *Why doesn't a tornado cloud last any longer than fifteen minutes?*
3. *According to the selection, what is one thing that ancient myths and modern technology have in common?*

Write

What would you do if you knew a tornado was coming? Write a set of directions telling what to do and what not to do during a tornado.

TORNADO ALERT!

CHILDREN'S CHOICE

Night of the Twisters
by Ivy Ruckman

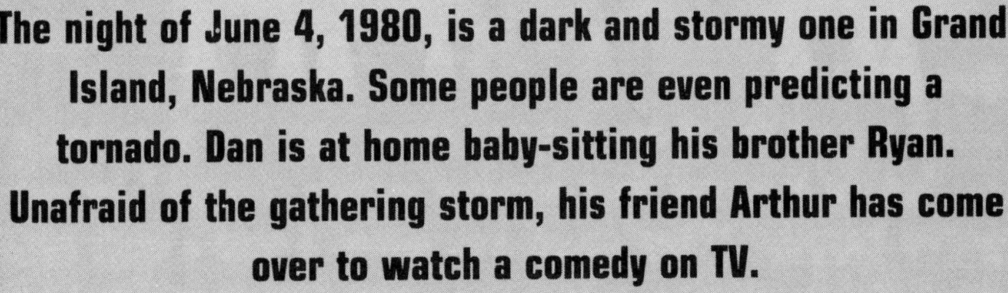

The night of June 4, 1980, is a dark and stormy one in Grand Island, Nebraska. Some people are even predicting a tornado. Dan is at home baby-sitting his brother Ryan. Unafraid of the gathering storm, his friend Arthur has come over to watch a comedy on TV.

by Ivy Ruckman

illustrated by Jeffrey Terreson

Sometime in there, in the middle of all that comedy on the screen, the siren began. Now, *that* is a very sobering sound. It's unlike anything else, having its own built-in chill factor.

I thought of Mom first. She'd hear it and come back, I told myself.

Then I thought of Dad and how far the farm was from town. They wouldn't even hear the siren out there.

In half a second, I was at the phone, dialing 555-2379.

Four rings. Then I heard Grandma's voice.

"Grandma!" I shouted into the phone. "Where have you been? There's a tornado just north of G.I. The siren's going, can you hear it?"

A voice said something, but it sounded so far away.

"Talk louder, Grandma! I can't hear you."

The voice faded away entirely. I wasn't even sure it was Grandma's now.

"There's a tornado coming! Can you hear me?"

Finally, there wasn't anything on the line but the sound of another phone ringing very faintly, as if it were in New York or someplace far away. I couldn't figure it out.

By then, Arthur was standing next to me. I was just about to hand him the phone when, abruptly, the siren stopped. It didn't taper off, it just quit, as if someone snipped it with scissors. Except for the TV, everything around us suddenly seemed very still.

"Hey," he said, raising his eyebrows, "they changed their minds."

I hung up the phone. I didn't know what was happening.

"Maybe they got their weather signals crossed," he suggested happily. "They could, you know. I read a book once about that happening, where this whole fleet of fishing boats put out to sea . . ." he rattled on.

I ran to the door, thinking I might see Mom pulling into the driveway, but no luck.

"It's quit blowing," I called over my shoulder to Arthur.

Sure enough, the wind had died down. Maybe the storm wouldn't amount to anything after all.

That nice comforting thought had hardly entered my mind when the siren blared forth again. With a jolt, I remembered what Mom had told us to do.

"We always turn on the radio," Arthur said, already on his way to the kitchen. "You want me to? I'll get the weather station."

I was hardly listening. I hurried down the bedroom hallway to Ryan's room at the end. I hated like everything to get him up. He'd cry. I knew he'd wake up and cry. Without Mom, Arthur and I would have him screaming in our ears the whole time.

When I saw him in his crib, peacefully sleeping on the side of his face, his rear end in the air, I just didn't have the heart to wake him up. I'd wait a minute or two. Mom would be back. Anyway, it's blowing over, I told myself, it won't last.

Quietly, I closed the door behind me.

That's when the lights started flickering.

In the hallway, I practically had a head-on with Arthur, who was coming at me real fast. The look on his face scared me.

"There's no . . . there's no . . ."

"What?"

"There's no radio reception anymore. It just went dead! This guy . . . He kept saying, 'Tornado alert, tornado alert!' Then it went dead."

We rushed back to the living room. The TV was flashing these big letters that filled the entire screen: CD . . . CD . . . CD . . .

"What's it mean?" Arthur cried.

"Civil Defense Emergency!" I whirled around. "I'm getting Ryan!"

The lights flickered again.

At the same time we heard these really strange sounds that stopped us in our tracks. They were coming from the bathroom and the kitchen. Sucking sounds. The drains were sucking! I felt this awful pulling in my ears, too, as if there were vacuums on both sides of my head.

"I've got to go home!" Arthur cried all of a sudden, bolting for the door.

I ran after him. "You're not—you can't!" I grabbed the back of his T-shirt, hauled him around, and pushed him toward the stairs. "Get *down* there. I have to get Ryan! Now *go*!"

I don't know what I'd have done if he hadn't minded me. We were catching the fear from each other, and even though the siren was screaming on and off again, so I didn't know what it was telling us, I knew we had to take cover fast.

The lights went out for good just before I reached Ryan's room. I smashed face first into Ryan's butterfly mobile. That's how I knew I was at the crib. I felt for him, got my hands under his nightshirt and diaper, rolled him over. I lifted him, but we didn't get far. He was caught in the mobile, his arm or his head . . . I couldn't see . . . I couldn't get him loose. . . .

"Mom!" I yelled, though I knew she wasn't there.

I tried to lay him down again, but he was so tangled, part of him was still up in the air. He started to cry.

"Wait, Ryan, I'll get you out!" But I couldn't.

Finally, holding him with my left arm, I climbed onto the side of the crib. My right hand followed the string up the mobile, way up to the hook. I yanked it loose. The whole thing came crashing down on top of us as I jumped backward off the crib.

The plastic butterfly poking me was poking Ryan, too, but I didn't care. The tornado was close, and I knew it. Both my ears had popped, and I had this crazy fear that those drains, sucking like monsters now, would get us if the storm didn't.

Arthur was at the bottom of the stairs, waiting. He'd found the flashlight! I jumped the last half-flight to the floor.

"Hurry!" I screamed. I swung into the doorway of the bathroom, with Arthur right behind me. We crouched under the towel rack.

"Shine it here, on Ryan," I gasped. "He's caught in this thing." By now Ryan was kicking and screaming, and his eyes were big in the light.

Once we got the mess of strings free of Ryan's sweaty nightshirt, Arthur kicked the mobile against the wall by the toilet.

"I have to go home!" he cried. "They won't go to the basement. Mama never does."

The beam of light bounced around the blackness of the bathroom as Arthur scrambled to his feet, but I grabbed and held on to him.

"You can't go! It's here! Can't you feel it?"

The siren quit again as I pulled him back down and threw my leg over him. The flashlight clattered to the floor and rolled away from us.

We heard it next. The lull. The deadliest quiet ever, one that makes you think you might explode. The heat in that room built until I couldn't get my breath.

Then I began to hear noises. A chair scraping across the kitchen floor upstairs.

"Your mom's back!" Arthur said, pushing at my leg.

I knew it wasn't my mother moving the chair.

The noises got worse. It seemed as if every piece of furniture was moving around up there . . . big, heavy things, smashing into each other.

A window popped.

Crash! Another.

Glass, shattering—everywhere—right next to us in the laundry room.

I pulled a towel down over Ryan and held him tight. If he was still crying, I didn't know it because I was *feeling* the sucking this time. It was like something trying to lift my body right up off the floor.

Arthur felt it, too. "We're going to die!"

Ten seconds more and that howling, shrieking tornado was upon us.

"The blanket!" I screamed at Arthur's ear.

He pulled it down from the countertop and we covered ourselves, our hands shaking wildly. I wasn't worrying about my mom then or my dad. Just us. Ryan and Arthur and me, huddled together there on the floor.

The roaring had started somewhere to the east, then came bearing down on us like a hundred freight trains. Only that twister didn't move on. It stationed itself right overhead, making the loudest noise I'd ever heard, whining worse than any jet. There was a tremendous crack, and I felt the wall shudder behind us. I knew then our house was being ripped apart. Suddenly chunks of ceiling were falling on our heads.

We'll be buried! was all I could think.

At that moment, as plain as anything above that deafening roar, I heard my dad's voice: *The shower's the safest place.*

I didn't question hearing it. Holding Ryan against me with one arm, I began crawling toward the shower stall. I reached back and yanked at Arthur's shirt. Somehow we got inside with the blanket. Another explosion, and the glass shower door shattered all over the bathroom floor.

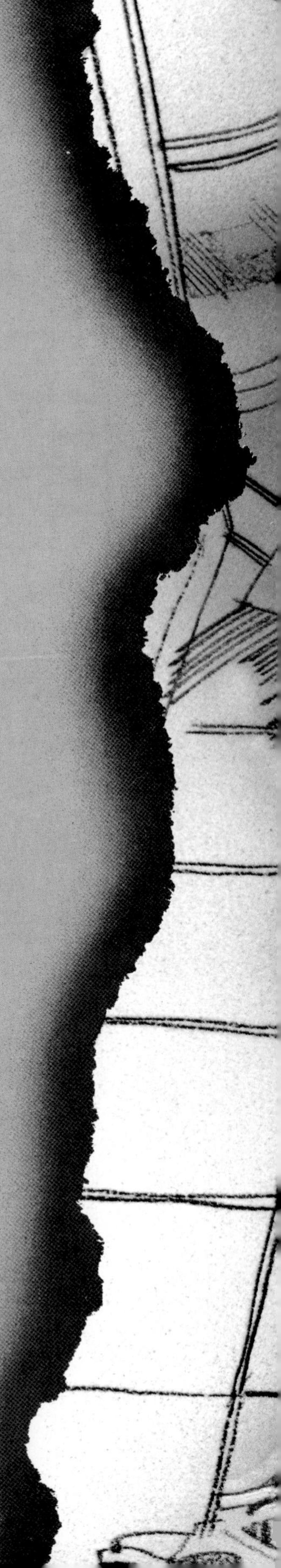

We pulled the blanket over our heads and I began to pray. I knew Arthur was praying, too, jammed there into my side. I could feel Ryan's heart beating through his undershirt against mine. Outside those places where our bodies touched, there was nothing but terror as the roar of that tornado went on and on. I thought the world was coming to an end, *had* come to an end, and so would we, any minute.

Then I felt Ryan's fat fingers close around one of mine. He pulled my hand to his mouth and started sucking on my finger. It made me cry. The tears ran down my cheeks and onto his head. With the whole world blowing to pieces around us, Ryan took my hand and made me feel better.

Afterward, neither Arthur nor I was able to say how long we huddled there in the basement shower.

"A tornado's forward speed is generally thirty to fifty miles an hour," the meteorologist had told us.

Our tornado's forward speed was zero. It parked right there on Sand Crane Drive. Five minutes or ten, we couldn't tell, but it seemed like an hour. Roaring and humming and shrieking, that twister was right on top of us. I'll never be that scared again as long as I live. Neither will Arthur.

Think It Over

1. *What problems does Dan face in the story?*
2. *Why does Dan drag Ryan and Arthur into the shower stall?*
3. *Dan and Arthur are not very worried in the beginning of the selection. What events lead them to realize that they are in great danger?*
4. *The story does not say that the boys are cold during the tornado. Why do they cover themselves with a blanket?*

Write

Think about Dan's behavior throughout the selection. How would you react in the same situation? Write a report that praises some of Dan's actions and criticizes others.

FROM

TORNADO! POEMS

BY ARNOLD ADOFF
ILLUSTRATED BY RONALD HIMLER

Poet Arnold Adoff lived through the fury of a tornado strike in his home near Xenia, Ohio. In these poems, he describes how the people rose up on the day after and went on with their lives.

CHILDREN'S CHOICE

In the morning

the sky is blue
and it is school
again

hungry
hungry hurry
up

at our school

the skylights have big holes
through their glass panes
there is glass all over
all the floors

it is a day for wearing shoes
even on the mats

the firemen start yelling

get away from there
these
buildings
can fall
at any time

will have to be
knocked
down as soon as the people
move their things away

one girl is carrying
her winter coat
her boots
out to a truck

one boy is playing
where
his
house had been
is not

you can see

a broken house
a street of broken
houses
a broken baby doll
in the boards

dogs and cats
are
sniffing
hungry
and
cows are strolling
down the
street

the woman

is telling about the wind

it was not just the wind
and the pressure
on your back
on your head
you couldn't get up
you couldn't
move

but the wind was full of dirt
and sand and filth and rocks
so many bits of
glass
and heavy things

heavy things
in the
air

momma says

that's why
the funnel
cloud
is
black

not the
color
of
the
wind

but dirt and boards
and trees
and stone

daddy says

there will be
storms for many springs
for many summers

momma says
we can be tougher
than some thunder
noise
some flash

grandma
says
the last time one came
through here was fifty
years ago and i can
wait another fifty
for the next

brother says

it never seems to rain
in a quiet way out here
just water
for the garden
and the corn fields
when they get dry

just wet
no
wind
it never seems to rain
in a quiet
way

i say
that's right
good
night

and anyway

no
old
tornado

i don't care
how
bad

is stronger
than the
people on the land

THEME WRAP-UP

NATURE'S FURY

According to the selections and poems, what impact does a tornado have on people's lives?

Based upon what you have read, do you think it would be exciting or frightening to see a tornado? Explain why you think so.

Writer's Workshop **WRITER'S WORKSHOP** Not all parts of the country experience tornadoes, but people everywhere are cautious of nature's fury. For example, people who live in some coastal states are concerned about hurricanes, while people living in northern states need to be prepared for ice storms. What sorts of weather emergencies does your community prepare for? Write a how-to paragraph explaining what to do in such an emergency, and read your "Weather Emergency Directions" before a group of your classmates.

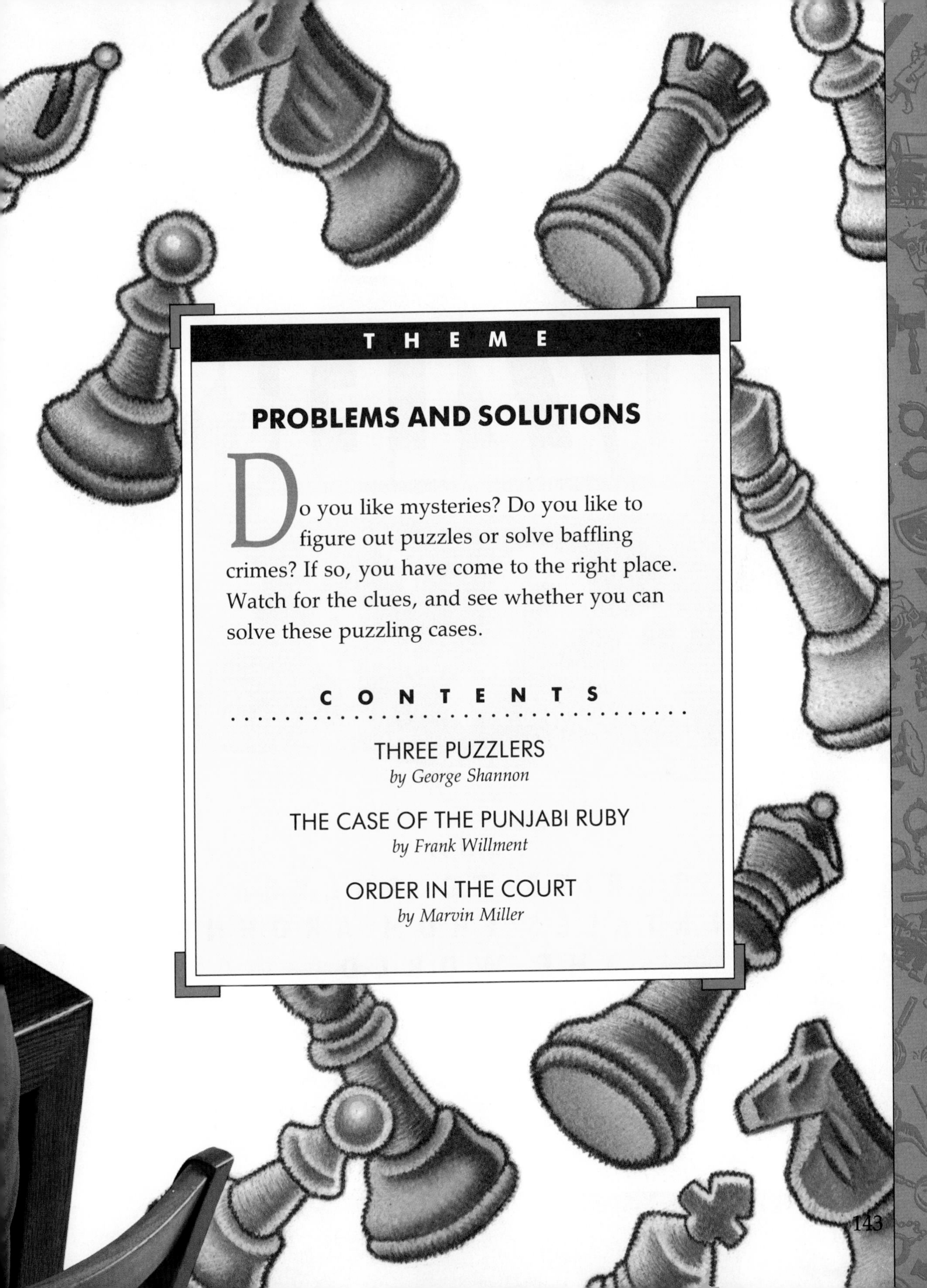

THEME

PROBLEMS AND SOLUTIONS

Do you like mysteries? Do you like to figure out puzzles or solve baffling crimes? If so, you have come to the right place. Watch for the clues, and see whether you can solve these puzzling cases.

CONTENTS

THREE PUZZLERS

FROM

STORIES TO SOLVE: FOLKTALES FROM AROUND THE WORLD

BY **GEORGE SHANNON**

ILLUSTRATED BY **PETER SIS**

THE STICKS OF TRUTH

Long ago in India judges traveled from village to village. One day a judge stopped at an inn to rest, but the innkeeper was very upset. Someone had just that day stolen his daughter's gold ring. The judge told him not to worry and had all the guests gather so that he could question them. When he could not figure out from their answers who the thief was, the judge decided to use some old magic. He told them all he was going to have to use the sticks of truth.

"These are magic sticks," he explained, "that will catch the thief."

He gave each guest a stick to keep under their bed during the night.

"The stick belonging to the thief will grow two inches during the night. At breakfast we will all compare sticks and the longest stick will be the thief's."

The next morning the judge had all the guests come by his table and hold their sticks up next to his to see if they had grown. But one after another all were the same. None of them had grown any longer. Then suddenly the judge called, "This is the thief! Her stick is shorter than all the rest."

Once caught, the woman confessed and the ring was returned. But all the guests were confused about the sticks of truth. The judge had said the longest stick would be the thief's, but instead it had been the shortest stick.

Why?

(The solution appears on page 148.)

FISHING

One fine summer day two fathers and two sons went fishing at their favorite lake. They fished and talked all morning long and by noon everyone had caught one fish. As the two fathers and two sons walked back home, everyone was happy because each had a fish even though only three fish had been caught.

Two fathers and two sons. Only three fish and no fish were lost. How can this have happened?

(The solution appears on page 149.)

THE CLEVEREST SON

Once there lived an old man who had three sons. When he grew old and ill and knew that he soon would die, he called all three sons into his room.

"There is no way I can divide the house and farm to support all three of you. The one who proves himself the cleverest will inherit the house and farm. There is a coin on the table for each of you. The one who can buy something that will fill this room will inherit all I own."

The eldest son took his coin, went straight to the marketplace, and filled his wagon full of straw. The second son thought a bit longer, then also went to the marketplace, where he bought sacks and sacks of feathers. The youngest son thought and then quietly went to a little shop. He bought two small things and tucked them into his pocket.

That night the father called them in to show what they had bought. The eldest son spread his straw about the floor, but it filled only one part of the room. The second son dumped out his sacks of feathers, but they filled only two corners of the room. Then the youngest son smiled, pulled the two small things out of his pocket, and soon filled the room.

"Yes," said the father, "you are indeed the cleverest and have filled my room when the others could not. You shall inherit my house and farm."

What had the youngest son bought and with what did he fill the room?

(The solution appears on page 149.)

SOLUTIONS

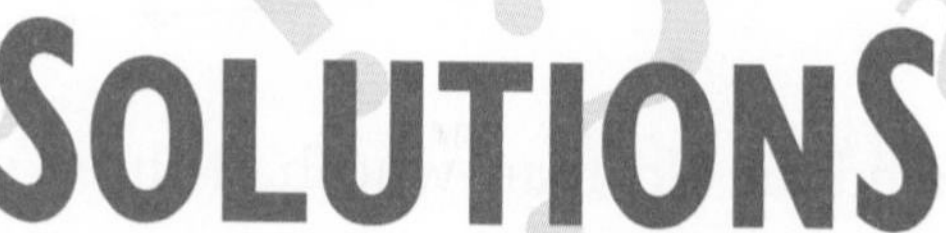

THE STICKS OF TRUTH

HOW IT WAS DONE

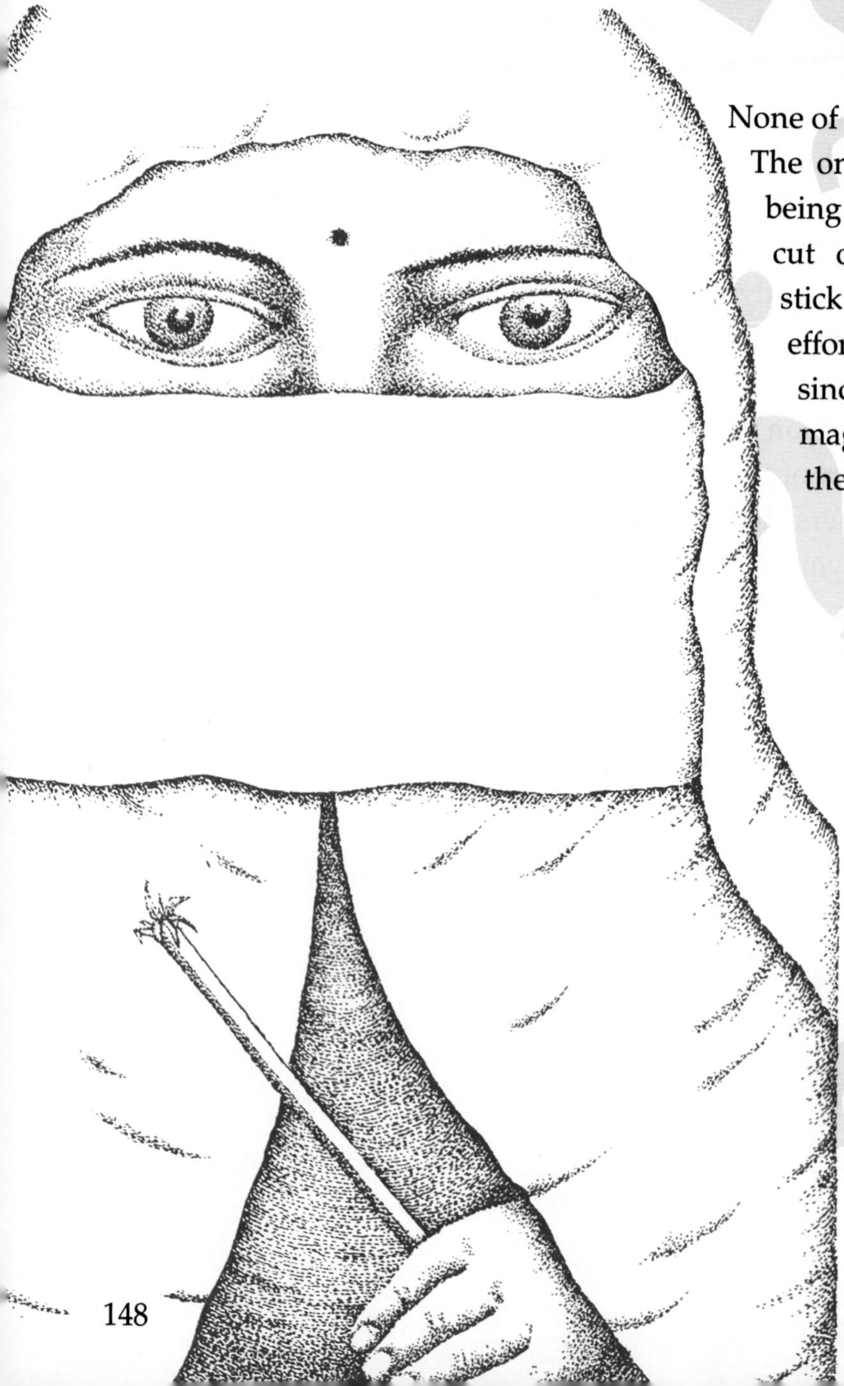

None of the sticks were magical. The only one to worry about being caught, the thief had cut off two inches of her stick during the night in an effort to hide its growth. But since the sticks were not magical, her stick ended up the only short one.

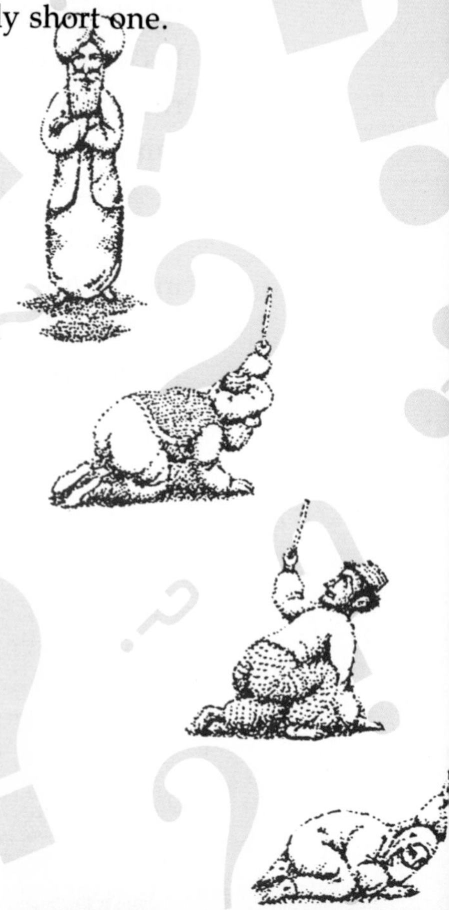

FISHING

HOW IT WAS DONE

Only three people went fishing. A boy, his father, and his grandfather: two sons and two fathers.

THE CLEVEREST SON

HOW IT WAS DONE

A match and a candle that filled the room with light.

THINK IT OVER

1. *Were you able to solve any or all of the puzzlers? Which puzzler did you find the hardest to solve?*
2. *What quality do the judge (from the first puzzler) and the youngest son (from the third puzzler) have in common?*

WRITE

Each puzzler ends with a clever solution. Think of another solution for one of them. Write a new ending based upon your solution.

THE CASE OF THE PUNJABI RUBY

BY
FRANK WILLMENT

ILLUSTRATED BY
MARCEL DUROCHER

CHARACTERS

MARLENA MARTINE
MONIQUE DUBOIS
PETER GOLDEN
SARDU SINGH
BRADFORD CABOT
SERGEANT O'SHEA
OFFICER BARNETT
INSPECTOR CONLON
AGATHA PRITCHETT

TIME: *Late afternoon.*

SETTING: *Golden room in the rear of Marlena Martine's jewelry shop. Table with five chairs around it is center. There are a few other chairs, an end table, etc., around room. There is a telephone on table upstage. Doors are right and left.*

AT RISE: SGT. O'SHEA *stands center in front of table, talking to* MONIQUE DUBOIS, *who sits at one end of table.* BRADFORD CABOT *stands behind her, listening.* MARLENA MARTINE *sits at opposite end of table, examining contents of her purse.* SARDU SINGH *is pacing back and forth at rear of room.* PETER GOLDEN *sits down at left, lost in thought, and* OFFICER BARNETT *guards door at right.*

MONIQUE DUBOIS *(Angrily):* Why are you keeping us here, Sergeant? We've all been searched by you or that officer. (*Waves hand in direction of* BARNETT) None of us has the missing ruby! The premiere of my latest film is tonight, and I simply must get back to my hotel to get ready.

O'SHEA: Just a few more minutes, Ms. Dubois. I know you Hollywood stars have busy schedules, but Inspector Conlon should be here soon. I called her at home as soon as the robbery was reported. It isn't every day we have a half-million-dollar jewel theft in this precinct, you know.

SINGH (*Angrily*): It was more than just a jewel. It was the Punjabi Ruby, a national treasure of my country, taken from us years ago.

GOLDEN (*Rising and crossing center*): *You* say it was the Punjabi Ruby, Singh. All we know is that we were looking at an extremely valuable stone when the lights went out and it was gone. (*To* O'SHEA) What can the Inspector do that you haven't done already, Sergeant? You've searched us, you've searched the room, and the gem isn't here. Why not let us go home while you continue your investigation?

O'SHEA: Sorry, Mr. Golden. My orders are, nobody leaves this room.

GOLDEN: What rubbish! I'm a busy man. (*Returns to seat*)

SINGH (*Confronting* O'SHEA): And I am the official representative of one of the wealthiest and most powerful men in India. If the Rajah knew you were keeping me prisoner here . . .

O'SHEA: You're not a prisoner, Mr. Singh. You'll be free to go shortly, I'm sure. (*Knock on door*) That must be the Inspector now. (*To* BARNETT) Let her in, Barnett. (BARNETT *nods, opens door right;* INSPECTOR CONLON *and* AGATHA PRITCHETT *enter.*)

CONLON: Hello, Barnett, O'Shea. Everybody still here?

O'SHEA: Still here, Inspector. They've been squawking, but we didn't let them go.

CONLON (*Sitting on edge of table as others gather around her*): Sorry to inconvenience you, folks, but we'll have a better chance of solving this mess if we keep you all together. By the way, this is Miss Agatha Pritchett (*Indicates* AGATHA, *who nods and smiles*), who taught me a few things years ago when she was my seventh-grade teacher. She happened to be paying me a visit when the Sergeant's call came, and she asked to tag along to see a police investigation firsthand.

O'SHEA: You picked a good one, Miss Pritchett. This case is a real humdinger.

AGATHA: Call me Miss Agatha, please. Everyone does. Now, all of you just pretend I'm not here. I'll just sort of fade into the draperies, and you won't even know I'm around.

CONLON: Now, then, let's get down to work. Will you fill us in on the facts, O'Shea?

O'SHEA: Sure, Inspector. (*Indicates* MARTINE) This is Marlena Martine, the owner of this shop, Martine's Jewels. (CONLON *nods.*) You passed through the main shop to get to this room. This is where she conducts private auctions of rare jewels.

CONLON: And I gather that an auction was going on here this afternoon.

MARTINE: Yes, we were holding a discrete auction of a valuable ruby. I had invited four clients who had expressed an interest in purchasing the gem.

CONLON: All four clients are present, I presume?

MARTINE: Yes, Inspector. This is Monique Dubois, the actress. (*She indicates* DUBOIS.)

DUBOIS: I realize that you have your job to do, Inspector, but if you could be brief—

INSPECTOR (*Nodding*): I'll do my best.

MARTINE: This gentleman is Sardu Singh. (*She indicates* SINGH.) The Rajah he represents is an old client of mine.

SINGH: I do not believe the Rajah will be kindly disposed toward the police when he hears that I have been held like a common criminal.

CABOT: The ruby was worth a million dollars, Singh. I'd say whoever stole it was an *uncommon* criminal.

CONLON (*To* CABOT): And who are you, sir?

CABOT: I'm Bradford Cabot, the curator of the City Museum. I'm here because I wanted to see if I could secure the ruby for our collection.

MARTINE: There is one more client you haven't met, Inspector. (*Gestures to* GOLDEN) This is Peter Golden, a prominent financier.

GOLDEN: I trust this won't take too long, Inspector. I'd like to get back to the stock exchange before closing time.

CONLON: I understand. Tell me, Mr. Golden, were you representing some business organization at the auction?

GOLDEN: No, I'm strictly a private collector. As a matter of fact, I would appreciate as little publicity as possible. The fewer people who know I collect rare gems, the less chance I have of being robbed.

AGATHA: I take it that you don't display or exhibit your collection, Mr. Golden.

GOLDEN: Never! I enjoy my jewels for their own sake. I share that pleasure with no one.

CONLON: Now, let's see if I have the facts straight. Ms. Martine was conducting a private auction in this room this afternoon, with four clients bidding on a valuable ruby.

MARTINE: We were sitting around the table with the ruby on a black cloth in the center.

CONLON: You, Ms. Martine, were sitting at the head, I suppose?

MARTINE: Yes. Ms. Dubois and Mr. Golden were on my right, and Mr. Cabot was on my left.

CONLON: Then at the far end of the table was Mr. Singh.

MARTINE: Correct.

CONLON: Now, Ms. Martine, tell us about your ruby.

MARTINE: It wasn't mine, Inspector. I merely had it on consignment for another client. I was working on a commission basis.

CONLON: How much of a commission would you have received?

MARTINE: Twenty percent. That's the standard fee in jewel auctions.

AGATHA: Then if the gem had been auctioned for a half a million dollars, your commission would have been $100,000.

MARTINE: True. But with the ruby gone, I receive nothing. You can see why I am so anxious for its return.

CONLON: Who owns the ruby?

MARTINE: A wealthy European aristocrat who wishes to remain anonymous.

CONLON: There's no doubt that the ruby was genuine, I take it.

CABOT: No doubt at all. I inspected it carefully, using a jeweler's loupe. In all modesty, I must say that I am an expert with jewels.

GOLDEN: Naturally I consider myself something of an expert also. I examined the gem, and I can say with certainty that it was genuine.

SINGH: I may not be an expert, but I would know the Punjabi Ruby anywhere. The gem on the table an hour ago *was* the Punjabi Ruby!

CONLON: I'll accept the fact that it was genuine. Now, what actually happened at the auction?

MARTINE: We met here at one o'clock, examined the ruby, placed it in the center of the table and began the bidding.

DUBOIS: We hadn't been bidding too long before there was a power failure. The lights went out, and since there are no windows in the room, it was completely dark.

CONLON: Sergeant O'Shea told me about the power failure when we spoke on the phone. How long were the lights out?

DUBOIS: Perhaps ten or fifteen seconds. Not very long.

SINGH: But quite long enough! When the lights came on again, the Punjabi Ruby was missing! (*Upset*) What will I tell the Rajah?

GOLDEN (*Heatedly*): Tell him what you did with it! You took it, didn't you? You came here to get the gem, one way or another!

SINGH: How dare you make such an accusation! The Rajah does not need to steal. He is one of the world's wealthiest men. I came prepared to outbid all of you. Had it not disappeared, the gem would be mine at this moment!

CONLON: Mr. Golden, let's not make unfounded charges. Now, could anyone have entered the room while the lights were out?

MARTINE: Impossible. There are two doors, and both were securely locked. And as Ms. Dubois pointed out, the room has no windows.

CONLON: Could anyone have hidden in the room before the auction began?

O'SHEA: No, Inspector. There's no place to hide. There isn't even a closet.

CONLON: Then that brings us back to the five people at the table when the lights went out. Now, what happened when the lights came back on?

GOLDEN: We discovered immediately that the ruby was missing.

CABOT: I insisted that the police be called at once and that no one leave the room.

AGATHA: There's a telephone in the room, I presume?

MARTINE: Yes, over on the corner table. (*Defensively*) I didn't leave the room to make a phone call, if that's what you're suggesting, Miss Aggie.

CONLON: How long did it take Sergeant O'Shea and Officer Barnett to arrive?

DUBOIS: Less than five minutes, I would say.

BARNETT: That's about right, Inspector. The station house is only two blocks away. We left as soon as we got the message.

CONLON: What did you do when you got here, Sergeant?

O'SHEA: Barnett and I searched the premises thoroughly after we questioned the witnesses.

SINGH: What witnesses? The lights were out. We witnessed nothing.

GOLDEN: What you mean to say is that we couldn't see you grab the ruby.

SINGH (*Outraged*): Another insult! I won't stand for it!

CONLON: I told you two before, stop the bickering. (*To* O'SHEA) Did you turn up anything in your search, O'Shea?

O'SHEA: Not a single clue. And of course, no sign of the ruby.

BARNETT: After that, we decided to search everyone who was here when the robbery took place.

CONLON: I gather the search proved fruitless.

O'SHEA: That's right. None of them had the ruby. I have complete lists of everything found on the suspects during the search. (*Takes papers from pocket, hands them to* CONLON)

DUBOIS (*Offended*): Suspects! I've never been so insulted in my life.

AGATHA (*Gently*): But, Ms. Dubois, one of you has to be guilty. So naturally all of you are suspects.

DUBOIS: I suppose you're right. It just doesn't sound very nice.

O'SHEA: As you can see, Inspector, there's nothing of any importance on those lists. Combs, keys, handkerchiefs—things of that sort.

CONLON (*Glancing at lists*): So I see.

AGATHA (*Timidly*): May I look at the lists, Ellen?

CONLON (*Hesitating*): Well, I don't know, Agatha.

GOLDEN: Why do you want to poke your nose into our affairs?

AGATHA: You seem to have reached a dead end, and I thought something on the lists might be helpful—give the Inspector another lead.

DUBOIS: I certainly have nothing to hide.

CABOT: Read them aloud. Somebody may get an idea. I'm sure we all want to find the ruby and get home.

CONLON (*Looking around*): Any objections?

OTHERS (*Ad lib*): No. Fine with me. Go ahead. (*Etc.*)

CONLON: All right. Why don't you read the lists, Miss Agatha? (*She hands lists to* AGATHA.)

AGATHA: Let's see. The first list is Mr. Golden's. (*Reading*) Handkerchief, aspirin, jeweler's loupe, checkbook, wallet, change.

CABOT: Nothing incriminating there.

GOLDEN (*Dryly*): Thanks for the vote of confidence.

AGATHA: Monique Dubois. (*Reads*) Doctor's prescription, credit cards, money clip, lipstick, address book, sunglasses, mints, keys, change, tissues.

DUBOIS (*Bored*): Makes me sound like a member of Murder Anonymous, doesn't it?

CONLON: I'll admit it sounds pretty innocuous. Carry on, Agatha.

AGATHA: Mr. Singh. (*Reads*) Passport, beads, letter, traveler's checks, wallet, vitamins, cold tablets. Ms. Martine: Compact, chewing gum, appointment book, tissues, keys, calculator, brush, and comb.

SINGH: The calculator was to figure her twenty percent commission on the Punjabi Ruby, no doubt!

MARTINE (*Heatedly*): A normal, legal commission, Mr. Singh!

AGATHA: Here's the last list—Mr. Cabot's. (*Reads*) Handkerchief, wallet, credit cards, nail file, parking ticket, comb, keys, jeweler's loupe.

GOLDEN (*In accusing tone*): Parking ticket, eh, Cabot?

CABOT: I put it in my pocket to pay later today. That hardly makes me a master criminal.

MARTINE: Are we quite finished with all this nonsense?

AGATHA: I've read all the lists, if that's what you mean.

DUBOIS: And they weren't much help, were they?

AGATHA: Oh, I wouldn't say that. I found them to be most interesting.

CONLON: If you saw something we didn't see, tell us, Agatha. You know, in school we always said that you had eyes in the back of your head. We couldn't put anything over on you, as I remember.

AGATHA (*Smiling modestly*): To be frank, I did notice one or two little things, but they're probably unimportant.

BARNETT: Then where do we go from here, Inspector?

CONLON: Let's review the facts. Fact one: The ruby must still be in this room. Fact two: It hasn't been found in the room or on anyone who was in the room when it disappeared. An interesting case!

GOLDEN (*Impatiently*): Interesting to you, maybe, but it's wasting my valuable time.

AGATHA: When I was a girl, we used to say, there's more than one way to skin a cat.

DUBOIS: What do you mean by that?

AGATHA: It means that there are many ways of looking at a problem. When you reach a dead end, try another angle.

SINGH: What angle do you suggest?

AGATHA: Let's see what the ruby's loss would mean to everyone. Perhaps it'll show us who had a motive for the theft.

GOLDEN: We all had a motive. We wanted a half-million-dollar gem!

AGATHA: But that jewel might have been more important to one person than to another. Now, Ms. Martine, if the gem had been sold for half a million dollars, your commission would have been $100,000. Is that correct?

MARTINE (*Dryly*): Yes, the theft cost me $100,000. How's that for a motive?

AGATHA: Wasn't the ruby insured?

MARTINE: Of course, for its full value. The owner will collect the insurance.

AGATHA: I see. The owner loses nothing. You lose your commission.

MARTINE: That's right.

AGATHA: Actually, the others have lost nothing except the chance to bid on the gem. Perhaps it would be enlightening to see what each person at the auction intended to do with the ruby and how much each was prepared to pay.

CONLON: That's a good angle to pursue, Miss Agatha.

AGATHA: Let's start with you, Ms. Dubois. Why did you want the stone?

DUBOIS: Frankly, wearing fabulous jewels is part of my image. They write it up constantly in the gossip columns. The ruby would be worth a lot of publicity to me.

AGATHA: I quite understand. And how much were you willing to pay?

DUBOIS: Unfortunately, this auction caught me at a bad time. I could raise only $275,000.

AGATHA: I see. And how high had the bidding gone when the lights went out?

MARTINE: The bidding was at $130,000, and the auction was far from over.

AGATHA: Mr. Cabot, you said you wanted to purchase the ruby for your museum. How high were you authorized to go, may I ask?

CABOT: I suppose there's no harm in telling you now. My top figure was to be $350,000. But I hoped to get it for less.

AGATHA: If you had been the successful bidder, the gem would be put on display at the museum?

CABOT: That's correct.

AGATHA: Now, Mr. Golden, if *you* had bought the ruby, it would have been hidden from the world, correct?

GOLDEN (*Defensively*): That's not a crime! As a private collector, I have no philanthropic inclinations, no wish to share my treasures. Gems are my hobby.

AGATHA: I see. And how much were you prepared to spend on your hobby?

GOLDEN: The auction was called at an inauspicious moment, to tell you the truth. Ordinarily, I would not have permitted anyone to outbid me, but I had to use most of my liquid assets to cover a margin call on the stock market last week. A bid of $225,000 would have been my top offer today.

AGATHA: Then you, like Ms. Dubois, would have lost to Mr. Cabot and the City Museum.

GOLDEN: It would seem so.

SINGH: Not quite! You seem to have forgotten that I was also bidding on the stone.

AGATHA: I was coming to you, Mr. Singh. What did you intend to do with the ruby?

SINGH: I was to return it to my homeland and to my Rajah, the rightful owner! Eighteen years ago it was stolen from the Shrine of Jind.

AGATHA: Then it would have been displayed in the shrine?

SINGH: Yes, along with other sacred relics. But this time it would be placed under constant armed guard.

GOLDEN: There's your man, Inspector. A fanatic who wanted the ruby any way he could get it!

SINGH: Yes, I wanted the ruby desperately, but there was no reason to steal it. My instructions were to outbid you all, and the Rajah is wealthy enough to do just that!

AGATHA: According to the others, the top bid would have been Mr. Cabot's $350,000.

SINGH: Then I would have secured the ruby for $360,000.

AGATHA: I see. I thank all of you for your frank answers, but I haven't been too much help so far, I'm afraid.

CONLON: Oh, one can't have too much information in a case like this. One slip of the tongue could provide the key to the mystery.

AGATHA (*Suddenly; brightly*): I just had an idea. Why don't we re-enact the crime?

SINGH: Re-enact the crime? What an idiotic idea!

AGATHA: Everybody could sit around the table. We could go through the bidding, turn out the lights at the proper moment, turn them on after ten seconds or so, and see if we learn anything.

CABOT: It sounds silly. What could we possibly learn?

AGATHA: Perhaps where the jewel is and who took it.

CONLON (*Shrugging*): What can we lose? The ruby is already gone. Let's try it. Everyone please take the places you had at the time of the auction. (*All take seats around table, with* MARTINE *at head,* SINGH *at opposite end,* DUBOIS *and* GOLDEN *to right of* MARTINE, CABOT *to her left.*) Now, let's put the black cloth in the center. (MARTINE *unfolds cloth on table.*)

DUBOIS (*Snippily*): This is a waste of time, Inspector!

CONLON: Maybe not. Please conduct the auction, Ms. Martine. Sergeant O'Shea, why don't you control the lights. (*Motions left*) When the bids reach $130,000, turn off the lights for ten seconds, and then switch them back on.

O'SHEA (*Going left to switch*): O.K., Inspector.

CONLON: Go ahead, Ms. Martine. (CONLON *stands behind table;* AGATHA *stands at head of table behind* MARTINE; BARNETT *is at other end of table behind* SINGH.)

MARTINE: Very well. You have all examined the ruby. May we begin the bidding?

GOLDEN: I bid $50,000.

DUBOIS: Make that $60,000.

CABOT: I say $70,000.

SINGH: Let's stop these trifling bids. I'll bid $100,000.

DUBOIS: $120,000.

CABOT: $130,000. (O'SHEA *pantomimes flipping light switch and there is a ten-second blackout. Lights come up again. Large "ruby" is in center of table on black cloth.*)

SINGH (*Incredulous*): Look! the ruby!

CONLON: I don't believe it! Where did it come from?

BARNETT: Is it the real Punjabi Ruby?

CABOT (*Taking out loupe and examining gem*): It's the real thing, all right.

GOLDEN: Let me see! (*Takes ruby from* CABOT, *examines it with loupe*) It *is* the Punjabi Ruby!

MARTINE (*Relieved*): It has been found! How wonderful! Now we can continue the auction.

SINGH: No auction is necessary. This woman (*Points to* AGATHA) made us reveal our top bids. I am obviously the high bidder at $360,000. Can anyone top it?

CONLON: You can't bid on stolen merchandise, Mr. Singh. A crime is involved.

MARTINE: But the ruby is back, even if we don't know who returned it!

AGATHA: I know who returned it.

DUBOIS: You do?

AGATHA: Yes. I returned it.

CABOT (*Shocked*): You? But you couldn't have. You weren't even here when the ruby was stolen!

AGATHA: Oh, I didn't steal the ruby. I simply discovered who did, guessed where it was hidden, and returned it to the table while the lights were out. That's why I wanted a re-enactment of the crime. I thought it would be more dramatic that way.

O'SHEA: Well, don't keep us in suspense. Who did it?

AGATHA: Let me first explain how I came to my conclusions. Ms. Dubois wouldn't steal the ruby. She wanted publicity, and she couldn't wear a stolen jewel in public.

CONLON: And Mr. Cabot couldn't display a stolen gem in his museum.

AGATHA: Precisely. Now, Mr. Singh wanted to return the ruby to India. Since he claims it was originally stolen from a temple, he might have been willing to steal it back.

GOLDEN: So it was Singh all the time! I knew it!

SINGH: Don't be stupid! Why would I steal a gem I was about to buy?

AGATHA: True. Also, if Mr. Singh had stolen the gem, how would he have gotten it out of the country? The police and customs officials would be watching him like hawks.

DUBOIS: Then it must have been Peter Golden! I should have known. I never did like his shifty look!

GOLDEN (*Coolly*): Be careful what you say, Ms. Dubois. A suit for slander isn't exactly the kind of publicity you want, is it?

AGATHA: Mr. Golden seemed obvious in the beginning. Once the ruby was in his private collection, no one would know he possessed it. On the other hand, any one of you might have stolen it, hoping to sell it later to some other private collector who wouldn't question where it came from.

BARNETT: Then we're right back where we started.

AGATHA: Not quite. While anyone might have had a motive for stealing the ruby, everyone except the thief lacked one important thing.

BARNETT: (*Fascinated*): What was that?

AGATHA: Opportunity!

O'SHEA: But everyone at the table had the same opportunity. They were all there when the lights went out.

AGATHA: But only one person knew *when* the lights would go out.

BARNETT: Who?

AGATHA: The thief. (*To* CONLON) Do you remember, Ellen, that I stopped to chat with the doorman when we entered the building?

CONLON: Yes. I wondered what you were talking to him about.

AGATHA: Well, Sergeant O'Shea had mentioned the power failure when he talked to you on the phone. I asked the doorman about it, but he said he wasn't aware of a power failure.

MARTINE: It lasted only ten seconds. He might not have noticed it.

AGATHA: I thought that, too. So I asked a woman who was leaving the building if the blackout had inconvenienced her, but she wasn't aware that there had been a power failure either.

BARNETT: Then what caused the lights to go out during the auction?

AGATHA: I wondered about that, too, so I looked around carefully when I first got here. You have rather elaborate lighting here, don't you, Ms. Martine?

MARTINE: Yes, to show off jewels to their advantage. It's one of the tricks of the trade.

AGATHA (*Pleasantly*): You know, at home I have a timing device attached to my radio. It allows me to go to sleep and wake up to the sound of music. It turns off my radio at night and turns it back on in the morning.

MARTINE (*Sharply*): So you like music. So what?

AGATHA: It occurred to me that a timing device could explain why the lights went out here and nowhere else.

CONLON: Ms. Martine, do you use timing devices here?

MARTINE (*Indignantly*): What if I do? Any one of us could have set the timers to turn off the lights!

AGATHA: I suppose that's true, but first let me explain how I found the ruby. It all started when Ms. Martine called me Miss Aggie.

MARTINE (*Suddenly*): I did?

AGATHA: Yes. Right then I knew you must be a former student of mine.

MARTINE: But the Inspector—you said that she was a former student of yours—and she's been calling you Miss Aggie.

AGATHA: No, she's been calling me Miss Agatha. As a matter of fact, I asked everyone to call me Miss Agatha.

MARTINE: So what?

AGATHA: In class, students always called me Miss Agatha. Behind my back some students called me Miss Aggie, and you were one of them, Molly.

MARTINE: Molly! What are you talking about?

AGATHA: When you said "Miss Aggie," it started to come back. Martine, I said. Take off the "e" and you have Martin. Molly Martin, a freckle-faced, gum-chewing, pony-tailed seventh grader!

MARTINE: I don't know what you're talking about.

AGATHA (*Ignoring her*): That's what I was looking for when I went over the lists. If you were Molly Martin, you'd still chew gum, I was certain. Sure enough, chewing gum was one of the things on your list.

MARTINE (*Impatiently*): All right. I was in your class, and I still chew gum. How does that add up to a jewel theft?

AGATHA (*To* CONLON): Ellen, did you chew gum in school?

CONLON (*Trying to remember*): Yes, I guess I did.

AGATHA: Did you chew it in my class?

CONLON: Of course not! You had no mercy for gum chewers.

AGATHA: Then what did you do with your gum when you came to my class?

CONLON (*Thinking a moment*): Well, we parked it under our chairs.

AGATHA: I thought you'd remember that. And I thought Molly Martin would, too! When the Sergeant turned off the lights, I reached under Molly's chair and found what I expected to find—a wad of chewing gum!

CONLON: With the Punjabi Ruby in the middle!

AGATHA: Right! I pulled the ruby out of the gum and put it back on the table before the lights came on again.

CONLON: Ms. Martine was the only one who could really have arranged for the lights to go out. She must have planned the whole thing!

MARTINE: You're crazy! Why would I steal the gem? I'd lose a huge commission.

AGATHA: Yes, but you'd have the ruby. At another time, when the stock market was better, Mr. Golden would have paid you the gem's full worth—$500,000.

GOLDEN: I would have, and Ms. Martine, or whatever her name is, knows it.

MARTINE: So I hid the ruby under the chair. What's the charge?

CONLON: It seems to me you were trying to steal the ruby from its rightful owner. We'll hold you for questioning, and get in touch with the owner to see if he wishes to press charges. In any case, I'm pretty sure he won't want you to handle any more auctions for him. (BARNETT *and* O'SHEA *escort* MARTINE *out.*)

AGATHA (*Shaking her head*): Molly Martin was never able to get away with anything, not even back in seventh grade.

CONLON: Miss Agatha, you should have been a detective.

AGATHA: No, Ellen, I'll let you be the detective. I'm just a retired schoolteacher. All I did was use one of the tricks of my trade. (*Quick curtain*)

THE END

THINK IT OVER

1. *What is the problem that brings all the characters together in this case?*
2. *Why don't the police find the Punjabi Ruby when they first search the room?*
3. *What first makes Agatha Pritchett suspicious of Marlena Martine?*
4. *Think about the characters Monique Dubois, Peter Golden, Sardu Singh, and Bradford Cabot. What makes each of these characters seem suspicious?*

WRITE

Do you think "The Case of the Punjabi Ruby" *is a good mystery? Pretend you are a journalist for a local newspaper. Write a positive or a negative review of the play.*

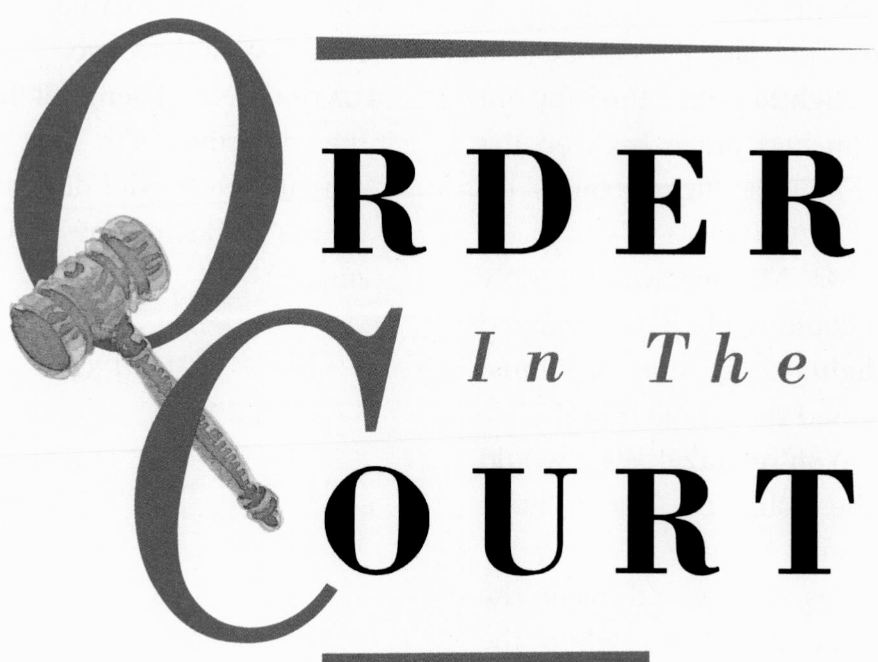

ORDER In The COURT

from **You Be the Jury**
by **Marvin Miller**
illustrated by **Harvey Chan**

Ladies and Gentlemen of the Jury:

This court is now in session. My name is Judge John Denenberg. You are the jury, and the trials are set to begin.

You have a serious responsibility. Will the innocent be sent to jail and the guilty go free? Let's hope not. Your job is to make sure that justice is served.

Read each case carefully. Study the evidence presented and then decide:

Innocent or Guilty?

Both sides of the case will be presented to you. The person who has the complaint is called the *plaintiff*. He has brought the case to court.

The person being accused is called the *defendant*. He is pleading his innocence and presents a much different version of what happened.

IN EACH CASE, THREE PIECES OF EVIDENCE WILL BE PRESENTED AS EXHIBITS A, B, AND C. EXAMINE THE EXHIBITS VERY CAREFULLY. A *CLUE* TO THE SOLUTION OF EACH CASE WILL BE FOUND THERE. IT WILL DIRECTLY POINT TO THE INNOCENCE OR GUILT OF THE ACCUSED.

Remember, each side will try to convince you that his version is what actually happened. BUT YOU MUST MAKE THE FINAL DECISION.

◆

◆ The Case of the Wrong Bag ◆

LADIES AND GENTLEMEN OF THE JURY:

A person who is found with stolen property is not necessarily a thief.

Keep this in mind as you go over the facts in this case. Since we are in criminal court today, the State is the accuser. In this case, the State, represented by the district attorney, has accused John Summers of robbing Kay's Jewelry Store. John Summers, the defendant, has pleaded innocent and claims that his arrest is a mistake.

The State called the owner of Kay's Jewelry Store as its first witness. She has testified as follows:

"My name is Wendy Kay, and I own Kay's Jewelry Store in Martinville. I was working alone in the store on Wednesday afternoon, December 2, when a man walked in. It was exactly 3:30. I noticed the time because I had just put a new collection of diamond watches from Switzerland on display. I noticed the man because he had a handkerchief over his face. I thought that was odd until I also noticed the outline of a gun projecting from his pocket. That's when I got scared."

The man ordered Wendy Kay to empty a case of jewels and all the store's cash into a black bag. The robbery took only minutes, and the thief escaped on foot.

At four o'clock the next afternoon, John Summers entered the lobby of the Bristol Hotel and walked over to the luggage checkroom. He pointed to a black bag, which the bellman gave him. As he handed the bellman a tip, a hotel detective noticed that Summers's bag matched the description of the bag used in the jewelry store robbery. He arrested Summers and called the police.

When the police opened the bag and emptied its contents, a look of shock and surprise spread over Summers's face. Inside was the stolen jewelry.

John Summers was dumbfounded. He claimed he had pointed to the wrong bag in the hotel checkroom. This bag was not his, he said, but an identical twin belonging to someone else. His own bag contained a blue toothbrush and underwear, and it was locked.

The police returned to the luggage checkroom and questioned the bellman. The man thought there might have been two bags in the checkroom, although a second black bag was nowhere to be found.

EXHIBIT A is a picture of the bag and jewelry. John Summers claims that he checked an identical bag and that he mistakenly picked up this bag from the luggage room.

The State has drawn your attention to the shape of this bag, its handle, and lock. The State submits that this is an unusual-looking bag, and that it is very unlikely, if not impossible, that another bag looking just like it would be checked into the same hotel on the same day.

The State also presented EXHIBIT B, a list of the contents of John Summers's pockets at the time he was arrested. His wallet contained $710 in cash, a sizable sum for a person spending only one night in town. The State alleges that the $710 in Summers's wallet is the money stolen from the jewelry store.

No gun was found in Summers's pocket. The State claims a simple explanation. John Summers robbed Kay's Jewelry Store by pretending the object in his pocket was a gun. In reality, it was only his pointed finger.

On the basis of all this evidence, John Summers was accused of the jewelry store robbery.

John Summers has given the following testimony:

"My visit to Martinville was supposed to be a simple overnight trip. Every year around this time, the Martinville Museum has its annual art sale, and I wanted to buy a painting. I just started collecting art last year. I may not know a lot about art, but I know what I like. I've already got two of those pictures of the sad-looking kids with the big eyes. But this time I wanted something really stupendous to go over the sofa in the living room. Maybe something with some purple in it to match the drapes. I saved up more than eight hundred bucks to buy a painting this trip."

Summers's schedule was easy to reconstruct. He arrived by bus on Wednesday morning and checked into the Bristol Hotel. The Museum opened at noon. Mr. Summers was one of the first persons to enter the Museum. He spent the entire afternoon there. But to his disappointment, he could not find any artwork he liked.

EXHIBIT C is a torn Museum ticket stub for the day in question. The Museum hours were noon to four o'clock. The robbery of Kay's Jewelry Store took place at 3:30. While there was no witness who can testify he saw John Summers in the museum the entire time, the stub shows he indeed visited the Museum.

When the Museum closed, John Summers went back to his hotel, disappointed his trip was in vain. The following day, he checked out of the hotel at noon. Since his bus did not leave until later that day, Summers locked his black bag, checked it in the hotel's luggage checkroom, and went sightseeing. Later he returned to pick up his bag, and he was promptly arrested.

John Summers claims that he is the victim of an unfortunate coincidence.

LADIES AND GENTLEMEN OF THE JURY: You have just heard the Case of the Wrong Bag. You must decide the merit of the State's accusation. Be sure to carefully examine the evidence in EXHIBITS A, B, and C.

Did John Summers rob Kay's Jewelry Store? Or had he indeed picked up the wrong bag?

(The jury's verdict appears on page 174.)

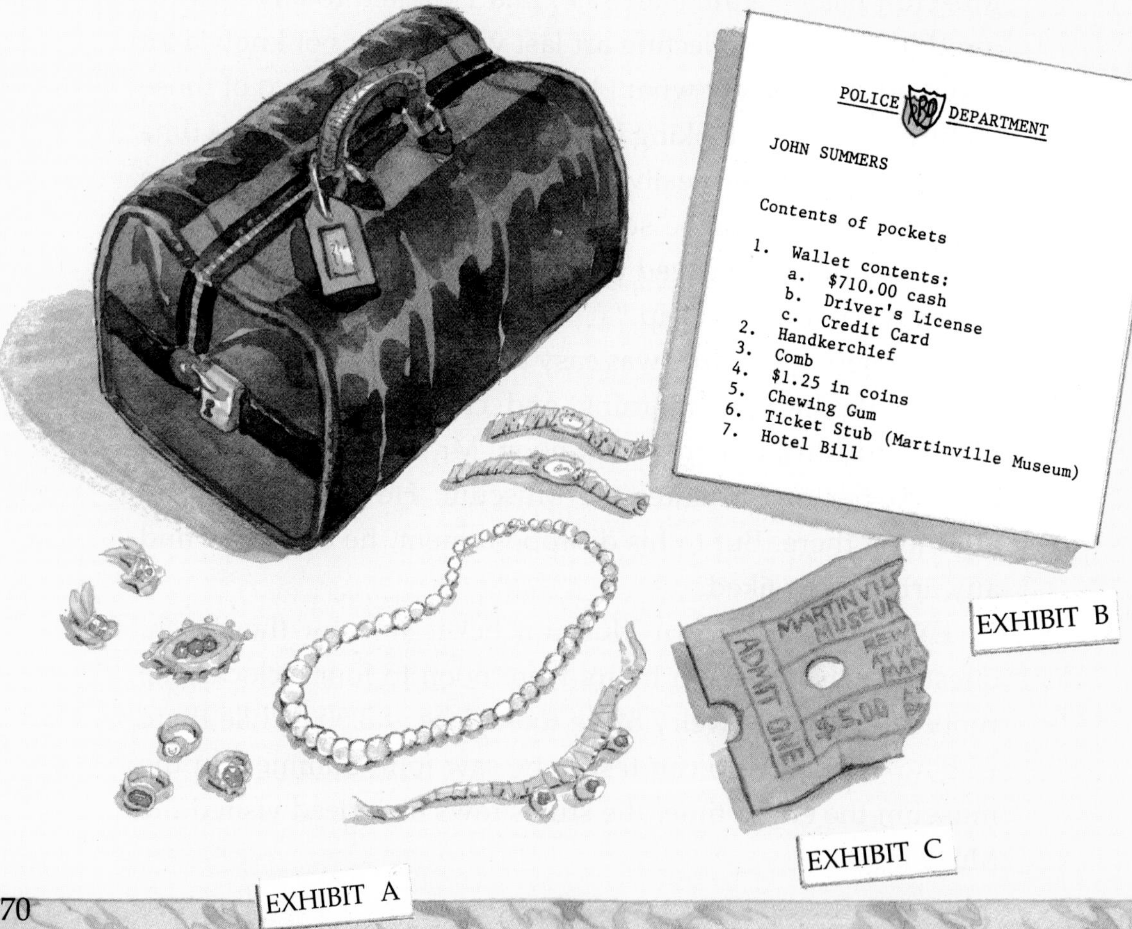

POLICE DEPARTMENT

JOHN SUMMERS

Contents of pockets

1. Wallet contents:
   a. $710.00 cash
   b. Driver's License
   c. Credit Card
2. Handkerchief
3. Comb
4. $1.25 in coins
5. Chewing Gum
6. Ticket Stub (Martinville Museum)
7. Hotel Bill

EXHIBIT B

EXHIBIT C

EXHIBIT A

◆ The Case of the Power Blackout ◆

LADIES AND GENTLEMEN OF THE JURY:

A company that provides a public service, such as a power company, has special responsibilities. When the service fails, the company is responsible for any damages that may happen.

Keep this in mind as you decide the case before you today. Mel Mudd, the plaintiff and owner of Mudd's Diner, claims that a power failure lasted sixteen hours and he was unable to serve his customers. Mr. Mudd wants to be paid for this lost business. Allied Utilities, the defendant, is a power company that provides electricity and gas to the people in Fairchester County. Allied Utilities admits to the power failure. But it claims to have repaired it three hours after it was reported.

Mel Mudd has given the following testimony:

"My name is Mudd. I'm the owner of Mudd's Diner. On Thursday, February 16 at 9:30 P.M., just as I was about to close up for the night, the lights went out. Do you know that old joke: Where was Thomas Edison when the lights went out? Well, the answer is: In the dark. And that's exactly where I was, too. I immediately called the power company and was assured the power would be restored promptly."

Mr. Mudd returned to his diner the following morning, opened the back door and flipped on the light switch. The room was totally dark.

He telephoned the power company several times, and each time the line was busy. After posting a "closed" sign on the front of the diner, Mudd returned to the back room and tried to telephone the company again. The line was still busy.

Mr. Mudd kept phoning the utility company and after two hours finally got through. The company told him they had fixed the problem the night before, but they promised they would send a repairman right away.

It took two hours for the repairman to arrive. By that time, Mr. Mudd had turned away the noon lunch crowd.

The repairman again checked the outside cable. He tightened the couplings but found nothing to indicate further repairs were needed. When the repairman went back to the diner to report his findings, the lights were on in the back room.

Mr. Mudd insisted the second visit was necessary to repair the lost power because the work had not been done properly the night before. He telephoned Allied Utilities and told them he planned to sue the company for lost business. A supervisor arrived at the diner in five minutes.

EXHIBIT A shows the lost business at Mudd's Diner during the time Mudd claims he had no power. You will note on that day he had only $146.35 in business. Entries for other days show he usually had up to $450.00 worth of business. This is the amount Mudd seeks from the utility company—$450.00.

Mel Mudd was extremely angry when the supervisor arrived at the back room of the diner. The man assured Mudd the power failure had been fixed the night before. Mudd strongly disagreed.

Allied Utilities enters as EXHIBIT B the repair work-order for the diner. This is a record kept for each customer complaint. You will note that the first call came in at 9:35 P.M. The repair order shows that the power failure lasted only three hours during the time the diner was closed. Power was claimed to have been restored by 12:36 A.M.

The company also enters EXHIBIT C, a photograph of the back room that was taken shortly after the supervisor arrived. You will note that the supervisor is holding up a light bulb. He had found it in a wastebasket in the diner's back room. Tests have shown this bulb is burned out and no longer in working order.

The company contends that while its repairman was outside checking the power the second time, Mudd somehow realized he may have been mistaken about the power failure.

The light in the back room had failed to go on because of a burned-out bulb. Mr. Mudd then replaced the bulb with a new one but said nothing to the company so he could sue them for lost business. Allied Utilities refuses to pay the money Mel Mudd has requested.

LADIES AND GENTLEMEN OF THE JURY: You have just heard the Case of the Power Blackout. You must decide the merit of Mel Mudd's claim. Be sure to carefully examine the evidence in EXHIBITS A, B, and C.

Should Allied Utilities pay Mr. Mudd for the income he lost during the power failure? Or did Mudd know that the power had been restored?

(The jury's verdict appears on page 174.)

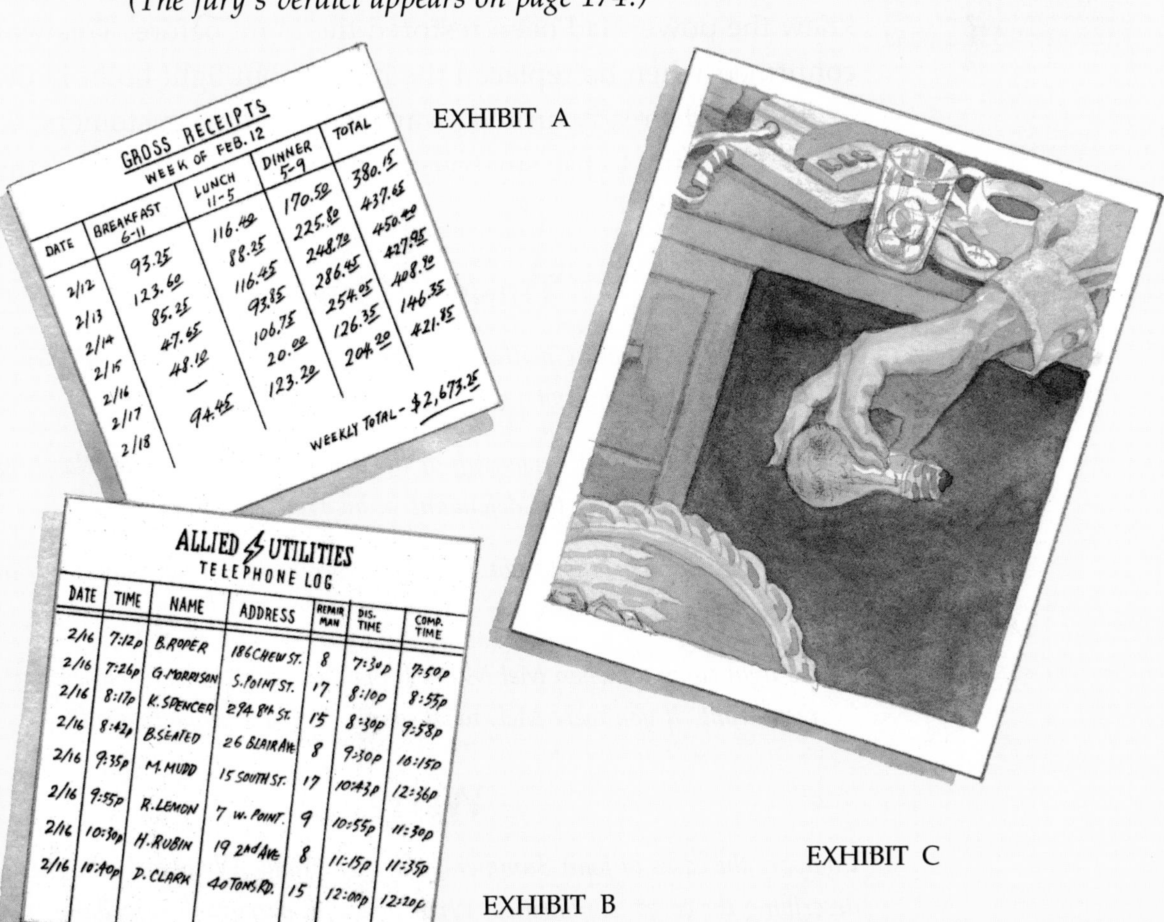

GROSS RECEIPTS
WEEK OF FEB. 12

DATE	BREAKFAST 6-11	LUNCH 11-5	DINNER 5-9	TOTAL
2/12	93.25	116.40	170.50	380.15
2/13	123.60	88.25	225.80	437.65
2/14	85.25	116.45	248.70	450.40
2/15	47.65	93.85	286.45	427.95
2/16	48.10	106.75	254.05	408.90
2/17	—	20.00	126.35	146.35
2/18	94.45	123.20	204.20	421.85

WEEKLY TOTAL - $2,673.25

EXHIBIT A

ALLIED UTILITIES
TELEPHONE LOG

DATE	TIME	NAME	ADDRESS	REPAIR MAN	DIS. TIME	COMP. TIME
2/16	7:12p	B.ROPER	186 CHEW ST.	8	7:30p	7:50p
2/16	7:26p	G.MORRISON	S.POINT ST.	17	8:10p	8:55p
2/16	8:17p	K.SPENCER	294 8th ST.	15	8:30p	9:58p
2/16	8:42p	B.SEATED	26 BLAIR AVE	8	9:30p	10:15p
2/16	9:35p	M.MUDD	15 SOUTH ST.	17	10:43p	12:36p
2/16	9:55p	R.LEMON	7 W. POINT.	9	10:55p	11:30p
2/16	10:30p	H.RUBIN	19 2nd AVE	8	11:15p	11:35p
2/16	10:40p	D.CLARK	40 TONS RD.	15	12:00p	12:20p

EXHIBIT B

EXHIBIT C

◆ The Case of the Wrong Bag ◆

VERDICT: JOHN SUMMERS WAS LYING.

John Summers claimed that the bag he stored in the checkroom was *locked*. But the contents of his pockets in EXHIBIT B showed he had no key. Summers was lying. He had indeed robbed Kay's Jewelry Store, and the bag with the jewelry was his.

◆ The Case of the Power Blackout ◆

VERDICT: MUDD KNEW THE POWER HAD BEEN RESTORED.

EXHIBIT C shows the back room of Mudd's Diner after the supervisor arrived. An empty glass with ice cubes is on a table. If the electricity was out until shortly before the supervisor got there, it would have been impossible for Mudd to have used ice cubes in the drink. When Mudd realized he had ice, he knew the power had been restored the night before. This was confirmed when he replaced the burned-out light bulb. However, he had already turned away his lunchtime customers, so he said nothing to the supervisor so he could illegally sue the power company.

Think It Over

1. *When you were acting as the jury, did you guess the right verdicts? Explain why or why not.*
2. *Was John Summers the plaintiff or the defendant in his trial? Was Mel Mudd the plaintiff or the defendant in his trial?*
3. *Why was it important to note that John Summers did not have a key in his pocket?*
4. *No light came on when Mel Mudd flipped the switch, so he closed his restaurant. If you were Mel, what would you have done instead?*

Write

Compare the cases of John Summers and Mel Mudd. Write one paragraph describing the cases' similarities. Write a second paragraph describing their differences.

THEME WRAP-UP

PROBLEMS AND SOLUTIONS

What qualities would help someone solve mysteries or problems? Support your opinion with examples from the selections.

Which of the selections would you like to share with a friend? Choose one of the selections, and tell why you think someone else would enjoy it.

WRITER'S WORKSHOP Imagine that you are Inspector Conlon and have just arrested Marlena Martine for the theft of the Punjabi Ruby. Write a police report to be used at the trial, explaining the facts of the case and how you know that Ms. Martine is the guilty party.

FLYING SOLO

Imagine that you are left alone in a small airplane. You don't know how to fly, but the plane seems to be able to fly itself. The problem is that it doesn't know how to land, and neither do you.

CONTENTS

NEWBERY HONOR
ALA NOTABLE BOOK
N702T

Brian is enjoying his first flight in a small plane when the unthinkable happens. The pilot suffers a heart attack, leaving Brian alone 7,000 feet above the Canadian wilderness.

Is There Anybody Listening?

from **Hatchet**
by Gary Paulsen

illustrated by Tomio Nitto

He was alone.

In the roaring plane with no pilot he was alone.

Alone.

For a time that he could not understand Brian could do nothing. Even after his mind began working and he could see what had happened he could do nothing. It was as if his hands and arms were lead.

Then he looked for ways for it not to have happened. Be asleep, his mind screamed at the pilot. Just be asleep and your eyes will open now and your hands will take the controls and your feet will move to the pedals—but it did not happen.

The plane.

Somehow the plane was still flying. Seconds had passed, nearly a minute, and the plane flew on as if nothing had happened and he had to do something, had to do something but did not know what.

Help.

He had to help.

He stretched one hand toward the pilot, saw that his fingers were trembling, and touched the pilot on the chest. He did not know what to do. He knew there were procedures, that you could do mouth-to-mouth on victims of heart attacks and push their chests—C.P.R.—but he did not know how to do it and in any case could not do it with the pilot, who was sitting up in the seat and still strapped in with his seatbelt. So he touched the pilot with the tips of his fingers, touched him on the chest and could feel nothing, no heartbeat, no rise and fall of breathing. Which meant that the pilot was almost certainly dead.

"Please," Brian said. But did not know what or who to ask. "Please . . ."

The plane lurched again, hit more turbulence, and Brian felt the nose drop. It did not dive, but the nose went down slightly and the down-angle increased the speed, and he knew that at this angle, this slight angle down, he would ultimately fly into the trees. He could see them ahead on the horizon where before he could see only sky.

He had to fly it somehow. Had to fly the plane. He had to help himself. The pilot was gone, beyond anything he could do. He had to try and fly the plane.

He turned back in the seat, facing the front, and put his hands—still trembling—on the control wheel, his feet gently on the rudder pedals. You pulled back on the stick to raise the plane, he knew that from reading. You always pulled back on the wheel.

He gave it a tug and it slid back toward him easily. Too easily. The plane, with the increased speed from the tilt down, swooped eagerly up and drove Brian's stomach down. He pushed the wheel back in, went too far this time, and the plane's nose went below the horizon and the engine speed increased with the shallow dive.

Too much.

He pulled back again, more gently this time, and the nose floated up again, too far but not as violently as before, then down a bit too much, and up again, very easily, and the front of the engine cowling settled. When he had it aimed at the horizon and it seemed to be steady, he held the wheel where it was, let out his breath—which he had been holding all this time—and tried to think what to do next.

It was a clear, blue-sky day with fluffy bits of clouds here and there and he looked out the window for a moment, hoping to see something, a town or village, but there was nothing. Just the green of the trees, endless green, and lakes scattered more and more thickly as the plane flew—where?

He was flying but did not know where, had no idea where he was going. He looked at the dashboard of the plane, studied the dials and hoped to get some help, hoped to find a compass, but it was all so confusing, a jumble of numbers and lights. One lighted display in the top center of the dashboard said the number 342, another next to it said 22. Down beneath that were dials with lines that seemed to indicate what the wings were doing, tipping or moving, and one dial with a needle pointing to the number 70, which he thought—only thought—might be the altimeter. The device that told him his height above the ground. Or above sea level. Somewhere he had read something about altimeters but he couldn't remember what, or where, or anything about them.

Slightly to the left and below the altimeter he saw a small rectangular panel with a lighted dial and two knobs. His eyes had passed over it two or three times before he saw what was written in tiny letters on top of the panel. TRANSMITTER 221 was stamped in the metal and it hit him, finally, that this was the radio.

The radio. Of course. He had to use the radio. When the pilot had—had been hit that way (he couldn't bring himself to say that the pilot was dead, couldn't think it), he had been trying to use the radio.

Brian looked to the pilot. The headset was still on his head, turned sideways a bit from his jamming back into the seat, and the microphone switch was clipped into his belt.

Brian had to get the headset from the pilot. Had to reach over and get the headset from the pilot or he would not be able to use the radio to call for help. He had to reach over . . .

His hands began trembling again. He did not want to touch the pilot, did not want to reach for him. But he had to. Had to get the radio. He lifted his hands from the wheel, just slightly, and held them waiting to see what would happen. The plane flew on normally, smoothly.

All right, he thought. Now. Now to do this thing. He turned and reached for the headset, slid it from the pilot's head, one eye on the plane, waiting for it to dive. The headset came easily, but the microphone switch at the pilot's belt was jammed in and he had to pull to get it loose. When he pulled, his elbow bumped the wheel and pushed it in and the plane started down in a shallow dive. Brian grabbed the wheel and pulled it back, too hard again, and the plane went through another series of stomach-wrenching swoops up and down before he could get it under control.

When things had settled again he pulled at the mike cord once more and at last jerked the cord free. It took him another second or two to place the headset on his own head and position the small microphone tube in front of his mouth. He had seen the pilot use it, had seen him depress the switch at his belt, so Brian pushed the switch in and blew into the mike.

He heard the sound of his breath in the headset. "Hello! Is there anybody listening on this? Hello . . ."

He repeated it two or three times and then waited but heard nothing except his own breathing.

Panic came then. He had been afraid, had been stopped with the terror of what was happening, but now panic came and he began to scream into the microphone, scream over and over.

"Help! Somebody help me! I'm in this plane and don't know . . . don't know . . . don't know . . ."

And he started crying with the screams, crying and slamming his hands against the wheel of the plane, causing it to jerk down, then back up. But again, he heard nothing but the sound of his own sobs in the microphone, his own screams mocking him, coming back into his ears.

The microphone. Awareness cut into him. He had used a CB radio in his uncle's pickup once. You had to turn the mike switch off to hear anybody else. He reached to his belt and released the switch.

For a second all he heard was the *whusssh* of the empty air waves. Then, through the noise and static he heard a voice.

"Whoever is calling on this radio net, I repeat, release your mike switch—you are covering me. You are covering me. Over."

It stopped and Brian hit his mike switch. "I hear you! I hear you. This is me . . .!" He released the switch.

"Roger. I have you now." The voice was very faint and breaking up. "Please state your difficulty and location. And say *over* to signal end of transmission. Over."

Please state my difficulty, Brian thought. My difficulty. "I am in a plane with a pilot who is—who has had a heart attack or something. He is—he can't fly. And I don't know how to fly. Help me. Help . . ." He turned his mike off without ending transmission properly.

There was a moment's hesitation before the answer. "Your signal is breaking up and I lost most of it. Understand . . . pilot . . . you can't fly. Correct? Over."

Brian could barely hear him now, heard mostly noise and static. "That's right. I can't fly. The plane is flying now but I don't know how much longer. Over."

". . . lost signal. Your location please. Flight number . . . location . . . ver."

"I don't know my flight number or location. I don't know anything. I told you that, over."

He waited now, waited but there was nothing. Once, for a second, he thought he heard a break in the noise, some part of a word, but it could have been static. Two, three minutes, ten minutes, the plane roared and Brian listened but heard no one. Then he hit the switch again.

"I do not know the flight number. My name is Brian Robeson and we left Hampton, New York headed for the Canadian oil fields to visit my father and I do not know how to fly an airplane and the pilot . . ."

He let go of the mike. His voice was starting to rattle and he felt as if he might start screaming at any second. He took a deep breath. "If there is anybody listening who can help me fly a plane, please answer."

Again he released the mike but heard nothing but the hissing of noise in the headset. After half an hour of listening and repeating the cry for help he tore the headset off in frustration and threw it to the floor. It all seemed so hopeless. Even if he did get somebody, what could anybody do? Tell him to be careful?

All so hopeless.

He tried to figure out the dials again. He thought he might know which was speed—it was a lighted number that read 160—but he didn't know if that was actual miles an hour, or kilometers, or if it just meant how fast the plane was moving through the air and not over the ground. He knew airspeed was different from groundspeed but not by how much.

Parts of books he'd read about flying came to him. How wings worked, how the propellor pulled the plane through the sky. Simple things that wouldn't help him now.

Nothing could help him now.

An hour passed. He picked up the headset and tried again—it was, he knew, in the end all he had—but there was no answer. He felt like a prisoner, kept in a small cell that was hurtling through the sky at what he thought to be 160 miles an hour, headed—he didn't know where—just headed somewhere until . . .

There it was. Until what? Until he ran out of fuel. When the plane ran out of fuel it would go down.

Period.

Or he could pull the throttle out and make it go down now. He had seen the pilot push the throttle in to increase speed. If he pulled the throttle back out, the engine would slow down and the plane would go down.

Those were his choices. He could wait for the plane to run out of gas and fall or he could push the throttle in and make it happen sooner. If he waited for the plane to run out of fuel he would go farther—but he did not know which way he was moving. When the pilot had jerked he had moved the plane, but Brian could not remember how much or if it had come back to its original course. Since he did not know the original course anyway and could only guess at which display might be the compass—the one reading 342—he did not know where he had been or where he was going, so it didn't make much difference if he went down now or waited.

Everything in him rebelled against stopping the engine and falling now. He had a vague feeling that he was wrong to keep heading as the plane was heading, a feeling that he might be going off in the wrong direction, but he could not bring himself to stop the engine and fall. Now he was safe, or safer than if he went down—the plane was flying, he was still breathing. When the engine stopped he would go down.

So he left the plane running, holding altitude, and kept trying the radio. He worked out a system. Every ten minutes by the small clock built into the dashboard he tried the radio with a simple message: "I need help. Is there anybody listening to me?"

In the times between transmissions he tried to prepare himself for what he knew was coming. When he ran out of fuel the plane would start down. He guessed that without the propellor pulling he would have to push the nose down to keep the plane flying—he thought he may have read that somewhere, or it just came to him. Either way it made sense. He would have to push the nose down to keep flying speed and then, just before he hit, he would have to pull the nose back up to slow the plane as much as possible.

It all made sense. Glide down, then slow the plane and hit.

Hit.

He would have to find a clearing as he went down. The problem with that was he hadn't seen one clearing since they'd started flying over the forest. Some swamps, but they had trees scattered through them. No roads, no trails, no clearings.

Just the lakes, and it came to him that he would have to use a lake for landing. If he went down in the trees he was certain to die. The trees would tear the plane to pieces as it went into them.

He would have to come down in a lake. No. On the edge of a lake. He would have to come down near the edge of a lake and try to slow the plane as much as possible just before he hit the water.

Easy to say, he thought, hard to do.

Easy say, hard do. Easy say, hard do. It became a chant that beat with the engine. Easy say, hard do.

Impossible to do.

He repeated the radio call seventeen times at the ten-minute intervals, working on what he would do between transmissions. Once more he reached over to the pilot and touched him on the face, but the skin was cold, hard cold, death cold, and Brian turned back to the dashboard. He did what he could, tightened his seat-belt, positioned himself, rehearsed mentally again and again what his procedure should be.

When the plane ran out of gas he should hold the nose down and head for the nearest lake and try to fly the plane kind of onto the water. That's how he thought of it. Kind of fly the plane onto the water. And just before it hit he should pull back on the wheel and slow the plane down to reduce the impact.

Over and over his mind ran the picture of how it would go. The plane running out of gas, flying the plane onto the water, the crash—from pictures he'd seen on television. He tried to visualize it. He tried to be ready.

But between the seventeenth and eighteenth radio transmissions, without a warning, the engine coughed, roared violently for a second and died. There was sudden silence, cut only by the sound of the windmilling propellor and the wind past the cockpit.

Brian pushed the nose of the plane down and threw up.

Going to die, Brian thought. Going to die, gonna die, gonna die—his whole brain screamed it in the sudden silence.

Gonna die.

He wiped his mouth with the back of his arm and held the nose down. The plane went into a glide, a very fast glide that ate altitude, and suddenly there weren't any lakes. All he'd seen since they started flying over the forest was lakes and now they were gone. Gone. Out in front, far away at the horizon, he could see lots of them, off to the right and left more of them, glittering blue in the late afternoon sun.

But he needed one right in front. He desperately needed a lake right in front of the plane and all he saw through the windshield were trees, green death trees. If he had to turn—if he had to turn he didn't think he could keep the plane flying. His stomach tightened into a series of rolling knots and his breath came in short bursts . . .

There!

Not quite in front but slightly to the right he saw a lake. L-shaped, with rounded corners, and the plane was nearly aimed at the long part of the L, coming from the bottom and heading to the top. Just a tiny bit to the right. He pushed the right rudder pedal gently and the nose moved over.

But the turn cost him speed and now the lake was above the nose. He pulled back on the wheel slightly and the nose came up.

This caused the plane to slow dramatically and almost seem to stop and wallow in the air. The controls became very loose-feeling and frightened Brian, making him push the wheel back in. This increased the speed a bit but filled the windshield once more with nothing but trees, and put the lake well above the nose and out of reach.

For a space of three or four seconds things seemed to hang, almost to stop. The plane was flying, but so slowly, so slowly . . . it would never reach the lake. Brian looked out to the side and saw a small pond and at the edge of the pond some large animal—he thought a moose—standing out in the water. All so still looking, so stopped, the pond and the moose and the trees, as he slid over them now only three or four hundred feet off the ground—all like a picture.

Then everything happened at once. Trees suddenly took on detail, filled his whole field of vision with green, and he knew he would hit and die, would die, but his luck held and just as he was to hit he came into an open lane, a channel of fallen trees, a wide place leading to the lake.

The plane, committed now to landing, to crashing, fell into the wide place like a stone, and Brian eased back on the wheel and braced himself for the crash. But there was a tiny bit of speed left and when he pulled on the wheel the nose came up and he saw in front the blue of the lake and at that instant the plane hit the trees.

There was a great wrenching as the wings caught the pines at the side of the clearing and broke back, ripping back just outside the main braces. Dust and dirt blew off the floor into his face so hard he thought there must have been some kind of explosion. He was momentarily blinded and slammed forward in the seat, smashing his head on the wheel.

Then a wild crashing sound, ripping of metal, and the plane rolled to the right and blew through the trees, out over the water and down, down to slam into the lake, skip once on water as hard as concrete, water that tore the windshield out and shattered the side windows, water that drove him back into the seat. Somebody was screaming, screaming as the plane drove down into the water.

Someone screamed tight animal screams of fear and pain and he did not know that it was his sound, that he roared against the water that took him and the plane still deeper, down in the water. He saw nothing but sensed blue, cold blue-green, and he raked at the seatbelt catch, tore his nails loose on one hand. He ripped at it until it released and somehow—the water trying to kill him, to end him—somehow he pulled himself out of the shattered front window and clawed up into the blue, felt something hold him back, felt his windbreaker tear and he was free. Tearing free. Ripping free.

But so far! So far to the surface and his lungs could not do this thing, could not hold and were through, and he sucked water, took a great pull of water that would—finally—win, finally take him, and his head broke into light and he vomited and swam, pulling without knowing what he was, what he was doing. Without knowing anything. Pulling until his hands caught at weeds and muck, pulling and screaming until his hands caught at last in grass and brush and he felt his chest on land, felt his face in the coarse blades of grass and he stopped, everything stopped. A color came that he had never seen before, a color that exploded in his mind with the pain and he was gone, gone from it all, spiraling out into the world, spiraling out into nothing.

Nothing.

Brian opened his eyes and screamed.

For seconds he did not know where he was, only that the crash was still happening and he was going to die, and he screamed until his breath was gone.

Then silence, filled with sobs as he pulled in air, half crying. How could it be so quiet? Moments ago there was nothing but noise, crashing and tearing, screaming, now quiet.

Some birds were singing.

How could birds be singing?

His legs felt wet and he raised up on his hands and looked back down at them. They were in the lake. Strange. They went down into the water. He tried to move, but pain hammered into him and made his breath shorten into gasps and he stopped, his legs still in the water.

Pain.

Memory.

He turned again and sun came across the water, late sun, cut into his eyes and made him turn away.

It was over then. The crash.

He was alive.

The crash is over and I am alive, he thought. Then his eyes closed and he lowered his head for minutes that seemed longer. When he opened them again it was evening and some of the sharp pain had abated—there were many dull aches—and the crash came back to him fully.

Into the trees and out onto the lake. The plane had crashed and sunk in the lake and he had somehow pulled free.

He raised himself and crawled out of the water, grunting with the pain of movement. His legs were on fire, and his forehead felt as if somebody had been pounding on it with a hammer, but he could move. He pulled his legs out of the lake and crawled on his hands and knees until he was away from the wet-soft shore and near a small stand of brush of some kind.

Then he went down, only this time to rest, to save something of himself. He lay on his side and put his head on his arm and closed his eyes because that was all he could do now, all he could think of being able to do. He closed his eyes and slept, dreamless, deep and down.

There was almost no light when he opened his eyes again. The darkness of night was thick and for a moment he began to panic again. To see, he thought. To see is everything. And he could not see. But he turned his head without moving his body and saw that across the lake the sky was a light gray, that the sun was starting to come up, and he remembered that it had been evening when he went to sleep.

"Must be morning now . . ." He mumbled it, almost in a hoarse whisper. As the thickness of sleep left him the world came back.

He was still in pain, all-over pain. His legs were cramped and drawn up, tight and aching, and his back hurt when he tried to move. Worst was a keening throb in his head that pulsed with every beat of his heart. It seemed that the whole crash had happened to his head.

He rolled on his back and felt his sides and his legs, moving things slowly. He rubbed his arms; nothing seemed to be shattered or even sprained all that badly. When he was nine he had plowed his small dirt bike into a parked car and broken his ankle, had to wear a cast for eight weeks, and there was nothing now like that. Nothing broken. Just battered around a bit.

His forehead felt massively swollen to the touch, almost like a mound out over his eyes, and it was so tender that when his fingers grazed it he nearly cried. But there was nothing he could do about it and, like the rest of him, it seemed to be bruised more than broken.

I'm alive, he thought. I'm alive.

Think It Over

1. *What are the problems that Brian Robeson faces in this story?*
2. *Why wouldn't air traffic controllers or any other authorities know the real path of Brian's flight?*
3. *Where does Brian hope to land the airplane?*
4. *What personal qualities does Brian exhibit in the selection? How do these qualities help him to survive?*

Write

Imagine that it is your job to contact Brian's father about the accident. Write down the message that you would leave for him.

WORDS FROM THE AUTHOR: GARY PAULSEN

The idea for *Hatchet* came from a combination of events. One was an incident that took place in Alaska. Two young girls went on a boating trip with their father. The boat began to leak, so he put the girls off on an island, telling them he'd come back as soon as he could. But he took ill, and he couldn't get right back. The girls didn't even have a hatchet! He expected they would be dead by the time he got back. Living on seaweed, and using an old piece of tarp for shelter, the girls somehow survived. I was very interested in that story because I've lived off the land, too. There was a time in my life when I got by with gardening, trapping, and hunting.

Most of the things that happen in the book have happened to me, too. I've been in a forced landing of a small plane, so I know about that kind of fear. I also know what it means to depend on yourself to survive. I wanted to write a book about young people being self-sufficient, on all levels—emotional, intellectual, physical. I decided to take a basically urban boy, put him in a hostile environment, and then see what happened.

When you're writing, there's no substitute for personal experience. When I realized that writing isn't just something I do, but is what I am, things changed for me. Like the storytellers of long ago, I'm the person who puts an animal skin on his back, dances around the fire, and tells what the hunt was like.

THEME WRAP-UP

FLYING SOLO

How might Brian's feelings about himself have changed from the beginning to the end of the selection?

What feelings and ideas about life might Brian share with his creator, Gary Paulsen?

WRITER'S WORKSHOP Think of an event you looked forward to, such as a trip, that did not turn out as you expected. Write one paragraph describing what you expected. Then write a second paragraph describing what actually happened.

CONNECTIONS

MULTICULTURAL CONNECTION

COURTS OF A DIFFERENT ORDER

Every society has written or unwritten laws and a system for enforcing those laws. The early Native Americans had a very efficient and just system. Wrongdoers were brought before tribal leaders, who were usually a council of elders, warriors, or religious heads. The council's goal was not to hand out punishments but to settle the case in a way that satisfied both sides.

This idea of justice lives on in modern tribal courts on Indian reservations. Such courts deal mostly with disputes between people.

The Oglala Sioux court is a good example. It has one chief judge and three other judges, all elected by the tribal council, as well as one "special judge," who must have legal training. Lawyers seldom appear. The judges' good sense and knowledge of tribal law enable them to hand down fair decisions.

■ *Imagine a problem that might come before a tribal court. With a group, create a dramatic skit in which you try a case and settle it in a way that satisfies both parties.*

SOCIAL STUDIES CONNECTION

TRACKING DOWN FACTS ABOUT DIFFERENT WAYS OF LIFE

Indian reservations are governed much as states are. With a group, find out about some of the differences between life on and off the Indian reservations. Share your findings in an oral report.

A chart like this one can help you organize facts.

	On reservations	Off reservations
Courts		
Lawmaking		
Law enforcement		
Education		
Economy		
Social life		

SCIENCE/LITERATURE CONNECTION

ANCIENT MYSTERIES

There were some natural mysteries the Indians of ancient times couldn't solve. So they made up "why" stories to explain nature's riddles. Read and summarize an Indian "why" story. Then write a scientific explanation of the condition or the event the story is about.

Eagle totem, Ketchikan, Alaska

A people without history is
like the wind on the buffalo grass.
a Sioux saying

How did General George Washington command his troops in battle? Why did free African American men and women risk their lives for others in the Underground Railroad? Who were the Chinese pioneers of the American west? Historians such as Ruthanne Lum McCunn seek answers to such questions. You too can find out about America's history by being curious and asking your own questions. As you read the selections in this unit, see how many of your questions are answered.

THEMES

BOOKSHELF

HANNAH'S FANCY NOTIONS

BY PAT ROSS

Hannah wants to create a special present for Rebecca, who goes away each week to work in the mills. Little does Hannah know that this present will change both their lives.

HBJ LIBRARY BOOK

TAKE A WALK IN THEIR SHOES

BY GLENNETTE TILLEY TURNER

The stories of fourteen great African Americans are told, first in short biographies and then in dramatic skits that allow you to "walk in their shoes."

SHH! WE'RE WRITING THE CONSTITUTION

BY JEAN FRITZ

Watch and listen to George Washington, Benjamin Franklin, and the other convention delegates as they try to agree on a form of government for a brand-new nation—the United States of America.
ALA NOTABLE BOOK

THUNDER AT GETTYSBURG

BY PATRICIA LEE GAUCH

On a July morning in 1863, two great armies clashed near the town of Gettysburg, Pennsylvania. This is a true account of that battle, told by a girl who was caught up in it.

TEAMMATES

BY PETER GOLENBOCK

The 1940s were years of great social change in America. In 1947, for example, Jackie Robinson became the first African American baseball player to be signed by a major league team—the Brooklyn Dodgers.

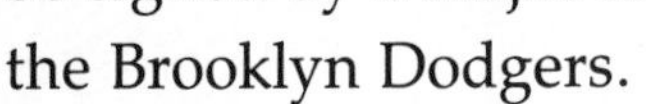

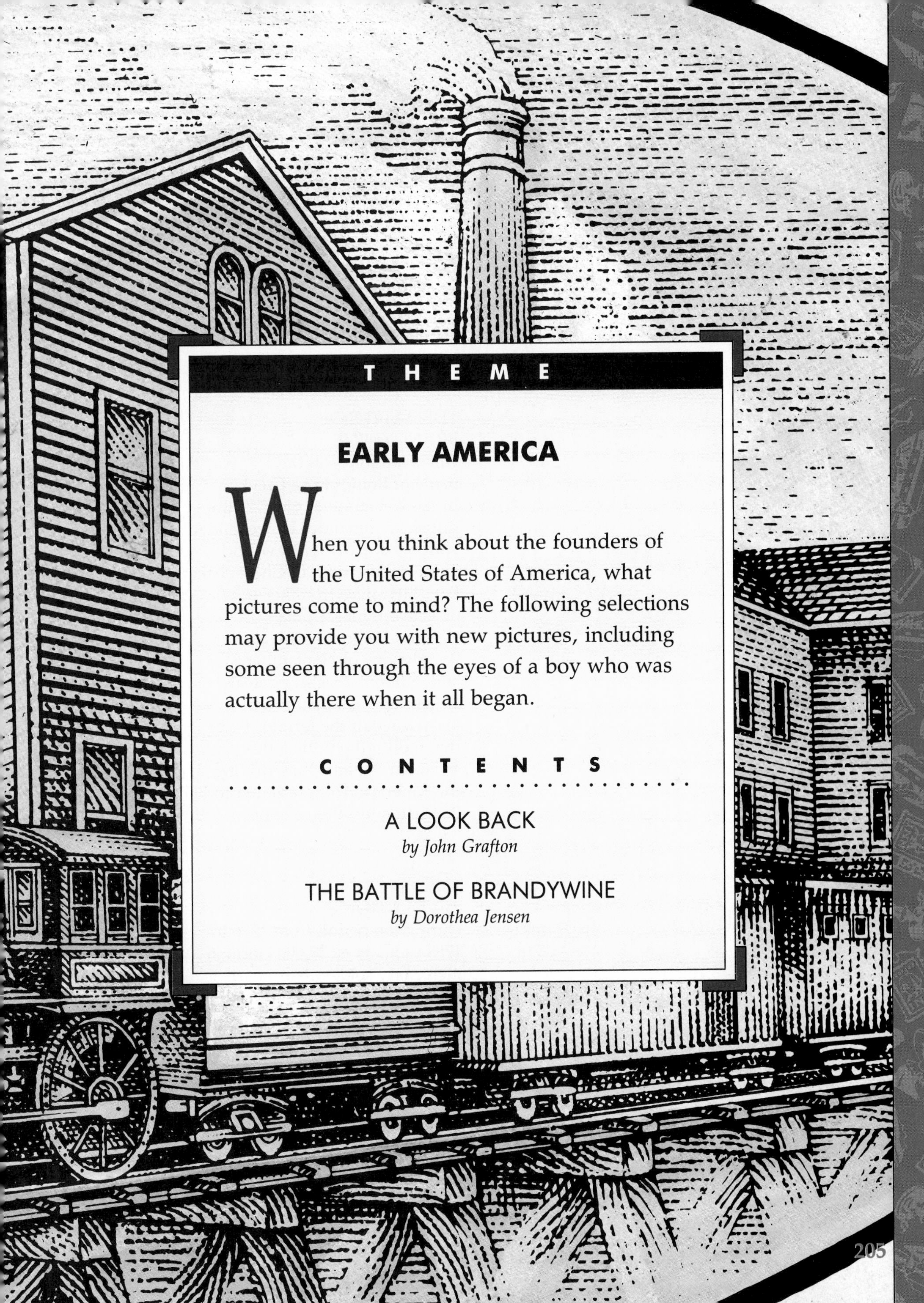

THEME

EARLY AMERICA

When you think about the founders of the United States of America, what pictures come to mind? The following selections may provide you with new pictures, including some seen through the eyes of a boy who was actually there when it all began.

CONTENTS

Engraving after a commemorative painting of an American soldier of the Revolution by George W. Maynard entitled simply "'76."

THE BATTLE OF BRANDYWINE

American forces at the battle of Brandywine Creek. In the late summer of 1777, the British Commander Howe landed with his army from New York at the northern tip of Chesapeake Bay, fifty miles from his objective, Philadelphia. Washington met Howe at the Brandywine on September 11 and suffered a tactical defeat largely through insufficient knowledge of the terrain. Later that month the British army occupied Philadelphia, driving the American Congress first to Lancaster and then to York.

THE HESSIANS IN THE REVOLUTION

During the period from 1776 to 1783 as many as 17,000 German mercenary soldiers—primarily from the state of Hesse-Cassel, thus the name Hessians—fought for the British in America.

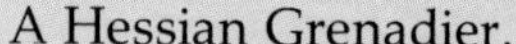

A Hessian Grenadier.

An American soldier.

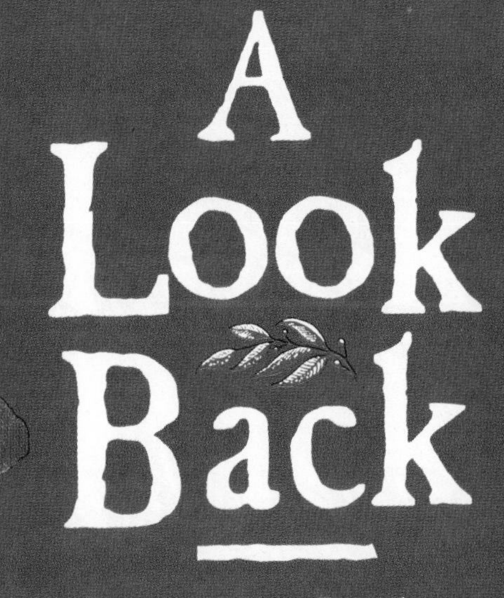

A British Grenadier.

This cartoon of a rattlesnake cut in segments representing parts of America with the legend "Join, or Die" was designed by Benjamin Franklin.

GEORGE WASHINGTON

FLAGS OF THE REVOLUTION

FIG. 1: The Grand Union Flag, America's first official flag with thirteen stripes symbolizing the Thirteen Colonies.

FIG. 2: Naval flag of Rhode Island with thirteen stars.

FIG. 3: An early version of the Stars and Stripes.

FIG. 4: Flag of a Continental Regiment at Yorktown.

FIGS. 5–6: The Pine Tree flag and a variant of the rattlesnake flag.

FIG. 7: South Carolina naval flag with the rattlesnake.

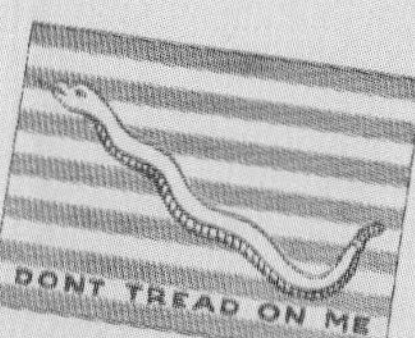

The Battle of Brandywine

from The Riddle of Penncroft Farm

by Dorothea Jensen

In the fall of 1777, in the midst of the American Revolution, Philadelphia has been taken over by George Washington's patriot forces. Many farmers in that area are Tories, colonists who side with the British.

Geordie's father, a stout Tory, is outraged when his oldest son, Will, leaves to fight for the patriot cause. He is angered further when the Continental Congress decrees that apples cannot be exported to England. In response, he sends Geordie to Philadelphia to try to peddle their farm goods.

---

illustrated by Gary Lippincott

map by Michelle Nidenoff

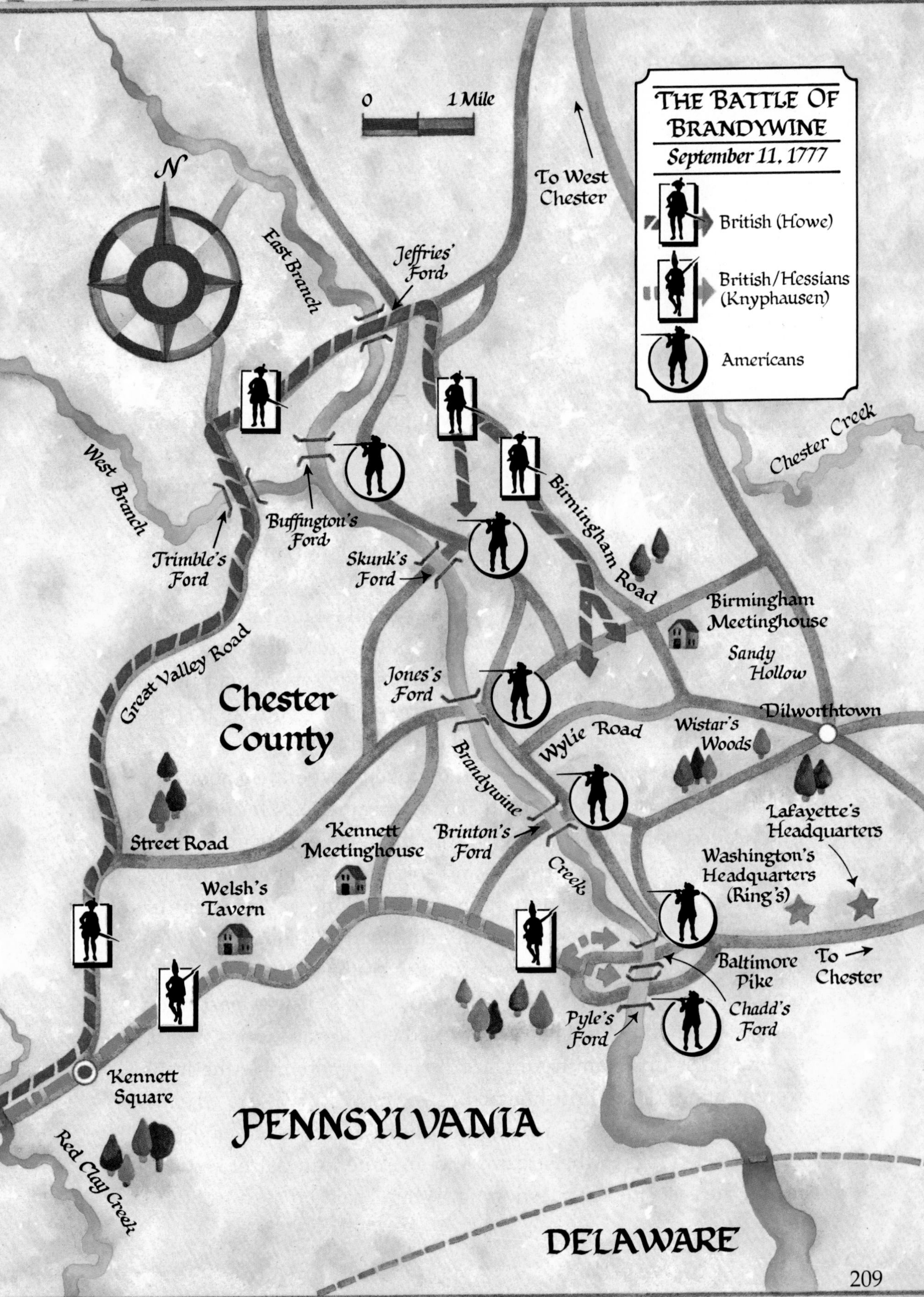
The Battle of Brandywine
September 11, 1777
British (Howe)
British/Hessians (Knyphausen)
Americans
0
1 Mile
N
To West Chester
East Branch
Jeffries' Ford
West Branch
Trimble's Ford
Buffington's Ford
Skunk's Ford
Birmingham Road
Birmingham Meetinghouse
Sandy Hollow
Chester Creek
Great Valley Road
Chester County
Jones's Ford
Wylie Road
Wistar's Woods
Dilworthtown
Brandywine
Creek
Brinton's Ford
Kennett Meetinghouse
Street Road
Welsh's Tavern
Lafayette's Headquarters
Washington's Headquarters (Ring's)
Baltimore Pike
To Chester
Chadd's Ford
Pyle's Ford
Kennett Square
Red Clay Creek
Pennsylvania
Delaware

Since the British columns blocked the road going west, I was forced to turn east, toward Chadd's Ford. Soon I came in sight of Kennett Meetinghouse. I could see that the Friends were assembled for midweek meeting, and I stopped to warn them that the British were not far behind me. What a waste of precious time! They thanked me for the warning but went calmly on with their meeting as if I had never interrupted, even though shots were now ringing out behind me on the road.

I hunkered down on the seat and looked desperately about for a place to turn off the main road. To my great relief, I found a lane that headed north. It was barely more than wheel ruts in the dirt, but at least 'twas clear of trees—and soldiers. Seemingly oblivious to my fears, Daisy and Buttercup ambled along at their regular snail's pace, despite my shaking the reins to urge them faster. Such efforts only delayed me further, for one of the reins snapped. It took the better part of an hour to mend. Thus, it was past noon before I reached Street Road and turned east toward Jones's Ford, several miles upstream from Chadd's Ford, where the Americans were waiting for the British attack.

Crossing at Jones's Ford was not easy—I had to pick my way around felled logs in the stream, and an American patrol stopped me on the east side for questioning. When I said I'd seen troops at

Welsh's but none since, the captain nodded. "Just what Major Spear reported. I don't know what that blind fool Colonel Bland saw going up to the fork, but it surely wasn't redcoats[1]! Now you'd best get along, boy," he said.

Mystified, I got along. Then, toiling up a steep slope, I heard rolling, distant thunder. I looked at the sky. It was cloudless—even the morning fog had burned away under the bright, hot sun. Again the rumbling rent the air, and this time I knew 'twas no thunderclap but the firing of guns, louder than I'd ever heard. I stopped the wagon to listen closely, trying to decide where the ominous sound was coming from. Panic rose in my chest until I could scarcely catch my breath. Instinctively, I reached into my pocket and brought out my lucky piece. The small, lead grenadier[2] in the red-painted tunic stood on my palm, aiming down his long musket. Clutching the toy, I made a childish wish that it could tell me what to do.

But a much larger and less silent figure decided my course of action. I heard a peculiar muttering in the woods nearby—a string of oaths. Without stopping to think, I raised up my lead soldier to throw at the mutterer. Then I saw his face: it belonged to Squire Thomas Cheyney, a swarthy, thickset man who had been a friend of my father's before the war had set them at odds. As the squire thrashed his way through the bushes with his riding crop, he scowled and swore like a madman. When he spotted me, his mouth opened into a perfect O of astonishment.

"Why, Geordie, what are you doing here?" he gasped.

"Been delivering perry[3] at Welsh's."

"Then your horses are fresh?" he inquired eagerly.

"If you want to call them that. Slowest nags in creation."

---

[1]British soldiers
[2]soldier
[3]pear cider

"At least they're not lame," he said with disgust. "I had to leave *my* infernal mount tied to a stile and was nearly caught by the redcoats! Give me a hand up, lad. We must hurry."

"What do you mean?" I asked, helping him up beside me.

"Why, we must warn Washington about this flanking action!"

"Flanking action?" I echoed, still not understanding.

"Aye. Ten thousand British are crossing the two branches of the Brandywine north of the fork, guided by the Tory Galloway. I saw them myself! They'll come down Birmingham Road behind the American line and fall upon the Continentals[4] from the rear. And by the cannon fire coming from the south, I judge Howe has sent some troops to make Washington believe that *that* is where the main attack will come."

"Aye, troops under Knyphausen[5] are moving against Chadd's."

Cheyney pounded his fist down on the seat. "I thought so! 'Tis the same trick Howe used to win at Long Island! I tried to warn General Sullivan of this, but he thought I was exaggerating! Well, at least the fool gave me a pass to Washington's headquarters. I'll need your wagon."

My expression must have resembled one of the idiots the Hessian[6] thought me to be, for the squire said, more kindly, "If you're too feared to come, wait here for me. I'll be back as soon as I can."

"Father will flay me if I help the Continentals, but . . ." Suddenly I thought of my brother, Will. I couldn't let him be taken by surprise. "Aye, I'm going with you!" I blurted out.

"That's a brave lad!" the squire cried. He seized the reins and whipped up the horses until they ran as if wolves were nipping at their hooves.

* * * * *

---

[4]American soldiers

[5]British/Hessian officer who had questioned Geordie earlier and thought him an "idiot"

[6]German soldier fighting for the British

As it turned out, Squire Cheyney and I didn't get far before the road along the creek grew too crowded with American troops for our wagon to pass. Nothing daunted, Cheyney said we must leave the wagon on Wylie Road and ride the three miles overland to Ring's house, Washington's headquarters near Chadd's Ford. With growing misgivings, I helped unhitch the team and conceal the wagon in the woods, and soon we were up on Daisy and Buttercup's bare backs, trotting over the rough ground. I clutched Buttercup's reins and mane for dear life as I followed Squire Cheyney up and down the steep wooded hills, more than once nearly sliding backwards off Buttercup's rump or forward over his head. Cheyney, all unheeding, allowed branches to whip behind him into my face.

As we came out of the trees on the hill behind Ring's house and paused to get our bearings, I quickly forgot my stinging face, for I could hear the sharp staccato of musketry coming from Brandywine Creek below. The thought that Will might be the target made me sick with fear.

Cheyney glanced at me. "Never heard muskets before, boy?" he asked brusquely, gathering up his reins.

I shuddered. "Not trained on men. And not when one of those men might be my brother, and he could be shot from the back."

"We'll prevent that if we get through in time! And Ring's is just below!" the squire cried, goading the winded Daisy into a gallop down the hill. As we reached the stone wall behind Washington's headquarters, a line of Continentals blocked our way. One grabbed Daisy's bridle and barked, "Don't you know there's a battle brewing? This is no place for farmers!"

"Don't be daft, sir!" Cheyney roared. "We've a pass from Sullivan to deliver urgent information to General Washington."

He held out a piece of paper. After the guard read it, he quickly motioned us on. Cheyney chirruped his horse down the hill, with mine wheezing along behind. We stopped beside the well. Dismounting, the squire sprinted around the side of the house and I scuttled behind him to the wide front door.

Two brawny sentries brought us both to a halt. Squire Cheyney, glaring at them, simply hallooed through the doorway in a voice Knyphausen likely could hear above the booming cannon beyond the Brandywine. I caught my breath, not only because my brother's life hung in the balance, but also because I was to see the man many revered as a god.

My suspense lasted but a trice.[7] A dignified figure in a buff-and-blue uniform appeared before us—General Washington.

Broad-shouldered, taller than anyone I'd ever seen, he regarded us through icy blue eyes. "There had better be an excellent reason for this interruption, sir," he exclaimed.

After all his sprinting and bellowing, Cheyney had little breath for speech. He panted like a landed fish for several long moments. Then, finally, he gasped out, " 'Tis the British, ten thousand strong, crossing upstream to attack from behind."

Washington narrowed his eyes, looked us over as if we stank of barn muck, and motioned us into the house.

---

[7]an instant

"I heard some such nonsense from Colonel Bland, but later reports proved this false," he said, frowning. "Local sources have assured me there is no ford above the fork that's close enough to offer a serious threat. No, it's here at Chadd's Ford that the British attack will come, and here at the Brandywine is where we'll hold them!" In an undertone, he added, "Indeed we must: no other obstacles lie 'twixt Howe and Philadelphia save the Schuylkill River—at the very doors of the city!"

The squire could barely contain his outrage. "Local sources!" he spluttered. "I *am* a local source. And a local source most loyal to your efforts! Don't you know that most of the farmers who've stayed nearby, in Howe's path, are neutrals or Tories who want to throw dust in your eyes?" His voice squeaked with fury, and with despair I perceived that he sounded too much like a bedlamite[8] to be taken seriously.

Washington dismissed Cheyney's words with a wave of his hand. "And why should I not think *you* are doing the same? Nay, I choose to believe the word of an innocent youth before that of a man puffed full of Tory guile!"

"Tory guile?!" Cheyney squawked, as ruffled as a fighting cock.

"Yes, an innocent such as this lad here."

Suddenly I felt pride and glory swelling within me. As puffed up as any guileful man, I stepped forward and gazed up expectantly at that lofty, grave countenance.

"Aye, this lad," repeated Washington. "Now confound the boy, where'd he get to? . . . Ned—Ned Owens?"

"Here, Excellency." As we stood in the corridor, I could see a pudgy boy standing at a sideboard in the room to the right. In one hand he held a meat pasty; in the other, a pewter tankard. Juice from one or the other was dribbling down his cheeks. Crestfallen, I watched him wipe his mouth on his sleeve.

"Have you heard what this man says, Owens?"

---

[8]insane person

"Aye, sir. And it be lies. I've been up and down the Brandywine—all the way north to the fork—and there's nary a ford you've not covered with patrols." He leveled a look at me that was brimming over with self-importance. 'Twas this barefaced conceit that gave me back my tongue.

"But the British crossed *above* the fork, at *Jeffries'* Ford!" I exclaimed. "The squire saw them, and I *know* him to be true to the patriot cause. Redcoats in the *thousands* will be coming south down Birmingham Road, behind you to the east! Don't let them flank your troops, sir. My brother, Will, is a Continental, and I couldn't bear . . ."

I shall never know why—'twas probably a storm of nerves after all I'd been through and my fears for Will—but then and there I burst into tears. No man would have done so, but 'tis likely my sobs did more than any man's vows (and surely more than Cheyney's dismayed howls) to convince Washington of the truth.

For a long moment those cool blue eyes took my measure. Just then an aide dashed into the room and thrust some papers into Washington's hand. From what he said, it appeared they were reports verifying all that Squire Cheyney and I had told the general. Washington immediately ordered word sent to Sullivan to meet the column advancing on his rear. After the aide's departure, the general buckled on his sword. As he did so, he asked, "What's your name, lad?"

"Geordie."

"We need drummer boys, Geordie. Join us, as Owens here has done." He threw these words over his shoulder as he strode from the room. Jealously, I glanced at Owens. How much I wanted to take up the drum—and how impossible that I do so!

Squire Cheyney cleared his throat. "Well done, Geordie." He mopped his brow with a handkerchief. "We'd best head back north to Wylie Road. 'Twill be safe enough—the main battle will surely be to the east, where the redcoats are."

We hurried outside, but before we could mount, one of Washington's aides sped up the path and stopped the squire.

"Go along with the courier and show Sullivan the way to Birmingham Road!" He cast a disparaging look at Daisy. "That nag will not be quick enough. Come, I'll find another for you."

Squire Cheyney handed me Daisy's reins with a warning to waste no time, then rushed away with the aide. By this time the gunfire was quickening, making Buttercup as skittish as an unbroken filly. I was still trying to get up on her when General Washington himself emerged from the house, calling for a guide to lead him to Birmingham Road.

I half hoped and half feared that I would be that guide, but instead his aides brought up an elderly man from the neighborhood, Mr. Joseph Brown. Old Mr. Brown made every possible excuse not to go, but in the end was convinced at swordpoint where his duty lay. When he protested his lack of a horse, one of Washington's aides dismounted from his own fine charger.

As Brown reluctantly climbed into the saddle, Washington sat impatiently on his own beautiful white horse. The instant the frightened farmer was in place, Washington snapped a whip at the rump of the reluctant guide's horse, which leapt into a gallop. The general followed, spurring his own mount. Even this didn't satisfy Washington, who cracked his whip and shouted, "Push along, old man, push along!" Spellbound, I watched the two race up the hill across the golden fields, jumping the fences as they came to them. I had never seen such horsemanship—superb on the part of the general, dreadful on the part of Mr. Brown. Behind them ran a ragged line of soldiers, rucksacks[9] bobbing as they sped over the uneven ground.

After the two mismatched leaders disappeared over the brow of the hill, I managed to get on Buttercup and take hold of Daisy's bridle. It took very little urging to hasten the two frightened horses

---

[9]backpacks

north, away from the sound of gunfire. By the time I got back to my wagon, my hands were too shaky for my fingers to work properly, and it took ages to harness the team. At the very moment I climbed to the seat and took up the reins, the valley behind me exploded with artillery fire. Terrified, Daisy and Buttercup reared in their traces. Up and up they went, pawing the smoke-filled air. Then they plunged back to the ground, landing at a dead run. For a few breathless moments I simply clung to the reins, pulling for all I was worth, but the horses were too panic-stricken to feel the bits sawing at their mouths. My arms ached from the effort, and I eased off to recover some strength for another try. *Perhaps my horses bolting might be a blessing in disguise,* I thought. It would surely get me away from the Brandywine much faster than their usual pace. Then I realized where we were headed: due east toward Birmingham Road, where the British and Americans were about to clash in battle.

With strength born of fear, I reached for the brake, only to have the lever break off in my hand. Clutching the reins, I shut my eyes and prayed. At the sound of gunfire, my eyes flew open once more. Up the hill to my left were two lines of soldiers. At the top of the ridge, one line raised their muskets in unconscious mimicry of the toy soldier in my pocket. Their tall caps were as pointed as my little grenadier's; their tunics as scarlet. But my toy had never spat forth puffs of smoke or blazes of fire as did the muzzles glinting in the sun. My eyes shifted down to the target below: the second line of soldiers, whose black cockaded hats proclaimed them Continentals. Under my horrified gaze, this American line wavered and broke, some few soldiers staying to return fire, but most wheeling in confusion toward the road down which my team was bolting.

As the wagon careened down the dusty lane, I glimpsed still, crumpled figures, their coats turning red with blood, lying in the field where the American line had stood. The thought that Will might be bleeding to death under the hot September sun made me steer my winded team into a thick copse of beech trees to consider what to do. 'Twas lucky I did, else I'd never have heard it—the faint but unmistakable sound of Will's whistle. I shook my head, thinking I must be imagining things. Then it came again more clearly from the thicket ahead.

I shot off the wagon seat and hurtled into the woods, crashing through underbrush in the manner of an animal fleeing a forest fire. My lips puckered soundlessly in the vain effort to whistle back. "Will! Where are you?" I finally called hoarsely.

Through the leaves, a gleam of pallid skin told me I'd found him. Will lay at the base of a beech tree looking much as he did napping in our orchard after a dip in our pond on a hot summer day. But the dark red daubs on his leg came from no pond.

"Geordie! I thought my eyes were playing tricks on me, seeing you pull up in our wagon. But when I whistled and you looked startled as a deer, I knew 'twas really you. Trust you to be in Wistar's Woods just when things got hot." Managing a feeble grin, he tried to sit up. Then, his face contorted with pain, and he fell back with a groan that tore at my heart.

"Don't you worry, Will," I said with a confidence I was far from feeling. "I'm taking you home."

"Nay," Will said weakly. "If the lobsterbacks[10] catch you . . ."

"Hush. I still have some perry in the wagon; I can bribe my way through the whole British army with you safely hidden under the hay. You look as if you could use a cupful." I ran to the wagon and fetched a tin cup full of perry for him. Will's hands shook so much I had to help him hold the cup, but the strong cider appeared to strengthen him a little.

With every moment, the sounds of battle crept closer. In my distraction, I noticed that golden leaves were sifting down upon us, but it was early for the trees to be shedding so much of their foliage. An odd buzzing sound drew my attention. I looked up and saw the cause of the early autumn: deadly grapeshot whizzing

---

[10]British soldiers

back and forth through the trees cutting down the leaves as it had cut down the young men in the field.

Frantically, I ripped off my shirt and tore it in two. As gently as I could, I wrapped one half around Will's wounded leg. It was agony for both of us, but I had to staunch the bleeding, else he'd die before I even got him into the wagon. If I could get him that far. He was at least a foot taller than I, and heavier by several stone.[11] Without daring to think of the impossibility of my task, I knotted the other piece of shirt round Will's wrists, slipped them over my head, and started to crawl for the wagon, dragging my brother beneath me. He cried out so piteously that I froze, but a burst of artillery fire shook the earth beneath me and I lunged forward convulsively. I don't know if Will struck his head or fainted, but suddenly he went slack, his dead weight bringing me down on top of him so abruptly that my face hit the ground. Everything swirled in a dizzy spiral.

It was the blood streaming down my own face that spurred me back into action. I clawed wildly to lift myself enough to give Will air. Then, slowly we inched forward to the wagon, stopped behind it, and I gently eased my head out from Will's hands. Leaving him below, I jumped up on the wagon and fixed the slats down at their loading angle. Grabbing the rope of the loading pulley, I tied it to Will's wrist and grasped the other end. Though I strained and heaved with every ounce of strength I possessed, I couldn't budge him.

Will's eyes flickered open and he moaned.

"Will," I cried. "Can you crawl any? I can't pull you. . . ."

But Will fell back senseless once more.

I was in such despair that I didn't hear anyone approaching until I saw him standing next to me—a man in a scarlet jacket with little wings on the shoulders and a tall helmet of black fur. Even without it, he was the tallest man I'd ever seen, that British grenadier.

---

[11]British unit of weight equal to 14 pounds

Without a word, we stared at each other. Then he drew one arm over his face to wipe the sweat out of his eyes. I didn't move, though I could feel the blood dripping down my own face and the sting of the sweat running into the cuts on my cheek.

His eyes flicked over me and then down to Will and the telltale cockade on his hat.

"My brother," I said, and opened my palms to him in appeal.

Still silent, the grenadier set down his musket and swung the pack off his back to the ground with a loud thud that showed how very heavy it was. Then he gathered Will up in his arms and carefully laid him down upon the wagon bed.

"Be that drink?" he asked, jutting his chin toward the barrel of perry.

I nodded my head, speechless.

"I could use a bit o' drink. Seventeen miles I've marched since dawn. Seventeen miles in all this heat. 'Tis enough to kill a man, even without the efforts of this lot." He jerked his thumb at Will.

I swarmed up the slats, filled a cup, and thrust it at him. The soldier drained it in one gulp and held the cup out for more. I hastily obliged. After downing the second cupful, he picked up his pack and musket.

"Thankee, lad," he growled, and plunged back into the woods before I could thank him in return.

I had no time to ponder what had happened. The sounds of muskets were all around me in the woods, and the next redcoat to come upon us might not be so helpful. Quickly, I replaced the slats across the wagon and flung myself back on the seat. Even in my hurry, I felt an uncomfortable lump under my breeches.

It was my lead soldier. I took him up in my hand and gazed at it. After the flesh-and-blood grenadiers I'd seen in the field and in the forest, the toy seemed different. With all the force that remained to me, I threw it down to the ground and left it behind me on the Brandywine battlefield.

I turned southeast past Sandy Hollow, joining a trickle of Continentals fleeing toward Dilworthtown. I slaked their thirst with the perry, while it lasted. The poor fellows deserved it.

It was midnight by the time we came up our lane. By great good fortune my father, exhausted by his harvest work, was sleeping too soundly to hear us arrive, but my mother's ear was sharpened with worry. She soon rushed out of the house, lantern in hand. As she stood there, the wind swirled her long white shift about her ankles and sent her long brown hair, loosened for bed, flying about her head.

"Geordie, I thought thee'd never get home!" she cried when she saw me.

"There was a battle at Brandywine, Mother. I found . . . "

"Geordie, thee knows I don't believe in bloodshed . . . no matter what the cause," she cut in. "It's bad enough to have thy brother run away and break thy father's heart, but now thee, too. . . ." Her voice faltered as she followed my mute gesture toward the wagon bed. "It's Will! Oh, Geordie, he isn't dead?"

"No, but grievously wounded."

Mother felt Will's forehead, then quickly looked over his wounds, murmuring under her breath all the while. "Ever since Will ran away, thy father has said he would treat him like the traitor he is should he return. I must think what's best to do." She pressed her hands to her head as if that would untangle her thoughts. Then, with an air of decision, she told me we would hide Will in Grampa's Folly.

This was a secret room my grandfather had insisted Father build into the barn foundation. Grampa had a fear of Indian raids and wanted a refuge handy in case of attack. Of course, there had never been any Indian raids—in fact, the only raids I heard about were the other way around. The Indians in our part of the colony had always been peaceful farmers. Indeed, they had taught the settlers the best ways to till the soil.

Now, however, we were heartily glad of Grandfather's stubbornness. The two of us managed to get Will to the barn, open the hidden door, and put him down on a pile of straw.

Will's eyes fluttered open. "Water," he murmured, then his eyelids closed once more.

Mother and I looked at each other, jubilant at this proof that he still lived. I ran for the spring, she for the herb garden to gather lamb's ear leaves to bandage and soothe his wounds.

It was not easy over the next few weeks to care for Will and keep Father ignorant of his presence in the barn. During that time I confided to my gentle Quaker mother the tale of how I had come to find Will in the beech grove. Though horror-struck by the dangers I had run and the sights I had seen, she conceded that my action had surely saved my brother's life.

Reports sifted in about the outcome of the Brandywine battle that had engulfed me and wounded Will. I heard that the American divisions, lacking the training to wheel and face the redcoats coming up behind them, had ended up dangerously separated from each other. Attempts to close the gap resulted in even more confusion—so much so that some Continentals had even fired on their own advance lines. As for the men pelting across the fields behind Washington and Mr. Brown, they had fought valiantly, but finally had had to retreat in disarray.

Still, 'twas said that Washington's men were not downcast by their defeat, especially since the British were too exhausted by their long day's march to pursue them. For a fortnight after Brandywine, the Continentals had done their best to keep Howe from crossing the Schuylkill, but to no avail. By late September, the British occupied Philadelphia.

Father was delighted, but Mother and I scarcely cared about the capture of the capital (if it could be called such after Congress had fled), for Will was safe at home again.

Think It Over

1. *Geordie's ride home from Philadelphia is filled with excitement and danger. Who are some of the people he meets on this journey?*
2. *What does the British grenadier do when he sees Geordie?*
3. *Why does Geordie throw away his toy grenadier when he drives from the battlefield?*
4. *Would you like to have lived in Geordie's time? Explain why or why not.*

Write

Imagine that you are Geordie, now safely at home. Write a letter to General Washington describing what happened to you at the Battle of Brandywine.

THEME WRAP-UP

EARLY AMERICA

Does the illustration of the British grenadier in "A Look Back" match the description given in "The Battle of Brandywine"? Tell why you think as you do.

In what ways were the flags of the American Revolution similar to the flag of the United States today? In what ways were they different?

WRITER'S WORKSHOP Imagine that you are a television reporter and your station is planning a series of reports about American history. Write a two-minute news story about the Battle of Brandywine, using details from the photo essay and the selection. Practice reading your report before presenting it to a group of your classmates.

THEME

WOMEN WHO LED THE WAY

Throughout American history, men and women have had to fight to win their freedoms. Names of leaders such as George Washington and Abraham Lincoln are well-known to us, but what are the names of some of the women who led the way? The following selections may help you find out.

CONTENTS

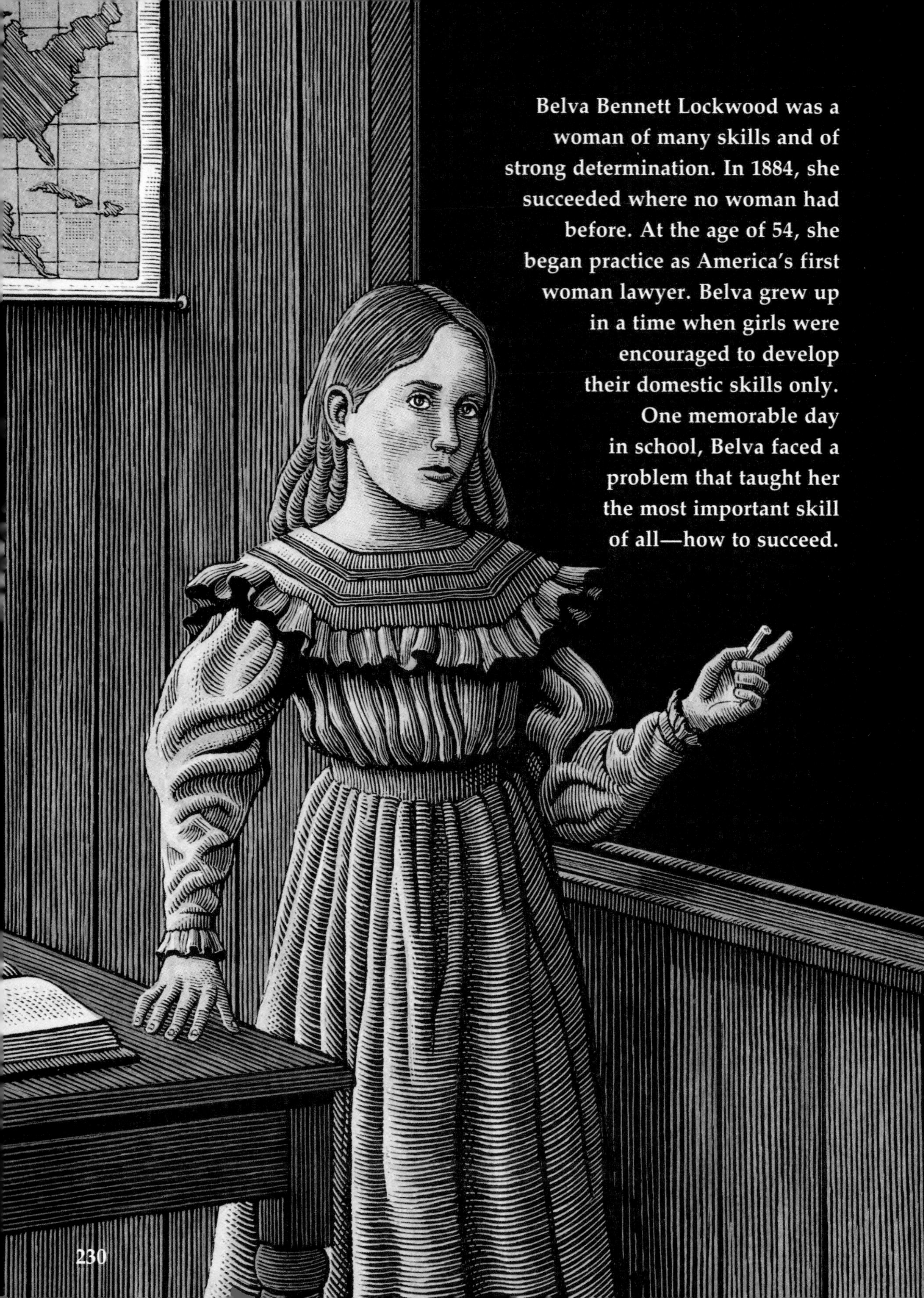

Belva Bennett Lockwood was a woman of many skills and of strong determination. In 1884, she succeeded where no woman had before. At the age of 54, she began practice as America's first woman lawyer. Belva grew up in a time when girls were encouraged to develop their domestic skills only. One memorable day in school, Belva faced a problem that taught her the most important skill of all—how to succeed.

Teacher for the Day

from

Lady for the Defense: A Biography of Belva Lockwood

by Mary Virginia Fox

illustrated by Douglas Smith

Mr. Bennett was a tall man, a straight man, even when pushing against a plow, yet he wore his tallness without authority. Within the house his wife's commands snapped the children to attention. He mouthed words of sternness, but his blue-gray eyes belied his toughness. Whether Papa recognized the fact or not, Mama quite frequently arranged to have her own will be done, and the master rarely complained.

Hannah Bennett sometimes paced with distraction because of her husband's lack of toughness and his willingness to share his neighbor's troubles.

"You've got work enough as it is, Lewis, without lending your team to the Anders. I saw a rock the size of a hog in the middle of our cornfield," she'd said one day.

"Now just how many ears of corn do you reckon would grow in that spot if I was to move that rock?" Lewis Bennett answered with a grin.

Hannah Bennett sighed, shook her head, and turned to her task of scouring the kettle with a sandstone billet.[1] "You can't always plow around your troubles, Lewis. Sometimes you have to work harder and heave them out."

"You talk as if we had a whole rock pile of troubles, Hannah." He had laughed and put his wife at ease, while she had strengthened his resolve to move that rock the following morning.

Belva's rocks weren't quite so easily moved. How could she prove she was faster than the Anders boy when she was told it was unladylike to race across the field on her way to school? There were so many things she liked to do that were forbidden. Thank goodness, book learning wasn't one of them. She loved to read.

Belva was the top student in her class at school, but this caused her little pride. Girls often did get better grades than boys.

[1]a short, thick piece of material

"Why aren't there any women doctors or lawyers or mayors or presidents if women are so smart?" Belva had asked her father.

"Probably because the Lord knew it takes more brains to run a family of children who are always asking questions."

He chuckled, but Belva ran from the room before she made a "sassy answer," which always did get her into trouble. It hurt her feelings when Papa refused to take her seriously.

History was Belva's favorite subject. It was strange to think that only a few years ago Indians had hunted wild game in the fields and forests that surrounded their own stand of corn and oats. Every spring at plowing time, Papa brought home a pocketful of finely chipped arrowheads, some small and heart-shaped to pierce the soft bodies of birds, others heavy and spearlike to bring down a deer, wildcat, or bear.

Often she tried to imagine what life would have been like if she had lived during a different chapter in her history book. If she had lived a hundred years ago, she would have been governed by a king. And there had been queens, too, who had ruled centuries ago, Elizabeth of England and Cleopatra of Egypt, and now a young girl, Victoria, had been crowned queen of the whole British Empire. Not all girls sat at home stitching on their samplers and kneading a plump hand of dough, she told herself. No sense in dreaming of queens, but she guessed she'd settle at least for being a schoolteacher one day like Miss Englehardt.

Belva knew she'd have to work hard to be a teacher like Miss Englehardt, but it was work that she loved.

Belva was only eleven years old when she had her first chance to step into Miss Englehardt's shoes. She would never forget that day. She had arrived early, as she often did, to help the teacher put slates and books on the proper desks, sometimes helping to stoke the coal stove that heated the drafty one-room shingled cottage that served as the schoolhouse.

Belva entered and hung her sweater on a hook at the back of the room and placed her lunch basket beneath that. Warren would be along later. Thirteen-year-old Rachel went to classes more or less when she felt like it. She considered school a waste of time, and Papa agreed. Only Mama kept urging her to stay on for a diploma for eighth grade, but today Mama was glad of help with the baby.

Belva turned to the bookshelf and noticed that Miss Englehardt was slumped at her desk, her head resting on her arm.

"Are you all right, Miss Englehardt?" Belva asked anxiously.

The teacher immediately straightened herself in her chair. "I'm so glad you came early, Belva. I don't know what is wrong, but I seem to be having a dizzy spell." Her usually neat auburn hair hung in damp strands around her flushed face.

"Can I get you some water from the pump?" Belva asked.

"No, thank you, but you can help, Belva. I'm going to let you take over the classes today. It is too late to cancel school, and I don't think I will be able to stay. I've already put out books and lessons. Ezra can read his paper on the pyramids. You can have a spelling bee, and the younger children might enjoy hearing a story from *Aesop's Fables.*"

Belva caught her breath. "Oh, but I couldn't be the teacher."

"Of course you can, Belva. You are the brightest one in the class. You know the lessons. It will be for only one day. I'm sure I'll be all right tomorrow."

Miss Englehardt rose from her chair unsteadily.

"Can you get home all right?" Belva asked with concern.

"I can manage if you can manage." Miss Englehardt smiled weakly. She put on her bonnet and shawl and left before Belva quite realized she was alone.

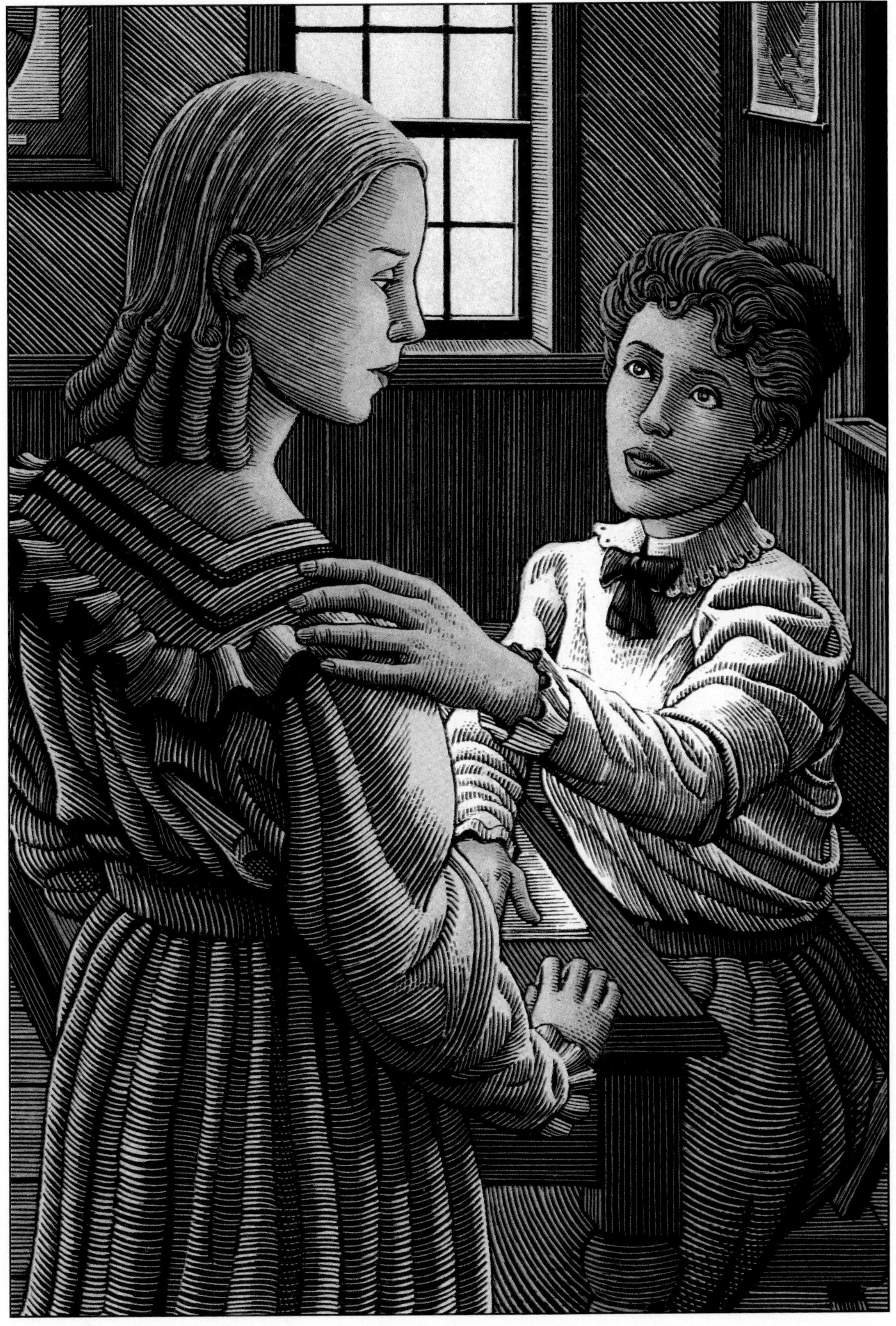

Hesitantly Belva moved to Miss Englehardt's desk. She seated herself in the straight, cane-bottom chair. Her feet barely touched the floor. Three lines of desks marched away from the blackboard in neat rows. There were eighteen places, but this year only fifteen pupils. Man-sized Ezra Zarit, called E.Z. by his peers, at sixteen was the oldest student. He would be the last to arrive because he always said he had a man-sized load of chores to finish at home. Most everyone knew that E.Z.'s early morning chore usually meant dropping a fishing line in the stream that cut across the Bennett meadow.

The youngest pupil in the school was five-year-old Toby Taylor, who was brought to school every day by his mother because the Taylor house was crowded with two-year-old twins and a four-year-old sister. He was the first one to arrive. Mrs. Taylor didn't take time to ask where Miss Englehardt was, which pleased Belva because she wondered what parents would say if they knew the teacher for the day had reached the hardly mature age of eleven. Belva felt nervous but not frightened.

When the clock on the wall read eight, she went outside and rang the school bell. The children had assembled, but from habit no one had bothered to enter the schoolhouse until summoned. There was the usual commotion as they deposited their lunches at the back of the room and found their places. Belva took a deep breath and stepped to the front of the class.

"We will now have the pledge of allegiance to the flag."

Everyone looked around in surprise. "Where's Miss Englehardt?" asked Warren.

"She's sick today," Belva explained, "but she was here and left all our lesson assignments."

"And here I got out of bed for nothin'." It was Ezra Zarit who had spoken.

"We will have classes just as usual, E.Z.," Belva said firmly. She placed her hand over her heart and faced the flag. "I pledge allegiance . . ."

Again from habit, fourteen voices joined hers. When they finished, all the students sat down except E.Z. "I don't have to stay if we don't have a teacher," he said.

"Miss Englehardt has assigned me to be the teacher," Belva answered clearly. Her eyes stared steadily at E.Z. "We can start with your paper on the pyramids. It should be of interest to all of us."

"Now don't she just sound like a teacher?" Ezra laughed. Then slowly he added, "But she sure don't look like one."

The classroom echoed with laughter. Belva flushed. She had to pass this first test of authority. "Ezra, we'd like to hear your paper."

"I haven't finished it."

"Well, then, that will give you something to do for the rest of the morning."

"I'm sure not going to mind a kid younger than me," he snorted, "and especially not a girl!"

Belva's voice remained calm. "If it isn't finished by tomorrow, I'm sure Miss Englehardt will arrange for an extra assignment, longer and harder than this one."

E.Z. hesitated, knowing Belva had spoken the truth. "Well, as long as I'm here, I might as well write a few lines, but I'm not takin' any bossin' from the likes of you."

Belva ignored the last threat. The rest of the morning went smoothly. She wrote the arithmetic problems on the blackboard for the older pupils. Verses to be memorized were assigned, and she sat with three of the younger children while they stumbled through a reading lesson. She was enjoying her day and was surprised to glance at the clock and see it was time to dismiss the class for lunch.

She waited until everyone had raced out the door before picking up her own lunch basket. E.Z. was waiting for her. She smiled a bit nervously. "Well, did you finish your paper?"

"As much as I aim to finish it. And as soon as I eat, me and the boys is takin' off. We'll leave the schoolin' for the sissy girls."

"What makes you think school is only for girls, Ezra?"

" 'Cause boys is naturally smarter and don't need to learn stupid things from books. Ever hear of a girl running a train? That's what I'm going to be in a year or two. I'm gonna work for the railroad and be an engineer."

"That's a fine idea," said Belva. "But I bet if a woman felt she wanted to, she could run a train just as well as a man. If they'd let her," she added quietly to herself.

Ezra laughed. "I ain't ever heard of a lady engineer."

The other boys began to snicker.

"I still say girls can do anything as well as boys."

"Bet you couldn't lift that rock over there." E.Z. grinned.

"That's not fair," said Belva. "I didn't say boys weren't stronger than girls, just that they weren't any smarter than girls."

"See, you're just making excuses. Watch me lift this one."

Ezra walked over to a large boulder that had been dumped in a pile where someone had started to build a stone gatepost. Rough timbers lay beside it. He strained to roll the stone over, but it was larger than he had bargained for and was half buried in the ground.

Belva watched thoughtfully for a moment. "I think I could move that stone," she said.

E.Z. slapped his knee and doubled up in laughter. "Hear it, boys. And she ain't joshin'. Why I can't even budge that hunk of stone."

"If I do move it," said Belva, "will you all promise to stay in class until the end of the day?"

"Sure, but if you don't move it, I'm gonna tell my folks teacher says I get a week off."

Belva first picked up a small stone and placed it near the bigger one. Then she chose a length of split timber about six feet long and wedged that against an undercut of the boulder. Using the smaller stone as a fulcrum for her lever, she put all her weight on the timber. The boulder slowly rolled onto its side.

E.Z.'s mouth dropped open in astonishment.

"Now if you'd read your lesson about how they built the pyramids, you would have won your challenge," said Belva. "And that's something you may want to remember when you're a railroad man."

She went back into the schoolhouse feeling she was now an experienced teacher.

Think It Over

1. *What character traits help Belva succeed at being a teacher for a day?*
2. *What women in history does Belva admire?*
3. *Ezra, who is sixteen, is upset because an eleven-year-old is left in charge of the class. How would you feel about having a teacher who is younger than you?*
4. *How might the story have changed if Ezra had read and understood his lesson about the Egyptian pyramids?*

Write

Imagine that you are Belva at the end of her teaching day. Write a note to Miss Englehardt describing what happened during your day as a substitute teacher.

ELIZABETH BLACKWELL

from INDEPENDENT VOICES ▪ by EVE MERRIAM

AWARD-WINNING AUTHOR

What will you do when you grow up,
nineteenth-century-young-lady?
Will you sew a fine seam and spoon dappled cream
under an apple tree shady?

Or will you be a teacher
in a dames' school
and train the little dears
by the scientific rule
that mental activity
may strain
the delicate female brain;
therefore let
the curriculum stress music, French, and especially
etiquette:
teach how to set
a truly refined banquet.
Question One:
What kind of sauce
for the fish dish,
and pickle or lemon fork?
Quickly, students,
which should it be?

Now Elizabeth Blackwell, how about you?
Seamstress or teacher, which of the two?
You know there's not much else that a girl can do.
Don't mumble, Elizabeth. Learn to raise your head.

"I'm not very nimble with a needle and thread.
"I could teach music—if I had to," she said,
"But I think I'd rather be a doctor instead."

"Is this some kind of joke?"
asked the proper menfolk.
"A woman be a doctor?
Not in our respectable day!
A doctor? An M.D.! Did you hear what she said?
She's clearly and indubitably out of her head!"

"Indeed, indeed, we are thoroughly agreed,"
hissed the ladies of society all laced in and prim,
"it's a scientific fact a doctor has to be a him.
"Yes, sir,
"'twould be against nature
"if a doctor were a her."

Hibble hobble bibble bobble
widdle waddle wag
tsk tsk
twit twit
flip flap flutter
mitter matter mutter
moan groan wail and rail
Indecorous!
Revolting!!
A scandal
A SIN

their voices pierced the air like a jabbing hat-pin.
But little miss Elizabeth wouldn't give in.

To medical schools she applied.
In vain.
And applied again
and again
and again
and one rejection offered this plan:
why not disguise herself as a man?
If she pulled back her hair, put on boots and pants,
she might attend medical lectures in France.
Although she wouldn't earn a degree,
they'd let her study anatomy.

Elizabeth refused to hide
her feminine pride.
She drew herself up tall
(all five feet one of her!)
and tried again.
And denied again.
The letters answering no
mounted like winter snow.

Until the day
when her ramrod will
finally had its way.
After the twenty-ninth try,
there came from Geneva, New York
the reply
of a blessed
Yes!
Geneva,
Geneva,
how sweet the sound;
Geneva,
Geneva,
sweet sanctuary found. . . .

. . . . and the ladies of Geneva
passing by her in the street
drew back their hoopskirts
so they wouldn't have to meet.

Psst, psst,
hiss, hiss
this sinister scarlet miss.
Avoid her, the hoyden, the hussy,
lest we all be contaminated!
If your glove so much as touch her, my dear,
best go get it fumigated!

When Elizabeth came to table,
their talking all would halt;
wouldn't so much as ask her
please to pass the salt.

In between classes
without a kind word,
Elizabeth dwelt
like a pale gray bird.

In a bare attic room
cold as a stone,
far from her family,
huddled alone

studying, studying
throughout the night
warming herself
with an inner light:

don't let it darken,
the spark of fire;
keep it aglow,
that heart's desire:

the will to serve,
to help those in pain—
flickered and flared
and flickered again—

until
like a fairy tale
(except it was true!)
Elizabeth received
her honored due.

The perfect happy ending
came to pass:
Elizabeth graduated . . .
. . . at the head of her class.

And the ladies of Geneva
all rushed forward now to greet
that clever, dear Elizabeth,
so talented, so sweet!

Wasn't it glorious
she'd won first prize?

Elizabeth smiled
with cool gray eyes

and she wrapped her shawl
against the praise:

how soon there might come
more chilling days.

Turned to leave
without hesitating.

She was ready now,
and the world was waiting.

Women in Washington

by Angela de Hoyos

First there was a teacher, then a lawyer, then a doctor . . . and the career fields for women in America continued to grow. Today, women's opportunities are unlimited, due to the leadership of people such as Belva Bennett Lockwood and Elizabeth Blackwell. The following portraits show six women who were and are leaders in their fields in our nation's capital, Washington, D.C.

FRANCES PERKINS (April 10, 1880–May 14, 1965)

Secretary of Labor

In 1933, Frances Perkins was appointed the first female member of the Cabinet, the group of official advisers to the president. As Secretary of Labor during the hard times of the Great Depression, Perkins helped to pass laws such as the Federal Emergency Relief Act and the Social Security Act. These laws led to programs that are still in effect and helping people today.

JEANNETTE RANKIN (June 11, 1880–May 18, 1973)

Congresswoman

In 1917, Jeannette Rankin from Montana became the first woman ever elected to the House of Representatives. Jeannette Rankin firmly believed in world peace. She was the only member of Congress to vote against the entry of the United States into both World War I and World War II. Of her first antiwar vote she said, "It was the most significant thing I ever did."

HELEN THOMAS (August 4, 1920–)

White House Bureau Chief

In 1974, Helen Thomas became the first woman to serve as the White House Bureau Chief for a major news service, the United Press International. This honor came after working for more than thirty years as a reporter. Thirteen of those years had been spent in the White House, which she calls "the most exciting place in the world." In 1976, the *World Almanac* named Helen Thomas as one of the most influential women in America.

SANDRA DAY O'CONNOR (March 26, 1930–)

Supreme Court Justice

In 1981, Sandra Day O'Connor was nominated to fill a vacant position on the Supreme Court of the United States. Sandra Day O'Connor was a successful lawyer, state senator, and judge from Arizona. Her appointment was approved unanimously, making one of her fondest dreams come true: to be "remembered as the first woman who served on the Supreme Court."

DR. ANTONIA NOVELLO (August 23, 1944–)

Surgeon General of the United States

In 1990, Dr. Antonia Novello became the first female Surgeon General, the highest-ranking officer in the United States Public Health Service. Dr. Antonia Novello, who was born in Puerto Rico, suffered from a serious birth defect throughout her childhood. This condition required frequent surgery and was not corrected until she was eighteen years old. She decided to become a doctor then, saying " . . . no other person is going to wait eighteen years."

SHARON PRATT DIXON (January 30, 1944–)

Mayor of Washington, D.C.

In January of 1991, Sharon Pratt Dixon was sworn in as the first woman mayor of Washington, D.C. During her campaign, she wore a pin in the shape of a shovel, the symbol of her promise to clean up the city. Sharon Pratt Dixon began her career as a successful lawyer. She is also the first woman to serve as national treasurer of the Democratic Party.

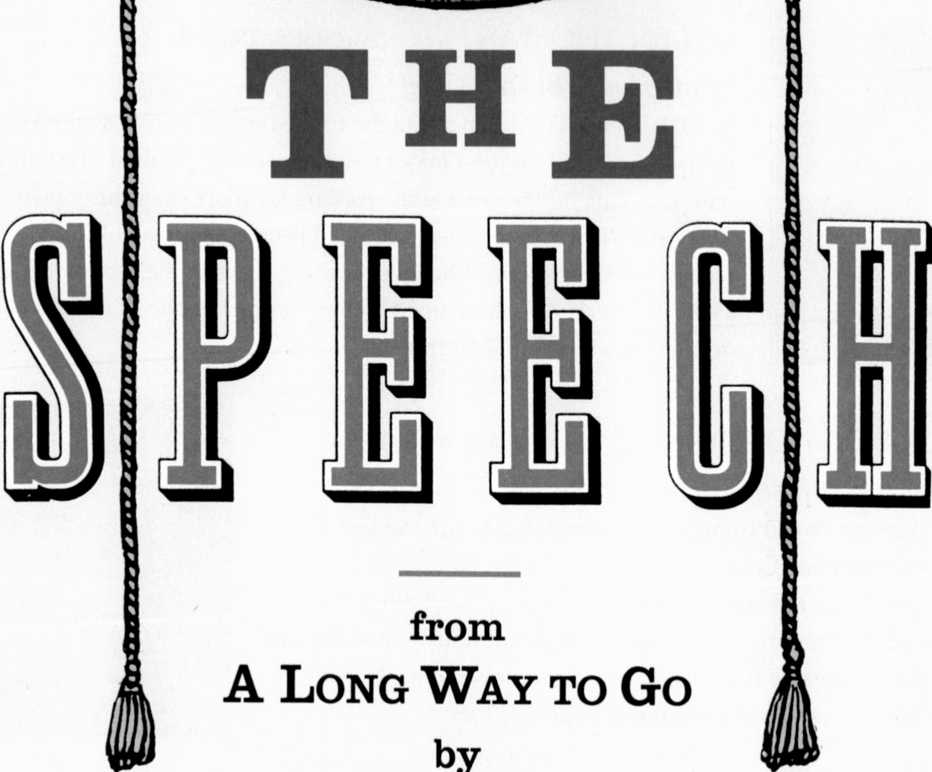

THE SPEECH

from

A Long Way to Go

by

Zibby Oneal

In 1917, Lila's proper family was scandalized by Grandmama, who wore a yellow chrysanthemum and spoke out for the right of women to vote. Lila, however, admired her grandmother's courage and tried to imitate her. Lila decided to prove to her friend Mike that women can do whatever men can do, including selling newspapers on a street corner.

Award-Winning Author

illustrated by
Sheldon Greenberg

"Now let's see you sell," Mike said, but he didn't wait to watch. Instead he began running after customers, waving papers, shouting, "Read all about the big fire in Brooklyn! Read about the flames forty feet high!"

Lila pulled a paper from the bag and looked at it. She couldn't see where he was getting all that. The paper didn't say a thing about flames. It didn't really say much about the fire. That was what he meant by imagination, she guessed, but it didn't seem quite fair to fool people that way.

She ran her eyes down the front page. The bond speech. The fire. But then she saw, down at the bottom of the page, not taking much space, a small article headed, SUFFRAGISTS REFUSE TO EAT. Lila read as fast as she could. There were suffragists in jail in Washington who wouldn't eat a bite. They said they'd rather starve than do without the vote. The paper called it a hunger strike.

Lila's eyes widened. This was news. This was something interesting. And, besides, it was true. She pulled a few more papers from her bag and stood herself right in the middle of the sidewalk. "Suffragists starving to death!" she yelled. "Read all about it!"

To her amazement, someone stopped to buy a paper. She tried again. "Read all about the ladies starving to death in Washington!" And, again, someone stopped.

"Crazy women," the man said, but he paid her and didn't seem to think it was strange at all to see a girl selling papers.

Lila felt encouraged. Over and over she waved her papers at people walking past. She shouted her headline until she was hoarse, but it felt good to be hoarse, to be shouting and running.

"President making women starve!" she cried. "They won't eat till they get to vote!" Anything she said seemed to work. People bought papers. Maybe they would have bought them anyway, thought Lila. She didn't know, but she didn't care. She was too busy selling. In no time, her bag was empty.

She hadn't had time to think about Mike, but now, bag empty, she turned around to look for him. He was leaning against a lamppost, watching her. "I sold them all," she said breathlessly.

"I noticed."

"Here's the money." She fished the change and a few bills from her pocket.

"You keep it."

"No. Why?"

"You earned it."

"But I didn't do it for that. You take the money. I just did it to show you I could."

"Yeah. Well." Mike kicked the lamppost with the toe of his shoe. "I guess you showed me."

There were things that Lila felt like saying, but she decided not to say them. Instead she picked up the empty canvas bag and slung it over her shoulder. Together they started back the way they had come.

* * * * *

"Lila, you've told me all about it three times."

She had. She couldn't help it. Saturday afternoon was like a story she didn't want to finish, like a book of beautiful colored pictures that she couldn't bear to close.

"Oh, I liked it all so much, but I'm not going to tell anyone else about it. Just you." Lila looked out the window at the sunlight on the fence around the park. "I wish girls could sell papers," she said a little sadly. "I mean all the time."

"There are more and more things that girls can do. Think of all the jobs women have now that there's a war on. When I was your age we didn't dream of working in offices and factories."

"That's women. I mean girls." And then, "Do you think that if women could vote, they'd let girls sell papers?"

Grandmama laughed. "I don't know. I suppose there'd be a better chance of that happening."

"Then I'm a suffragist," Lila said. "I *thought* I was, but now I'm sure."

"That's fine."

Lila frowned. "But what can I do?"

"Believe that women have rights the same as men."

That wasn't what Lila had in mind. She wanted action. She wanted to shout headlines, run around yelling. "I could give speeches," she said. She imagined herself standing on a wooden box speaking to crowds in the street. It would be a lot like selling papers.

But Grandmama only laughed again. "You're still too young to make speeches."

"But I want to do *something*. It's no use just sitting around believing things."

Grandmama looked thoughtful. "Well, there's a suffragist parade a week or so before the state election. We're going to march up Fifth Avenue all the way from Washington Square to Fifty-ninth Street."

"With signs?" said Lila. "And banners?"

"Oh, yes, and music, too. We're going to make people notice us."

"Would you take me?"

"Well, I was thinking—"

Lila sat up straight. "I'm coming."

"But not without permission you aren't. Not unless your mama and papa agree."

"I'll make them agree," said Lila, though she had no idea how she'd do that.

"Well, I'll try to help you," Grandmama said. "At least I'll mention the parade."

Lila sat quietly in church with her hands in her lap. She played nicely with George until lunchtime, rolling his ball to him over and over though this was the most boring game in the world. She sat straight at the table and ate all of her lunch, though that included beets. Really, Lila thought, she was being so perfect it was hard to see how Mama and Papa could say no.

But that was what Papa said. While they were waiting for dessert, Grandmama brought up the parade. She did it in a kind of offhanded way, as if it were something she'd only just remembered. "And I think Lila would like to march, too," she said. Lila looked down at her napkin and crossed her fingers. But Papa said no.

It was such a small word, no, but it seemed to Lila that it was the biggest word in her life. So many nos. She felt tears of disappointment prickling in her eyes. She couldn't look up.

When, after lunch, Papa said, "Come on, Lila, it's time for our Sunday walk," Lila felt like saying, "No!" She didn't want to go for a walk with her father. She felt too mad and disappointed. All the same, she went to get her coat, because a little girl didn't say no to her father.

"Which way shall we walk?" he asked her when they were standing on the pavement.

"I don't care." And she didn't. She didn't care at all.

"What about Fifth Avenue then?"

Lila had known he'd choose that. Papa liked walking along Fifth Avenue, looking at the new motorcars pass by. One day, he said, he thought he might buy one.

And so they walked over to Fifth Avenue. Lila was wearing her best coat again and clean white gloves because Papa liked her to look like a lady when they went walking. But her hands felt crowded in the gloves and her shoulders felt crowded in her coat. She felt crowded all over.

At the corner of Fifth Avenue, they turned and walked north, past banks and office buildings, past shops and department stores. Usually Lila liked looking into the department store windows, but today they didn't seem exciting. Fifth Avenue was dull.

"Has the cat got your tongue?" Papa said.

"No. I'm thinking."

"About important things?"

"I was thinking about the parade. It's going to come right up this street."

"Lila, you must forget the parade."

But how could she? She couldn't stop thinking about it, even though the thinking made her sad.

They waited to cross the street while a car passed. "That's a Pierce Arrow," Papa said. "It's really something, isn't it?"

Lila nodded. She supposed so.

"Maybe when George is older we'll buy one like that. He can learn to drive it."

"What about me?"

"Oh, you'll be a beautiful grown lady by then. You can ride in the back and tell George where to take you. You'll have all kinds of pretty clothes to wear. We'll go shopping for things like the dress in that window."

Lila glanced at the dress in the shop window. She had to admit it was pretty. She wondered why she didn't like it more, and then she knew. It looked like the kind of dress that was for sitting around doing nothing.

"I'd rather learn how to drive a motorcar," she said. "I'd rather be *doing* something."

Papa didn't understand. "There'll be plenty for you to do. Tea dances and parties and all that sort of thing."

"Those aren't the things I want to do."

"No? What then?"

"Oh!" Lists of things came tumbling into Lila's head. She wanted to march in the parade, turn cartwheels, walk on her hands, roll her stockings down. She wanted to run and yell, sell papers—but that was not what Papa meant. He meant later, when she was grown-up. What did she want to do *then?* Lila closed her eyes and squeezed them tight. "I want to vote," she said.

The words were out before she knew she was going to say them, but suddenly they seemed just right. "I want to be able to vote same as George."

When she opened her eyes, Papa was looking at her. "That's what you want more than anything?"

Lila nodded. She dug her fists into her pockets and looked up at Papa bravely. "It's what Grandmama says. Girls are people, too. They have rights. It isn't fair the way it is. Billy Ash says he's smarter than me just because he's a boy. But I'm the one who gets all *A*'s, not him. So why should he be allowed to vote and not me? Why should George if I can't? It's not fair, Papa. It's not fair to girls."

Lila paused for breath, but she couldn't stop talking. "When I grow up, I want to be just like Grandmama. I want to make things fair for everyone. That's why I want to march in the parade—to show people that's what I think. And if they put me in jail for marching, then I just won't eat, like the ladies in Washington."

Then Lila stopped. She didn't have anything else to say.

"Well," said Papa, "that was quite a speech."

Lila couldn't tell what he was thinking. His face was very serious. She wondered if he would stop loving her now because of all she'd said. She wondered if he'd already stopped. She waited for him to say something more, but he said nothing at all. He took her hand and they kept on walking.

Lila's feet slapped along beside him. It was too late now to take it back, and, anyway, she couldn't take it back without lying. She'd said what she meant. But Papa wasn't saying anything at all. He was looking straight ahead as if he had forgotten all about her, as if he didn't know she was there any more.

Lila felt hollow in the middle. She bit the insides of her cheeks to keep from crying. On the way home, she counted cracks in the sidewalk.

When they reached the corner of Twenty-first Street and were almost home, Papa said, "How did you happen to know about those women in Washington, the ones who aren't eating? Did Grandmama tell you?"

Lila shook her head, still counting cracks. "No," she said. "I read it in the paper."

"Did you really? For heaven's sake." Lila could have sworn, if she hadn't known better, that he sounded proud of her.

After supper, she had her bath and watched Katie Rose laying out her clothes for school the next day. The same old stockings. The same old dress. Lila sighed. Everything was the same old thing again, except that now it would be different with Papa. She climbed out of the tub and wrapped herself in a towel. She went into her room to put on her nightgown.

And that was when Grandmama came in. She had a funny, puzzled sort of expression. "It looks as if we'll be going to the parade together," she said.

Lila paused. The damp ends of her hair swung against her shoulders. "What?"

"Your father says you may go."

"With you? To the parade?" Lila felt as if she couldn't take it all in so fast.

"That's what he says."

"But why?"

Grandmama shrugged. "I don't know what you said to him on that walk, but you must have said something."

Lila swallowed. He had called it a speech. She had made a speech and he'd listened! A bubble of happiness began to rise inside her. He had listened and it was all right.

Think It Over

1. *What is Lila's problem in this story? How does she solve it?*
2. *What does Lila do to increase her newspaper sales?*
3. *If you were Mike, would you have accepted the newspaper money from Lila? Explain why or why not.*
4. *As they walk along Fifth Avenue, Lila tells Papa about the things she wants to do in her life. What are some of these things?*

Write

Imagine that you are a newspaper headline writer. Write headlines that describe what might happen to Mike, to Lila, to Grandmama, and to Papa.

WOMEN WHO LED THE WAY

What do the selections reveal about obstacles in the paths of women who wanted to do something different? What qualities helped the women overcome these obstacles?

In "The Speech," Grandmama explains to Lila what a suffragist is. What other women in the selections, poem, or photo essay do you think could be described as suffragists? Why?

WRITER'S WORKSHOP Belva Lockwood and Lila are about the same age in the selections you have read. In what other ways are they alike? In what ways are they different? Make two lists, one of similarities and one of differences, and use your lists to write paragraphs of comparison and contrast.

INTERPRETING THE PAST

Do you ever think about the vast amount of history that has gone before you? Every event that has ever happened is a part of history, but not every event is worth writing about. Think about how authors, such as Virginia Hamilton, decide what is important to write about when they interpret the past.

CONTENTS

An Interview with the Author: Virginia Hamilton

Writer Ilene Cooper had the opportunity to talk with Virginia Hamilton about two of her novels: *The House of Dies Drear* and *The Bells of Christmas*. This is what Virginia Hamilton had to say about interpreting the past for her readers.

COOPER: You write about history from both historical and personal points of view. In your work they often blend together, don't they?

HAMILTON: My personal history does enhance my fiction. In *The House of Dies Drear*, I started with the town history as well as the stories that I heard growing up. For one thing, my grandfather, a fugitive from slavery, had come north to Ohio. The area where I live in Ohio had been a station on the Underground Railroad. Because of that there were many houses in my town that had hidden rooms and secret passages. In fact, here in Yellow Springs is the Octagon House, one of the few buildings left that was designed specifically to hide slaves. The eight corners of the house were made into little cubby holes that could be used as hiding places. I knew all this and found it fascinating. Enough so that when I started writing *The House of Dies Drear*, I called on what I knew. In the first chapter, when the family is traveling north, they are using one of the same routes that the fugitives had used a century before. Though you don't know that from reading the book, I called on that information to make it historically correct.

AWARD-WINNING AUTHOR

COOPER: Where did you get the idea for *The Bells of Christmas*?

HAMILTON: One of my editors said to me, "You've never done a Christmas book." The idea appealed to me greatly because of the stories I had heard growing up about the way my mother's family spent the holiday. There were sleighs and sleigh bells, big snows, and lots of family around.

COOPER: So that was personal history. Did you research facts for the story as well?

HAMILTON: Oh, yes. I'm lucky enough to live near the National Road. I've often used aspects of the National Road in books. The Midwest was opened up by people using that road, and so that became a part of the story. I also wanted a big snow in my book. I began researching the newspapers from one hundred years or so back to see what year there was a huge snowfall at Christmas. I couldn't find one! I was dying. Finally, I found one; you see, it is very important to me that details be historically correct. I would never say in a book that there was a snow during a particular year if there wasn't one.

COOPER: Can we say that when the story is historical, you still inject some of your personal history, and when the story is personal, you still make sure the facts are correct?

HAMILTON: Yes, I'm lucky enough to have a personal history to draw on *and* an area to draw on that is important to our country's history. I used to say it was serendipity that helped me find material. Now I believe that all of the things a writer needs are out there waiting; you just have to be able to recognize them.

A New Home in Ohio

from The House of Dies Drear

ALA Notable Book

SLJ Best Books of the Year

by Virginia Hamilton

illustrated by Jack Molloy

Thomas Small and his family are in a car traveling to their new home in Ohio. Although he has yet to see it, their new home is fascinating to Thomas because of its history. It was once a stopover for the runaway slaves who fled north along the Underground Railroad.

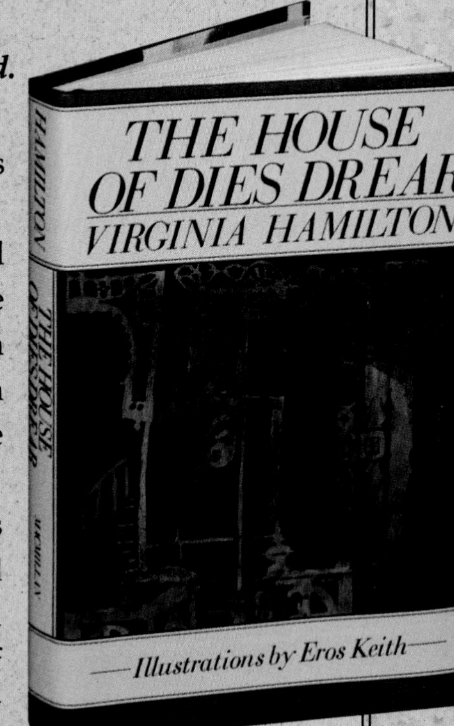

"I wish we'd hurry and get there," Thomas said. "It feels like we've been riding forever."

They lapsed into silence. Thomas could think of no better birthday present than to have the new house suit him. He wanted to like it in the same way he liked the masses of clouds in front of a storm or the dark wood of the pine forest back home.

His father had given him a book for his birthday. It was a volume, bound in real leather, about the Civil War, the Underground Railroad and slaves. Thomas loved the smell of real leather, and he rubbed the book lightly back and forth beneath his nose. Then he leaned back, flipping idly through the pages. In a moment his brothers were nestled against him, but Thomas did not even notice.

He had come across a curious piece of information earlier. Of the one hundred thousand slaves who fled from the South to Canada between 1810 and 1850, forty thousand of them had passed through Ohio. Thomas didn't know why this fact surprised him, yet it did. He knew a lot about slaves. His father had taught Civil War history in North Carolina. He would be teaching it in Ohio in the very town in which they were going to live. He had taught Thomas even more history than Thomas cared to know. Thomas knew that Elijah Anderson had been the "superintendent" of the Underground Railroad in Ohio and that he had finally died in prison in Kentucky. He knew that in the space of seven years, one thousand slaves had died in Kentucky. But the fact that forty thousand escaping slaves had fled through Ohio started him thinking.

Ohio will be my new home, he thought. A lot of those slaves must have stayed in Ohio because Canada was farther than they could have believed. Or they had liked Elijah Anderson so much, they'd just stayed with him. Or maybe once they saw the Ohio River, they thought it was the Jordan and that the Promised Land lay on the other side.

The idea of exhausted slaves finding the Promised Land on the banks of the Ohio River pleased Thomas. He'd never seen the Ohio River, but he could clearly imagine freed slaves riding horses up and down its slopes. He pictured the slaves living in great communities as had the Iroquois, and they had brave leaders like old Elijah Anderson.

"Papa . . ." Thomas said.

"Yes, Thomas," said Mr. Small.

"Do you ever wonder if any runaway slaves from North Carolina went to Ohio?"

Mr. Small was startled by the question. He laughed and said, "You've been reading the book I gave you. I'm glad, it's a good book. I'm sure some slaves fled from North Carolina. They escaped from all over the South, and it's likely that half of them passed through Ohio on their way to Canada."

Thomas sank back into his seat, arranging his sprawling brothers against him. He smoothed his hand over the book and had half a mind to read it from cover to cover. He would wake the twins and read it all to them. They loved for him to read aloud, even though they couldn't understand very much.

No, thought Thomas. They are tired from being up late last night. They will only cry.

Thomas' brothers were named Billy and Buster and they knew all sorts of things. Once Thomas had taken up a cotton ball just to show them about it. They understood right away what it was. They had turned toward Great-grandmother Jeffers' house. She had a patch of cotton in her garden, and they must have seen her chopping it.

They loved pine, as Thomas did, although they couldn't whittle it. Thomas' papa said the boys probably never would be as good at whittling as he was. Thomas had a talent for wood sculpture, so his father said. There were always folks coming from distances offering Thomas money for what he had carved. But Thomas kept most of his carvings for himself. He had a whole box of figures tied up in the trailer attached to the car. He intended placing them on counters and mantles all over the new house.

Thomas could sit in front of his brothers, carving an image out of pine, and they would jump and roll all around him. When the carving was finished, the twin for whom it was made would grab it and crawl off with it. Thomas never need say, and never once were the twins wrong in knowing what carving was for which boy.

They were fine brothers, Thomas knew.

If the new house is haunted, he thought, the twins will tell me!

* * * * *

The sedan headed through the Pisgah National Forest in the Blue Ridge Mountains, and then out of North Carolina. Thomas had seen a sign and knew exactly when they entered Virginia.

"That's done with," he said to himself.

If Mr. Small noticed they had left their home state, he gave no hint. Mrs. Small slept or at least kept her eyes closed. The twins awoke, and Mr. Small told Thomas to give them their lunch. Soon the boys were subdued, staring out the windows and eating, looking far below at the bank upon bank of mist nestled in the deep valleys of the Blue Ridge.

Thomas was thinking about the new house in Ohio. The house was a relic with secret passages and rooms. In Civil War times it had been one of the houses on the Underground Railroad system, which was a resting and hiding place for slaves fleeing through the North to Canada. Such houses had been secretly called "stations."

When Thomas' father read about the station house for rent in Ohio, he had written to the foundation that owned it for a full report. For years he had hoped to explore and possibly live in a house on the Underground Railroad. Now was his chance. But not until he saw the report did he find out how important the Ohio station had been. Those who ran the house in Ohio had an even greater task than the care and concealment of running slaves. They actually encouraged the slaves to let themselves be caught and returned to slavery!

Thomas hadn't believed slaves went willingly back into slavery until his father had explained it to him.

"If you'll recall your history, Thomas, you'll remember that the incredible history of the Underground Railroad actually began in Canada," his father had told him. Slaves who had reached Canada in the very early 1800s and established settlements there returned by the thousands to this country in order to free others. They came back for their families; they became secret "conductors" on the Underground Railroad system. And they returned to bondage hoping to free masses of slaves.

"But slaves continued to flee by whatever means," Mr. Small had said, "with or without help. Upon reaching the Railroad, they might hide in our house in Ohio, where they would rest for as little as a week. Some of them were given rather large sums of money and returned again to slavery."

"What would slaves need with money?" Thomas had wanted to know.

"Even a fleeing slave needs maneuvering money," his father had said. "He would need food and shelter and the best and safest way for him to get it was to buy it from freed Negroes."

"But the slaves connected with the house in Ohio were going back *into* slavery," Thomas had said.

"Yes," said Mr. Small. "And after they were caught and went back, they passed the hidden money on to other slaves, who would attempt to escape."

Still Thomas couldn't believe slaves could successfully hide money on themselves without having it found.

Some slaves did have their money found and taken away, his father said. It was dangerous work they were involved in. But others managed to return to bondage with the money still in their possession.

"Remember," his father had told him, "the slaves we're talking about weren't ordinary folks out for a peaceful stroll. Many had run for their lives for weeks from the Deep South. They had no idea how far they had to travel and they were armed with little more than the knowledge that moss grew only on the northern side of trees. Any who managed to get as far as Ohio and the Underground Railroad line had to be pretty brave and strong, and very clever. Most of them were young, with a wonderful, fierce desire to free themselves as well as others. It was the best of these who volunteered to return to slavery. They were hand-picked by Dies Drear himself, the abolitionist who built our house in Ohio. He alone conceived of the daring plan of returning numbers of slaves to the South with sizable amounts of money hidden on them."

"He must have been something!" Thomas had said.

"He was a New Englander," Mr. Small said, "so independent and eccentric, most Ohio abolitionists thought him crazy. He came from an enormously wealthy family of shipbuilders, and yet his house in Ohio was fairly modest. To give you an idea how odd he was," said Mr. Small, "his house was overflowing with fine antiques, which he neither took any interest in nor sold for profit. All the furniture remained in great piles, with just enough space to get through from room to room, until the house was plundered and Drear was killed.

"But when his plan to send slaves back to slavery worked," said Mr. Small, "there grew among freemen and slaves an enormous respect for him. You know, they never called him by his name, partly because they feared he might be caught, but also because they were in awe of him. They called him Selah. Selah, which is no more than a musical direction to raise the voice. And yet, Selah he was. *Selah*, a desperate, running slave might sigh, and the name—the man—gave him the strength to go on."

Selah. Freedom.

THINK IT OVER

1. *Why is Thomas so excited about seeing his family's new home in Ohio?*
2. *Why does Mr. Small know so much about the Underground Railroad?*
3. *This story is told through the thoughts of Thomas Small. What are some of the things that you learn about Thomas through his narration?*
4. *Why did Dies Drear hand-pick certain slaves to go back into slavery?*

WRITE

Thomas is fascinated by people such as Elijah Anderson and Dies Drear. Choose a person from history, and write a short report about why that person interests you.

VIRGINIA HAMILTON

THE BELLS OF CHRISTMAS

ILLUSTRATED BY LAMBERT DAVIS

A Great Caravan On The National Road

from *The Bells of Christmas*
by Virginia Hamilton

illustrated by Lambert Davis

ALA Notable Book
Coretta Scott King Award

It is Christmastime in 1890. Jason Bell, his sister Lissy, and his brother Bob are waiting for their relatives, who are traveling down the National Road in Ohio.

The National Road, a part of American history, is the way west for the pioneers. It is also a part of the Bells' family history because it is the place where Papa lost his leg in an accident.

Lissy smiled and looked happy as she could be. Well, it was Christmas, and to me it felt like she was less of a bother as the day wore on.

We broke out of the trees, away from the patches of cattails, and stood a few feet off the Road.

"Ah, me!" I exclaimed.

"Ah, me!" said copy-cat Lissy.

"That makes the three of us—ah, me!" said Bob.

All was a sight to see on this Great Day. On the National Road!

And bells. Bells! No, not my relative Bells, not yet!

But bells, sets of three or five attached to the collars around horses' necks. Sometimes there was a whole string of bells tied to horses' harnesses. As the horses of a team moved, guided by the driver holding the reins, the bells sounded *jing-jing, jing-a-ling!* up and down the Road. And *ching, ching-aling.*

"Never in my life!" said I.

"Never in my life!" said Lissy.

Bob laughed. "Then feast your eyes!" said he. "This is the best part of a deep-snow day."

The snow kept on snowing, all over us and everything. Horses, teams of two and four, pulled sleighs! And the sleighs were full of laughing, talking, shouting Christmas folks. Whole families sometimes, if a sleigh was large enough. Whole families out for a sleigh ride before the favorite, Great Day supper.

The sky emptied its heart out. I knew I would hear the scudding sound of sleigh runners gliding through snow even in my dreams. And the muffley clip-clop of teams as snow deepened on the Road.

"Bob, will our sleigh work—can we sleigh ride?" I asked.

"Yes! Yes!" shouted Melissy. "Let's go before the snow stops!"

"This snow won't stop, Lissy, not for a good while," Bob said. "We'll sleigh ride when the relatives get here."

The snowfall and the sleigh bells must have heard him. For all at once there was a shout down the Road. We all turned as a four-horse team pulling a large, covered sleigh swung into view. The riders had spied me and Bob and Lissy before we spied them.

"Ho-ho!" shouted Bob.

"Ho-ho-ho-o-o!" came the return call.

"Bells!" I shouted. "It's Uncle Levi!"

"They're here!" shouted Lissy.

We jumped up and down for joy.

The horses came on, decorated with harness bells. They trotted briskly and snorted loudly at the driver's directions.

The covered sleigh top was homemade and fashioned to look like an old Conestoga wagon top.

Oh, it was a sight, that sleigh of merry Bells. "Tisha! Tisha!" we called out.

"You look like pioneers!" I hollered.

And they all waved and laughed and shouted, "Merry Christmas, Bells!"

"Same to you!" I called.

"Jason! Lissy! Bob! Jason! Jason! Merry Christmas!" called Tisha.

Then they were with us. Tisha was just the prettiest girl! She wore a hooded cloak of dark wool and a skirt with back drapery.

"You look all new!" I told her, gaping. "Haven't seen you in *so* long!"

"And you!" she said, eyes big and wide. "Jason, you look thirteen!"

Uncle Levi and Aunt Etta Bell gave hugs all around. The older brothers, Anthony and Chester, and cousin Sebella, took in Christmas packages.

The best gifts for the younger relatives had been exchanged. But there were some few gifts, such as Jason's from Tisha, and goods for the best meal, that had come with the Bells on this Great Day.

My present for Tisha was waiting for her under the tree.

"My pa has brought his grand surprise for Uncle James," whispered Tisha. "Remember, I said it was a secret, and I can't tell."

"Yes," I said. And I wondered all over again what it could be.

"You'll be surprised," she said.

Then brother Bob and Chester, my oldest Bell cousin, took Lissy, me, and Tisha for a sleigh ride. Just a short one. For the team was tired and needed tending to.

"Oh, now!" I said to Tisha. We were settled under the blanket, and we were a grand sight through the snow on our lane by the National Road. "How are you—shall we stop for Matthew?"

We did stop for him. We talked excitedly about everything as we neared his house. Tisha called from the sleigh: "Here, Matthew. I've come to get you!"

The door of Matthew's house flew open. Matthew sprang out so quickly he fairly slid halfway to us.

"Ah, gee! A fine sleigh this is, is it new?" he asked, climbing in next to Tisha. I was on her other side. Lissy sat in the front seat between Bob and Chester, listening to their eager talk.

"Poor Matthew! I suppose you've forgotten me as well as this sleigh. Now then, shall we ride, or shall we take you back before you forget where you came from?" she asked.

Matthew sat grinning from ear to ear. But his tongue was tied. Speechless.

"We ride! We glide!" I said. Matthew stole glances at Tisha. She looked just perfect, I thought. I was proud she was my relative and here for the Great Day.

"Aunt Lou Rhetta made this wonderful cloak," Tisha was telling Matthew, about Mama. "There's no other like it," said Tisha.

"It looks so nice on you, too," said Matthew, shyly.

I smothered a laugh so as not to disturb their talk.

"And this muff my ma found for me. I put it to my face when my nose gets cold," said Tisha. "I declare, I no longer can feel my feet!"

Matthew looked ready to wrap her feet in the blanket and run to the fire with them.

I grinned and looked away. I knew Bob and Chester smiled as Lissy chattered about the snow making her a white cloak with a hood, like Tisha's.

Soon we headed back, and in no time we were home. The house was a supper house, full of smells of good food—a mixture of sauces and meats and desserts. The spicy-sweet scent of pumpkin pie rode high above everything. My big brothers Ken and Samuel were here now with their families. The house was just full to bursting with relatives. Tisha and I circled the tree. I gave her the present I had picked out for her.

"Oh!" she exclaimed. "I did hope for a toilet set!" It had a brush, a comb, and a mirror. "It's so pretty, thank you, Jason."

She gave me a pocketknife of quality, and I praised it highly and showed Matthew.

"That's the finest I've seen," he said. Shyly, he handed Tisha his gift for her.

"I adore presents at Christmas," she said, and opened it. It was a bracelet with charms upon it. Quite pretty, too, and Tisha was delighted.

"Matthew, you weren't to spend a great lot of money, don't you know," she told him. But I could tell Tisha was pleased. Matthew had saved for months.

Then he went home for his supper. I thought he might refuse altogether to leave Tisha's side. "You can come back for pie," she said.

"I will," said Matthew.

Oh, but Christmas lasted long on its Great Day! I was filling up with it, and each sweet morsel of it was the best yet.

Mama received wonderful bead necklaces from Aunt Etta. She presented Aunt Etta with a silk umbrella. Aunt Etta loved it. She and Tisha and I went outside to open it. We three got under the umbrella.

Large flakes of snow came streaming down upon it as we stood there, shivering.

Papa gave his brother, Uncle Levi, a spokeshave, a cutting tool with a blade set between two handles. Uncle Levi was pleased.

We all waited eagerly to see what Uncle Levi would give to Papa. But they took Papa's present and went into the sitting room. They were gone a short while. And in that time, we children helped out. We moved tables, spread tablecloths, and arranged chairs for supper. Tisha and I placed the plates and silverware.

* * * * *

When Papa and Uncle Levi made their appearance, we were all back in the parlor. Mama had herded us there to sing carols. We had finished a sweet "Silent Night" when in came Papa, empty-handed. I couldn't see the present. It had been wrapped in a big box, too. Uncle Levi didn't have it either. What had happened to it?

Everybody stared at the two of them. Papa cut quite a figure in his Christmas suit. As he walked toward all of us and the tree, he held onto Uncle Levi's shoulder.

"Well, I declare," said Aunt Etta Bell. "Lou Rhetta, it sure is a wonder!" And she smiled brightly at Mama and all around. Mama looked Papa up and down and then, she, too, broke into a smile. "It's a wonder, indeed!" she said.

"And takes some getting use to, I'll wager," said cousin Chester Bell.

My brother Bob nodded agreement. "Papa will get used to it as quick as you please, if I know him," he said.

Well, I wondered! I gazed at my papa and he looked just like my papa, which he was. It was Christmas, with everybody and Tisha and oh, so many new things and goings on. That was the wonder, that I could see anything atall.

"What in the world is everybody talking about?" I asked.

"Yes, what are you all talking . . ." Lissy began.

I cut her off. "Hush up!" I said. I did not like being left out of things.

Papa smiled at me and said, "Calm down, son." He took his hand from Uncle Levi's shoulder.

"Now," said Papa, "come see what your Uncle Levi made me."

There was silence as I came up close to Papa. Lissy was right behind me with her walking doll. Everybody else crowded around. To my surprise, Papa raised his pant leg.

"Just look," said Papa. "Two true feet!"

I bent near with my hands on my knees. Well, it was a shock! Sure enough, where once there had been only the tip of a peg leg, there was now a shoe. And I hadn't noticed atall. And in Papa's stocking in the shoe was a foot. It matched the foot he'd always had. Attached to the foot was an ankle and then a leg. Not a peg leg atall. It was a wonder, all right.

"Knock on it, Jason," said Papa. And I did. I knocked on the leg, and it was wood. Very gently, I touched it with my fingers, and it was smooth oak, turned and made perfect by a master carver. It looked true, like the one that was real.

I shook my head, it was so hard to believe. "Is it a mechanical thing?" I asked Uncle Levi, for I knew he had made it.

"In some ways it is," said he. "There are wonders going on in mechanics."

"The foot moves up and down, like any foot," said Papa, "and it walks comfortable. For now, I will wear Levi's fine 'mechanical thing' on special occasions, such as this Great Day."

We all applauded wildly.

"You should both take a bow," said brother Bob. And they did. Uncle Levi and Papa bowed, holding onto each other for support. Each swept his free arm back in a grand gesture. They gave us a swell stage bow.

"It's a great wonder," I said, "to have a mechanical leg and foot. Papa, you look just like everybody!"

The grown-ups laughed at that. I was not too embarrassed. Tisha knew what I meant. So did Papa. It was a good son that wanted his papa to be just like folks. Oh, I liked him fine in his wheel-a-chair or on his peg leg. He was only different to me because he was such a fine carpenter and woodworker. But his two true feet did look the marvel. And then I just swelled up with pride at my papa and Uncle Levi.

"I'm glad of you both!" I couldn't help saying. "What true brothers you are!" And then Papa put his arm around me. And it was me and Uncle Levi who helped him to the dining room, and then into his wheel-a-chair, off his new leg for a while.

Well, it was a wonderful Christmas, 1890. A Great Day. The meal made our long supper table groan. Everybody talked and ate turkey and rabbit, sweet potatoes and turnips from our own root cellar, and hot bread and rolls and apple butter.

And, oh, that pumpkin pie! I could've cried, it tasted so good. Tisha said she could've died over it.

Well, that made Matthew laugh. He was back with us for the dessert. I gave him a spin top for Christmas, and he gave me the same! He gave Lissy a fine ball. And, besides the boa I gave her for dress-up, I gave her paper dolls with sets of paper clothes for play, which she loved. And Matthew got what he wanted from Uncle Levi, too. Matthew looked amazed when Tisha gave him what he would call ever after his *grand* muffler. It was long and striped, and Tisha knitted it herself. It looked comical draped around Matthew's thin neck. The fringed ends fell almost to his knees.

"It looks just right on you, Matthew," Tisha said, eyes shining.

"It does!" I agreed, chuckling out loud.

"What's so funny?" said little Lissy to a giggling Matthew. "What are all those stripes?"

And then we three—Matthew, Tisha, and me—*did* just about die laughing.

There was quiet talk, over coffee and chocolates made by Tisha and Aunt Etta. Everybody stayed close, leaning elbows on the table now as the table was cleared.

"Another Christmas," said Mama, happily.

"Another Christmas," said Uncle Levi, "and all of us, together."

"Still prosperous," said Aunt Etta, her face like sunshine.

"A hundred years of us Bells," said Papa, "who've lived long by the National Road. And this house," he added. "This house that Grandpa built."

"My great-grandpa Joshua Levi Bell," I said.

Uncle Levi nodded. "Grandpa was a drover along the Road out there. He and his helpers drove turkeys and sheep to market for landholders," Uncle Levi said. "East they went, a few miles each day. At nighttime, Grandpa rented pasture pens along the Road to keep the stock safe. He had some few of his own stock in there, too. Oh, it was quite a time, with thousands of head of animals in pens overnight, to be driven out on the Road by morning. And all kinds of easy transport—wagons, fast coaches, sleighs, sulkies all mixed in with the animals. And troops of immigrants, walking, driving cows and hogs . . ."

"And, did you know, Sherman and his army came eastward and passed along the Road after the Civil War?" Papa asked.

"No!" said Matthew and Tisha and I.

"No!" said Lissy.

"Good times and bad times," added Uncle Levi. "And all times of this family."

There was silence then at the table. Mama's cider was warmed and poured into glasses with cinnamon sticks, and we children loved the steam from it up our noses, and the taste.

It wasn't ten minutes later that Mama said, "Goodness! Look at the time! The church!"

We scrambled then. All of us, rushing to fix ourselves up, then jumping into coats and hats, mufflers. For the entertainment at church on Christmas night was the height of it all.

"It's still snowing!" I yelled, surprised as I could be.

"It's never going to stop," said Tisha.

"Then you'll stay here forever!" whispered Matthew, just for her, but I overheard.

Outside, our sleigh was ready, pulled up behind Uncle Levi's Conestoga.

My older brothers had brought their own sleighs for their families.

"We're going to be a parade of Bells!" I hollered, and all the Bell fellows called, "Yes! Yes, indeed!"

"And Matthew!" cried Tisha.

And we all shouted, "Matthew, too! Matthew, too!"

The next thing and we paraded our sleighs down the lane, with all of our Christmas bells *ching-ching-chinging* in time with the horses' trotting.

Other sleighs, more and more of them, formed a great caravan on the National Road.

THINK IT OVER

1. *What are some of the things that make the Christmas of 1890 so memorable for Jason?*
2. *What is Uncle Levi's Christmas present to Papa?*
3. *This selection comes from the book* The Bells of Christmas. *Why might Virginia Hamilton have chosen that as the title?*

WRITE

Think of a past holiday that is as memorable to you as this holiday is to Jason. Write a narrative paragraph telling about this holiday.

THEME WRAP-UP

INTERPRETING THE PAST

What do the stories "A New Home in Ohio" and "A Great Caravan on the National Road" have in common? How do these stories reflect the interests and beliefs of Virginia Hamilton?

How are these stories different from nonfiction articles about American history? Why do you think some writers choose to present information as historical fiction?

WRITER'S WORKSHOP Think about the way history seems to "stick" to the house and the road described in the selections. Picture a place, such as the Drear house or the National Road, that might call up memories of the past. As you imagine the place, make notes on what you see in your mind. Then use your notes to write one or more descriptive paragraphs. You might make a drawing to go with your description. Then share your work with your classmates.

CONNECTIONS

MULTICULTURAL CONNECTION

March Fong Eu,
California Secretary of State

KEEPING OUR YESTERYEARS ALIVE

What picture comes to your mind when you hear the word *pioneers*? You should have a vision of men, women, and children of every age and race.

Years ago one San Francisco teacher decided that not enough people were aware of the contributions of Chinese pioneers. Ruthanne Lum McCunn also felt that she could understand how the pioneers felt living in a new country because she had spent her own childhood in Hong Kong.

To share the fascinating stories of Chinese Americans, McCunn wrote a book for young readers called *An Illustrated History of the Chinese in America.* Since that book was published, she has become a full-time writer and historian. Besides a folktale called *Pie Biter,* she has written three more books about America's Chinese heritage.

■ *Use research books and other materials to make a classroom display that highlights the contributions of Chinese pioneers and their descendants.*

Judge Thomas Tang,
State Bar of Arizona

SOCIAL STUDIES/ART CONNECTION

OUR PAST IS MANY PEOPLE

From what parts of the world did the people who settled in your community come? How did they contribute to the history of your region? Find the answers to these questions, and then work with classmates to create a mural that reflects your community heritage.

Making a drawing like the one below can help you as you collect information.

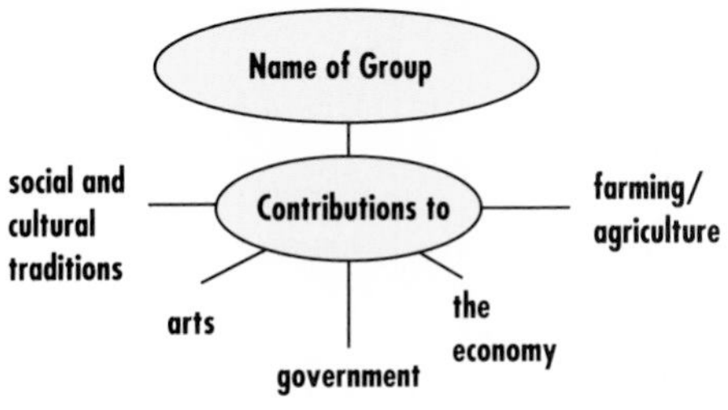

MUSIC CONNECTION

SONGS THAT SAVE THE PAST

In addition to books, songs keep our history and heritage alive. With a group, find two songs about political or social events that took place between 1750 and 1950. If the songs are in another language, you should provide a translation. Before singing the songs, tell your classmates why these songs were popular.

O once upon a time in Arkansas,
An old man sat in his little cabin door,
And fiddled a tune that he lik'd to hear,
A jolly old tune that he'd play by ear.

an American folk song

Entertainers seem to speak in a universal language, a language to which people all over the world can respond. How might a television newscaster such as Ed Bradley go about sharing world events with an audience of millions? Do you ever wonder how writers such as Gary Soto and Kazue Mizumura consistently dream up images and adventures that entertain readers? Think about what entertains and enlightens you as you read the selections in this unit.

THEMES

BOOKSHELF

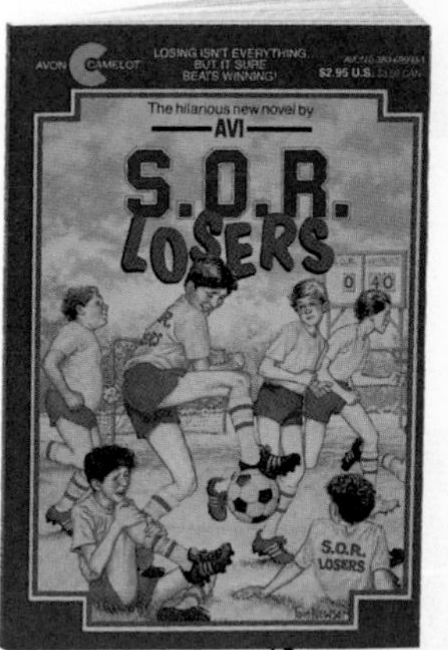

S.O.R. LOSERS

BY AVI

South Orange Regional (S.O.R.) is a middle school with a long tradition of winning at sports. That tradition could end, however, now that Ed and his friends have been drafted for a misfit soccer team. PARENTS' CHOICE

HBJ LIBRARY BOOK

FERRET IN THE BEDROOM, LIZARDS IN THE FRIDGE

BY BILL WALLACE

All Liz wants to do is lead a normal life. But Liz's dad works with some strange and unusual animals, and he keeps bringing his work home. CHILDREN'S CHOICE

NO ONE IS GOING TO NASHVILLE

BY MAVIS JUKES

Sonia, a future veterinarian, already has an alligator lizard and a goose as pets. What harm could a small stray dog cause? SCHOOL LIBRARY JOURNAL BEST BOOK AWARD

RAMONA: BEHIND THE SCENES OF A TELEVISION SHOW

BY ELAINE SCOTT

Have you ever wondered what goes on behind the scenes of a television series? Follow the writers, cast, and crew of the television series *Ramona,* from the first auditions to the final filming.
ALA NOTABLE BOOK

LENTIL

BY ROBERT McCLOSKEY

Lentil can't sing. He can't even whistle. How will he manage to save the day with his musical skill?

GOING BUGGY

How do you feel about bugs? They share the planet with us, yet we usually try to avoid them. The following selections are based upon some of the relationships that have developed between people and insects.

CONTENTS

JOYFUL
NOISE
Poems for Two Voices
PAUL FLEISCHMAN
illustrated by Eric Beddows

·F·I·R·E·F·L·I·E·S·

from Joyful Noise: Poems for Two Voices

by Paul Fleischman

illustrated by Eric Beddows

Light	Light
	is the ink we use
Night	Night
is our parchment	
	We're
	fireflies
fireflies	flickering
flitting	
	flashing
fireflies	
glimmering	fireflies
	gleaming
glowing	
Insect calligraphers	Insect calligraphers
practicing penmanship	
	copying sentences
Six-legged scribblers	Six-legged scribblers
of vanishing messages,	
	fleeting graffiti
Fine artists in flight	Fine artists in flight
adding dabs of light	
	bright brush strokes
Signing the June nights	Signing the June nights
as if they were paintings	as if they were paintings
	We're
flickering	fireflies
fireflies	flickering
fireflies.	fireflies.

LIKE JAKE AND ME

by Mavis Jukes · pictures by Lloyd Bloom

Jukes · Bloom LIKE JAKE AND ME Knopf

NEWBERY HONOR
ALA NOTABLE BOOK
CHILDREN'S CHOICE

THE RAIN HAD STOPPED. The sun was setting. There were clouds in the sky the color of smoke. Alex was watching his stepfather, Jake, split wood at the edge of the cypress grove. Somewhere a toad was grunting.

"Jake!" called Alex.

Jake swung the axe, and wood flew into the air.

"Jake!" Alex called again. "Need me?" Alex had a loose tooth in front. He moved it in and out with his tongue.

Jake rested the axe head in the grass and leaned on the handle. "What?" he said. He took off his Stetson hat and wiped his forehead on his jacket sleeve.

Alex cupped his hands around his mouth. "Do . . . you . . . need . . . me . . . to . . . help?" he hollered. Then he tripped over a pumpkin, fell on it, and broke it. A toad flopped away.

Jake adjusted the raven feather behind his hatband. "Better stay there!" he called. He put his hat back on. With powerful arms, he sunk the axe blade into a log. It fell in half.

"Wow," thought Alex. "I'll never be able to do that."

Alex's mother was standing close by, under the pear tree. She was wearing fuzzy woolen leg warmers, a huge knitted coat with pictures of reindeer on the back, and a red scarf with the name *Virginia* on it. "I need you," she said.

Alex stood up, dumped the pumpkin over the fence for the sheep, and went to Virginia.

"I dropped two quarters and a dime in the grass. If I bend down, I may never be able to get up again," she said. Virginia was enormous. She was pregnant with twins, and her belly blocked her view to the ground. "I can't even see where they fell."

"Here!" said Alex. He gave her two quarters. Then he found the dime. He tied her shoe while he was down there.

"Thanks," said Virginia. "I also need you for some advice." She pointed up. "Think it's ready?"

One of the branches of the pear tree had a glass bottle over the end of it. Inside were some twigs and leaves *and* two pears. In the spring, Virginia had pushed the bottle onto the branch, over the blossoms. During the summer, the pears had grown and sweetened inside the bottle. Now they were fat and crowding each other.

The plan was that when the pears were ripe, Virginia would pull the bottle from the tree, leaving the fruit inside. Then she'd fill the bottle with pear nectar and trick her sister, Caroline. Caroline would never guess how Virginia got the pears into the bottle!

"Shall we pick it?" asked Virginia.

"Up to you!" said Alex.

Months ago, Virginia had told him that the pears, and the babies, would be ready in the fall. Alex looked away at the hills. They were dusky gray. There were smudges of yellow poplars on the land. Autumn was here.

Alex fiddled with his tooth. "Mom," he asked, "do you think the twins are brothers or sisters?"

"Maybe both," said Virginia.

"If there's a boy, do you think he'll be like Jake or like me?"

"Maybe like Jake *and* you," said Virginia.

"Like Jake *and* me?" Alex wondered how that could be possible.

"Right," said Virginia.

"Well, anyway," said Alex, "would you like to see something I can do?"

"Of course," she said.

Alex straightened. Gracefully he lifted his arms and rose up on his toes. He looked like a bird about to take off. Then he lowered his arms and crouched. Suddenly he sprang up. He spun once around in midair and landed lightly.

Virginia clapped. "Great!"

Alex did it again, faster. Then again, and again. He whirled and danced around the tree for Virginia. He spun until he was pooped. Jake had put down the axe and was watching.

"Ballet class!" gasped Alex. "Dad signed me up for lessons, remember?"

"Of course I remember," said Virginia. "Go show Jake!"

"No," panted Alex. "Jake isn't the ballet type."

"He might like it," said Virginia. "Go see!"

"Maybe another time," said Alex. He raced across the field to where Jake was loading his arms with logs. "Jake, I'll carry the axe."

"Carry the axe?" Jake shook his head. "I just sharpened that axe."

Alex moved his tooth with his tongue and squinted up at Jake. "I'm careful," he said.

Jake looked over at the sheep nosing the pumpkin. "Maybe another time," he told Alex.

Alex walked beside him as they headed toward the house. The air was so cold Jake was breathing steam. The logs were stacked to his chin.

Virginia stood under the pear tree, watching the sunset. Alex ran past her to open the door.

Jake thundered up the stairs and onto the porch. His boots were covered with moss and dirt. Alex stood in the doorway.

"Watch it!" said Jake. He shoved the door open farther with his shoulder, and Alex backed up against the wall. Jake moved sideways through the door.

"Here, I'll help you stack the wood!" said Alex.

"Watch it!" Jake came down on one knee and set the wood by the side of the woodstove. Then he said kindly, "You've really got to watch it, Alex. I can't see where I'm going with so big a load."

Alex wiggled his tooth with his tongue. "I just wanted to help you," he said. He went to Jake and put his hand on Jake's shoulder. Then he leaned around and looked under his Stetson hat. There was bark in Jake's beard. "You look like a cowboy in the movies."

"I have news for you," said Jake. "I *am* a cowboy. A real one." He unsnapped his jacket. On his belt buckle was a silver longhorn steer. "Or was one." He looked over at Alex.

Alex shoved his tooth forward with his tongue.

"Why don't you just pull out that tooth?" Jake asked him.

"Too chicken," said Alex. He closed his mouth.

"Well, everybody's chicken of something," said Jake. He opened his jacket pocket and took out a wooden match. He chewed on the end of it and looked out the windows behind the stove. He could see Virginia, still standing beneath the tree. Her hands were folded under her belly.

Jake balled up newspaper and broke some sticks. He had giant hands. He filled the woodstove with the wadded paper and the sticks and pushed in a couple of logs.

"Can I light the fire?" Alex asked.

"Maybe another time," said Jake. He struck the match on his rodeo belt buckle. He lit the paper and threw the match into the fire.

Just then Alex noticed that there was a wolf spider on the back of Jake's neck. There were fuzzy babies holding on to her body. "Did you know wolf spiders carry their babies around?" said Alex.

"Says who?" asked Jake.

"My dad," said Alex. He moved his tooth out as far as it would go. "He's an entomologist, remember?"

"I remember," said Jake.

"Dad says they only bite you if you bother them, or if you're squashing them," said Alex. "But still, I never mess with wolf spiders." He pulled his tooth back in with his tongue.

"Is that what he says, huh," said Jake. He jammed another log into the stove, then looked out again at Virginia. She was gazing at the landscape. The hills were fading. The farms were fading. The cypress trees were turning black.

"I think she's pretty," said Alex, looking at the spider.

"I do, too," said Jake, looking at Virginia.

"It's a nice design on her back," said Alex, examining the spider.

"Yep!" said Jake. He admired the reindeer coat, which he'd loaned to Virginia.

"Her belly sure is big!" said Alex.

"It has to be big, to carry the babies," said Jake.

"She's got an awful lot of babies there," said Alex.

Jake laughed. Virginia was shaped something like a pear.

"And boy! Are her legs woolly!" said Alex.

Jake looked at Virginia's leg warmers. "Itchy," said Jake. He rubbed his neck. The spider crawled over his collar.

"She's in your coat!" said Alex. He backed away a step.

"We can share it," said Jake. He liked to see Virginia bundled up. "It's big enough for both of us. She's got to stay warm." Jake stood up.

"You sure are brave," said Alex. "I like wolf spiders, but I wouldn't have let that one into my coat. That's the biggest, hairiest wolf spider I've ever seen."

Jake froze. "Wolf spider! Where?"

"In your coat getting warm," said Alex.

Jake stared at Alex. "What wolf spider?"

"The one we were talking about, with the babies!" said Alex. "And the furry legs."

"Wolf spider!" Jake moaned. "I thought we were talking about Virginia!" He was holding his shoulders up around his ears.

"You never told me you were scared of spiders," said Alex.

"You never asked me," said Jake in a high voice. "Help!"

"How?" asked Alex.

"Get my jacket off!"

Alex took hold of Jake's jacket sleeve as Jake eased his arm out. Cautiously, Alex took the jacket from Jake's shoulders. Alex looked in the coat.

"No spider, Jake," said Alex. "I think she went into your shirt."

"My shirt?" asked Jake. "You think?"

"Maybe," said Alex.

Jake gasped. "Inside? I hope not!"

"Feel anything *furry* crawling on you?" asked Alex.

"Anything *furry* crawling on me?" Jake shuddered. "No!"

"Try to get your shirt off without squashing her," said Alex. "Remember, we don't want to hurt her. She's a mama."

"With babies," added Jake. *"Eek!"*

"And," said Alex, "she'll bite!"

"Bite? Yes, I know!" said Jake. "Come out on the porch and help me! I don't want her to get loose in the house!"

Jake walked stiffly to the door. Alex opened it. They walked out onto the porch. The sky was thick gray and salmon colored, with blue windows through the clouds.

"Feel anything?" asked Alex.

"Something . . ." said Jake. He unsnapped the snaps on his sleeves, then the ones down the front. He opened his shirt. On his chest was a tattoo of an eagle that was either taking off or landing. He let the shirt drop to the floor.

"No spider, back or front," reported Alex.

They shook out the shirt.

"Maybe your jeans," said Alex. "Maybe she got into your jeans!"

"Not my *jeans!*" said Jake. He quickly undid his rodeo belt.

"Your boots!" said Alex. "First you have to take off your boots!"

"Right!" said Jake. He sat down on the boards. Each boot had a yellow rose and the name *Jake* stitched on the side. "Could you help?" he asked.

"Okay," said Alex. He grappled with one boot and got it off. He checked it. He pulled off and checked the sock. No spider. He tugged on the other boot.

"You've got to pull harder," said Jake, as Alex pulled and struggled. "Harder!"

The boot came off and smacked Alex in the mouth. "Ouch!" Alex put his tongue in the gap. "Knocked my tooth out!" He looked in the boot. "It's in the boot!"

"Yikes!" said Jake.

"Not the spider," said Alex. "My tooth." He rolled it out of the boot and into his hand to examine it.

"Dang," said Jake. "Then hurry up." Alex dropped the tooth back into the boot. Jake climbed out of his jeans and looked down each leg. He hopped on one foot to get the other sock off.

"She won't be in your sock," said Alex. "But maybe—"

"Don't tell me," said Jake. "Not my shorts!"

Alex stared at Jake's shorts. There were pictures of mallard ducks on them. "Your shorts," said Alex.

"I'm afraid to look," said Jake. He thought he felt something creeping just below his belly button.

"Someone's coming!" said Alex. "Quick! Give me your hat! I'll hold it up and you can stand behind it."

"Help!" said Jake in a small voice. He gave Alex the hat and quickly stepped out of his shorts. He brushed himself off in the front.

"Okay in the back," said Alex, peering over the brim of the hat.

Jake turned his shorts inside out, then right side in again. No spider. When he bent over to put them on, he backed into his hat, and the raven feather poked him. Jake howled and jumped up and spun around in midair.

"I didn't know you could do ballet!" said Alex. "You dance like me!"

"I thought I felt the spider!" said Jake. He put on his shorts.

"What on *earth* are you doing?" huffed Virginia. She was standing at the top of the stairs, holding the bottle with the pears inside.

"We're hunting for a spider," said Jake.

"Well!" said Virginia. "I like your hunting outfit. But aren't those *duck*-hunting shorts, and aren't you cold?"

“We’re not hunting spiders,” explained Jake. “We’re hunting *for* a spider.”

“A big and hairy one that *bites!*” added Alex.

“A wolf spider!” said Jake, shivering. He had goose bumps.

“Really!” said Virginia. She set the bottle down beside Jake’s boot. “Aha!” she cried, spying Alex’s tooth inside. “Here’s one of the spider’s teeth!”

Alex grinned at his mother. He put his tongue where his tooth wasn’t.

Jake took his hat from Alex and put it on.

“Hey!” said Virginia.

“What?” said Jake.

“The spider!” she said. “It’s on your hat!”

“Help!” said Jake. “Somebody help me!”

Alex sprang up into the air and snatched the hat from Jake’s head.

“Look!” said Alex.

“Holy smoke!” said Jake.

There, hiding behind the black feather, was the spider.

Alex tapped the hat brim. The spider dropped to the floor. Then off she swaggered with her fuzzy babies, across the porch and into a crack.

Jake went over to Alex. He knelt down. “Thanks, Alex,” said Jake. It was the closest Alex had ever been to the eagle. Jake pressed Alex against its wings. “May I have this dance?” Jake asked.

Ravens were lifting from the blackening fields and calling. The last light had settled in the clouds like pink dust.

Jake stood up holding Alex, and together they looked at Virginia. She was rubbing her belly. “Something is happening here,” she told them. “It feels like the twins are beginning to dance.”

“Like Jake and me,” said Alex. And Jake whirled around the porch with Alex in his arms.

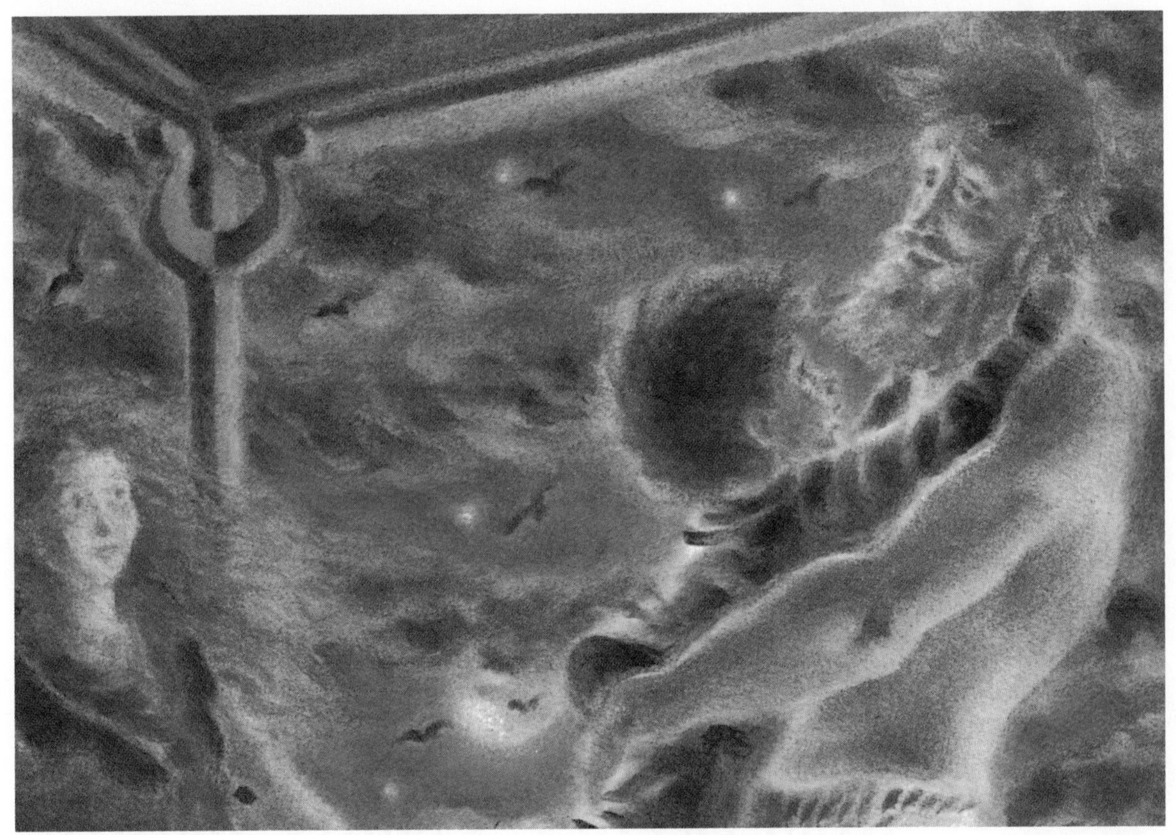

Think It Over

1. *How does Jake change from the beginning to the end of the story?*
2. *While Alex is talking about the wolf spider, Jake is talking about something else entirely. What is it?*
3. *Why doesn't Alex want to show Jake what he learned at his ballet class?*

Write

Alex is fascinated by the look of the wolf spider. Write a paragraph describing an insect that looks interesting to you.

WHO WON THE CONTEST

from *Beetles, Lightly Toasted*

by Phyllis Reynolds Naylor

After weeks of preparing and testing his bug recipes, Andy entered the Roger B. Sudermann Contest. Andy felt confident that his essay about using beetles, bugs, and worms as food was good enough to win first prize.

illustrated by Katy Farmer

ON JUNE 4, TWO DAYS BEFORE SCHOOL WAS OUT, Mrs. Haynes' class sat waiting as Luther Sudermann's car pulled up outside the window. As they watched him shake hands with the principal, the teacher said, "No matter who wins the contest, I want you to know that I read all the essays myself before I sent them to Mr. Sudermann, and I think that every one of them was good. *All* of you who entered the contest deserve to feel proud of what you've done."

There were footsteps in the hall, then the principal came in, followed by a gray-haired man in a blue suit. His eyes seemed to take in the whole room at once, and he smiled as the principal introduced him. Then he sat down on the edge of Mrs. Haynes' desk and looked the students over.

"I was disappointed," he said, "that only nine of you decided to enter my contest this year, but I'm delighted with those who did. It just goes to show that imagination is alive and well in these United States, and if the future of our country depends on people like you, then we're in good hands."

The principal beamed.

Mr. Sudermann went on to talk about his son Roger when he was alive, and how Roger was always building something or taking it apart.

"If something broke around the house, Roger would say, 'Maybe I can fix it, Dad,' and when he saw something new, he'd say, 'Show me how it works.' He was intellectually curious—always tried to improve things, make them a little better." Mr. Sudermann bowed his head for a moment and stared at the floor. "Needless to say, I miss him," he told the class, "but through this contest, I can keep the idea of him alive—I can keep his imagination going, and reward others who show the same inventiveness as Roger."

Andy had never known anything about Roger Sudermann before, and could almost see the boy that Mr. Sudermann was talking about. He was wondering, too, if *he* ever died young, what his dad would say about *him*. That Andy was imaginative? Helpful? Open to new ideas?

"To the nine of you who entered my contest," Mr. Sudermann went on, "I want you to know that I have read your essays carefully—some of them several times. I narrowed my choice down to five, then four, then three, and I had a very hard time narrowing it down to two. But once I had eliminated all but two, I simply could go no further, and so—for the first time in the history of the Roger B. Sudermann Contest—I am declaring two winners this year, and each will receive a check for fifty dollars. The two winning essays were: 'Saving Energy When You Cook,' by Jack Barth, and 'How Beetles, Bugs, and Worms Can Save Money and the Food Supply Both,' by Andy Moller. Would you two boys come up here, please?"

The class began to clap as Andy, swallowing, stood up and moved numbly to the front of the classroom beside Jack. The teacher and principal were clapping too.

Mr. Sudermann shook both boys' hands. "I saw a little of my son in what each of you boys wrote," he said, "and I know that if Roger were alive, he'd want to be your friend. You have both shown the spirit of initiative and creativity that Mrs. Sudermann and I so admire, and on June 10, I am going to feel very honored to shake your hands again on the steps of the library."

"Thank you," said Jack.

"Thank you," said Andy, barely audible.

The principal walked Mr. Sudermann back out to his car again, and Mrs. Haynes beamed at Jack and Andy.

"Read their essays out loud!" someone said.

"Yes!" said the others.

"Isn't it lucky that I made copies?" Mrs. Haynes smiled, and took them out of her drawer. Andy stared down at his feet.

Mrs. Haynes read Jack's essay first. Everybody laughed when she read the part about the hamburgers almost catching fire under the hood of the car. The class clapped when the essay was over, and Mrs. Haynes said she was looking forward to cooking fish in her dishwasher. Then she picked up Andy's essay.

When it was clear that Andy was talking about *eating* beetles, bugs, and worms, there were gasps.

"Oh, gross!" someone giggled.

"Eeeyuuk!" said somebody else.

Andy saw Sam look over at him nervously and smile. He tried to smile back but his face felt frozen. When Mrs. Haynes read about using little bits of beetles, lightly toasted, in brownies, the room suddenly got very quiet. And when at last she finished reading, nobody clapped. Sam started to, then stopped. Mrs. Haynes looked around, puzzled.

"Wasn't that a good essay, class?" she said. "I suppose it might take some getting used to, but there is really no reason why we can't use insects as a source of protein."

Dora Kray raised her hand. "What if somebody gives you a brownie with beetles in it and doesn't tell you?"

The teacher thought about it. "Well, I think everyone has the right, certainly, to know what he's eating, but . . ." She looked around, puzzled. "Andy wouldn't do . . ." She stopped.

The room was embarrassingly quiet, and Mrs. Haynes didn't quite know what to do. Finally she asked everyone to take out his arithmetic book, and she started the morning's lesson.

"Listen, they had to find out sooner or later," Sam said to Andy at recess when the others walked by without talking to him. "Heck, they'll get over it. They'll forget."

"Go on and play kickball with them," Andy said. "I don't want them mad at you, too."

It was one of the most horrible days Andy had ever spent. Whenever the other students walked by his desk, they either looked the other way or glared at him. Jack, strangely, spoke to him on the bus going home, but no one else did. Andy didn't know just how he was going to tell his family. He was relieved, when he reached the house, that Mother had forgotten what day it was, and she and Aunt Wanda were busily putting up pints of strawberry jam.

In a matter of minutes, however, the phone rang and it was Aunt Bernie, telling Mother that both Jack and Andy had won the contest together, and Mother said she would call her back later, that the preserves were boiling.

"For heaven's sake, Andy, you didn't even tell us," Mother said, turning back to the stove. "How wonderful!"

Andy faked a smile.

"You're going to have to tell us all about it at supper," she went on. "Won't your dad be pleased, though?"

"What did you write about?" Aunt Wanda asked, pouring a pitcherful of sugar into the pot of boiling berries.

"Oh, saving money on groceries," Andy said.

"Well, I'll be glad to hear how to do that!" Mother told him.

Andy went out in the barn and began shoveling out the stalls. The whole fifth-grade class was mad at him, and he couldn't much blame them. In another hour or so, the entire family would be angry, too. He didn't see how saying that he was sorry would help. What was done was done, and no one would ever forget it.

At supper that evening, Dad had no sooner asked the blessing than Mother said, "Andy has some good news tonight. Tell them, Andy."

Andy swallowed. His cheeks felt as though they would crack if he tried to make them smile once more. "I was one of the winners of the Roger B. Sudermann Contest," he said. "There were two winners this year, and Jack was the other one."

"Isn't that marvelous?" said Mother. "Did Mr. Sudermann come to school and announce the winners himself?"

Andy told them about the little speech Mr. Sudermann had given the class, glad to turn the attention away from himself. He said how Luther Sudermann had told them that Roger was always inventing things, trying to find out how something worked.

"He *was* the boy who came to school as a TV set!" Lois said suddenly. "I remember now! He was wearing this box with knobs, and his face was where the screen would be. When you turned one knob, he gave you a dog food commercial, and when you turned the other one, he shut up."

"Well!" said Andy's father. "We'll have to read that essay you wrote. What was it about?"

"Saving money on groceries," said Aunt Wanda. "I'd certainly like to know how Andy knows anything about that."

"What did you call your essay?" Wendell asked, reaching for another slice of beef.

Andy took a deep breath and put down his fork. "'How Beetles, Bugs, and Worms Can Save Money and the Food Supply Both,'" he said.

The family stared at him.

"How can they do *that?*" asked Mother.

Andy's face felt flushed. His tongue seemed to be swelling. "You eat them," he said.

"*Eat* them?" cried Lois.

Andy continued staring down at his hands. "I wrote to a man at the University and he told me how to fix them."

"*Safely?*" said Mother.

Andy nodded.

"Did you *try* it?" she asked.

"I cooked them," Andy said, not quite answering.

Suddenly no one was eating.

"What . . . did . . . you . . . cook?" came Aunt Wanda's voice, slow and steady.

Andy closed his eyes. "Brownies . . .," he said.

He heard Wendell cough.

"Deep-fried worms . . ."

The family seemed to have stopped breathing.

"And . . . grubs in egg salad."

"Egg salad!" Lois leaped up, tipping over her chair. "Not *my* egg salad!"

Andy didn't answer.

A long, piercing shriek filled the kitchen, rattling the walls. "Arrrrgggggh!" Lois lunged for the sink, stuck her mouth under the faucet and turned the water on full force. "Yauuugghh!" she screamed again, gargling and screeching, both at the same time.

"Andy," said Aunt Wanda, and her voice was like lead weights. "Did you touch my Okra Surprise?"

Andy couldn't answer that either, and continued staring down at his lap. And at that very moment, the phone rang.

Andy got up from the table and answered the phone because he needed an excuse to leave. If he could have sailed out the window and over the treetops, he would have done so gladly. A ringing telephone was the next best thing. It saved him from simply getting up from the table and going upstairs to his room, which was what he was about to do anyway.

"Could I speak to Andy Moller, please?" said a man's voice at the other end.

"I'm Andy."

"Good! This is Frank Harris, a photographer from the *Bucksville Gazette*. Mr. Sudermann told me about you winning the essay contest—you and another boy—and we'd like to get a photo of the winners."

It was what Andy had been waiting for for two years—the reason he had entered the contest. Now, the last thing in the world he wanted was his picture in the *Bucksville Gazette,* but there was no way he could get out of it.

"You're the one who wrote about beetles and bugs, aren't you?" the photographer asked.

"Yes . . ."

"Well, what Mr. Sudermann has in mind, see, is a photo of you right there on the steps of the library eating one of those meals you wrote about."

Think It Over

1. *What is Andy's problem in the story?*
2. *Why does Mr. Sudermann sponsor a contest every year?*
3. *Why doesn't anyone in the classroom applaud after Mrs. Haynes reads Andy's essay?*
4. *What different reactions do people have when they hear about Andy's bug recipes?*
5. *How would you react if you were in Andy's class and realized you had eaten one of his brownies?*

Write

Put yourself in Andy's place. Write a dialogue between Andy and Mr. Sudermann. Decide whether Andy will accept or back down from the challenge of eating one of his insect dishes on the steps of the library.

A Matter of Taste

by Margery Nichelason
illustrated by Normand Cousineau

Does your stomach grumble at the thought of the same old burger and fries for lunch? Then it's time to tempt your taste buds with something different.

Perhaps a piping-hot serving of "hopster Newburg" would please your palate. But if cooked grasshoppers sound too filling, how about a sliver of poached cockroach? Sound yummy? Probably not. But *entomophagy,* or insect eating, has been popular for a long, long time.

Thousands of years ago our prehistoric ancestors thrived on insects. In fact, they dined on so many of them that some species almost became extinct.

In ancient Greece and Rome, grasshoppers and other insect dishes were a delicacy. Wealthy Romans found beetles so tasty that they fattened the insects with meal before eating them!

Pioneer farmers, on the other hand, consumed insects out of necessity. From time to time hordes of grasshoppers ravaged the farmlands, leaving Great Plains settlers without crops for food. The pests that destroyed dinner then became dinner.

Some American Indian tribes pulverized insects into powder and added this protein-rich substance to other foods during the winter. In the summertime, tribes went grasshopper hunting. Men, women, and children stood in an enormous ring out on the grasslands. Gradually everyone moved toward the center, making the circle smaller. As they walked, they beat the grasses with long sticks, which caused the grasshoppers to hop toward the middle in a huge pile. The Indians set the pile ablaze and devoured the roasted grasshoppers by the handful.

Entomophagy isn't in style in the United States today. But many people throughout the world eat insects with great enjoyment. For example, African Bushmen in the Kalahari Desert feast on cockroaches. In Bogotá, Colombia, vendors sell fried ants along the street. Australians have a lemonade-like beverage whose main ingredient is green weaver ants. And many East Africans enjoy dragonflies sautéed with onions.

The most commonly eaten insect is the grasshopper. People serve these little creatures toasted, fried, broiled, ground, dried, and salted. What variety!

Why would anyone deliberately want to eat bugs? There are a lot of reasons. First of all, insects are the most abundant form of life on earth, and with the right recipes and seasonings, many people find them irresistibly delicious.

Insects are also nutritious. Termites, for example, have more protein than fish and less fat than steak. A daily handful of insects would provide not only vitamins, but also necessary fats and carbohydrates.

Insects are such a healthy food source that large-scale insect production has been suggested. Many hungry people in the world are in desperate need of protein, and insects are an excellent source. They are easy to find and can be prepared easily and inexpensively. In fact, if we processed just the bees we destroy each year, tons of pure protein would be available for the hungry.

Now, before you head into the jungle to gobble termites like Tarzan, keep this in mind. Not all insects are safe to eat, and certain types *must* be avoided, especially those you find dead. If you're interested in entomophagy, why not visit your library and see what you can find out about it.

And if entomophagy still makes you squeamish, don't despair. As the Roman poet Lucretius said, "What's food to one man may be fierce poison to another."

Now there's food for thought!

Think It Over

1. *Why did some settlers on the Great Plains consume grasshoppers?*
2. *Explain how you would feel about using insects as food.*

Write

Imagine that you are the food critic for a magazine. Write a review of a fast-food restaurant that specializes in some of the insect dishes described in the story.

THEME WRAP-UP

GOING BUGGY

Insects play a big part in the outcome of both "Like Jake and Me" and "Who Won the Contest." How do insects make life better for Alex and worse for Andy?

Which story character's feelings about insects are much like yours? Explain why you agree with this character.

WRITER'S WORKSHOP Think about some of the insect recipes Andy mentions in "Who Won the Contest." What would an *Andy Moller Insect Cookbook* include? Write an insect recipe of your own. Make a list of the ingredients, and write a paragraph giving directions for making the insect dish.

MOONLIGHT

The same moon shines down upon us all with the same light. Yet each person looks back at the moon with different thoughts and different feelings.

CONTENTS

MOON

from *Flower Moon Snow: A Book of Haiku*
written and illustrated by Kazue Mizumura

ALA Notable Book

Following me all along the road,
The moon came home
With me tonight.

Coming home late,
Only my moonlit shadow
Dances on the street.

Again and again,
The wind wipes away the clouds
And shines up the moon.

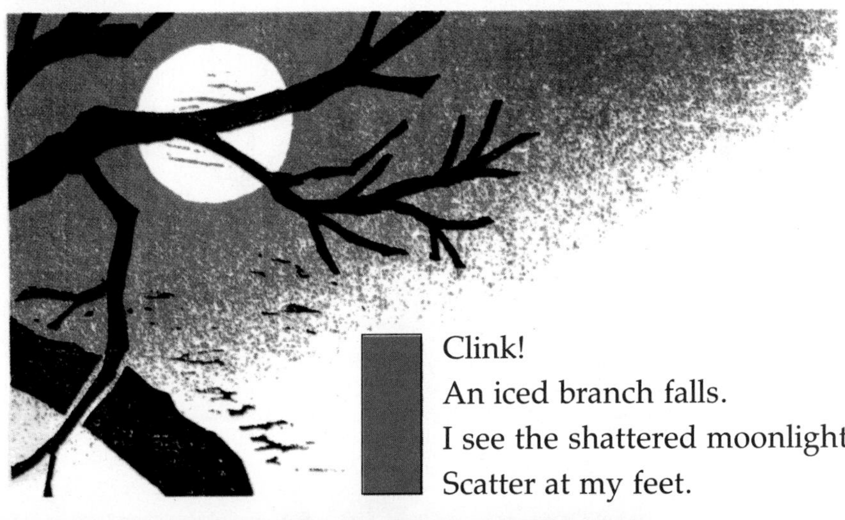

Clink!
An iced branch falls.
I see the shattered moonlight
Scatter at my feet.

The party is over.
The moon in the swimming pool
Is all alone.

Many Moons
by JAMES THURBER
Illustrated by MARC SIMONT

ONCE UPON A TIME, in a kingdom by the sea, there lived a little Princess named Lenore. She was ten years old, going on eleven. One day Lenore fell ill of a surfeit of raspberry tarts and took to her bed.

The Royal Physician came to see her and took her temperature and felt her pulse and made her stick out her tongue. The Royal Physician was worried. He sent for the King, Lenore's father, and the King came to see her.

"I will get you anything your heart desires," the King said. "Is there anything your heart desires?"

"Yes," said the Princess. "I want the moon. If I can have the moon, I will be well again."

AWARD-WINNING AUTHOR

Now the King had a great many wise men who always got for him anything he wanted, so he told his daughter that she could have the moon. Then he went to the throne room and pulled a bell cord, three long pulls and a short pull, and presently the Lord High Chamberlain came into the room.

The Lord High Chamberlain was a large, fat man who wore thick glasses which made his eyes seem twice as big as they really were. This made the Lord High Chamberlain seem twice as wise as he really was.

"I want you to get the moon," said the King. "The Princess Lenore wants the moon. If she can have the moon, she will get well again."

"The moon?" exclaimed the Lord High Chamberlain, his eyes widening. This made him look four times as wise as he really was.

"Yes, the moon," said the King. "M-o-o-n, moon. Get it tonight, tomorrow at the latest."

The Lord High Chamberlain wiped his forehead with a handkerchief and then blew his nose loudly. "I have got a great many things for you in my time, your Majesty," he said. "It just happens that I have with me a list of the things I have got for you in my time." He pulled a long scroll of parchment out of his pocket.

"Let me see, now." He glanced at the list, frowning. "I have got ivory, apes, and peacocks, rubies, opals, and emeralds, black orchids, pink elephants, and blue poodles, gold bugs, scarabs, and flies in amber, hummingbirds' tongues, angels' feathers, and unicorns' horns, giants, midgets, and mermaids, frankincense, ambergris, and myrrh, troubadours, minstrels, and dancing women, a pound of butter, two dozen eggs, and a sack of sugar—sorry, my wife wrote that in there."

"I don't remember any blue poodles," said the King.

"It says blue poodles right here on the list, and they are checked off with a little check mark," said the Lord High Chamberlain. "So there must have been blue poodles. You just forget."

"Never mind the blue poodles," said the King. "What I want now is the moon."

"I have sent as far as Samarkand and Araby and Zanzibar to get things for you, your Majesty," said the Lord High Chamberlain. "But the moon is out of the question. It is 35,000 miles away and it is bigger than the room the Princess lies in. Furthermore, it is made of molten copper. I cannot get the moon for you. Blue poodles, yes; the moon, no."

The King flew into a rage and told the Lord High Chamberlain to leave the room and to send the Royal Wizard to the throne room.

The Royal Wizard was a little, thin man with a long face. He wore a high red peaked hat covered with silver stars, and a long blue robe covered with golden owls. His face grew very pale when the King told him that he wanted the moon for his little daughter, and that he expected the Royal Wizard to get it.

"I have worked a great deal of magic for you in my time, your Majesty," said the Royal Wizard. "As a matter of fact, I just happen to have in my pocket a list of the wizardries I have performed for you." He drew a paper from a deep pocket of his robe. "It begins: 'Dear Royal Wizard: I am returning herewith the so-called philosopher's stone which you claimed—' no, that isn't it." The Royal Wizard brought a long scroll of parchment from another pocket of his robe. "Here it is," he said. "Now, let's see. I have squeezed blood out of turnips for you, and turnips out of blood. I have produced rabbits out of silk hats, and silk hats out of rabbits. I have conjured up flowers, tambourines, and doves out of nowhere, and nowhere out of flowers, tambourines, and doves. I have brought you divining rods, magic wands, and crystal spheres in which to behold the future. I have compounded philters, unguents, and potions, to cure heartbreak, surfeit, and ringing in the ears. I have made you my own special mixture of wolfbane, nightshade, and eagles' tears, to ward off things that go bump in the night. I have given you seven-league boots, the golden touch, and a cloak of invisibility—"

"It didn't work," said the King. "The cloak of invisibility didn't work."

"Yes, it did," said the Royal Wizard.

"No, it didn't," said the King. "I kept bumping into things, the same as ever."

"The cloak is supposed to make you invisible," said the Royal Wizard. "It is not supposed to keep you from bumping into things."

"All I know is, I kept bumping into things," said the King.

The Royal Wizard looked at his list again. "I got you," he said, "horns from Elfland, sand from the Sandman, and gold from the rainbow. Also a spool of thread, a paper of needles, and a lump of beeswax—sorry, those are things my wife wrote down for me to get her."

"What I want you to do now," said the King, "is to get me the moon. The Princess Lenore wants the moon, and when she gets it, she will be well again."

"Nobody can get the moon," said the Royal Wizard. "It is 150,000 miles away, and it is made of green cheese, and it is twice as big as this palace."

The King flew into another rage and sent the Royal Wizard back to his cave. Then he rang a gong and summoned the Royal Mathematician.

The Royal Mathematician was a bald-headed, nearsighted man, with a skullcap on his head and a pencil behind each ear. He wore a black suit with white numbers on it.

"I don't want to hear a long list of all the things you have figured out for me since 1907," the King said to him. "I want you to figure out right now how to get the moon for the Princess Lenore. When she gets the moon, she will be well again."

"I am glad you mentioned all the things I have figured out for you since 1907," said the Royal Mathematician. "It so happens that I have a list of them with me."

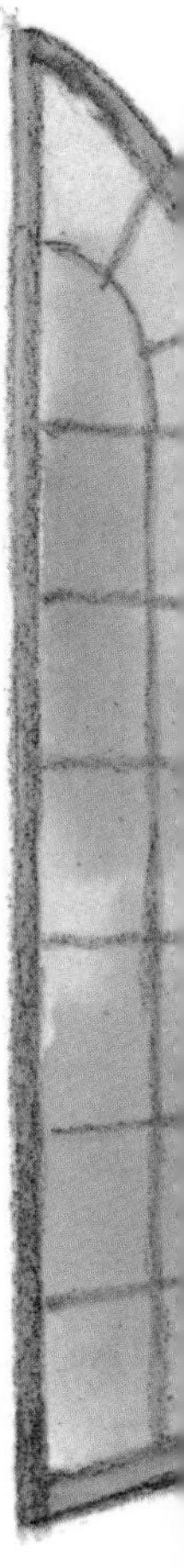

He pulled a long scroll of parchment out of a pocket and looked at it. "Now, let me see. I have figured out for you the distance between the horns of a dilemma, night and day, and A and Z. I have computed how far is Up, how long it takes to get to Away, and what becomes of Gone. I have discovered the length of the sea serpent, the price of the priceless, and the square of the hippopotamus. I know where you are when you are at Sixes and Sevens, how much Is you have to have to make an Are, and how many birds you can catch with the salt in the ocean—187,796,132, if it would interest you to know."

"There aren't that many birds," said the King.

"I didn't say there were," said the Royal Mathematician. "I said if there were."

"I don't want to hear about seven hundred million imaginary birds," said the King. "I want you to get the moon for the Princess Lenore."

"The moon is 300,000 miles away," said the Royal Mathematician. "It is round and flat like a coin, only it is made of asbestos, and it is half the size of this kingdom. Furthermore, it is pasted on the sky. Nobody can get the moon."

The King flew into still another rage and sent the Royal Mathematician away. Then he rang for the Court Jester.

The Jester came bounding into the throne room in his motley and his cap and bells, and sat at the foot of the throne.

"What can I do for you, your Majesty?" asked the Court Jester.

"Nobody can do anything for me," said the King mournfully. "The Princess Lenore wants the moon, and she cannot be well till she gets it, but nobody can get it for her. Every time I ask anybody for the moon, it gets larger and farther away. There is nothing you can do for me except play on your lute. Something sad."

"How big do they say the moon is," asked the Court Jester, "and how far away?"

"The Lord High Chamberlain says it is 35,000 miles away, and bigger than the Princess Lenore's room," said the King. "The Royal Wizard says it is 150,000 miles away, and twice as big as this palace. The Royal Mathematician says it is 300,000 miles away, and half the size of this kingdom."

The Court Jester strummed on his lute for a little while. "They are all wise men," he said, "and so they must all be right. If they are all right, then the moon must be just as large and as far away as each person thinks it is. The thing to do is find out how big the Princess Lenore thinks it is, and how far away."

"I never thought of that," said the King.

"I will go and ask her, your Majesty," said the Court Jester. And he crept softly into the little girl's room.

The Princess Lenore was awake, and she was glad to see the Court Jester, but her face was very pale and her voice very weak.

"Have you brought the moon to me?" she asked.

"Not yet," said the Court Jester, "but I will get it for you right away. How big do you think it is?"

"It is just a little smaller than my thumbnail," she said, "for when I hold my thumbnail up at the moon, it just covers it."

"And how far away is it?" asked the Court Jester.

"It is not as high as the big tree outside my window," said the Princess, "for sometimes it gets caught in the top branches."

"It will be very easy to get the moon for you," said the Court Jester. "I will climb the tree tonight when it gets caught in the top branches and bring it to you."

Then he thought of something else. "What is the moon made of, Princess?" he asked.

"Oh," she said, "it's made of gold, of course, silly."

The Court Jester left the Princess Lenore's room and went to see the Royal Goldsmith. He had the Royal Goldsmith make a tiny round golden moon just a little smaller than the thumbnail of the Princess Lenore. Then he had him string it on a golden chain so the Princess could wear it around her neck.

"What is this thing I have made?" asked the Royal Goldsmith when he had finished it.

"You have made the moon," said the Court Jester. "That is the moon."

"But the moon," said the Royal Goldsmith, "is 500,000 miles away and is made of bronze and is round like a marble."

"That's what you think," said the Court Jester as he went away with the moon.

The Court Jester took the moon to the Princess Lenore, and she was overjoyed. The next day she was well again and could get up and go out in the gardens to play.

But the King's worries were not yet over. He knew that the moon would shine in the sky again that night, and he did not want the Princess Lenore to see it. If she did, she would know that the moon she wore on a chain around her neck was not the real moon.

So the King sent for the Lord High Chamberlain and said, "We must keep the Princess Lenore from seeing the moon when it shines in the sky tonight. Think of something."

The Lord High Chamberlain tapped his forehead with his fingers thoughtfully and said, "I know just the thing. We can make some dark glasses for the Princess Lenore. We can make them so dark that she will not be able to see anything at all through them. Then she will not be able to see the moon when it shines in the sky."

This made the King very angry, and he shook his head from side to side. "If she wore dark glasses, she would bump into things," he said, "and then she would be ill again." So he sent the Lord High Chamberlain away and called the Royal Wizard.

"We must hide the moon," said the King, "so that the Princess Lenore will not see it when it shines in the sky tonight. How are we going to do that?"

The Royal Wizard stood on his hands and then he stood on his head and then he stood on his feet again.

"I know what we can do," he said. "We can stretch some black velvet curtains on poles. The curtains will cover all the palace gardens like a circus tent, and the Princess Lenore will not be able to see through them, so she will not see the moon in the sky."

The King was so angry at this that he waved his arms around. "Black velvet curtains would keep out the air," he said. "The Princess Lenore would not be able to breathe, and she would be ill again." So he sent the Royal Wizard away and summoned the Royal Mathematician.

"We must do something," said the King, "so that the Princess Lenore will not see the moon when it shines in the sky tonight. If you know so much, figure out a way to do that."

The Royal Mathematician walked around in a circle, and then he walked around in a square, and then he stood still. "I have it!" he said.

"We can set off fireworks in the gardens every night. We will make a lot of silver fountains and golden cascades, and when they go off, they will fill the sky with so many sparks that it will be as light as day and the Princess Lenore will not be able to see the moon."

The King flew into such a rage that he began jumping up and down. "Fireworks would keep the Princess Lenore awake," he said. "She would not get any sleep at all and she would be ill again." So the King sent the Royal Mathematician away.

When he looked up again, it was dark outside and he saw the bright rim of the moon just peeping over the horizon. He jumped up in a great fright and rang for the Court Jester. The Court Jester came bounding into the room and sat down at the foot of the throne.

"What can I do for you, your Majesty?" he asked.

"Nobody can do anything for me," said the King mournfully. "The moon is coming up again. It will shine into the Princess Lenore's bedroom, and she will know it is still in the sky and that she does not wear it on a golden chain around her neck. Play me something on your lute, something very sad, for when the Princess sees the moon, she will be ill again."

The Court Jester strummed on his lute. "What do your wise men say?" he asked.

"They can think of no way to hide the moon that will not make the Princess Lenore ill," said the King.

The Court Jester played another song, very softly. "Your wise men know everything," he said, "and if they cannot hide the moon, then it cannot be hidden."

The King put his head in his hands again and sighed.

Suddenly he jumped up from his throne and pointed to the windows. "Look!" he cried. "The moon is already shining into the Princess Lenore's bedroom. Who can explain how the moon can be shining in the sky when it is hanging on a golden chain around her neck?"

The Court Jester stopped playing on his lute. "Who could explain how to get the moon when your wise men said it was too large and too far away? It was the Princess Lenore. Therefore the Princess Lenore is wiser than your wise men and knows more about the moon than they do. So I will ask *her.*" And before the King could stop him, the Court Jester slipped quietly out of the throne room and up the wide marble staircase to the Princess Lenore's bedroom.

The Princess was lying in bed, but she was wide awake and she was looking out the window at the moon shining in the sky. Shining in her hand was the moon the Court Jester had got for her. He looked very sad, and there seemed to be tears in his eyes.

"Tell me, Princess Lenore," he said mournfully, "how can the moon be shining in the sky when it is hanging on a golden chain around your neck?"

The Princess looked at him and laughed. "That is easy, silly," she said. "When I lose a tooth, a new one grows in its place, doesn't it?"

"Of course," said the Court Jester. "And when the unicorn loses his horn in the forest, a new one grows in the middle of his forehead."

"That is right," said the Princess. "And when the Royal Gardener cuts the flowers in the garden, other flowers come to take their place."

"I should have thought of that," said the Court Jester, "for it is the same way with the daylight."

"And it is the same way with the moon," said the Princess Lenore. "I guess it is the same way with everything." Her voice became very low and faded away, and the Court Jester saw that she was asleep. Gently he tucked the covers in around the sleeping Princess.

But before he left the room, he went over to the window and winked at the moon, for it seemed to the Court Jester that the moon had winked at him.

Think It Over

1. *Why are the King and his advisers in such an uproar?*
2. *Why is the King still worried on the day after the Princess gets the moon?*
3. *Why does the Court Jester want to hear Princess Lenore's opinions about the moon?*
4. *Who is your favorite character in the story? What qualities make this character likable?*

Write

The Lord High Chamberlain, the Royal Wizard, the Royal Mathematician, and the Royal Goldsmith all provide information about the moon. Compile a list of "facts" about the moon, based upon their statements.

Words from the ILLUSTRATOR:

MARC SIMONT

I first met James Thurber and his family when they moved to Cornwall, Connecticut, during the late 1940s. *Many Moons* had already been written. It was illustrated by Louis Slobodkin and had won the Caldecott Medal. A few years ago, when Mrs. Thurber was asked about doing a newly illustrated edition, she had qualms. But she and her family finally decided to do it. Since I had illustrated other James Thurber books, *The Wonderful O* and *The Thirteen Clocks,* she asked me to do this one.

Usually, I don't like to meet the authors of the books I'm illustrating. They have their own ideas, and it creates conflicts. But James Thurber was my friend before he was my collaborator. We had talked about various things in *Many Moons* before I ever knew that I would one day illustrate it.

Some people have asked me how I felt about reillustrating a book that is so famous. To tell you the truth, when I illustrate a book, I decide to make it all my own, my personal interpretation of the story. Yes, I was interested in seeing how Louis Slobodkin had done it, but in no way did his work affect my vision, which was quite different. There are some things I like about Slobodkin's version, but his *Many Moons* had no impact on my own. When it comes to an artist's vision, every artist is in a different world.

THEME WRAP-UP

MOONLIGHT

Which characters in "Many Moons" do you think are wise? Which ones are foolish? Explain why you think as you do.

Think about the descriptions of the moon in the story and in the poetry. Explain how they are alike and different.

WRITER'S WORKSHOP According to the Court Jester, the moon is exactly what each person thinks it is. If the moon could really be anything you imagine, what would your moon be? Decide what your moon would be made of and how far away it would be. Think of as many creative details as you can. Then write a descriptive paragraph telling about your moon.

THEME

UNFORGETTABLE PERFORMANCES

Have you ever performed before a large audience? Or even before an audience of one? If so, you probably learned what the characters in these selections learned: You just never know what might happen!

CONTENTS

Oliver Hyde's DISHCLOTH CONCERT

from

Richard Kennedy: Collected Stories

CHILDREN'S CHOICE

by Richard Kennedy

illustrated by Marcia Sewall

Now maybe it's sad and maybe it's spooky, but there was a man who lived just out of town on a scrubby farm and no one had seen his face for years. If he was outside working, he kept his hat pulled down and his collar turned up, and if anyone approached him he ran up the hill to his house and shut himself inside. He left notes pinned to his door for a brave errand boy who brought him supplies from town. The people asked the boy what he heard up there in that tomblike house when he collected the notes and delivered the supplies. "Darkness and quietness," said the boy. "I hear darkness and quietness." The people nodded and looked at the boy. "Aren't you afraid?" The boy bit his lip. "A fellow has to make a living," he said.

Sometimes the children would come out of town and sing a little song up at the house and then run away. They sang:

"The beautiful bride of Oliver Hyde,
Fell down dead on the mountainside."

Yes, it was true. The man was full of grief and bitterness. He was Oliver Hyde, and his young bride's wagon had been washed into a canyon by a mudslide and it killed her, horse and all. But that was years ago. The children sang some more:

"Oliver Hyde is a strange old man,
He sticks his head in a coffee can,
And hides his face when there's folks about,
He's outside in, and he's inside out."

It was too bad. Oliver used to have many friends, and he played the fastest and sweetest fiddle in the county. And for the few short weeks he was married his playing was sweeter than ever. But on the day his wife was buried he busted his fiddle across a porch post, and now he sat cold, dark, and quiet on his little hill. No one had visited him for years. There was a reason. You shall see.

One day a man came from the town and walked up the hill toward Oliver's house. He was carrying a fiddle case. Two or three times he stopped and looked up at the house and shook his head and continued on. He arrived at the porch steps. All the window shades were pulled down and it was dead quiet inside. The three porch steps creaked like cats moaning in their dreams, and the man knocked on the door. For a little bit it was quiet, then there was the sound of a chair being scooted across the floor. A voice said, "Come in."

The man opened the door a crack and peeked inside.

"Oliver?" he said. "It's me, Jim." No answer. Jim opened the door farther and put a foot inside. It was dark, and smelled stale. Jim opened the door all the way.

Off in the corner where the light didn't touch sat a figure in a chair, perfectly upright, with his hands on his knees like a stone god, as still and silent as a thousand years ago. The head was draped completely with a dishcloth.

Jim swallowed and spoke. "Haven't seen you around lately, Oliver." No answer.

People used to visit Oliver for a while after his beautiful bride fell down dead on the mountainside, but this is how it was—Oliver sitting in the dark with a dishcloth over his head, and he never spoke to them. It was too strange. His friends stopped visiting.

All Jim wanted was a single word from Oliver—yes or no.

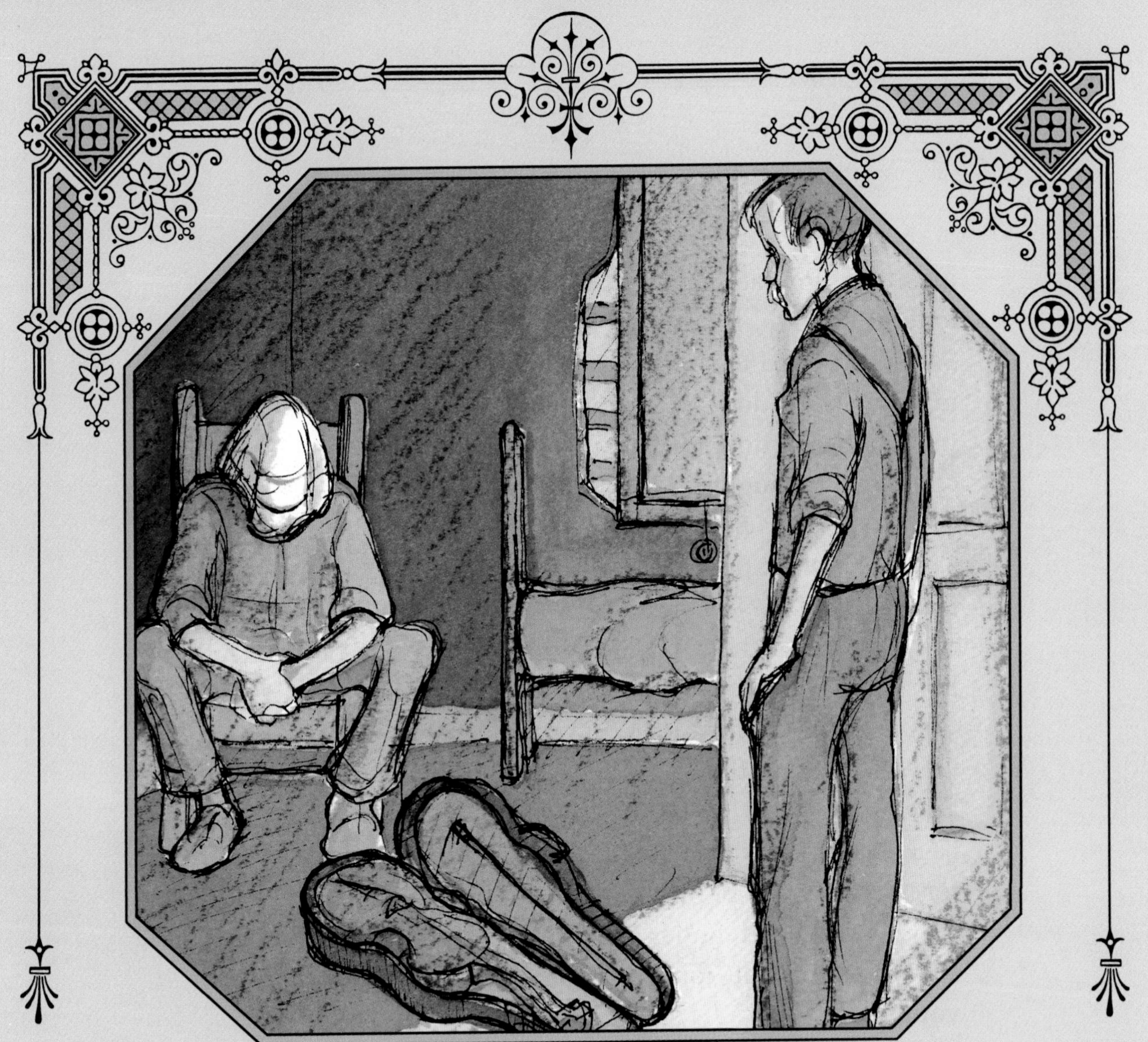

He had a favor to ask. He was Oliver's oldest friend. He moved inside.

"Sue's getting married, Oliver," he said. No answer. "You remember my little girl, Sue? She's all growed up now, Oliver, and mighty pretty, too." For all the notice he got, Jim might just as well have been talking to a stove. He cleared his voice and went on. "The reason I came, Oliver, was to ask you to come and play the fiddle for us at the dance. We was the best friends, and I don't see how I can marry off Sue without you being there to fiddle for us. You can just say yes or no, Oliver."

Now Oliver wasn't dead himself yet, so he still had feelings, and Jim had been his best friend. They had played and fought together, fished and hunted, and grown up together. So Oliver hated to say "No" just flat out like that, so he said instead, "No fiddle." Jim was prepared for that, and he laid the fiddle case down on the floor and flipped it open.

"Here, I brought a fiddle, Oliver. Porky Fellows was happy to make a lend of it."

Oliver felt trapped now. He was silent for a long time, then finally he said, "Tell you what. I can't wear this dishcloth on my head and fiddle, but if everyone else wears a dishcloth I'll come."

Jim was quiet for a long time, but at last he said, "All right, Oliver, I'll ask if they'll do it. The dance is tomorrow night at Edward's barn. I'll leave the fiddle here, and if I don't come back to pick it up, then you got to come to the dance and fiddle for us. I got your promise."

Oliver smiled under his dishcloth. They'd be fools to agree to that. You can't have any fun with a dishcloth over your head.

"So long, Oliver," Jim said. Oliver didn't answer. Jim went back on down the hill.

Oliver took the dishcloth off. The fiddle was laying in the light of the open door. He sucked a whisker and looked at it. Oliver knew the fiddle, and it was a good fiddle. He wondered if it was in tune and wanted to pick it up, but he let it lay there. His foot was tapping, and he slapped his knee to make it stop. He laughed to himself and muttered, "Them donkeys—what do they know?" Then he got up and moved around the little house on his dreary business.

The sun went down and the shadow of the fiddle case stretched across the floor. Oliver's eyes kept landing on the

fiddle, and he stepped over the shadow when he crossed that way. It looked to him like the bow had new horsehair on it. But it didn't make any difference to him. He figured he'd never be playing that fiddle, and he never touched it.

Next morning Oliver watched down the hill for Jim to come and tell him the deal was off and to get the fiddle. Noon came. Oliver ate some beans. Afternoon came on. Jim didn't show. Oliver began to get mad. He was mad that he had ever made the promise. It started to get dark. "Those cluckheads!" Oliver said, pulling the window shut. "They can't dance with dish-cloths on their heads, or drink punch, either. They'll have a rotten time."

But a promise is a promise.

Finally he decided it was time to put his hat and coat on. "They tricked me," Oliver grumbled, "but I got a trick for them, too. They'll be sorry I came to their party." It wasn't a great trick Oliver had in mind, but just a miserable little one to make sure nobody could have any fun while he was there. He figured they'd ask him to leave shortly. He wouldn't even bother to take off his hat and coat.

He headed down the hill with the fiddle and into the little town. He entered Edward's barn with his hat pulled down and his collar turned up. It was dark except for two bare, hanging light bulbs, one over the center of the barn and one at the end where a sort of stage was built up. Oliver had played at shindigs there many times. He kept his head down, and only from the corners of his eyes could he see all the people sitting around the walls. "It's awfully dark," Oliver thought to himself, "and quiet. I figure they know that's the way I like it." He got under the light bulb that hung over the stage and took out the fiddle.

He tuned down to a fretful and lonesome sound, and then he played.

Of course he knew they were all looking for happy dancing tunes, so first off he played a slow and sad tune about a man who was walking down a long road that had no ending and was gray all about, and the man was looking forward to being dead because it might be more cheerful. Nobody danced, naturally, and didn't clap either when Oliver finished it. "That's just right," Oliver thought. "I'll give them a wretched time." And he started on another.

The second tune he played was even slower and sadder, about a man who thought his heart was a pincushion and it seemed to him that everyone was sticking pins and needles into it, and it was hurtful even to listen to it. Nobody danced, and nobody even moved to the punch bowl. "Now they're sorry I came," Oliver thought. Still, he had played that last tune especially sweet, and he expected that someone might have clapped a little just for that, even if it was sad.

Oliver looked out a little under his hat as he retuned a bit. He tried to see Jim. He ought to come up and say hello at least, not just let him stand there completely alone. And he wondered where the other musicians were. Four people were sitting down off to the right of the stage. That would be them. Oliver considered it would be nice to have a little slide guitar on these slow ones, sort of mournful played, and a mouth harp and mandolin would fit in nice. "Naw! This is just the way I want it. One more gloomy song and they'll ask me to leave."

So then he played another, this one about a man who had a wife that just recently moved to heaven, and how roses grew all over her tombstone even in the winter. Oliver was halfway through that before he remembered that he'd played that tune at his own wedding party. He pulled up short a bit then, but kept on playing it out, and a tear rolled down his cheek. Well, nobody could see. He wiped his eyes when he was finished.

Nobody clapped and nobody moved, just sat against the dark walls perfectly still. Among the dark figures was a lighter shape. Probably the bride in her wedding gown. Oliver remembered how lovely and happy his bride had been, and he felt a little mean when he thought about that, giving out such sad tunes.

He spoke out loud, the first words that were spoken since he came in. "Well, I guess you're all ready for me to leave now, and I will. But first I want to play just one happy tune for the bride, and so you can dance, and then I'll go." Then he did play a happy one, a fast one, carrying on with fiddling lively enough to scramble eggs. But nobody got up to dance, and when he was finished nobody moved or made a sound.

"Look here," Oliver said. "I reckon you can't dance with those dishcloths over your heads, I forgot about that. So take 'em off. I'll give you another dancing tune, then I'll go." And then he went into another, as sweet and light and fast as any-

one ever could, something to get even a rock up and dancing, but nobody moved. And when he was finished they all sat silent with the dishcloths still on their heads.

"Come on," Oliver said. "Take those things off your heads. You other fellows get up here with your music and help me out. Let's have some dancing, drink some punch, let's get alive now." He stomped his foot three times and threw into a tune that would churn butter all by itself. But the other four musicians sat perfectly still, and so did everybody else, and Oliver was standing there under the light bulb in silence when he finished the tune.

He stood there with his head down, understanding things, and how it felt to be on the other side of the darkness and silence when all you wanted was some sign of life to help out. Then he leaned over and put the fiddle in the case and closed it. He said one last thing, then walked out from under the light toward the door. "Okay," he said. "That's a hard lesson, but I got it."

When he opened the door he bumped into someone sitting next to it against the wall, and the fellow fell off his chair. Oliver put a hand down to help him up. But the fellow just lay there. Oliver touched him. "What's this?" He felt around, then shoved back his hat for a look. It was a sack of grain he'd knocked over. And the next person sitting there was a sack of grain, too. And the next was a bale of hay.

Oliver walked completely around the barn. All the people were sacks of grain and bales of hay sitting against the dark walls, and the bride was a white sack of flour. The four musicians sitting off to the right of the stage were four old saddles setting on a rail.

When Oliver came around to the door again he heard music. He stepped outside and looked down the street. A barn down near the end was all lit up, and lots of people were moving about. He went back up on the stage, got the fiddle, and headed down the street.

Jim was standing by the door. "Waiting for you, Oliver," he said. "We're just getting under way—come on in." When he led Oliver inside everyone became quiet, first one little group of people, then another, until at last everyone was silent and looking at Oliver. The bride and groom were holding hands. Jim made a motion and everyone headed for a chair against the walls. They all took out dishcloths to put over their heads.

"Edward's got himself a new barn, huh?" Oliver said.

"Yeah," said Jim. "I guess you didn't know that. Uses the old one to store stuff. I shoulda told you."

"It's all right," Oliver said. He looked up on the stage. Four musicians were sitting there with dishcloths over their heads. Then Jim took out a large dishcloth. Oliver touched him on the arm.

"Never mind that. And everyone else, too. Just be regular and dance. I'll fiddle for you."

Jim slapped him on the back and shouted out the good news. Oliver went up on the stage. Someone got him a mug of punch. The musicians tuned up. Oliver took off his hat and dropped it, and tossed his coat on a chair. They lit into a fast, happy tune. They danced and played and sang half the night.

Ah, they had a wonderful time. Oliver included.

Think It Over

1. *Why did Oliver Hyde shut himself off from the world?*
2. *Why does Oliver demand that the wedding guests wear dishcloths on their heads?*
3. *Do you think Oliver Hyde has the right to behave as he does? Explain why you feel as you do.*
4. *If Oliver Hyde were your friend, would you have asked him to play at a wedding? Explain your answer.*

Write

Oliver Hyde goes through a great change during the story. Write the lyrics to a song describing what happens to him.

Arkansas TRAVELER

a traditional American folk song

from *Tom Glazer's Treasury of Songs for Children*

illustrated by Bill Russell

1. O once upon a time in Arkansas,
An old man sat in his little cabin door,
And fiddled at a tune that he lik'd to hear,
A jolly old tune that he'd play by ear.
It was raining hard, but the fiddler didn't care,
He sawed away at the popular air,
Tho' his roof tree leaked like a waterfall,
That didn't seem to bother the man at all.

2. A traveler was riding by that day,
And stopped to hear him a-practicing away;
The cabin was afloat and his feet were wet,
But still the old man didn't seem to fret.
So the stranger said: "Now the way it seems to me,
You'd better mend your roof," said he,
But the old man said, as he played away:
"I couldn't mend it now, it's a rainy day."

3. The traveler replied: "That's all quite true,
But this, I think, is the thing for you to do;
Get busy on a day that is fair and bright,
Then patch the old roof till it's good and tight."
But the old man kept on a-playin' at his reel,
And tapp'd the ground with his leathery heel;
"Get along," said he, "for you give me a pain;
My cabin never leaks when it doesn't rain."

La Bamba

from Baseball in April and Other Stories

Best Books for Young Adults

by Gary Soto

illustrated by David Diaz

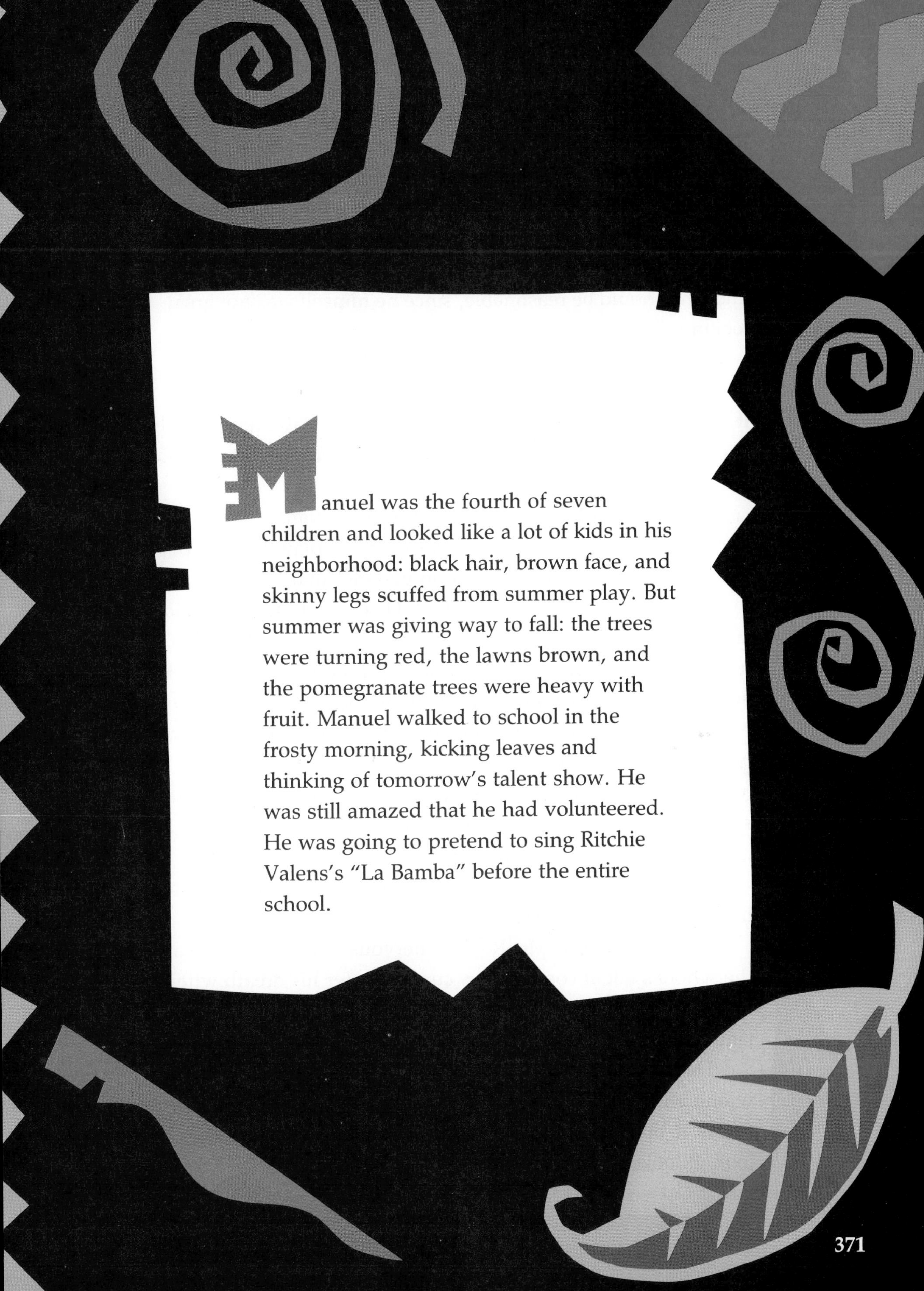

Manuel was the fourth of seven children and looked like a lot of kids in his neighborhood: black hair, brown face, and skinny legs scuffed from summer play. But summer was giving way to fall: the trees were turning red, the lawns brown, and the pomegranate trees were heavy with fruit. Manuel walked to school in the frosty morning, kicking leaves and thinking of tomorrow's talent show. He was still amazed that he had volunteered. He was going to pretend to sing Ritchie Valens's "La Bamba" before the entire school.

Why did I raise my hand? he asked himself, but in his heart he knew the answer. He yearned for the limelight. He wanted applause as loud as a thunderstorm, and to hear his friends say, "Man, that was bad!" And he wanted to impress the girls, especially Petra Lopez, the second-prettiest girl in his class. The prettiest was already taken by his friend Ernie. Manuel knew he should be reasonable, since he himself was not great-looking, just average.

Manuel kicked through the fresh-fallen leaves. When he got to school he realized he had forgotten his math workbook. If the teacher found out, he would have to stay after school and miss practice for the talent show. But fortunately for him, they did drills that morning.

During lunch Manuel hung around with Benny, who was also in the talent show. Benny was going to play the trumpet in spite of the fat lip he had gotten playing football.

"How do I look?" Manuel asked. He cleared his throat and started moving his lips in pantomime. No words came out, just a hiss that sounded like a snake. Manuel tried to look emotional, flailing his arms on the high notes and opening his eyes and mouth as wide as he could when he came to *"Para bailar la baaaaammmba."*

After Manuel finished, Benny said it looked all right, but suggested Manuel dance while he sang. Manuel thought for a moment and decided it was a good idea.

"Yeah, just think you're like Michael Jackson or someone like that," Benny suggested. "But don't get carried away."

During rehearsal, Mr. Roybal, nervous about his debut as the school's talent coordinator, cursed under his breath when the lever that controlled the speed on the record player jammed.

"Darn," he growled, trying to force the lever. "What's wrong with you?"

"Is it broken?" Manuel asked, bending over for a closer look. It looked all right to him.

Mr. Roybal assured Manuel that he would have a good record player at the talent show, even if it meant bringing his own stereo from home.

Manuel sat in a folding chair, twirling his record on his thumb. He watched a skit about personal hygiene, a mother-and-daughter violin duo, five first-grade girls jumping rope, a karate kid breaking boards, three girls singing, and a skit about the pilgrims. If the record player hadn't been broken, he would have gone after the karate kid, an easy act to follow, he told himself.

As he twirled his forty-five record, Manuel thought they had a great talent show. The entire school would be amazed. His mother and father would be proud, and his brothers and sisters would be jealous and pout. It would be a night to remember.

Benny walked onto the stage, raised his trumpet to his mouth, and waited for his cue. Mr. Roybal raised his hand like a symphony conductor and let it fall dramatically. Benny inhaled and blew so loud that Manuel dropped his record, which rolled across the cafeteria floor until it hit a wall. Manuel raced after it, picked it up, and wiped it clean.

"Boy, I'm glad it didn't break," he said with a sigh.

That night Manuel had to do the dishes and a lot of homework, so he could only practice in the shower. In bed he prayed that he wouldn't mess up. He prayed that it wouldn't be like when he was a first-grader. For Science Week he had wired together a C battery and a bulb, and told everyone he had discovered how a flashlight worked. He was so pleased with himself that he practiced for hours pressing the wire to the battery, making the bulb wink a dim, orangish light. He showed it to so many kids in his neighborhood that when it was time to show his class how a flashlight worked, the battery was dead. He pressed the wire to the battery, but the bulb didn't respond. He pressed until his thumb hurt and some kids in the back started snickering.

But Manuel fell asleep confident that nothing would go wrong this time.

The next morning his father and mother beamed at him. They were proud that he was going to be in the talent show.

"I wish you would tell us what you're doing," his mother said. His father, a pharmacist who wore a blue smock with his name on a plastic rectangle, looked up from the newspaper and sided with his wife. "Yes, what are you doing in the talent show?"

"You'll see," Manuel said.

The day whizzed by, and so did his afternoon chores and dinner. Suddenly he was dressed in his best clothes and standing next to Benny backstage, listening to the commotion as the cafeteria filled with school kids and parents. The lights dimmed, and Mr. Roybal, sweaty in a tight suit and a necktie with a large knot, wet his lips and parted the stage curtains.

"Good evening, everyone," the kids behind the curtain heard him say. "Good evening to you," some of the smart-alecky kids said back to him.

"Tonight we bring you the best John Burroughs Elementary has to offer, and I'm sure that you'll be both pleased and amazed that our little school houses so much talent. And now, without further ado, let's get on with the show." He turned and, with a swish of his hand, commanded, "Part the curtain." The curtains parted in jerks. A girl dressed as a toothbrush and a boy dressed as a dirty gray tooth walked onto the stage and sang:

Brush, brush, brush
Floss, floss, floss
Gargle the germs away—hey! hey! hey!

After they finished singing, they turned to Mr. Roybal, who dropped his hand. The toothbrush dashed around the stage after the dirty tooth, which was laughing and having a great time until it slipped and nearly rolled off the stage.

Mr. Roybal jumped out and caught it just in time. "Are you OK?"

The dirty tooth answered, "Ask my dentist," which drew laughter and applause from the audience.

The violin duo played next, and except for one time when the girl got lost, they sounded fine. People applauded, and some even stood up. Then the first-grade girls maneuvered onto the stage while jumping rope. They were all smiles and bouncing ponytails as a hundred cameras flashed at once. Mothers "awhed" and fathers sat up proudly.

The karate kid was next. He did a few kicks, yells, and chops, and finally, when his father held up a board, punched it in two. The audience clapped and looked at each other, wide-eyed with respect. The boy bowed to the audience, and father and son ran off the stage.

Manuel remained behind the stage shivering with fear. He mouthed the words to "La Bamba" and swayed from left to right. Why did he raise his hand and volunteer? Why couldn't he have just sat there like the rest of the kids and not said anything? While the karate kid was on stage, Mr. Roybal, more sweaty than before, took Manuel's forty-five record and placed it on a new record player.

"You ready?" Mr. Roybal asked.

"Yeah . . ."

Mr. Roybal walked back on stage and announced that Manuel Gomez, a fifth-grader in Mrs. Knight's class, was going to pantomime Ritchie Valens's classic hit "La Bamba."

The cafeteria roared with applause. Manuel was nervous but loved the noisy crowd. He pictured his mother and father applauding loudly and his brothers and sisters also clapping, though not as energetically.

Manuel walked on stage and the song started immediately. Glassy-eyed from the shock of being in front of so many people, Manuel moved his lips and swayed in a made-up dance step. He couldn't see his parents, but he could see his brother Mario, who was a year younger, thumb-wrestling with a friend. Mario was wearing Manuel's favorite shirt; he would deal with Mario later. He saw some other kids get up and head for the drinking fountain, and a baby sitting in the middle of an aisle sucking her thumb and watching him intently.

What am I doing here? thought Manuel. This is no fun at all. Everyone was just sitting there. Some people were moving to the beat, but most were just watching him, like they would a monkey at the zoo.

But when Manuel did a fancy dance step, there was a burst of applause and some girls screamed. Manuel tried another dance step. He heard more applause and screams and started getting into the groove as he shivered and snaked like Michael Jackson around the stage. But the record got stuck, and he had to sing

Para bailar la bamba
Para bailar la bamba
Para bailar la bamba
Para bailar la bamba

again and again.

Manuel couldn't believe his bad luck. The audience began to laugh and stand up in their chairs. Manuel remembered how the forty-five record had dropped from his hand and rolled across the cafeteria floor. It probably got scratched, he thought, and now it was stuck, and he was stuck dancing and moving his lips to the same words over and over. He had never been so embarrassed. He would have to ask his parents to move the family out of town.

After Mr. Roybal ripped the needle across the record, Manuel slowed his dance steps to a halt. He didn't know what to do except bow to the audience, which applauded wildly, and scoot off the stage, on the verge of tears. This was worse than the homemade flashlight. At least no one laughed then, they just snickered.

Manuel stood alone, trying hard to hold back the tears as Benny, center stage, played his trumpet. Manuel was jealous because he sounded great, then mad as he recalled that it was Benny's loud trumpet playing that made the forty-five record fly out of his hands. But when the entire cast lined up for a

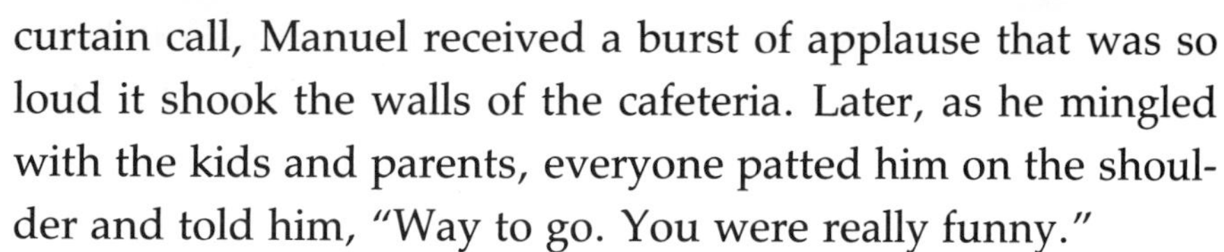

curtain call, Manuel received a burst of applause that was so loud it shook the walls of the cafeteria. Later, as he mingled with the kids and parents, everyone patted him on the shoulder and told him, "Way to go. You were really funny."

Funny? Manuel thought. Did he do something funny?

Funny. Crazy. Hilarious. These were the words people said to him. He was confused, but beyond caring. All he knew was that people were paying attention to him, and his brothers and sisters looked at him with a mixture of jealousy and awe. He was going to pull Mario aside and punch him in the arm for wearing his shirt, but he cooled it. He was enjoying the limelight. A teacher brought him cookies and punch, and the popular kids who had never before given him the time of day now clustered around him. Ricardo, the editor of the school bulletin, asked him how he made the needle stick.

"It just happened," Manuel said, crunching on a star-shaped cookie.

At home that night his father, eager to undo the buttons on his shirt and ease into his recliner, asked Manuel the same thing, how he managed to make the song stick on the words *"Para bailar la bamba."*

Manuel thought quickly and reached for scientific jargon he had read in magazines. "Easy, Dad. I used laser tracking with high optics and low functional decibels per channel." His proud but confused father told him to be quiet and go to bed.

"Ah, *que niños tan truchas,*[1]" he said as he walked to the kitchen for a glass of milk. "I don't know how you kids nowadays get so smart."

Manuel, feeling happy, went to his bedroom, undressed, and slipped into his pajamas. He looked in the mirror and began to pantomime "La Bamba," but stopped because he was tired of the song. He crawled into bed. The sheets were as cold as the moon that stood over the peach tree in their backyard.

He was relieved that the day was over. Next year, when they asked for volunteers for the talent show, he wouldn't raise his hand. Probably.

Think It Over

1. *Why is Manuel confused by the crowd's reaction to his performance?*
2. *What happened to Manuel with his first-grade science experiment?*
3. *Manuel experiences many different feelings during the story. What are some of the feelings that he has?*
4. *After his embarrassing performance, why was Manuel so angry at Benny?*

Write

Imagine that you performed in the talent show, too. Write a paragraph describing your act and the audience's reaction to it.

---

[1]what clever little rascals

THEME WRAP-UP

UNFORGETTABLE PERFORMANCES

In the selections, why is each public performance unforgettable for the person who gives it as well as for the audience?

Do the performances of Oliver Hyde, the Arkansas fiddler, or Manuel remind you of any performance you have witnessed or taken part in? Describe the similarities.

WRITER'S WORKSHOP Which of the three stories do you like the best? List all of the reasons for your choice. Use the most persuasive reasons from your list to write a paragraph to convince other people that your choice is the best story.

CONNECTIONS

MULTICULTURAL CONNECTION

PERFORMING IN FRONT OF THE NATION

Your family is watching the top-rated television news show in the nation. The team of newscasters on the show tell you not only what is happening but why it's happening.

Ed Bradley is a key member of that team. He's a special type of newscaster called a broadcast journalist. This means that he doesn't read stories written by other people but researches and writes his own. He flies all over the world to interview people and find out facts. He tells camera crews what he needs taped. After he creates a program from the facts and the tape, he goes on television to present the news.

Bradley's hard work, attention to detail, and fair presentations have won him the respect of his co-workers. He has won the Emmy, television's top award, three times.

■ *Choose a broadcaster from a local or a national news program. Write a brief "TV Profile" describing that person's usual subject matter and style of reporting.*

SOCIAL STUDIES CONNECTION

THE WEEK IN REVIEW

Collect the top newspaper stories about community events for one week. With a small group, use the facts from these to write a script for a news report that you and your classmates will perform. Have someone record your performance on videotape or audiotape.

This chart can remind you of the facts you need to find out.

What happened?	
Why did it happen?	
When did it happen?	
Where did it happen?	
Who made it happen?	
How did it happen?	

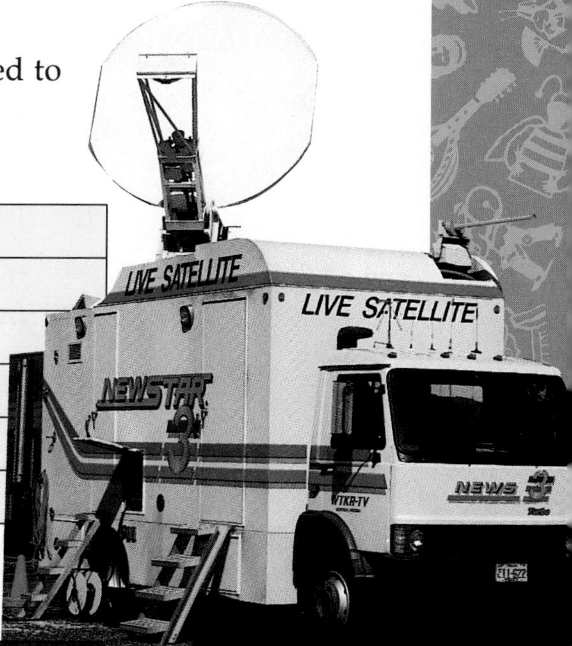

SCIENCE CONNECTION

PERFORMING EVERYWHERE AT ONCE

How is the news broadcast across the world so fast? What part do satellites play? How are signals passed from place to place? Find out how our communication systems work. With a partner, create a diagram or a mural that shows the facts you learned.

UNIT FIVE
LIFELINES

In time of silver rain
The earth
Puts forth new life again.
Langston Hughes

Nature can be kind, but it can also be challenging. A Papago Indian girl faces the challenge of a raging flood in the Sonoran Desert. Environmentalists such as Rachel Carson and Harrison Ngau urge people to meet the challenge of befriending the earth. As you read the selections in this unit, think about what you can do to treat the earth with kindness.

THEMES

BOOKSHELF

SEA OTTER RESCUE: THE AFTERMATH OF AN OIL SPILL

BY ROLAND SMITH

In March of 1989, thousands of sea otters became trapped in the deadly slick of the Exxon *Valdez* oil spill. Follow the heroic efforts of the people who headed north to try to save them.

HBJ LIBRARY BOOK

SUGARING TIME

BY KATHRYN LASKY

PHOTOGRAPHS BY CHRISTOPHER G. KNIGHT

Wade out into the deep snow with the Lacey family as they harvest their own maple syrup during the season they call "sugaring time."

NEWBERY HONOR

A MAN NAMED THOREAU

BY ROBERT BURLEIGH

Henry David Thoreau was considered a very strange man by the people in his village. He spent every day simply watching and listening to nature and writing down all that he learned. ALA NOTABLE BOOK

MOJAVE

BY DIANE SIEBERT

Unique paintings accompany this book-length poem about the beauties and mysteries of the Mojave Desert. TEACHERS' CHOICE

50 SIMPLE THINGS KIDS CAN DO TO SAVE THE EARTH

BY THE EARTHWORKS GROUP

This step-by-step guide shows you exactly what you can do in your home, school, neighborhood, and state to help clean up and preserve our planet.

LIFE IN THE DESERT

When you think of a desert, do you think of a hot, dry, lifeless place? Would you be surprised to read about the desert as a place overflowing with life and activity? To its many inhabitants, including humans, that's precisely what it is.

CONTENTS

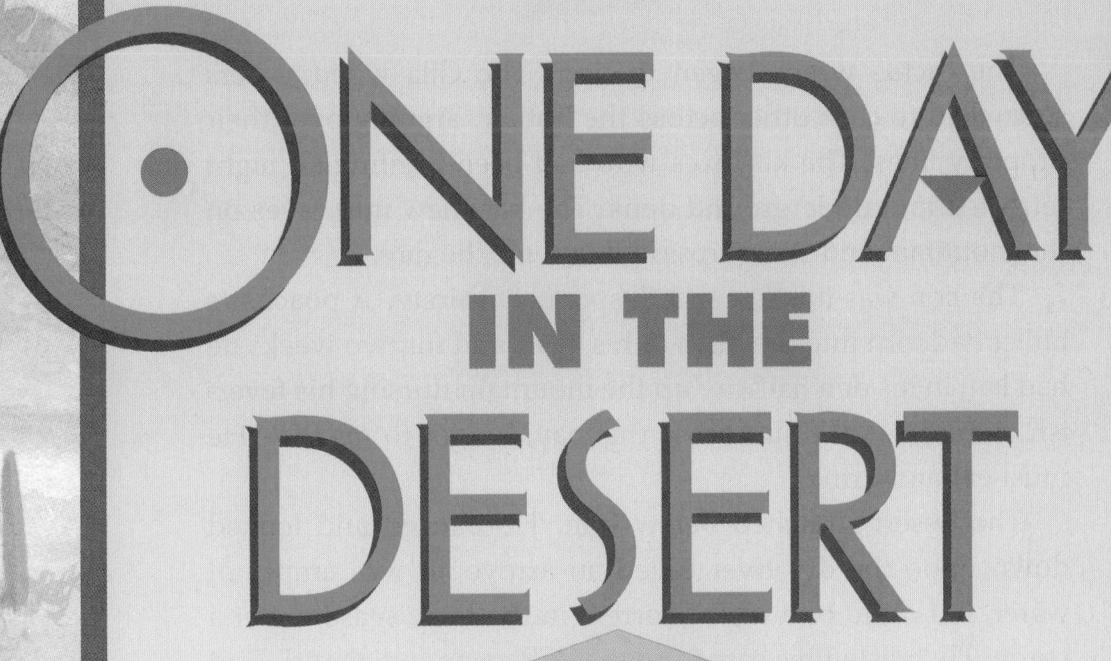

One Day in the Desert

by Jean Craighead George

illustrated by Oleana Kassian

At daybreak on July 10th a mountain lion limped toward a Papago Indian hut, a small structure of grass and sticks on the bank of a dry river in the Sonoran Desert of Arizona. Behind it rose Mount Scorpion, a dark-red mountain. In all directions from the mountain stretched the gray-green desert. It was dry, hot and still.

The cactus wrens began to sing. The Gila woodpeckers squawked to each other across the hot air, arguing over their property lines. The kit foxes who had been hunting all night retreated into underground dens. The bats flew into caves on the mountain and hung upside down for the day.

The lion was hungry and desperately thirsty. A poacher's bullet had torn into the flesh of his paw, and for two weeks he had lain in his den halfway up the mountain nursing his feverish wound. As the sun arose this day, he got to his feet. He must eat and drink.

The desert stretched below him. He paused and looked down upon the dry river called an arroyo. It was empty of water, but could be a raging torrent in the rainy season after a storm. He twisted his ears forward. A Papago Indian girl, Bird Wing, and her mother were walking along the bank of the dry river. They entered the hut.

The lion smelled their scent on the air and limped toward them. He was afraid of people, but this morning he was desperate.

Six feet (1.8 meters) in length, he stood almost 3 feet (a meter) tall. His fur was reddish brown above and white beneath. A black mustache marked his face. The backs of his ears and the tip of his tail were also black.

He growled as he came down the mountain, which was a huge clinker thrown up from the basement of the earth by an ancient volcano. Near its summit were pools where beaver and fish lived in the desert and which the mountain lion normally visited to hunt and drink. But today he went down, for it took less energy than going up.

The rising sun burned down from space, heating the rocks and the soils until they were hot even through the well-

padded feet of the lion. He stood in the shade of a rock at 8 A.M. when the temperature reached 80° Fahrenheit (26.6° Celsius).

This day would be memorable. Bird Wing, her mother, the lion and many of the animals below Mount Scorpion would be affected by July 10th. Some would survive and some would not, for the desert is ruthless.

The Sonoran Desert is one of four deserts marked by distinctive plants that make up the great North American Desert, which extends from central Mexico to almost the Canadian border. The North American Desert covers more than 500,000 square miles (1,300,000 square kilometers).

All of the four deserts have one thing in common—little rain. Less than 10 inches (24 centimeters) a year fall on the greater parts of these deserts. The temperatures, however, vary from below freezing to the low 120s F. (about 50° C.).

Each one is slightly different. The Great Basin desert of Oregon, California, Idaho, Nevada, Utah and Wyoming—the most northern and the coldest—is largely covered with sagebrush, a plant that has adapted to the dry cold.

The Mojave Desert of California is the smallest and driest, with less than 4 inches (10 centimeters) of rain a year. The teddy-bear cactus called cholla (choy • ya), a cactus so spiny it seems to have fur, dominates this desert.

The third, the Chihuahuan (chee • wa • wan) Desert, lies largely in Mexico. Only 10 percent of it is in the United States, in New Mexico, Arizona and Texas. On this desert the yuccas and agaves, or century plants, have adapted and grow abundantly, lending a special look to the land.

The fourth and most magnificent is the Sonoran Desert of Mexico and Arizona. Unlike the other deserts, it has two rainy seasons—showers in March and deluges in July and August. The rains nourish magnificent plants that support a great variety of creatures. The outstanding plant in this desert is the giant saguaro cactus, a tall plant that resembles a telephone pole with upturned arms. All the cacti—the saguaro, barrel, teddy bear and prickly pear—are unique to North America. They have evolved nowhere else in the world.

The North American Desert is dry because it is robbed of rain by the Pacific coast mountains. The clouds coming in from the ocean strike the high cold peaks and dump most of their moisture on the western side of the mountains. Practically no rain reaches the eastern side, which is in what is called the "rain shadow" by scientists.

All deserts are lands of extremes: too hot, too dry, too wet. Yet they abound with living things that have adjusted to these excesses. To fight dryness, plants store water in their tissues or drop their leaves to prevent evaporation from their broad surfaces. They also grow spines, which do not use much water and which cast shadows on the plant to protect it from the blazing sun. They thicken stems and leaves to hold water.

The animals adapt by seeking out cool microclimates, small shelters out of the terrible heat. The microclimates are burrows in the ground where it is cool, crevices and caves in rocks, or the shade. Because of the dryness, the thin desert air does not hold heat. Shady spots can be 20° F. (11° C.) cooler than out in the sun.

A few animals adapt to the harsh conditions by manufacturing water from the starch in the seeds they eat. The perky kangaroo rat is one of these. Others move in the cool of the night.

The coyote hunts in the dark, as do the deer, ring-tailed "cat" (cacomistle), desert fox, raccoon and lion. The honeypot ant, on the other hand, has such a tough outer skeleton that it can walk in extremely hot sunshine.

On July 10th the wounded mountain lion was forced to hunt in the heat of the day. He could not wait for darkness. He made his way slowly down the trail toward the Papago Indian hut.

By 9 A.M. he was above the dwelling on a mountain ledge. The temperature climbed another degree. He sought the shade of a giant saguaro cactus and lay down to rest.

The scent of lion reached the nose of a coyote who was cooling off under the dark embankment of the dry river not far from the Papago Indian hut. He lifted his head, flicked his ears nervously and got to his feet. He ran swiftly into his burrow beneath the roots of the ancient saguaro cactus that grew beside the hut.

The huge cactus was over 100 years old, stood 75 feet (22.5 meters) tall and weighed more than 6 tons (5.5 metric tons). The last of its watermelon-red fruits were ripe and on the ground. Bird Wing and her mother were going to gather them and boil them in the water they had carried in buckets from the village. The fruit makes a sweet, nourishing syrup.

At 11 A.M. they stretched out on their mats in the hut. It was much too hot to work. The temperature had reached 112° F. (44.4° C.).

The old cactus was drying up in the heat. It drew on the last of the water in the reservoir inside its trunk and shrank ever so slightly, for it could expand and contract like an accordion.

The mountain lion's tongue was swollen from lack of moisture. He got to his feet again.

A roadrunner, a ground-dwelling bird with a spiny crest and a long neck and legs, saw the lion pass his shady spot in the grass. He sped down the mountain, over the riverbank and into the dry riverbed. He stopped under the embankment where the coyote had been. There he lifted his feathers to keep cool. Bird feathers are perhaps the best protection from both heat and cold, for they form dead air space, and dead air is one of the best insulations.

The roadrunner passed a family of seven peccaries, piglike animals with coarse coats, tusks and almost no tails. They stay alive in the dry desert by eating the water-storing prickly pear cactus, spines and all. They were now lying in the cool of the paloverde trees that grow in thickets. Like the pencil-straight ocotillo and almost all the desert leafy plants, the paloverdes drop their leaves when the desert is extremely hot and dry. On July 10th they began falling faster and faster.

The scent of the lion reached the old boar. He lifted his head and watched the great beast. The lion turned away from the peccary family and limped toward the Indian hut. All the pigs, big and little, watched him.

A warm moist wind that had been moving northwest across the Gulf of Mexico for a day and a night met a cold wind blowing east from the Pacific coast mountains. The hot and cold air collided not far from the Mexico-Arizona border and exploded into a chain of white clouds. The meeting formed a stiff wind. It picked up the desert dust and carried it toward Mount Scorpion.

As the lion limped across the embankment under which the roadrunner was hiding, the air around him began to fill with dust.

Near the coyote den dwelled a tarantula, a spider almost as big as a man's fist and covered with furlike hairs. She looked like a long-legged bear, and she was sitting near the top of her burrow, a shaft she had dug straight down into the ground. The hot desert air forced her to let go with all eight of her legs. She dropped to the bottom of her shaft, where the air was cooler. The spider survives the heat by digging underground and by hunting at night. The moist crickets and other insects she eats quench her thirst.

A headstand beetle felt the heat of the day and became uncomfortable. He stopped hunting in the grass and scurried into the entrance of the tarantula hole. He was not afraid of the spider, with her poison fangs that kill prey, but he was wary of her. Hearing the spider coming up her shaft to see who was there, the headstand beetle got ready to fend her off. He stood on his head, aimed his rear end and mixed chemicals in his abdomen. The tarantula rushed at him and lifted her fangs. The headstand beetle shot a blistering-hot stream of a quinonoid chemical at the spider. She writhed and dropped to the bottom of her den. The headstand beetle hid under the grass plant by the tarantula's door.

The temperature rose several more degrees.

At 12:30 P.M. a desert tortoise, who was protected from the heat by two unusually thick shells of bone, went on eating the fruit of a prickly pear cactus. He was never thirsty. The moisture from the plants he ate was stored in his enormous bladder, a reservoir of pure water that desert tortoises have devised over the ages to adapt themselves to the dry heat. The water cools the reptiles on the hottest days and refreshes them on the driest.

The temperature reached 117° F. (47.2° C.). At last the tortoise felt warm. He turned around and pushed up on his toes. On his short legs he walked to his burrow under the paloverde bushes where the peccaries hunched, their eyes focused on the lion.

Inside his burrow the tortoise came upon a cottontail rabbit who had taken refuge there out of the hot sun. The tortoise could not go on. The heat poured in, and to lower the temperature he plugged up the entrance with his back feet. On the ceiling above his head clung a spiny-tailed lizard and a Texas banded gecko, reptiles who usually like the heat. At 12:30 P.M. on July 10th they sought the protection of the tortoise's burrow.

The temperature rose one more degree. A cactus wren who had sung at dawn slipped into her nest in a teddy-bear cactus at the edge of the paloverde thicket. She opened her beak to release heat.

The peccaries heard soft sounds like rain falling. Hundreds of small lizards who usually hunted the leaves of the paloverde, even on the hottest days, could no longer endure the high temperature. They were dropping to the ground and seeking shelter under sticks and stones.

A kangaroo rat was in her labyrinth under the leafless, pencillike ocotillo plants. She awakened when the temperature reached 119° F. (47.3° C.). Her bedroom near the surface of the desert floor had become uncomfortably hot. Her body was drying out. She scurried along a tunnel, turned a corner and ran down a slope toward a room under the giant saguaro cactus. She paused at her pantry to eat seeds of the mesquite tree before retiring to the cool, deep chamber. While she slept, her internal system converted the starch of the seeds into water and revived her dry body.

The lion walked into the paloverde bushes. The peccaries squealed in fright and trotted out into the terrible sunshine. In a cloud of dust they sped into the dry riverbed and frightened the roadrunner. He ran out from under the overhang and flew into the saguaro forest on the far side of the dry river. The pigs hid under the embankment where the roadrunner had been.

The injured lion could not chase the peccaries. He lifted his head, smelled the sweet piglets and climbed up the Indian trail till he was at the hut. Bird Wing and her mother were sleeping. He stared at them and crouched. Slinking low, he moved to a bucket, drank long and gratefully, then lay down in the doorway of the hut.

The temperature climbed one more degree. The birds stopped singing. Even the cicadas, who love hot weather and drum louder and faster in the heat, could no longer endure the fiery temperature. They stopped making sounds with their feet and wings and sat still. The Gila woodpecker flew into his hole in the giant saguaro. Below him, in one of his old nests, sat the sparrow-sized elf owl. He opened his beak and lifted his feathers.

Bird Wing was awakened by thirst. She tipped one of the water buckets and drank deeply. The desert was so quiet she became alarmed.

Clouds were racing toward Mount Scorpion. They were black and purple. Constant flashes of lightning illuminated them from within. She crept to the back of the hut and lay down beside her mother. She closed her eyes.

At 1:20 P.M. the temperature reached 121° F. (49.4° C.).

This hour on July 10th was the hottest hour on record at the bottom of Mount Scorpion.

Even the well-insulated honeypot ants could not tolerate the temperature. They ran toward the entrance of their labyrinth near a pack rat nest by the hut. Some managed to get underground in the caverns where sister ants hung from the ceilings. Forager honeypot ants store the sweets from plants they have gathered in the bellies of hanging ants, some of which become as round as balloons and as big as marbles. The last two foraging ants ran across the hot soil to get home. They shriveled and died in seconds.

The peccaries under the embankment dug into the earth to find coolness.

The clouds covered the sun.

Instantly, the temperature dropped four degrees.

The tortoise shoveled more dirt into the mouth of his burrow.

The thunder boomed like Indian drums.

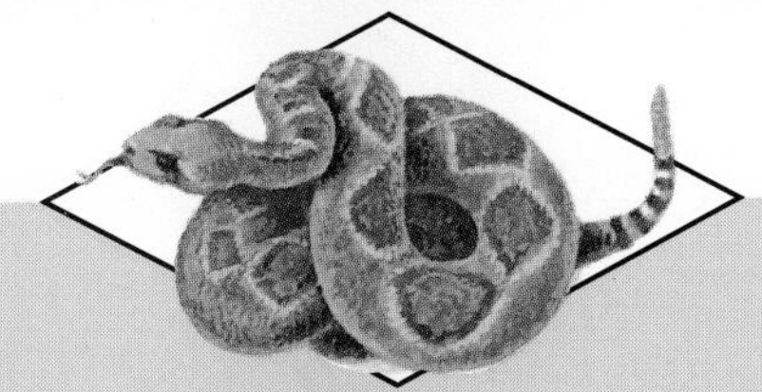

The kangaroo rat felt the earth tremble. She ran to her door, smelled rain on the air and scurried to a U-shaped tunnel. She went down it and up to a room at the top. There she tucked her nose into her groin to sleep.

The temperature dropped five more degrees. A rattlesnake came out of the pack rat's nest and slid back to his hunting spot at the rear of the hut. The cicadas sang again. The cactus wren looked out of the entrance of her ball nest in the teddy-bear cactus.

A thunderclap exploded sharply. Bird Wing awoke. She saw the lion stretched in the doorway. She took her mother's arm and shook her gently until she awoke. Signaling her to be quiet, she pointed to the mountain lion. Bird Wing's mother parted the grass at the rear of the hut and, after pushing Bird Wing out, backed out herself.

The rattlesnake buzzed a warning.

The sky darkened. Lightning danced from saguaro cactus to saguaro cactus. Bird Wing's mother looked at the clouds and the dry arroyo.

"We must get out of here," she said. "Follow me up the mountain." They scrambled over the rocks on hands and feet without looking back.

Huge raindrops splattered onto the dust. Bird Wing and her mother reached an overhanging rock on the mountain. Lightning flashed around them like white horsewhips.

The thunder cracked and boomed. Then water gushed out of the sky. The rain fell in such torrents that Bird Wing and her mother could not see the dry river, the hut or the old saguaro. They sat quietly, waiting and listening.

A flash of lightning shot out of a cloud and hit the old saguaro cactus. It smoked, split and fell to the ground. The elf owl flew into the downpour. His wings and body became so

wet, he soared down to the grass beneath the paloverde bushes. The woodpecker stayed where he was, bracing himself with his stiff tail.

The crash of the saguaro terrified the coyote. He darted out of his den under the tree and back to the dry riverbed. The peccaries dug deeper into the embankment. The roadrunner took to his feet and ran up the slope beyond the giant saguaro forest.

The rain became torrents, the torrents became waterfalls and the waterfalls cascaded out of the sky until all the moisture was wrung from the clouds. They drizzled and stopped giving rain. The storm clouds rumbled up the canyon above the dry riverbed.

The sun came out. Bird Wing and her mother did not move. They listened. The desert rocks dripped and the cacti crackled softly as they swelled with water. Cactus roots lie close to the surface, spreading out from the plants in all directions to absorb every possible drop of water. The roots send the water up into the trunks and barrels and pads to be stored.

A drumroll sounded up Scorpion Pass.

The peccaries heard it and darted out from under the embankment. They struggled up the bank and raced into the saguaro forest.

The lion got to his feet. He limped through the door.

The coyote rushed out of the dry riverbed. The wet elf owl hooked his beak around a twig of a paloverde and pulled himself upward toward higher limbs.

Water came bubbling and singing down the arroyo. It filled the riverbed from bank to bank, then rose like a great cement wall, a flash flood that filled the canyon. It swept over the embankment, over the hut, over the old saguaro cactus. It rose higher, thundered into the paloverdes and roared over the

rocks at the foot of the mountain. It boomed into the valley, spread out and disappeared into the dry earth.

The coyote was washed out from under the embankment. He tumbled head over heels, swam to the surface and climbed onto an uprooted mass of prickly pears. On this he sailed into the valley and was dropped safely onto the outwash plain when the water went into the ground. Stunned, he shook himself and looked around. Before him the half-drowned pack rat struggled. Recovering his wits, the coyote pounced upon him.

The lion was lifted up by the flood and thrown against a clump of ocotillo. He clung to it for a moment, then, too weak to struggle, slipped beneath the water.

The flash flood that had trickled, then roared, trickled and then was gone. The banks of the arroyo dripped. Bird Wing and her mother walked to the spot where their hut had been. There was no sign of house, pack rat nest, saguaro or lion.

"But for the lion, we would be dead," said Bird Wing. "We must thank him." She faced the mountain and closed her eyes for a moment. Her mother picked up an ocotillo stick and turned it over in her hand.

"We will rebuild our house up the mountain above the flood line," she said. Bird Wing nodded vigorously and gathered sticks, too.

The kangaroo rat sat in her room above the U trap that had stopped the water from reaching her. She waited until the floodwaters seeped into the ground. Then she began to repair her labyrinth.

The peccaries came out of the saguaro forest and rooted for insects among the billions of seeds that had been dumped on the land by the flood. The land was greening, the sky was blue. The roadrunner came back to the saguaro forest, ran down a young snake and ate it. The cactus wren and owl did not call. The rattlesnake did not rattle. They had not survived the wrath of the desert on this day, July 10th.

Bird Wing walked to the arroyo edge. The earth trembled at her feet. She looked down. Plugs of sand popped out of the wet bank like corks. In each hole sat a grinning spadefoot toad, creatures who must grow up in the water. Then what were they doing in the desert? Waiting for just this moment.

They hopped into the brilliant sunshine and leaped into the puddles in the arroyo. Quickly they laid eggs and quickly they ate and dug backward into the sand with the spades on their feet. Far underground their skins secreted a sticky gelatin that would prevent them from drying up. In this manner they survived the hot waterless desert.

The warm sunlight of late afternoon heated the water in the puddles, speeding up the development of the toad eggs. They must hatch into pollywogs and change into toads before the blazing heat dried up the puddles.

At 7:33 P.M. soft blue and purple light swept over the beautiful desert. In the puddles pollywogs swam.

THINK IT OVER

1. *Describe the changes in weather in the Sonoran Desert on July 10th, from 8 A.M. to 7:33 P.M.*
2. *Why had the mountain lion not hunted for two weeks?*
3. *Do you think the author is correct when she says, "the desert is ruthless"? Explain your answer.*
4. *After the flood, why does Bird Wing say that she wants to thank the mountain lion?*

WRITE

The author describes many different animals in this story. Choose one desert animal that interests you and write a name poem about it. Use each letter in the animal's name to start a line of the poem.

WORDS ABOUT THE AUTHOR:

Jean Craighead George

Jean George doesn't mind getting up at 5:30 on Sunday morning if she can share the wonders of nature. That is what she does when she leads nature walks in the town where she lives. She has been in love with nature since she was a child.

"All through my childhood, my parents had taken the three of us (I have identical twin brothers) into the forests along the Potomac River outside of Washington, D.C., where I was born," she remembers.

Jean George spent summers on a farm in Pennsylvania, where she learned a lot about nature. She learned about trees, flowers, birds, and insects. She camped on the sandy islands and went canoeing and fishing. She felt close to nature even though she grew up in a big city, and she has kept this feeling all her life.

Jean George's family helped get her love for nature started. Her father was an entomologist. He studied insects. Her twin brothers grew up to be ecologists. They study the ways plants and animals live in nature. Ms. George and her family often took care of wild animals right in their home. When Jean George won the Newbery Medal for *Julie of the Wolves,* she especially thanked her parents. She said they gave her "a love of nature and a deep respect for the earth and its precious cargo of life."

JACKRABBIT

from *Desert Voices*

by Byrd Baylor
illustrated by Peter Parnall

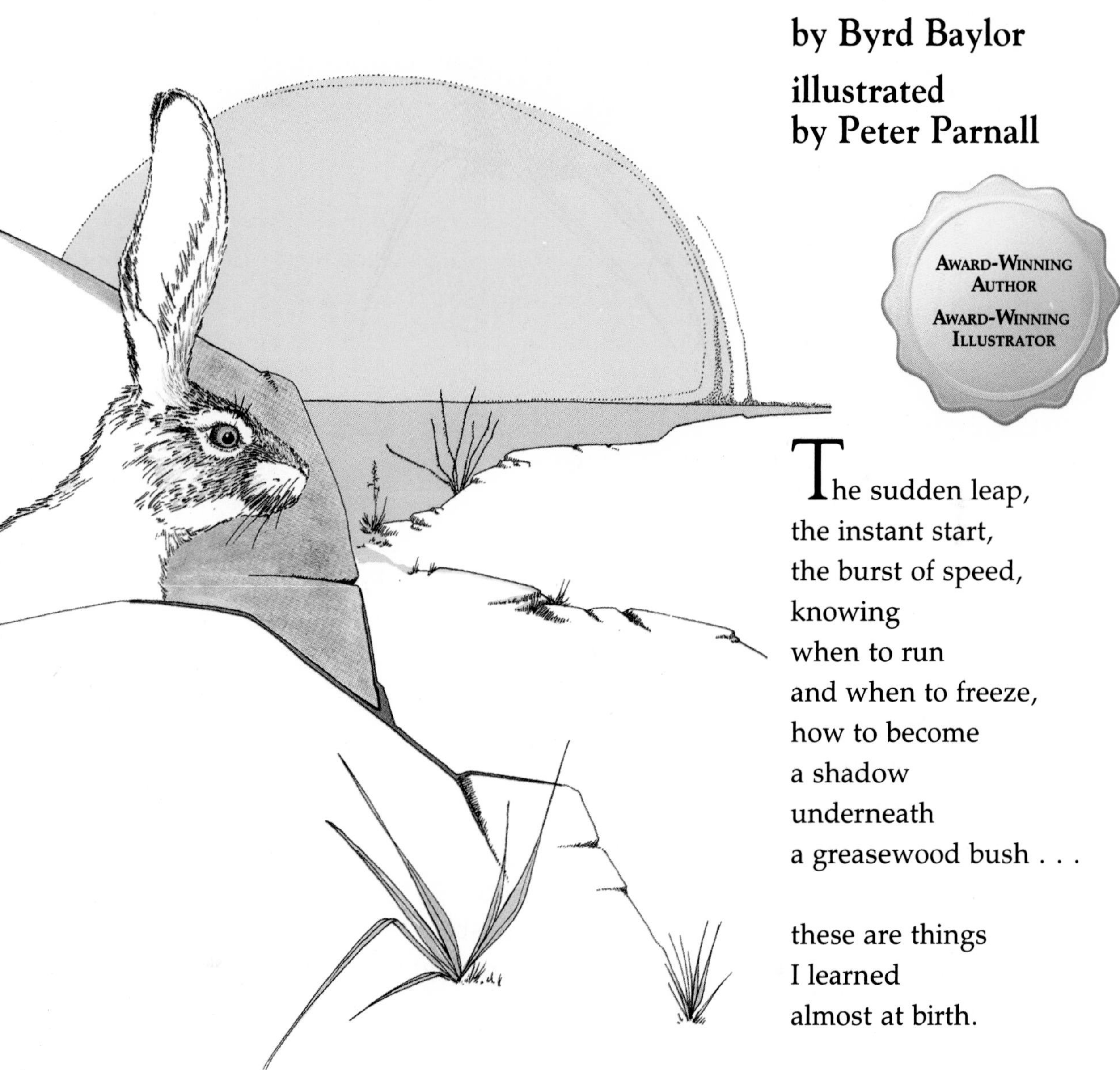

Award-Winning Author
Award-Winning Illustrator

The sudden leap,
the instant start,
the burst of speed,
knowing
when to run
and when to freeze,
how to become
a shadow
underneath
a greasewood bush . . .

these are things
I learned
almost at birth.

Now
I lie
on the shadow-side
of a clump of grass.
My long ears bring me
every far-off footstep,
every twig that snaps,
every rustle in the weeds.

I watch
Coyote move
from bush to bush.

I wait.
He's almost here.

Now . . .

Now I go
like a zig-zag
lightning flash.
With my ears laid back,
I sail.

Jumping gullies
and bushes and rocks,
doubling back,
circling,
jumping high
to see where my enemy is,
warning rabbits
along the way,
I go.

I hardly touch
the ground.

And suddenly
I disappear.

Let Coyote stand there
sniffing
old jackrabbit trails.

Where I am now
is a
jackrabbit secret.

THEME WRAP-UP

LIFE IN THE DESERT

What difficulties and dangers are faced by the desert animals in the selections? What characteristics do they have in common that help them survive these dangers?

Which do you think are better equipped to live in the desert, the animals you have read about, or people? Explain your reasons for thinking as you do.

WRITER'S WORKSHOP How are other American deserts different from the Sonoran Desert of Arizona? In the library, find information about other deserts, and choose one that is different from the Sonoran Desert. Make notes about the differences, and use your notes to write a paragraph of contrast. Be sure to include any photographs or other interesting material you find in your research.

wolfe
No.830806
250ml
KIMAX

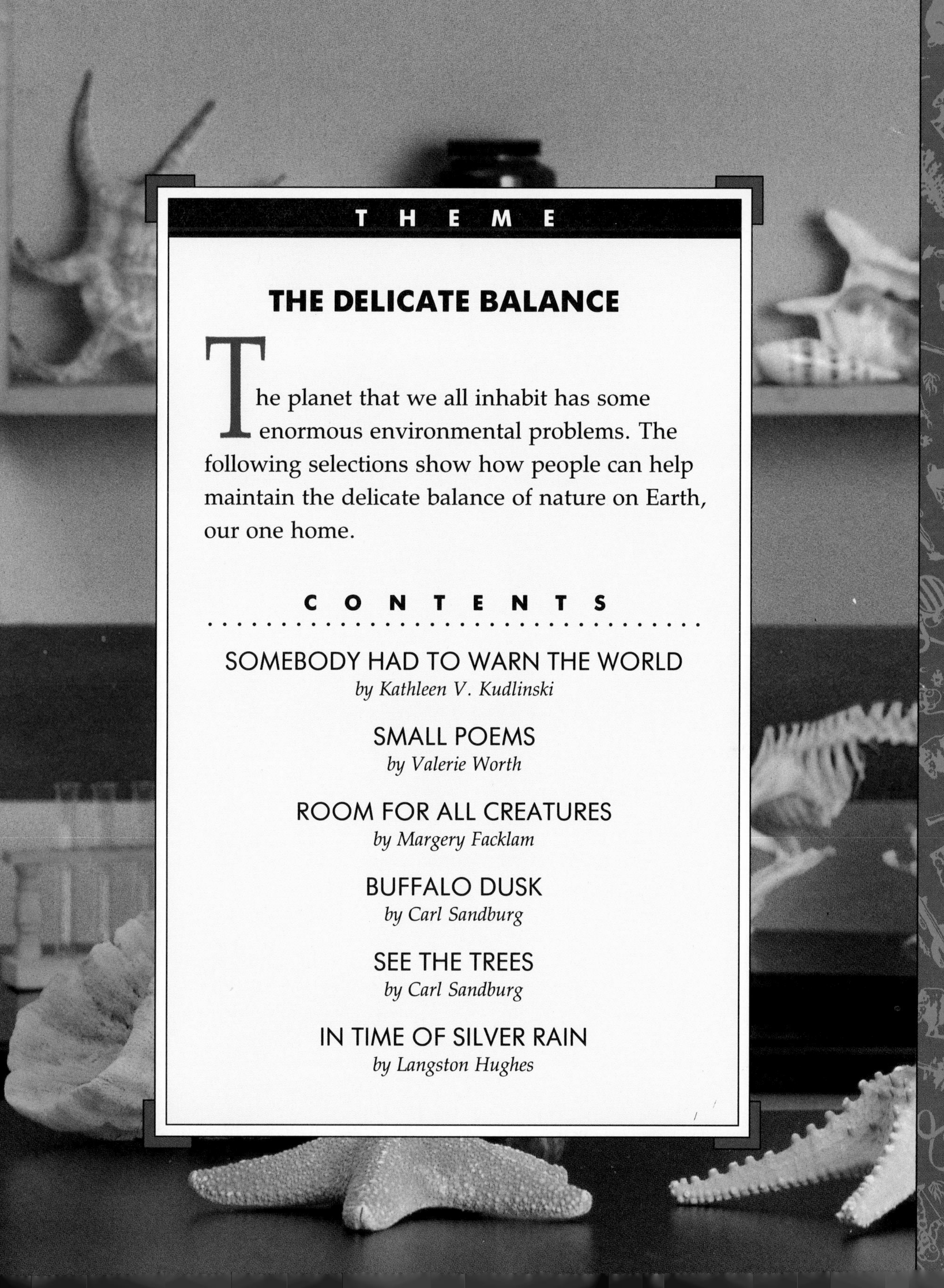

THEME

THE DELICATE BALANCE

The planet that we all inhabit has some enormous environmental problems. The following selections show how people can help maintain the delicate balance of nature on Earth, our one home.

CONTENTS

SOMEBODY HAD TO WARN THE WORLD

As a child, Rachel Carson had two loves —studying about the sea, and writing. Rachel expected that a day would come when she would have to choose between the two, but she was wrong. By 1955, Rachel Carson was known the world over as a scientist who studied and wrote about the sea.

Whenever she could, Rachel traveled along the Atlantic seacoast, taking notes for her third book, *The Edge of the Sea*. Once she bragged that she and her mother had driven 2,000 miles in just a few months. Muffy, a favorite cat, traveled with them. They visited coral beaches in Florida, sandy beaches in North Carolina, and her own rocky Maine coast. Rachel wanted to know which animals lived where, and why.

from *Rachel Carson: Pioneer of Ecology* by Kathleen V. Kudlinski

illustrated by Goro Sasaki

The Edge of the Sea needed many drawings. Rachel asked Bob Hines, the Fish and Wildlife artist, to illustrate her book. Bob joined Rachel, her mother, and Muffy in their wanderings up and down the Atlantic coast whenever he could. He drew pictures of the live animals Rachel found. Often when she was working, Rachel forgot all about time. She would stand for hours in icy-cold tide pools in Maine, watching tiny animals. Sometimes her legs would get so numb she couldn't walk. Bob would pick her up like a stack of books, and carry her back to the warmth of her car.

Then Rachel would head back to Silver Spring or to Maine to write and rewrite the book. She described hundreds of the animals she had seen on coral, sandy, and rocky beaches. She explained how the animals' lives were shaped by these different environments. And her book showed the readers that they, too, fit into an environment.

from *The Edge of the Sea*

The edge of the sea
is a strange and beautiful place.
All through the long history of Earth
it has been an area of unrest
where waves have broken heavily against the land,
where the tides have pressed forward over the
continents, receded, and then returned.
For no two successive days
is the shoreline precisely the same.

In October of 1955, *The Edge of the Sea* reached bookstores. It was another instant best-seller. Everyone wanted to meet the famous Rachel Carson. Her fans found her in beauty parlors when her hair was up in curlers. They even knocked on her hotel room door before she was dressed in the morning.

Only in tiny West Southport, Maine, could she relax.

Rachel had become close friends with her neighbors, Stanley and Dorothy Freeman. Rachel and Dorothy shared a love of nature, fine music, and the sea.

Rachel's niece Marjie often came on visits to Maine with her son, Roger. She was ill with arthritis and needed help with her little boy. When Roger was a baby, his father had died. Now Rachel was like a loving grandmother to him. Some of Roger's first words were the names of seashells that Rachel had shown him as they walked along beaches.

From their times together, she wrote a magazine article about sharing nature with children. The most important thing for them to learn, she wrote, is "a sense of the beautiful, the excitement of the new and the unknown."

When the Freemans' grandchildren came to play with Roger, Rachel would lead them all down the steps behind her house to the ocean. "Rachel answered all their questions. A microscope always sat ready in the living room for closer looks at the animals they found," the children's mother remembered. "Before we could have snacks, we had to carry everything back down the steps to the water and put each animal right back where we had found it."

There were fireworks shot from Rachel's rocky cliffs on the Fourth of July, and many nature walks through the quiet Maine woods. But Rachel the writer was restless. The strain of family problems, fame, and her own poor health were wearing her out. She needed a new project to give her life a fresh direction.

The idea came in a letter. A friend wrote to tell her of the horrible deaths of fourteen robins after a bug poison, DDT, was sprayed over her yard. Could Rachel do something?

In the 1950s, chemical companies were allowed to sell almost any kind of poison to kill bugs, weeds, molds, and other pests. Millions of tons of these pesticides were used.

Many scientists were worried. What were all those poisons doing to other animals, to the soils, and to the seas?

Rachel decided to write an article. No magazine would print it. They didn't think her facts were right. The chemical companies had told everyone that their poisons were safe. So had the government. Yet the more research Rachel did, the more upset she became.

The poisons were spreading through the world, making people and animals sick. If people knew how dangerous the poisons were, they wouldn't buy them anymore. They would be angry with the people who made them and with the government that said pesticides were safe. The powerful companies that made pesticides would fight to keep her story quiet. The Department of Agriculture would argue that she was wrong.

But somebody had to warn the world. Somebody who was both a scientist and a writer.

Was sharing the truth worth the battle Rachel knew she would face? "Even knowing that it would force her into the spotlight, a role that she hated, she was sure she was right," a friend remembered. Rachel *had* to write the book.

Rachel kept her new book, *Silent Spring*, a secret. The book had to be as strong as it could be before its enemies found out about it. Rachel double-checked every fact. She asked other scientists to read parts of the book to be sure she was right. And she asked them to help her keep the secret of *Silent Spring*.

The pesticide problem was worse than anyone knew. In the 1950s, most people had never heard of pollution. They believed that the government would protect them from any danger. Rachel was learning that this was not true.

Scientists had made dreadful poisons that could end all life on Earth. If people kept using these chemicals, springtime might someday come silently, with no birds left to sing, and no people left to hear them. The more Rachel learned, the more determined she was to write the book. It wasn't easy for her.

A neighbor remembered that "Rachel would do all the household chores first and try to take care of the family, and then she would try to find time to work." Twice a year, everything was moved to Maine or back to Maryland. It was no wonder that work on *Silent Spring* went slowly.

Rachel went back to writing, working through one illness after another. First it was the flu, then a painful stomach ulcer. Arthritis and infections in her knees kept her from walking for months. An eye infection made her blind for a few weeks. So many bad things were happening that Rachel said she felt like she was under an evil spell that would never let her finish *Silent Spring*.

Worst of all, she learned that she had cancer, and that it was going to kill her. Another person might have given up writing, but Rachel said, "Knowing the facts as I did, I could not rest . . ."

Now she studied about cancer, as well as pesticides. These facts went into new chapters about how poisons in the environment cause cancer. Did she have time to finish *Silent Spring*? She had to. All life on Earth was in danger, not just her own.

from *Silent Spring*

There was a strange stillness. The birds,
for example—where had they gone? Many people
spoke of them, puzzled and disturbed. The feeding
stations in the backyards were deserted.
The few birds seen anywhere were moribund;
they trembled violently and could not fly.
It was a spring without voices.
On the mornings that had once throbbed with
the dawn chorus of robins, catbirds, doves, jays, wrens,
and scores of other bird voices there was now no sound;
only silence lay over the fields and woods and marsh.

Early in 1962, *Silent Spring* was done. After four years, the article no one would publish had grown into an enormous book, beautifully written and full of complicated scientific ideas. But would it work as a warning? Would it make people want to change things? Marie[1] sent *Silent Spring* to Rachel's publisher and to *The New Yorker* magazine. Rachel wanted to hear what the editors thought.

Within a week, she got a late-night phone call. Mr. William Shawn, editor of *The New Yorker*, had just finished reading her work. He couldn't wait until the next morning to tell her how wonderful it was. He was horrified by the things he had learned from *Silent Spring*. How could this have happened? What could be done about it?

[1]Marie Rodell, Rachel's agent

That was exactly what Rachel wanted to hear. She knew now that *Silent Spring* would work. Rachel picked up her cat and walked stiffly into her study. In spite of all her sickness, Rachel had reached her goal. Finally she could rest. She put on a classical record, sank into a deep chair, and cried with relief.

Rachel didn't get much of a rest. When parts of *Silent Spring* were printed in *The New Yorker* a few months later, it shocked the whole country. Readers sent thousands of angry letters to newspapers, to the chemical companies, and to the government. As Rachel had expected, pesticide makers were furious.

Men from the chemical companies and the Department of Agriculture argued with her in newspapers, magazines, the TV, and radio. Some tried to prove her facts wrong. Others said she didn't know enough about science to understand the things she was writing about. One said, "Her book is even more poisonous than the pesticides."

President John F. Kennedy asked for a special report from top scientists to decide who was right. When the report came out, it agreed with Rachel. New laws were made to limit chemical pollution in the United States and to find other ways to control insect pests.

Awards and offers to travel and speak flooded in to Rachel. She was too sick to do very much. She worked to make her article about children and nature into a book. She never finished it, but *The Sense of Wonder* was published after she died.

from *The Sense of Wonder*

One stormy autumn night when my nephew Roger
was about twenty months old I wrapped him in a blanket
and carried him down to the beach in the rainy darkness.
Out there, just at the edge of where-we-couldn't-see,
big waves were thundering in,
dimly seen white shapes that boomed and shouted
and threw great handfuls of froth at us.
Together we laughed for pure joy—he a baby
meeting for the first time the wild tumult of Oceanus,
I with the salt of half a lifetime of sea love in me.
But I think we felt the same spine-tingling response
to the vast, roaring ocean and the wild night around us.

Even though she was in pain most of the time, Rachel agreed to be on television. Many thousands of people had read her book, but on TV, she could tell millions more about the danger of using too many pesticides. On the same show, a man from a chemical company tried to prove she was wrong. Rachel was still a nervous speaker, but she knew her facts were true. She said, "Man is a part of nature, and his war against nature is . . . a war against himself." The viewers believed her.

Silent Spring was published in dozens of other countries in 1963. No matter what language it was printed in, the message was the same: We must be more careful about what we do to the Earth. Around the world, new laws were made about pesticides.

Rachel spent the next summer in Maine. One afternoon, she and Dorothy Freeman sat at the top of a rocky cliff near Rachel's house. They listened to the sounds of the sea below them and watched monarch butterflies heading south for the winter. As the butterflies danced along the cliff's edge, Rachel and Dorothy wondered how many would ever be back. Most would never live to return, they realized. The two friends were not sad about it. That was how life was for butterflies.

Later that day, Rachel wrote a note to explain to Dorothy what "those fluttering bits of life taught me this morning." She said she had found a "deep happiness" in knowing that "it is a natural and not unhappy thing that a life comes to its end."

A few months after Rachel returned to Silver Spring, her own life came to its end. She died on April 14, 1964. But the work of her books went on.

Her writings about the sea showed how all life was tied together. *Silent Spring* showed how the future of all life depended on what we do. Over the years, Rachel Carson's love of nature and her beautiful writing have helped to change the way a world of people looks at the life of their planet.

Think It Over

1. *Why did somebody like Rachel Carson have to warn the world?*
2. *How did Rachel do the research for her book* The Edge of the Sea?
3. *Why did Rachel give the title* Silent Spring *to her book about pesticides?*
4. *Why were the chemical companies and the Department of Agriculture furious with Rachel Carson?*
5. *In what sense does Rachel Carson's work "live on," even after her death?*

Write

Rachel Carson described the wonders of nature with careful detail. Select a particular shell, rock, or plant that interests you. Write a paragraph describing your choice.

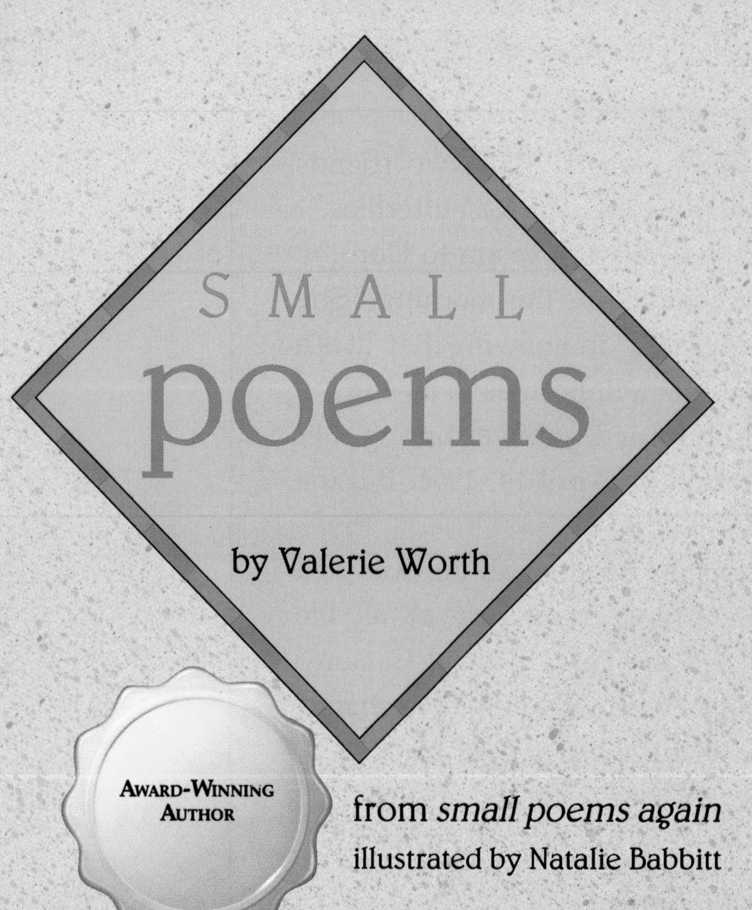

AWARD-WINNING AUTHOR

from *small poems again*
illustrated by Natalie Babbitt

seashell

My father's mother
Picked up the shell
And turned it about
In her hand that was
Crinkled, glossy and
Twined with veins,
The fingers rumpled
Into soft roses
At the knuckles, and
She said, "Why did
That little creature
Take so much trouble
To be beautiful?"

robins

Look how
Last year's
Leaves, faded
So gray
And brown,

Blunder
Along
Like flimsy
Flightless
Birds,

Stumbling
Beak over
Tail
Before
The wind.

But no,
Wait:
Today
They right
Themselves,

And turn
To the
Stout slate
And ruddy
Rust

Of robins,
Running
On steady
Stems across
The ground.

starfish

Spined
With sparks,
Limbed
With flames,

Climbing
The dark
To cling
And shine

Until the
Slow tide
Turns
Again:

Not even
Knowing
What stars
Are,

But
Even so,
The
Same.

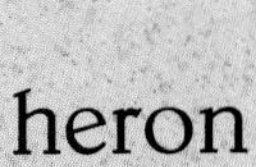

heron

Only
Fools
Pursue
Their
Prey.

Mine
Comes to
Me, while
I stand and
Reflect:

Quick silver
Visions
Swimming into
My glassy
Reverie,

Seized
By a mere
Nod of
My wise
Beak.

ROOM FOR ALL CREATURES

from
And Then There Was One

by Margery Facklam

illustrated by Pamela Johnson

NO PLACE TO LIVE

When it was first developed, everyone welcomed the pesticide DDT as the best thing ever to happen to agriculture. Here at last was a way to wipe out crop-eating insects. And no more mosquitoes! But no one counted on the other things DDT would do.

When a lot of polar bears were dying in the Arctic, scientists wanted to know why. They were surprised to discover the bears were full of DDT. How could that be? No one had sprayed the Arctic with pesticide.

AND·THEN·THERE·WAS·ONE
The Mysteries of Extinction

Polar bear and cubs

What we hadn't known was that DDT works its way up the food chain. The DDT that reached the polar bears actually came from California fruit orchards. When fruit growers sprayed their trees, DDT was carried by winds out over the ocean. There it settled on algae and seaweed and on the masses of tiny floating animals called plankton, which many fish and whales feed on. When the fish swam north, they were eaten by polar bears. DDT stayed in the fish, but even more stayed in the polar bears. The bigger the animal, the more DDT built up in its system.

If a person eats fruit sprayed with DDT, the pesticide does not leave the body for a long time. It was only when human babies began getting sick because their mothers' milk contained DDT that the pesticide was finally outlawed.

In a wide belt around the equator, tropical rain forests are swarming with life. Although rain forests take up only a sixth of the earth's surface, they are home to almost half the world's plant and animal species. Scientists believe there are thousands, and maybe millions, of species in the rain forests that haven't even been described and named, or perhaps even found yet. Among these may be plants we could use for medicine or food. What fascinating birds or reptiles or insects are we missing?

We may never know. The tropical rain forests are disappearing at the rate of 50 acres every minute! That's like mowing down the whole state of West Virginia every year. Trees are cut for lumber or bulldozed down to make room for farms and towns. When Dr. Jane Goodall went to Africa to study chimpanzees in Kenya in 1960, the chimpanzees had a territory of sixty square miles. Today the chimps of Kenya are limited to a two-mile strip of forest. The great jungles of Indonesia, home of the orangutans, are being cut down for lumber, and much of the exported wood is used to make throwaway plywood forms to mold concrete for buildings.

It's been said that when America was new, with only thirteen states, the forests were so thick that a squirrel could hop from tree to tree all the way from Maine to Florida and never touch ground. Not so today. Our large forests are few and far between, and even those are now in danger. A major problem is *acid rain*. It sounds like something from a monster movie, but it's not. It's real rain, but it's full of chemicals from factories, and it eats tree bark and leaves. It seeps into the forest floor and poisons the soil. It falls into lakes and ponds and kills the fish. Acid rain is carried around the world on currents of air. Silent and invisible, it kills plants and animals and even eats into stone.

Wetlands are not wastelands. They teem with life, but they're disappearing fast. Bogs, swamps, and marshes are being filled in to make room for waterfront apartments and hotels. The Everglades in Florida is a shallow river of grass that once covered seven million acres. It was alive with millions of water birds and other animals. But now, more than half of it has been drained to make room for farms, industries, and homes. Miami is one of the world's fastest growing cities. One hundred thousand people settle there each year, and ten million tourists visit. Each person uses 200 gallons of water a day, and all of it must come from the Everglades. It's no wonder there is less and less space for alligators, manatees, and water birds.

In the United States alone, we are paving over more than 3 million acres for cities, highways, airports, and water projects *each year*. Where mankind moves in, must animals always move out? Or can we find ways to make room for all creatures?

American alligator

AND NOW THE GOOD NEWS

A "doomsday" book lists all the animals in danger of extinction. Its official name is *The Red Data Book.* It's published each year by the International Union for Conservation of Nature and Natural Resources. In a book of so much bad news, can we ever find anything good?

The good news is that some animals get off the list, when they make a comeback. The American alligator was once in danger of extinction because a lot of people thought that alligator skin looked better on shoes and luggage than on the alligator. Then a law was passed in the 1970s to protect the big reptiles from harm. Now there are so many alligators that they are causing problems. They are turning up on golf courses and in private lakes. One huge alligator was found basking in the sun on a runway at the West Palm Beach International Airport. The alligator population is up to a million, and some way must be found for alligators and people to live side by side.

When a large predator like the alligator thrives, dozens of smaller animals thrive with it. Alligators make room for an entire community in their water holes. Fish, turtles, snakes, frogs, and snails settle in. Herons, ibis, egrets, spoonbills, and other birds stay close because they can find food, and so do raccoons, muskrats, wild pigs, and other mammals. As long as the alligator keeps the water hole weeded and open, the whole community lives well.

Bald eagle chick

Zoos and wildlife sanctuaries are part of the good news. About 90 percent of the mammals and 75 percent of the birds in American zoos were born in captivity. No longer can an expedition go into the jungle and capture a tiger or monkeys. No one is allowed to catch a dolphin in the open ocean for a marine exhibit or research without permission from the government. Unfortunately, many dolphins, seals, and sea turtles are trapped illegally in fishing nets that trail for miles behind commercial fishing ships. People are trying to design safer nets that will allow turtles and sea mammals to escape if they are caught. They are also trying out different regulations that would require fishing ships to haul in nets more frequently, which could save large animals caught in them from drowning.

For many wildlife experts, the big goal is to breed animals in captivity and return them to their native homes. But that's not as easy as it sounds. You might think that all you'd have to do is open a cage to let an animal know it's free, but that doesn't always work. In Indonesia, workers at one rehabilitation center try to move once-captive orangutans back into the jungle, but many of the animals won't go. The big red apes like to hang around the feeding station, where bananas and other good food are handed out. When workers take them by the hand and lead them into the forests, some orangutans drag their feet like ornery children. A few may stay alone in the forest overnight, but the next morning they are back in time for breakfast. Part of the problem is too little forest and too many captured orangutans that need homes in it.

The National Wildlife Refuge System cares for 400 habitats from the Florida Keys to Alaska. They protect green sea turtles and monk seals in Hawaii, whooping cranes in Texas, and trumpeter swans in Montana. They provide safe feeding and resting grounds for the annual migrations of thousands of ducks, geese, and other birds.

Bald eagles have found help in the refuge system, too. When the eagle was chosen as our national symbol in 1782, there were probably 75,000 of the big birds nesting in the U.S. territory. Today there are fewer than 3,000. It wasn't until 1940, when bald eagles were on the edge of extinction, that Congress passed a law to protect them. But even when they were safe from hunters, eagles' eggs were destroyed by DDT because the adult birds had eaten fish contaminated by the pesticide.

Now the wildlife experts take the first clutch of eggs from an eagle's nest and put them in an incubator until they hatch. With her eggs gone, the eagle will lay a second clutch of eggs, which she will raise. When an eagle is found without eggs, or whose chicks have died, the scientists place three-week-old eaglets from an incubator in its nest. The foster parents usually adopt the chicks and raise them as their own.

Carolina parakeet, extinct 1910

The whooping crane is another success story. In 1941, there were only sixteen whooping cranes, but now there are more than 200. They are still on the endangered list, but their numbers are growing.

The Endangered Species Act became law in 1973. It makes it a crime for anyone to sell or transport an endangered species or a product made from the body of an endangered species. That means people can't sell rhinoceros horns or tiger skins. No longer can certain tropical birds be transported or sold or kept as pets. It is illegal for an endangered animal to be "killed, hunted, collected, harassed, harmed, pursued, shot, trapped, wounded, or captured." The law also sets aside some "critical" habitats for some species. That means that no federal government agency can use the habitat of an endangered species.

Unfortunately, it does not protect the same area from private projects. For example, where an eagle is nesting, a federal highway or an army base can't be built because it's paid for by our taxes. But someone might be able to build houses or a shopping mall or a factory, unless state or local governments protect the land.

The shy, bashful marine mammal called a manatee is a distant cousin to the elephant, although it looks like a cross between a seal and a baby hippo. Some grow to be 12 feet long and weigh 3,000 pounds. They used to live a quiet life in Florida's waterways, but there are few left. Now they must compete with hundreds of thousands of small power boats. Someone has said that the manatee is going off the earth for the same reason that television shows go off the air—no sponsor. Who will sponsor the gentle manatee and other animals that cannot speak for themselves?

We tend to forget that we are the only creatures who can make choices. Instead of adapting to an environment, we can change it. If we're cold, we can put on warm clothes and turn up the heat. Too hot? Just turn on the air conditioner. Want to fly? Just get on an airplane. Run out of food? Buy groceries from anywhere on earth at the supermarket. We can change the rules. We are the animals with imagination and power.

Manatee

All creatures large and small have the right to live because they share their home planet with us. We can do nothing about the way animals adapt to the changes in the environment, but we *can* do something about how the environment changes. We can keep the earth clean. We can stop polluting and destroying the habitats of other living things. We can learn from the past and begin planning for the future.

Sea otter

Think It Over

1. *What problems have people caused for animals? What are some of the solutions to these problems?*
2. *How did DDT sprayed in California end up in polar bears in the Arctic?*
3. *Why does the author tell us that "we are the animals with imagination and power"?*
4. *Name some animals that have been saved from the brink of extinction. What are some reasons why they are making comebacks?*

Write

Choose one animal mentioned in this selection that you would like to protect. Create a poster that urges people to help save the animal.

BUFFALO DUSK

by Carl Sandburg

The buffaloes are gone.
And those who saw the buffaloes are gone.
Those who saw the buffaloes by thousands
   and how they pawed the prairie sod
   into dust with their hoofs,
   their great heads down pawing
   on in a great pageant of dusk,
Those who saw the buffaloes are gone.
And the buffaloes are gone.

SEE THE TREES

by Carl Sandburg

See the trees lean
   to the wind's way of learning.
See the dirt of the hills shape
   to the water's way of learning.
See the lift of it all
   go the way
   the biggest wind
   and the strongest water
   want it.

Detail of *The Buffalo Trail*, 1867–68
Courtesy, Museum of Fine Arts, Boston
Karolik Collection

In Time of Silver Rain

by Langston Hughes

In time of silver rain
The earth
Puts forth new life again,
Green grasses grow
And flowers lift their heads,
And over all the plain
The wonder spreads
    Of life,
    Of life,
    Of life!

In time of silver rain
The butterflies
Lift silken wings
To catch a rainbow cry,
And trees put forth
New leaves to sing
In joy beneath the sky
As down the roadway
Passing boys and girls
Go singing, too,
In time of silver rain
    When spring
    And life
    Are new.

Springtime Fantasy by Adolphe Faugeron, French, Born 1866

THEME WRAP-UP

THE DELICATE BALANCE

What message do the selections and poems have in common? Why is it an important message?

Which do you think is a more effective warning about ecological problems, a poem such as "Buffalo Dusk" or a nonfiction selection such as "Room for All Creatures"? Tell why you think as you do.

WRITER'S WORKSHOP Choose an endangered animal, one of those described in the selections or another endangered animal that you know about, and write a poem about it. Include details about the animal's appearance, its habitat, and the reason it is endangered. The purpose of your poem should be to convince people of the importance of saving the animal. Trade poems with a partner, and discuss whether adding or taking out details would improve the poems.

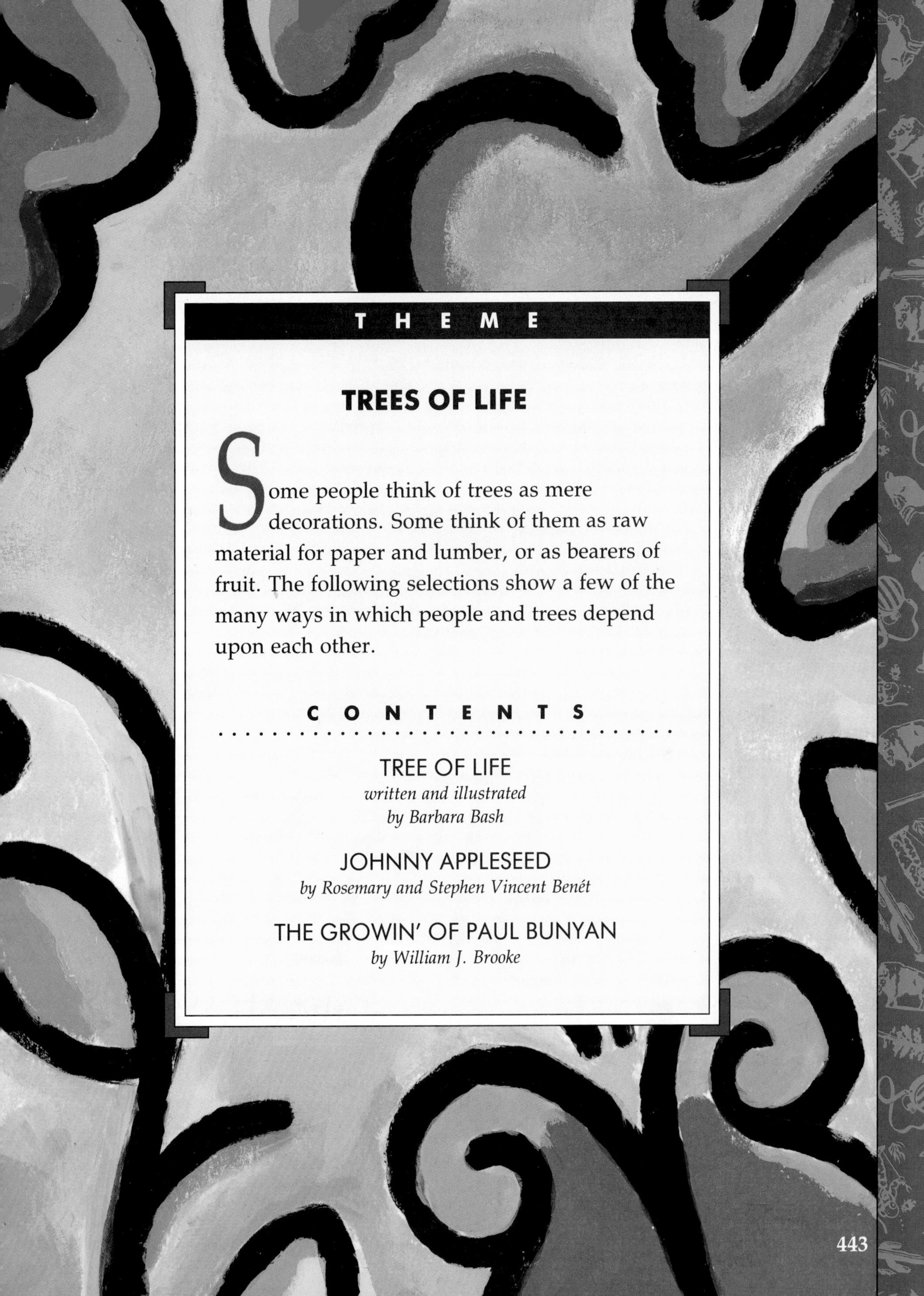

THEME

TREES OF LIFE

Some people think of trees as mere decorations. Some think of them as raw material for paper and lumber, or as bearers of fruit. The following selections show a few of the many ways in which people and trees depend upon each other.

CONTENTS

TREE TALES
TREE OF LIFE
The World of the African Baobab
BARBARA BASH

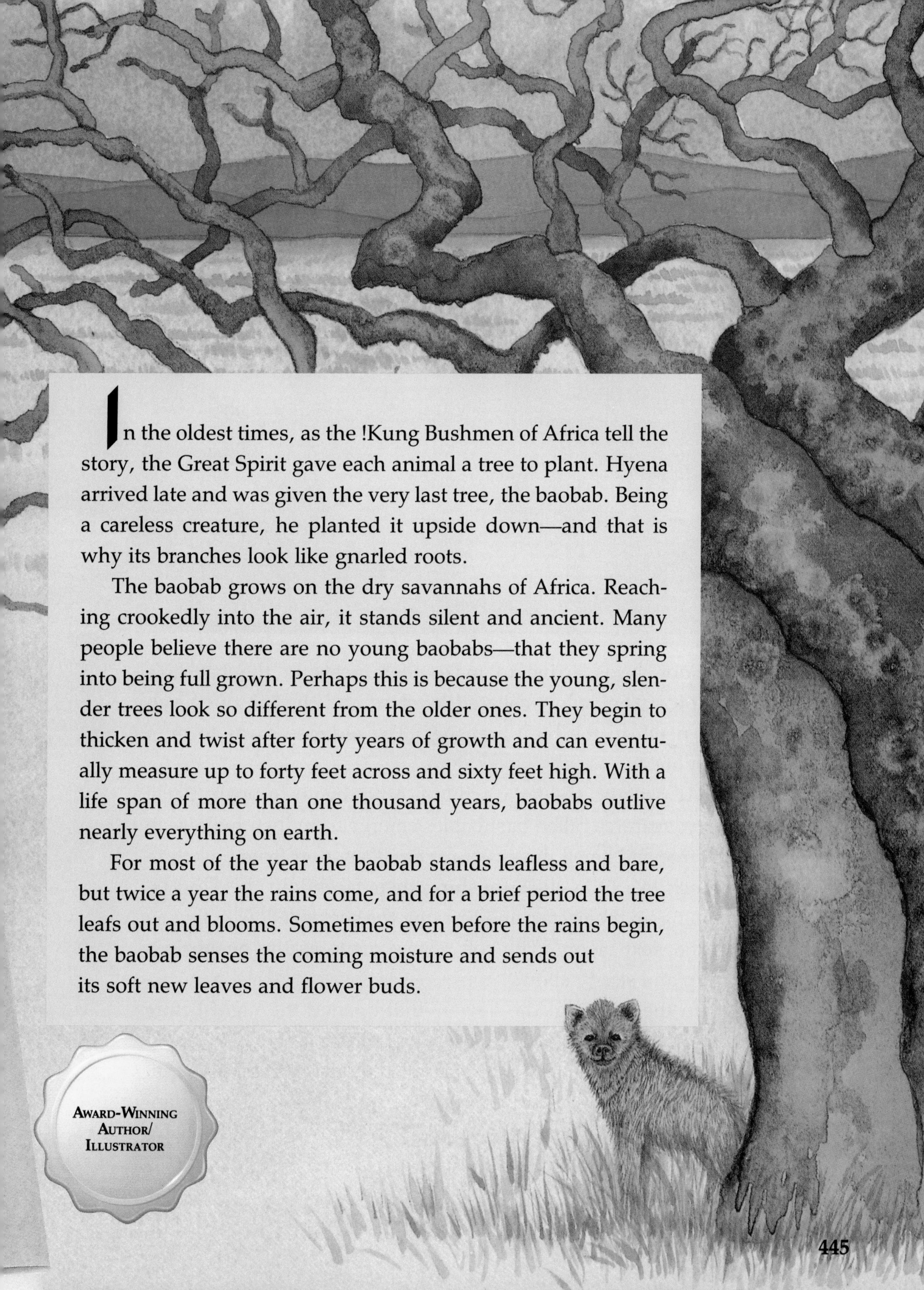

In the oldest times, as the !Kung Bushmen of Africa tell the story, the Great Spirit gave each animal a tree to plant. Hyena arrived late and was given the very last tree, the baobab. Being a careless creature, he planted it upside down—and that is why its branches look like gnarled roots.

The baobab grows on the dry savannahs of Africa. Reaching crookedly into the air, it stands silent and ancient. Many people believe there are no young baobabs—that they spring into being full grown. Perhaps this is because the young, slender trees look so different from the older ones. They begin to thicken and twist after forty years of growth and can eventually measure up to forty feet across and sixty feet high. With a life span of more than one thousand years, baobabs outlive nearly everything on earth.

For most of the year the baobab stands leafless and bare, but twice a year the rains come, and for a brief period the tree leafs out and blooms. Sometimes even before the rains begin, the baobab senses the coming moisture and sends out its soft new leaves and flower buds.

Soon birds arrive to make their nests in the baobab's hollows. The yellow-collared lovebird and the mosque swallow perch in the high branches. The old tree starts to hum with life.

At twilight, the large white flowers begin to open. Small furry creatures called bushbabies emerge from their hollows in the tree and smell the sweet nectar. They dart from branch to branch like little elves, pushing their faces into the flowers, lapping up the nectar, and carrying the sticky yellow pollen on to the next bloom. The soft leaves rustle as the bushbabies chirp and scurry about.

In the morning, the flowers that opened the night before have fallen to the ground, and a pair of eland comes to lap up the soft petals. A trio of impalas also munches the petals quietly, keeping a watchful eye on the horizon for signs of danger. In the distance, a lone giraffe reaches for the baobab's tender leaves.

In a few weeks, the rains end and the baobab's leaves begin to fall, exposing the weaver nests. The male red-headed weaver has been weaving a hanging nest with a long entrance spout at the end of a branch, while the buffalo weaver has built a spiky clump of twigs. Both nests protect the birds' eggs from dangerous snakes. When the nests are complete, the male weavers attract females to the new homes they've built. But if the females don't like the nests, the males must start all over again! The tree is full of weaver nests, and the birds dart busily in and out.

When all the leaves have fallen, the fruit begins to develop. Soon hundreds of big melon shapes hang from the bare branches. Before long, a family of baboons arrives to feast on the fresh fruit. They spend the whole day in the baobab, cracking open the hard velvety shells and scooping out the sweet pulp of all the fruit they can reach. Seeds fall to the ground as the baboons scamper and chortle.

After the fruit is gone, the baobab is very still. A boomslang snake drapes its long body over a gnarled branch and waits. A praying mantis turns its head, its large eyes ever-watchful. A stick insect hides from the snake in plain sight, looking very much like a twig. A flap-eared chameleon is also camouflaged in the branches; it turns the color of its surroundings and does not move.

Sometimes the stillness is broken by the call of the honey guide bird—*aje-je-je-je*—and the voices of tribesmen who follow close behind. The bird dips and swoops, flashing its white tail feathers, until it gets close to a hive in the baobab. Then the honey guide perches quietly nearby and waits for the hunters to find the hive. The men climb the baobab, smoke out the bees, and scoop out the honey. But they always leave some beeswax behind, as thanks to the honey guide bird.

To the African people, the baobab is more than a source of honey. Its bark is stripped for baskets and rope; its fruit is made into candy and sweet drinks; and its roots and leaves are used as medicine. On the hot, dry savannah, the hollow trunks of ancient baobabs can also become water containers and even shelters.

At the end of the long, dry season, the thirsty elephants arrive and begin to eat the baobab bark, extracting juices from the soft fiber. With their enormous strength, the elephants strip away all the bark and pull down large chunks of wood, leaving gaping holes in the trunk. But the baobab heals its wounds, produces new bark, and keeps growing.

Finally, after many, many years, the old baobab dies. Perhaps too many elephants have chewed the wood and weakened its structure, or insects have broken down its inner core.

One day it collapses in on itself, a melted heap of ruins. Over time, only a soft mound of powdery fragments is left. The wind will blow these away until nothing of the baobab remains.

In the sky, the clouds begin to build for the coming rains. Near the dust of the dead tree, a baobab seed has sprouted. It is all alone on the wide savannah. Now the story of the baobab begins all over again.

Think It Over

1. *For what reasons might the African baobab be called the "tree of life"?*
2. *Why does the !Kung legend explain that the hyena planted the first baobab tree upside-down?*
3. *For how many years might a baobab tree live?*
4. *Name some of the animals and people that depend on the baobab tree.*

Write

Imagine that you lived for a year in a tree house in your neighborhood. Write four brief journal entries, one for each season, describing events such as those in "Tree of Life."

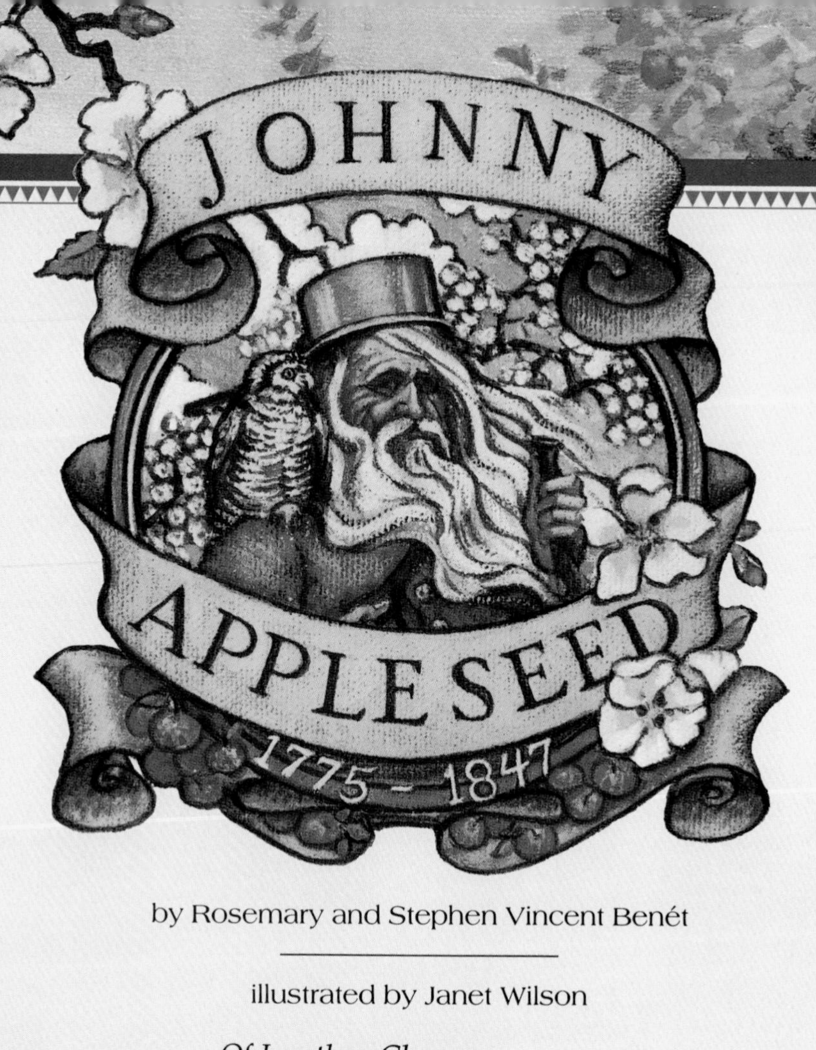

by Rosemary and Stephen Vincent Benét

illustrated by Janet Wilson

Of Jonathan Chapman
Two things are known,
That he loved apples,
That he walked alone.

At seventy-odd
He was gnarled as could be,
But ruddy and sound
As a good apple tree.

For fifty years over
Of harvest and dew,
He planted his apples
Where no apples grew.

The winds of the prairie
Might blow through his rags,
But he carried his seeds
In the best deerskin bags.

From old Ashtabula
To frontier Fort Wayne,
He planted and pruned
And he planted again.

He had not a hat
To encumber his head.
He wore a tin pan
On his white hair instead.

He nested with owl,
And with bear-cub and possum,
And knew all his orchards
Root, tendril and blossom.

A fine old man,
As ripe as a pippin,
His heart still light,
And his step still skipping.

The stalking Indian,
The beast in its lair
Did no hurt
While he was there.

For they could tell,
As wild things can,
That Jonathan Chapman
Was God's own man.

Why did he do it?
We do not know.
He wished that apples
Might root and grow.

He has no statue.
He has no tomb.
He has his apple trees
Still in bloom.

Consider, consider,
Think well upon
The marvelous story
Of Appleseed John.

The Growin' of PAUL BUNYAN

by William J. Brooke illustrated by Alex Murawski

CHILDREN'S CHOICE

THIS IS A STORY about how Paul Bunyan met up with Johnny Appleseed an' what come about because o' that meetin'. But it all got started because o' the problems Paul had with his boots one mornin'.

The hardest thing for ole Paul about gettin' started in the mornin' was puttin' on his boots. It wasn't so much the lacin' up that got him down (although when your bootlaces are exactly 8,621 feet an' four an' three quarters inches long, an' each one has to be special ordered from the Suwanee Steamship Cable Company in New York City, an' if because you're strong as ole Paul you tend to snap about two laces a week as a rule, then just tyin' your boots can be a bit of an irritation, too).

No, the hardest part o' puttin' on his boots was makin' sure he was the only one in 'em. Because, you see, they was so big an' warm that all the critters liked to homestead in 'em. So he'd have to shake 'em for nine or ten minutes just to get out the ordinary rattlesnakes an' polecats. Then he'd reach in an' feel around real careful for mountain lions an' wolf packs an' the occasional caribou migration. Fin'ly he'd wave his hand around real good to see if any hawks or eagles was huntin' game down around the instep. Then he could start the chore o' lacin'.

But ever' now an' then, no matter how careful he was, he'd miss a critter or two an' then he'd just have to put up with it. 'Cause once he had those laces all done up, it just wasn't worth the trouble to untie 'em all again.

So on this partic'lar day ole Paul is out o' sorts because of a moose that's got stuck down betwixt his toes. Paul's appetite is so spoiled he can't get down more than three hunnert pancakes an' about two an' a half hogs worth o' bacon afore he grabs up his ax an' takes off to soothe his ragged nerves in his usual way by shavin' a forest or two.

Well, the more his toes itch, the faster he chops; an' the faster he chops, the more his toes itch. Fin'ly, he can't stand it no more, so he sets down on a medium-size mountain an' undoes all 8,621 feet, four an' three quarters inches o' his right bootlace an' takes it off an' shakes it out for twenty minutes afore he remembers it was his left foot that was itchin'. So he gives a big sigh an' starts in on the other boot.

Fin'ly, both boots is off an' a slightly bruised moose is shakin' his head an' blinkin' his eyes an' staggerin' off betwixt the stumps. An' Paul has his first chance to take a deep breath an' have a look round. An' he's surprised, 'cause he can't see any trees anywheres, only stumps. So he gets up on a stump an' looks around an' he still can't see any standin' timber. He'd been so wrought up, he'd cleared all the way to the southern edge o' the big woods without noticin'.

Now this annoys Paul, 'cause he's too far from camp to get back for lunch, an' nothin' upsets him like missin' grub. An' when he's upset, the only thing to soothe him is choppin' trees, an' all the trees is down so that annoys him even worse.

There he sits, feelin' worse by the minute, with his stomach growlin' like a thunderstorm brewin' in the distance. An' then he notices somethin' way off at the horizon, out in the middle o' them dusty brown plains. All of a sudden there's somethin' green. As he watches, that green starts to spread in a line right across the middle of all that brown.

Now the only thing I ever heard tell of that was bigger than ole Paul hisself was ole Paul's curiosity. It was even bigger than his appetite. So quick as he can get his boots on, he's off to see what's happenin'. What he sees makes him stop dead in his tracks. 'Cause it's trees, apple trees growin' where nothin' but dirt ever growed before. A whole line of apple trees stretchin' in both directions as far as you can see.

It makes him feel so good he just has to take up his ax an' start choppin'. An' the more he chops, the better he feels. An' as he marches westward through all the flyin' splinters an' leaves an' applesauce, he sees that the trees is gettin' shorter until they're just saplin's, then green shoots, then just bare earth.

Paul stops short then an' leans on his ax handle to study the funny little man who turns around an' looks up at him. He's barefoot an' wears a gunnysack for clothes with a metal pot on his head for a hat. He looks up at Paul for a second, then he reaches in a big bulgy bag hangin' at his side an' takes out somethin' teeny-tiny, which he sticks in the ground. He gathers the dusty brown dirt around it an' pats it down. He stands up, an' out of a canvas waterbag he pours a little bit o' water on the spot. Then he just stands an' watches.

For a few seconds nothin' happens, then the tiniest littlest point o' green pokes out o' the dust an' sort o' twists around like it's lookin' for somethin'. All at once, it just stretches itself toward the sky an' pulls a saplin' up after it. An' it begins to branch an' to fill out an' its smooth green skin turns rough an' dark an' oozes sap. The branches creak an' groan an' stretch like a sleeper just wakin' up. Buds leaf out an' turn their damp green faces to the sun. An' the apples change from green to red an' swell like balloons full to bustin' with sweet cider.

The funny little man looks up an' smiles an' says, "My name's John Chapman, but folks call me Johnny Appleseed."

"Pleased to meet you," says Paul.

The little man points at his tree. "Mighty pretty sight, don't you think?"

"Sure is," says Paul, an' with a quick-as-a-wink flick o' his ax, he lays the tree out full length on the ground. "My name's Paul Bunyan."

The little man lifts his tin pot an' wipes his bald head while he stares at the tree lyin' there in the dirt. Then he squints up at Paul an' kneels down an' puts another seed in the ground. Paul smiles down at him while the tree grows up, then he lays it out by the first. The little man pops three seeds into the ground fast as can be. Paul lets 'em come up, then he lops all three with one easy stroke, backhand.

"You sure make 'em come up fast," says Paul, admirin'-like.

"It's a sort o' gift I was born with," says Johnny Appleseed. He looks at the five trees lyin' together. "You sure make 'em come down fast."

"It's a talent," says Paul, real humble. "I have to practice a lot."

They stand quiet awhile with Paul leanin' easy on his ax an' Johnny lookin' back along the line o' fallen trees to the horizon. He lifts his tin pot again an' rubs even harder at his head. Then he looks up at Paul an' says, "It seems like we got somethin' of a philosophical difference here."

Paul considers that. "We both like trees," he says real friendly.

"Yep," Johnny nods, "but I like 'em vertical an' you like 'em horizontal."

Paul agrees, but says he don't mind a man who holds a differin' opinion from his own, 'cause that's what makes America great. Johnny says, "Course you don't mind, 'cause when my opinion has finished differin' an' the dust settles, the trees is in the position you prefer. Anybody likes a fight that he always wins."

Paul allows he's sorry that Johnny's upset. "But loggin's what I do, an' a man's gotta do what he does. Besides, without my choppin' lumber, you couldn't build houses or stoke fires or pick your teeth."

"I don't live in a house an' I don't build fires an' when I want to clean my teeth I just eat an apple. Tell me, when all the trees are gone, what'll you cut down then?"

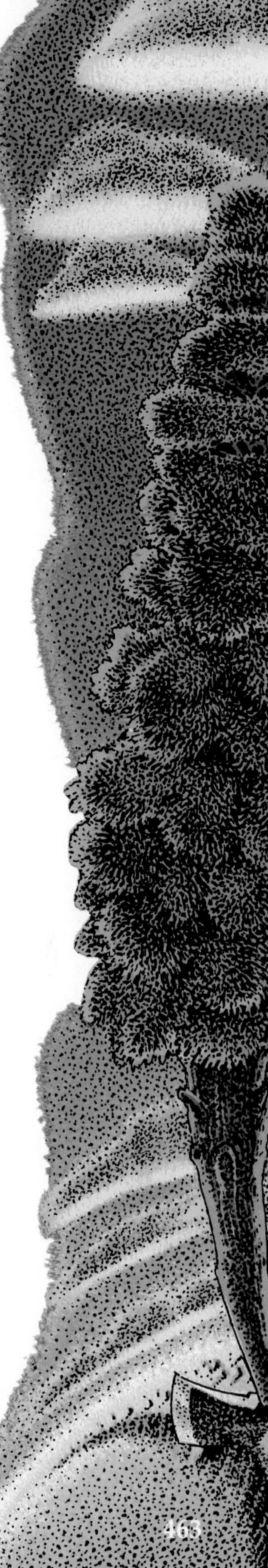

Paul laughs. "Why, there'll always be trees. Are you crazy or somethin'?"

"Yep," says Johnny, "crazy to be wastin' time an' lung power on you. I got to be off. I'm headin' for the Pacific Ocean an' I got a lot o' work to do on the way. So why don't you head north an' I'll head west an' our paths won't cross till they meet somewheres in China."

Paul feels a little hurt at this, but he starts off north, then stops to watch as Johnny takes off at a run, tossin' the seed out in front o' him, pressin' it down into the ground with his bare toes an' tricklin' a little water behind, all without breakin' stride. In a minute he's vanished at the head o' his long line of apple trees.

Now Paul has figured that Johnny hadn't really meant to offend him, but it was more in the nature of a challenge. An' Paul loves any kind of a challenge. So he sets down an' waits three days, figurin' he should give a fair head start to Johnny, who's a couple hunnert feet shorter'n he is. Then at dawn on the fourth day, he stands up an' stretches an' holds his ax out level a foot above the ground. When he starts to run, the trees drop down in a row as neat as the cross ties on a railroad line. In fact, when it came time to build the transcontinental railroad, they just laid the iron rails down on that long line o' apple trees an' saved theirselves many thousands o' dollars.

Anyways, Paul runs for two days an' two nights, an' when the sun's settin' on the third day, he sees water up ahead. There's Johnny Appleseed plantin' a last tree, then sittin' on a high bare bluff lookin' out over the Pacific Ocean. Paul finishes the last o' the trees an' swings the ax over his head with a whoop an' brings it down on the dirt, buryin' its head in the soil an' accident'ly creatin' the San Andreas Fault. He mops his brow an' sits down beside Johnny with his feet danglin' way down into the ocean.

Starin' out at the orange sun, Johnny asks, "Are they all gone?" Paul looks back over his shoulder an' allows as how they are. Paul waits for Johnny to say somethin' else, but he just keeps starin', so Paul says, "It took you six days to plant 'em and it took me only three days to chop 'em down. Pretty good, huh?"

Johnny looks up an' smiles sadly. "It's always easier to chop somethin' down than to make it grow." Then he goes back to starin'.

Now that rankles Paul. When he beats somebody fair an' square, he expects that someone to admit it like a man. "What's so hard about growin' a tree anyway?" he grumps. "You just stick it in the ground an' the seed does all the work."

Johnny reaches way down in the bottom o' his bag an' holds out a seed. "It's the last one," he says. "All the rest o' my dreams is so much kindlin' wood, so why don't you take this an' see if it's so easy to make it grow."

Paul hems an' haws, but he sees as how he has to make good on his word. So he takes the little bitty seed an' pushes it down in the ground with the tip o' one fingernail. He pats the soil around it real nice, like he seen Johnny do. Then he sits down to wait as the sun sets.

"I'm not as fast as you at this," Paul says, "but you've had more practice. An' I'm sure my tree will be just as good as any o' yours."

"Not if it dies o' thirst," says Johnny's voice out o' the dark.

Paul hasn't thought about that. So when the moon comes up, he heads back to a stream he passed about two hunnert miles back. But he don't have nothin' to carry water in, so he scoops up a double handful an' runs as fast as he can with the water slippin' betwixt his fingers. When he gets back, he's got about two drops left.

"Guess I'll have to get more water," he says, a mite winded.

"Don't matter," says Johnny's voice, "if the rabbits get the seed."

An' there in the moonlight, Paul sees all the little cottontails hoppin' around an' scratchin' at the ground. Not wishin' to hurt any of 'em, he picks 'em up, one at a time, an' moves 'em away, but they keep hoppin' back. So, seein' as how he still needs water, he grabs 'em all up an' runs back to the stream, sets the rabbits down, grabs up the water, runs back, flicks two more drops on the spot, pushes away the new batch o' rabbits movin' in, an' tries to catch his breath.

"Just a little more water an' a few less rabbits an' it'll be fine," Paul says between gasps.

Out o' the dark comes Johnny's voice. "Don't matter, if the frost gets it."

Paul feels the cold ground an' he feels the moisture freezin' on his hands. So he gets down on his knees an' he folds his hands around that little spot o' dirt an', gentle as he can, breathes his warm breath onto that tiny little seed. Time passes and the rabbits gather round to enjoy the warmth an' scratch their soft little backs up against those big callused hands. As the night wears on, Paul falls into a sleep, but his hands never stop cuppin' that little bit o' life.

Sometime long after moonset, the voice o' Johnny Appleseed comes driftin' soft out o' the dark an' says, "Nothin's enough if you don't care enough."

Paul wakes up with the sun. He sets up an' stretches an' for a minute he can't remember where he is. Then he looks down an' he gives a whoop. 'Cause he sees a little tiny bit o' green pokin' up through the grains o' dirt. "Hey, Johnny," he yells, "look at this!" But Johnny Appleseed is gone, slipped away in the night. Paul is upset for a minute, then he realizes he don't need to brag to anybody, that that little slip o' green is all the happiness he needs right now.

As the sun rises, he fetches more water an' shoos away the crows an' shields that shoot from the heat o' the sun. It grows taller an' straighter an' puts out buds an' unfurls its leaves. Paul carries in all the animals from the surroundin' countryside, coyotes an' sidewinders an' Gila monsters, an' sets 'em down in a circle to admire his tree growin' tall an' sturdy an' green.

Then Paul notices somethin'. He gets down on his hands an' knees an' looks close. It's a brown leaf. "That's not too serious," he thinks an' he shades it from the sun. Then he sees another brown leaf an' he runs back to get more water. When he gets back, the little saplin' is droopin' an' shrivelin'. He gets down an' breathes on it, but as he watches, the leaves drop off an' the twigs snap. "Help me, somebody," he cries out, "help me!" But there's no answer 'cept the rustlin' o' the critters as they slink away from him. An' while he looks down at the only thing he ever give birth to, it curls up an' dies.

For a second he just stands there, then he pounds his fists on the ground an' yells, "Johnny! Johnny! Why didn't you tell me how much it could hurt?"

He sets down an' he stares till the sun begins settin'. Then he jumps up an' says, "Only one thing's gonna make me feel better. I'm gonna cut me some timber! Maybe a whole forest if I can find one!" He reaches for his ax.

An' that's when he sees it. It stretches right up to the sky, with great green boughs covered with sweet-smellin' needles an' eagles nestin' in its heights. Johnny must have worked some o' his magic afore he left, 'cause when Paul struck it into the ground it wasn't nothin' but an ax. But now, in the light o' the settin' sun, it shines like a crimson column crowned in evergreen.

"I'll call it a redwood," says Paul, who knew now he'd never want an ax again as long as there was such a tree.

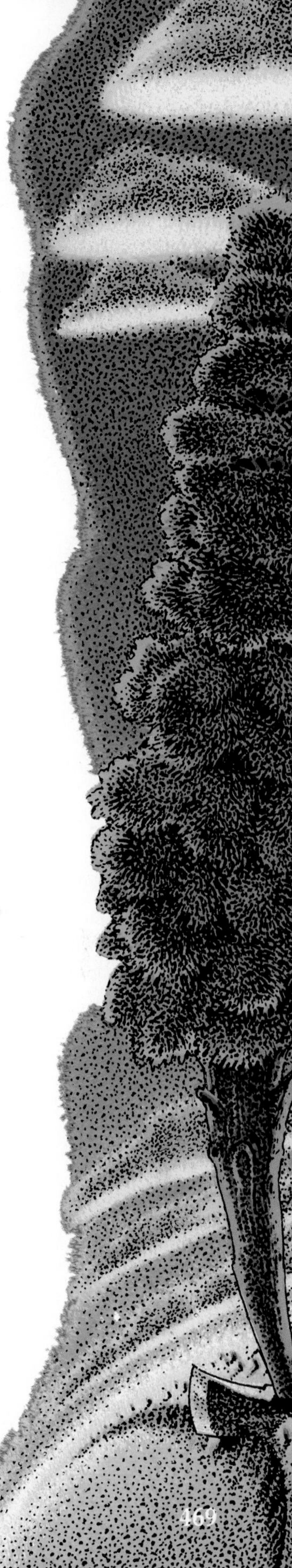

So he waited for the cones with the seeds to form an' drop, an' he planted them all over the great Northwest an' nurtured them an' watched a great woodland spring up in their shelter. An' he never felled a tree again as long as he lived.

For years he worked, an' there are those who say you can still catch a glimpse o' him behind the highest mountains in the deepest woods. An' they say he's always smilin' when you see him.

'Cause Paul learned hisself somethin': A little man who chops somethin' down is still just a little man; but there's nobody bigger than a man who learns to grow.

THINK IT OVER

1. *In what way does Paul Bunyan grow in this story?*
2. *How does the author let you know that this is a legend and not a true story?*
3. *What is Johnny Appleseed's special talent?*
4. *What is Paul Bunyan's special talent?*
5. *Why does Johnny Appleseed give his very last seed to Paul Bunyan?*

WRITE

Paul Bunyan and Johnny Appleseed have very different opinions about trees. Make a list of other differences between these two characters.

THEME WRAP-UP

TREES OF LIFE

For what reasons might the trees described in the selections be called "trees of life"?

Think about how the !Kung Bushmen and Johnny Appleseed treat trees. How are their attitudes similar?

WRITER'S WORKSHOP What other important message about protecting nature could a tall tale deliver? With your classmates, brainstorm some living things that might be in danger. For example: *A baobab might be threatened by an African woodcutter. A wild bear might be in danger from Davy Crockett.* Choose the one you would most like to save, and brainstorm humorous ways in which a wise character might save it. Use your ideas to write a tall tale.

CONNECTIONS

MULTICULTURAL CONNECTION

PRIZING OUR WORLD

Harrison Ngau grew up in the rain forests of Sarawak, a state in northern Borneo. He watched these forests being slowly destroyed by timber companies who sold the lumber worldwide. He knew that all rain forests are important to the health of our planet. He also knew that these forests were home to the Irak and other native peoples.

To save the Irak culture as well as the forests, Ngau organized people to halt the logging in every way they could. For his efforts, Harrison Ngau was awarded the Goldman Environmental Prize in 1990. He quickly put his $60,000 prize money to work and financed a successful bid for a seat in his nation's parliament.

■ *Ngau has shown that one person can do a lot to help our environment. Write a character sketch about someone you know who is making a difference in our world.*

Harrison Ngau

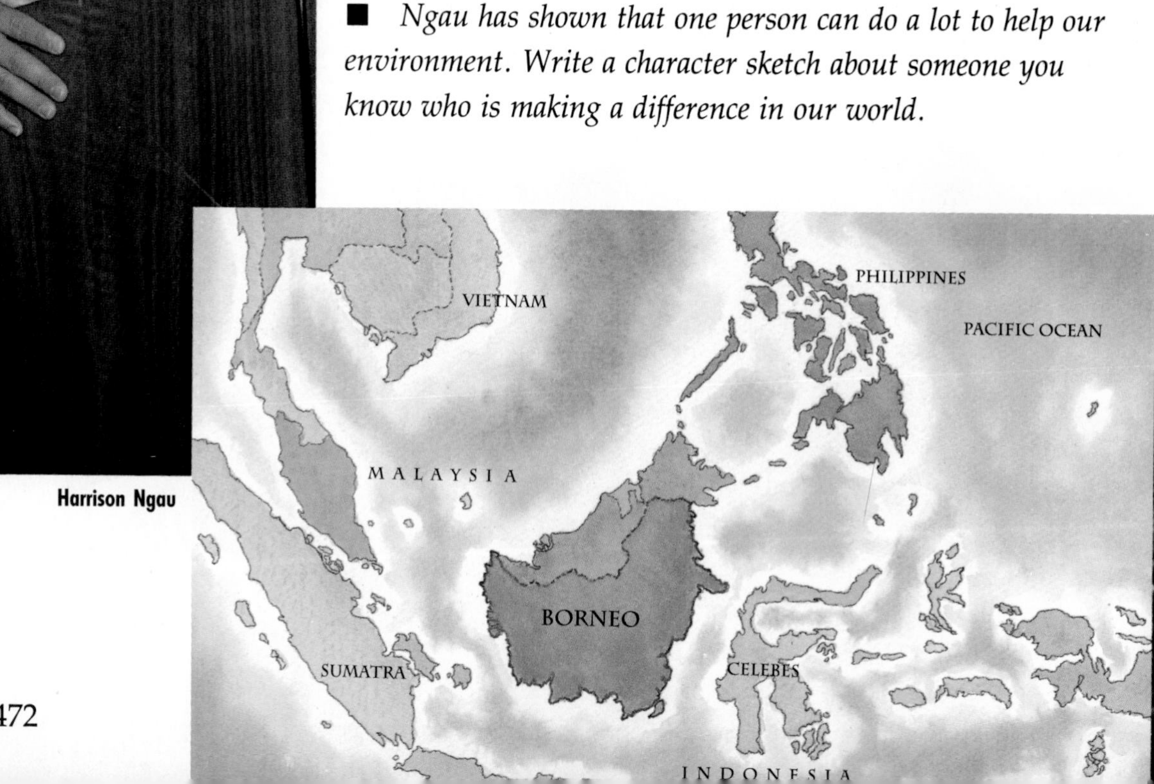

SOCIAL STUDIES CONNECTION

SAVING THE WORLD BEGINS AT HOME

People all over the world are working to save the environment. What are your community's environmental problems? What groups are already trying to solve these problems? Create posters that tell how people can make a difference in your community.

You and your classmates might use a web like this one to help you record facts.

MATH CONNECTION

CALCULATING THE FUTURE

What percentage of the earth's surface is covered by rain forest? How fast are the forests being destroyed? Collect these and other statistics that show how our environment is changing. Use the information to compute the changes that may take place on our planet in the next ten years. Report your conclusions.

We have always been fascinated by the skies above us. This fascination goes back over 3,000 years, to the ancient astronomers of China, Babylonia, and Egypt. Our fascination has now led us beyond mere looking. We actually travel into space for close-up views. Find out what fascinates you about the skies as you read the selections in this unit.

THEMES

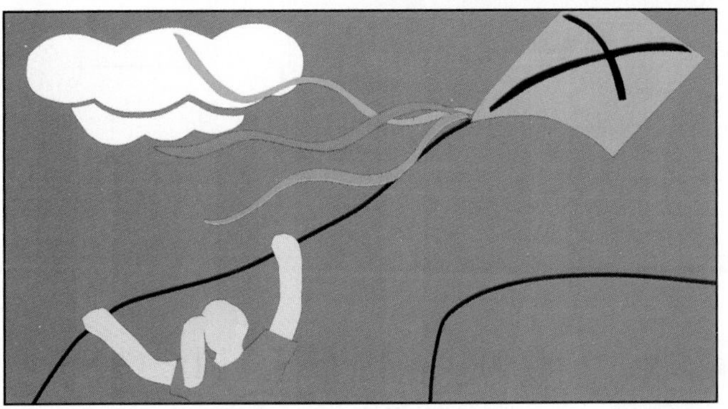

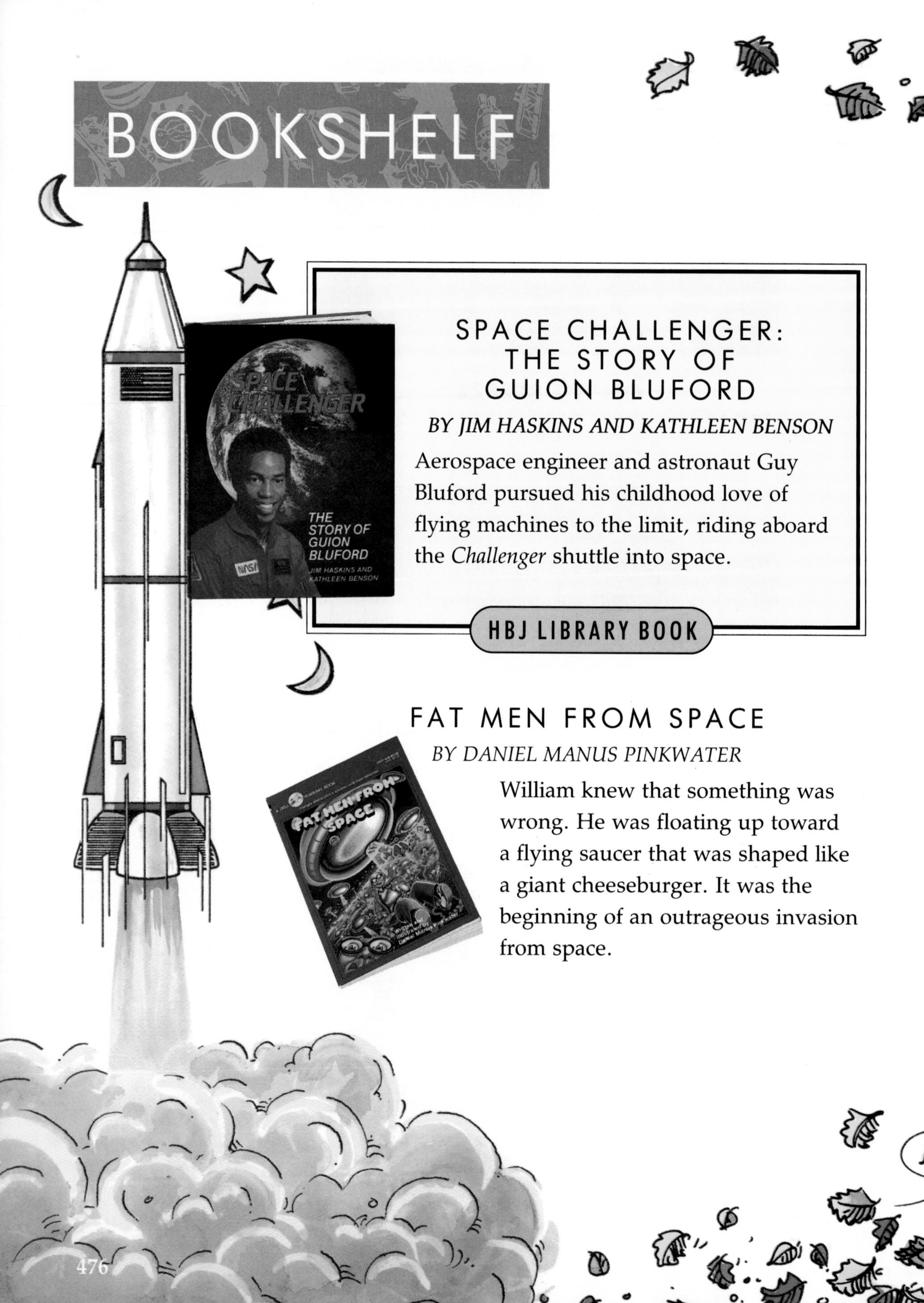

BOOKSHELF

SPACE CHALLENGER: THE STORY OF GUION BLUFORD

BY JIM HASKINS AND KATHLEEN BENSON

Aerospace engineer and astronaut Guy Bluford pursued his childhood love of flying machines to the limit, riding aboard the *Challenger* shuttle into space.

HBJ LIBRARY BOOK

FAT MEN FROM SPACE

BY DANIEL MANUS PINKWATER

William knew that something was wrong. He was floating up toward a flying saucer that was shaped like a giant cheeseburger. It was the beginning of an outrageous invasion from space.

BEFORE THE WRIGHT BROTHERS

BY DON BERLINER

Who were the first people to plan, build, and take to the air in flying machines? Find out in this collection of short biographies.

STINKER FROM SPACE

BY PAMELA F. SERVICE

Space alien Tsynq Yr (Stin-ker), hiding in the body of a skunk, enlists the help of two Earth children to borrow one of NASA's space shuttles.

THE WONDERFUL FLIGHT TO THE MUSHROOM PLANET

BY ELEANOR CAMERON

Two boys answer an advertisement for amateur spaceship designers and set out on an extraordinary adventure to an undiscovered planet.

ON THE BREEZE

Have you ever wondered what it feels like to fly—not on a seat in a commercial airliner, but on the currents of the breeze? The authors of these selections try in different ways to express that feeling.

CONTENTS

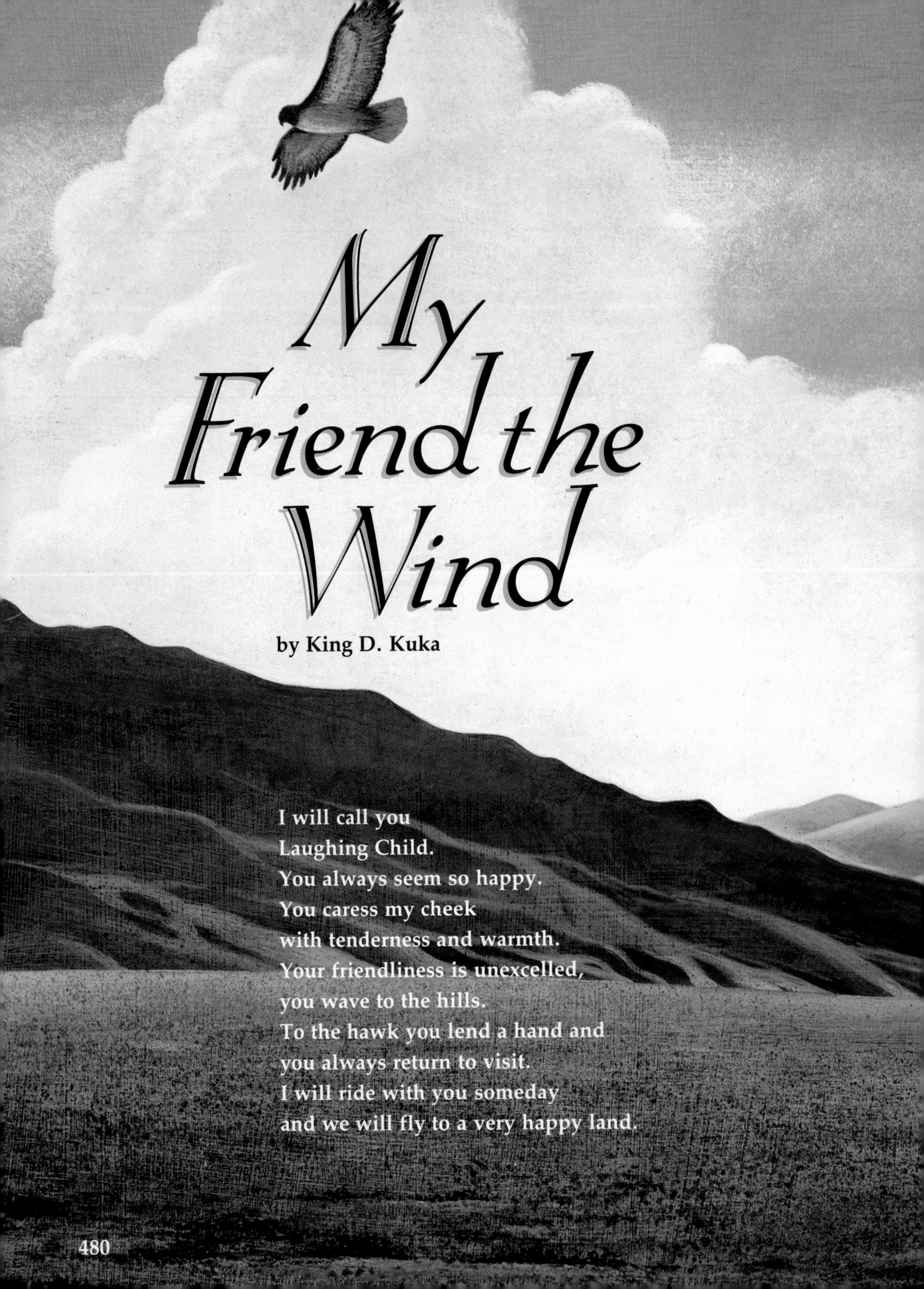

My Friend the Wind

by King D. Kuka

I will call you
Laughing Child.
You always seem so happy.
You caress my cheek
with tenderness and warmth.
Your friendliness is unexcelled,
you wave to the hills.
To the hawk you lend a hand and
you always return to visit.
I will ride with you someday
and we will fly to a very happy land.

FROM *VOICES OF THE RAINBOW: CONTEMPORARY POETRY BY AMERICAN INDIANS*

EDITED BY KENNETH ROSEN

ILLUSTRATED BY WENDELL MINOR

Wishes

by Ya-Ka-Nes

Over the rainy day mountain
Past the laughing blue rainbow
Gliding in the cloudless ivory sky
The young Happiness bird
In the freedom of quiet solitude or
with a loved-one friend

Always follow the beauty road
Gliding in the cloudless ivory sky
Past the laughing blue rainbow
Over the rainy day mountain
Forever in happiness
Forever in beauty
Always

CHINESE KITES
How to Make and Fly Them

AN ARRAY OF CHINESE KITES

from *Chinese Kites: How to Make and Fly Them*
by David F. Jue

Kites were in use in China long before the beginnings of written history. Bamboo for frames was native to the land. Silk has been produced in China since stone-age times, as long ago as 2600 B.C. With bamboo available for frames and silk for the coverings and the flying lines, the art of kite-making arose.

The origin of paper in China has been traced back at least as far as 200 B.C. When paper became commonplace, the cheaper material put kite-making into the reach of all. The kite became a folk art of the people and as such survives today.

On a breezy day, you may see kites flying above the water with a long string tied to the tail. At the end of this string, a hook with the bait is submerged under the water. When a fish bites, the fisherman pulls the kite in.

Kite fighting is very popular in China and is the most exciting sport of the kite-flying season. The object is to engage the strings and saw the opponent's flying line in two. The victor obtains right of ownership of the vanquished kite.

Think It Over

1. *What are some of the uses of kites in China?*
2. *What is your opinion of the Chinese kites illustrated in this selection?*

Write

Imagine that you have one of the kites in this selection. Write a how-to paragraph for a young child, telling how to launch the kite into the air.

FLYING

Eleven-year-old Jennifer Rosen wishes she could fly across the ice as gracefully as a champion skater. So when her mother gives her a set of colored pencils, it seems natural for Jennifer, idly wishing she had wings, to draw a "Self-Portrait with Wings." What isn't so natural is to wake up the next morning and discover she actually has them. Not ordinary bird or angel wings but beautiful gossamer wings arching over her back, invisible except in mirrors. Real wings!

Jennifer's best friend, Angela, is the only one who knows the secret. Angela keeps after Jennifer to use her extraordinary gift—to spread her wings and fly!

from *Self-Portrait with Wings*
by Susan Green
illustrated by Gordon Sauve

"Fly? Are you on that again?"

"But don't you even want to fly?"

"I guess so. But this is New York, remember? Where do you think I can go without thousands of people seeing me?" Her skates were swinging over her shoulder, her wings brushing against her legs in an easy, gentle motion.

The two girls were walking through Central Park. The trees were turning a faint, whispery apple green and the sky was a very deep blue. And no matter which way they turned, there were people—people roller-skating and people walking, people jogging, biking, dog walking, kiting on Sheep's Meadow.

"Wow! Look at that one!" A kite, fifteen feet long, looking like a rainbow, danced across the sky. Jennifer shaded her eyes and watched it spiraling and shimmering as it twirled. A long tail ribboned out, flickering in the sun.

Angela stopped on the path. "Jen . . ."

"What?"

"Do you remember the hang glider kite we saw? It was like a giant balloon." Her voice was slow, as if she were thinking aloud and trying to figure something out.

"Well, I'm not sure."

"Oh, you remember. We were walking over by the Met. Your mom saw it first, remember? It was life-size. We all thought it was a man up there." Her voice was rising, building with excitement. "Remember? Think! Everyone was pointing. It came out from over the trees and . . . Come on, Jen, you were as excited as everyone else. You thought he was going to crash."

"Oh, yeah . . ."

"It was a kite!"

"Yeah?" Jennifer's voice was slow and suspicious. "So?"

"Well, I have lots of string."

"No."

"All we have to do is tie it on and everyone would think you were a kite."

"No!"

"Why not? You'd find out if you could really fly! You'd be up there!" She pointed toward the streaming, spiraling rainbow, its tail floating out across the cloudless sky. "Can't you even think what it would feel like?"

"NO!"

They walked along in silence. Angela looked mad. "I don't see why you won't do it."

"You act as if I'm spoiling your fun. First of all, I don't know if I can really fly. And I don't want to get killed, OK?"

"OK."

Jennifer kicked at a bottle cap on the path. "Besides," she paused, "people would be around to see me take off."

Angela spun around to face her. "Not if we do it right. All we have to do is find one little isolated spot, really early. And once you're even ten feet off the ground no one would dream you were real. I mean, people just don't think that way."

"But you just said . . ."

"Besides, I'd have this string on you. I've got a whole long roll of it from that plastic kite Dad got me at the beach. It's not even tangled or anything."

"Yeah. You never even got it off the ground."

"And if you really can't do it you'll never get off the ground."

"I don't know, Angela." Jennifer suddenly had a vision of herself up there, spiraling with the kite, floating in that immaculate, blue, immense space. She held her breath. She could almost feel herself weightless, free.

"I know what I'm talking about," Angela rattled on. "You'll be fine. Look, it's logical. If you can fly at the rink you can fly in the sky, right?"

"You really think so?" The sky was getting bluer.

"I'm your best friend, right? If I weren't so sure I'd say so."

"Well, I'll think about it."

"You will? Wow!"

Early the next morning the sky was blue again and the wind ruffled along, a perfect little breeze. The two girls were walking toward Sheep's Meadow. It was a huge expanse with a few clumps of trees here and there. A gray cement footpath ran around it and then, beyond, man-made forests with walks, rinks, ponds, and playgrounds were tucked in here and there. Sheep's Meadow was the one place where Jennifer could feel space, real space, opening up like a dome and widening out around her, forever.

But she wasn't thinking about that now. She was feeling her heartbeat. With each step, each slap of the wings against her legs, her heart jumped too. "Oh, Ange, I'm scared. What if . . ."

"There's nothing to be nervous about. Look," she said as she opened her PBS tote bag, "we've got plenty of string." The shiny nylon string was wound around a plastic tube shaped like a rolling pin, with bright red wings on either side.

"It doesn't look like very much."

"No problem. It goes on for miles and miles. Now, what we'll do is tie it around your wrist and that way you can signal me if you have to. I've got it all figured out. One tug means you're headed for the trees. Two tugs means that you should turn right, and three even tugs means you have to turn left. Two short tugs, like this, de-dum, means that people are coming, and . . ."

Panic was rising. "I'll never remember all of this."

"That's why I wrote it all down." She pulled a piece of paper out of her pocket and unfolded it. "See. Just put it in your pocket and if you get confused, you can take it out and read it." She sounded triumphant. Jennifer was looking over the list of directions. It looked like a long one. She closed one eye and looked at Angela cockeyed.

"Up there?"

"Sure. What difference does it make where you are? You can still read, can't you?"

Jennifer groaned as she stuffed it into her pocket.

"Hey, this looks like a great spot." Spread out before them was the great lawn of Sheep's Meadow.

Jennifer took a deep breath as she looked out over it. There was only one other person there; another kiter, the one with the spiral kite of the day before. It was already unraveling against the sky, way across on the other side of the field.

"OK." Angela put down the tote bag and sat down on the grass. "Here, you need some strength. I brought apples and some juice"—she was emptying her bag on the lawn—"the string, a camera . . ."

"Don't you dare!"

"OK, OK, don't be so touchy. Oh, yes, sunglasses. It might be really glary up there. Knee pads from skating. I guess that's it." She cheerfully bit into an apple. "Don't you want one?"

"I'm too nervous."

"Don't worry. It'll be fine. I know . . ."

"If you say 'I know what I'm talking about' one more time, I'm leaving."

"Sorry." Angela turned to the field. "See, it looks good. I told you there wouldn't be anyone here."

"What about him?" Jennifer nodded toward the man on the other side of the Meadow. He was running along, his head tilted back, watching his kite.

Angela barely looked up. "Not to worry. He's too far away to notice anything. Besides, he's not paying any attention. Now, just put out your hand and I'll tie on the string." She leaned over Jennifer's outstretched arm. "I think it ought to go around twice, just to make sure. Oh, Jen, I'm so excited! I can't stand it! How do you feel?"

"You're not listening to me, Angela." Then she sighed. "I don't know. I really do wonder what it's like up there; if it's like flying in a plane or swimming or something." She felt her heart lurch again. "Scared," she said. "Really scared. And if my mother ever finds out . . ."

"OK. Now." Angela really didn't seem to hear her. She was too involved with the string. "Is it tight enough?"

"I guess so."

"Now, I don't want to make a bow. It might come undone . . . there, that's better." Jennifer looked down. The string was tied tightly in a series of little knots like her mother put on packages. She was attached. And Angela was unraveling the rolling pin. "Now, how do we do this?"

"What?"

"I'll keep hold of the string and you start running."

It's supposed to be the other way around," said Jennifer. "A kite can't run."

"But you're not a normal kite. Now, if you run against the wind, you ought to go up easy." She wet her finger and put it out to test the wind. "It's coming from up there," she said. "Perfect."

Jennifer stared up at the sky. The spiral kite was tumbling, then drifting in the air, its rainbow colors dancing in space. In a few minutes she'd be up there, too. She couldn't believe it. A surge of excitement filled her. She wanted to be up there. She really did.

"Jennifer!" She jumped. "Look, you've got to pay attention. You ought to test them out first. Just a little flutter to make sure you can really get off the ground."

"Is anyone watching?"

Angela looked around slowly, then shook her head. "No." There was no one in sight.

Jennifer nodded solemnly. She stood up as straight as she could and unfurled her wings. She let them out against the air. It felt wonderful. For a moment she just let the delicious breeze play against them, running off behind and into space.

Angela's voice brought her back again. "Jen, are you fluttering? Nothing's happening."

"Not yet. You're sure no one's there?"

"Positive."

Jennifer hesitated, holding back.

"Come on, Jen, we don't have that much time. It's a quarter of eight already. The Jog-a-Thon starts at nine."

"Oh, I forgot that."

"Don't worry about it. Just get started, OK?"

"OK. Here goes." She looked at Angela one more time. "Wish me luck." Her throat felt dry. Her breath was shallow and gasping.

Angela gulped. "Good luck."

"This is it." She felt herself stalling.

"Yep."

"OK. Here goes." She stood in the vast, empty field. Her eyes followed the string floating out from her wrist, attached, at the other end, to the bobbin in Angela's hands. She took one last deep breath, then wiggled her shoulders just a little. Behind her she could feel the breeze caught then released from her trembling wings. Her feet lifted from the ground, then touched down again. It was working. She opened her wings to a half span.

There was a surge she had never felt before, a thrilling, open release as she fanned her wings out behind her and felt the wind rushing up beneath them, lifting her up. She felt the string pull taut.

"Run!" she shouted.

Angela took off. At the end of the string she could feel Jennifer's weight rising, tugging for more and more string to be let out. The holder whirled in her hands.

Jennifer was climbing, whirling like the ballerina on her music box, round and round, higher and higher. Angela was the center of an invisible whirlpool, getting smaller and smaller, way down below. Branches with their tiny traces of buds passed by, and then the uneven brush of the treetops. And she was still going up. Over and beyond the trees, the hazy, gray city of skyscrapers was circling. And then, the sky.

Down below, Angela was motionless. Jennifer lifted her arm to wave and tilted. Her heart plummeted. She heard a long, faint scream and righted herself. She had never thought about steering. She'd have to do some experimenting.

She put both arms out to the side and they seemed to balance her. She lowered one arm slightly and her body tilted; both arms over her head and she lay horizontally. She tilted to the right. She turned, straightened out, and tilted to the left. She raised a shoulder and her whole body swerved again. She S-curved through the sky and did a figure eight. A new current swept under her body and she tipped and swooped with it. The wind changed and her wings automatically began to pump to hold her afloat. It was like dancing. She felt like singing. Up and up she went, then over and down.

She discovered subtle twists and movements of her body, changed her speed and direction, learned to listen to the wind. Her wings spread out behind her, opened fully, then snapped shut, and she twisted like a corkscrew; she swept them open again and she soared. Jennifer looked down. All of Central Park was budding and a thin veil of green hung over the trees. Here and there the park was splashed with brilliant streaks of yellow flowers and sprinkled with pink and white clouds of blossoming trees.

Above her space went on forever and she was a part of it; part of the air, of the power of the sky, held by the currents yet free. Tentatively she raised one leg and began to sing: "On the wings of a snow white dove." She laughed and the laughter rippled out around her. She really was the dove, as she started her freestyle routine. She turned and flowed into it, skating in the sky. "He sends His perfect . . ." She swirled and twirled.

There was a tug on her wrist. She stopped midair, slowed, and peered down. She could hardly see Angela anymore. She was just a tiny dot in the field. To her right another dot was traveling quickly. Another tug pulled at her wrist. She remembered the list in her pocket. She crossed her arm over her body to get at it. She twisted and plummeted.

Sky and trees spun by as she dropped. She heard a long scream. Instinctively her arm went out and she was righted. A stream carried her upward again and she let herself be carried. Her whole body pounded and trembled, she could hear her breath wheezing and gasping. She had dropped so quickly! She steadied herself and felt her heartbeat slow.

Oh, they'd put the list in the pocket she couldn't reach.

Suddenly she was aware of where she was. All that sky! And she was so tiny in it, hanging in it . . . alone . . . up there. All alone. Everything was so still; only her wings, swinging up and down, moved.

Another tug pulled her back. One tug. What did that mean? She'd have to get into her pocket. She took a deep, shivering breath and kept her wings moving. She'd have to use the hand with the string attached. With a quick motion she thrust her hand into her jeans pocket and then out again. Nothing.

She waited for a moment, gliding, preparing herself, then poised to try it again. Her wings whipped back and forth behind her. "One, two." She thrust more quickly. The tips of her fingers caught the paper and drew it out. Three frantic tugs jerked her arm like the strings would a marionette. Her fingers opened. The paper flew out into space. She made a grab for it, but the breeze had already taken it. She dove awkwardly and timidly, no longer sure of what to do. It fluttered, twirling, out of her reach, turning silver then dark as the sun caught it.

Desperately she leaned over and looked down. On the field the dot seemed to be jumping up and down. Angela was dancing wildly, waving her arms and pulling on the string like a bell ringer. Jennifer's arm was cranked up and down like a puppet's. She fluttered frantically, trying to hold herself upright, peering down. What did Angela want?

Then Jennifer saw it: the other kite. Its spirals were turning, churning in the wind. Its tail was floating out gracefully behind. It was coming toward her.

She tried to dive, then caught herself. Somehow she had gotten too close to the trees and her line was caught. The kite was still coming. She had to get away. She plucked at the knot they'd tied on her wrist. It was too tight! She flapped desperately, trying to keep steady. And the spiraling kite chugged methodically toward her.

She started to struggle, feeling as if she were doing some strange, uncontrollable dance up there in the middle of nothing. The kite made its way evenly, calmly, toward her. She tugged on the string, pulling, trying to break it. It wouldn't budge. Her sunglasses tipped off an ear and dangled for a second before they fell off altogether, and the sun's full glare hit her full force. She blinked against it. And as her arm went up to shield her eyes she lost her bearings and dropped. She struggled to open her wings.

Something hit her kite string.

The impact sent her swaying wildly back and forth like a pendulum. When she finally slowed enough to look down, she saw the kite. Her string was caught, wrapped around it. It was struggling in the wind to free itself, opening and closing like an accordion. She was losing control, her wings flapping in one direction, the string pulling in the other, the thing getting more and more tangled.

There was a ripping sound as something beneath her went limp. As she watched, the bright colors of the kite tore apart. Pieces of it went sailing down through the sky. The string snapped. The whole, mangled contraption fell hurtling toward the earth while she spun in confusion toward the trees.

She reached out for the branches.

"Jennifer! Jennifer!"

She opened her eyes. Angela was racing toward her, tears streaming down her horrified face. "Jen . . . talk to me. Are you all right? Oh, Jen!"

She was clinging desperately to a branch in a tree, heaving, scrabbling for a foothold.

She closed her eyes and managed a nod. "I can't move," she said. She was trembling uncontrollably.

"Are you hurt? Oh, Jen!"

"No . . . I . . . I . . ."

"Jen, you've got to get down. He's coming!"

"I can't."

"The man with the kite is really mad! He . . ."

"I can't." She felt totally and horribly helpless. She held on tighter.

"But . . ."

From around the bend a furious man charged toward them, dragging the remains of his mangled kite.

"What do you think you're doing!" he screamed at Angela. "Look at this! Look at this! It's ruined! This kite cost me a hundred and fifty bucks and look at it!"

He stopped midscream and stared up at Jennifer, lopsided and clinging in a crook of the tree, her eyes tightly shut.

"Where's the rest of my kite?" he screamed at her.

She cringed and pointed to the ground behind the tree where the tangled mess of string and torn rainbow lay in a heap.

"Look at it! Just look at . . ." He stopped and gaped. "Where did you come from?"

Angela looked at her feet. Jennifer shook her head. She looked at his ruined kite and felt a sob rising. It had been so beautiful floating up there. She whimpered and tried to swallow.

"I . . . I'm sorry."

"How did you get up there?"

"She flew." Angela turned her face up toward Jennifer. "Come on, let's get out of here."

Think It Over

1. *How do Jennifer's feelings about flying differ from Angela's feelings about it?*
2. *Why does Angela think that Jennifer can fly over crowds of people without causing a great commotion?*
3. *What steps do the girls have to go through to get Jennifer airborne?*
4. *How do the girls communicate while Jennifer is flying?*
5. *Do you think Jennifer was right to accept Angela's challenge to fly? Why?*

Write

Imagine that you too could fly like a kite! What words would you use to describe your experience? Use these words to write a poem about flying.

THEME WRAP-UP

ON THE BREEZE

In what ways do you think Jennifer is like a kite?

Which of the selections or poems gives you the most vivid picture of the wind? Explain your choice.

WRITER'S WORKSHOP What if other people started to grow wings, too? Imagine that two friends wake up one morning to discover that they both have wings. Work with a partner to create a dialogue in which the friends discuss their new wings and what to do with them.

THEME

SPACE FLIGHTS

What would it be like to report to work in the morning and be blasted into space? In the selections that follow, you will read about some extraordinary things that happened, and some that never came to be, in our quest to explore space.

CONTENTS

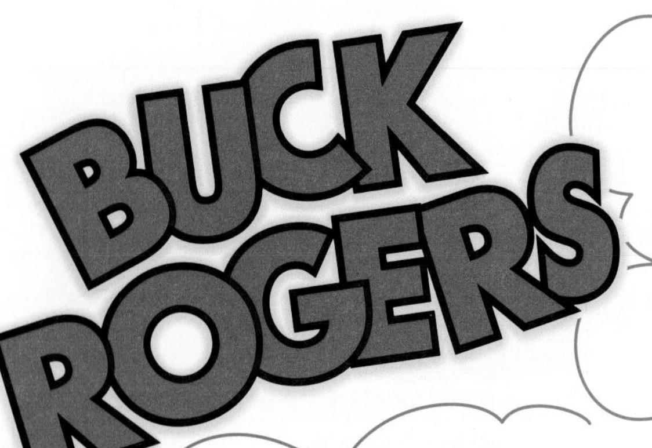

The idea of space travel was once so fantastic that it was confined to the comics pages. There, writers and illustrators could let their imaginations soar to describe what the future might hold. Were they right? Were they even close? You be the judge.

IN THE 25TH CENTURY

In 1929, writer Phil Nowlan and illustrator Dick Calkins began to chronicle the adventures of Buck Rogers, a man trapped in a cave who woke up 500 years into the future. Running until 1967, this comic strip entertained Americans well into the real space age.

ABOVE THE STRATOSPHERE THERE WAS NO AIR. I COULD MAKE SPEED.

THEN I REVERSED THE SHIP AND DROPPED DOWN OVER NIAGARA.

ROARING CROWDS WELCOMED US.
QUICK, STODDARD! RUSH REPAIRS! LOAD SUPPLIES!
I'LL REPORT TO THE PRESIDENT RIGHT AWAY
LT. DICK CALKINS
380
TO BE CONTINUED

WHILE SUPPLIES WERE RUSHED ABOARD —
COPYRIGHT JOHN F. DILLE CO.
REG. U. S. PAT. OFF.

WE MUSTERED OUR CREW FOR THE FIRST MARTIAN EXPEDITION EVER TO LEAVE EARTH—
I, MYSELF WAS CAPTAIN
I WAS FIRST MATE
I WAS SECOND MATE
I WAS CHIEF ENGINEER AND CHEMIST
I CAME ALONG AS ASTRONOMICAL NAVIGATOR AND GRAVITATIONIST
I WAS ELECTRONIST
I WAS CHIEF ROCKET GUNNER
BUCK ROGERS
WILMA DEERING
LIEUTENANT BURKE
PROFESSOR STODDARD
BOB BYRON
JOE MARTIN
JUD HANCOCK

WHAT'S THE DELAY?
THE PRESIDENT IS COMING! WE HAVE TO CHRISTEN THE SHIP PUBLICLY. WHAT SHALL WE CALL IT?
LT. DICK CALKINS
381
TO BE CONTINUED

WE WERE ABOUT TO LAUNCH THE MOST DARING EXPEDITION EVER ATTEMPTED BY MAN – A TRIP TO MARS – TO RESCUE SALLY, WILMA'S LITTLE SISTER, AND ILLANA THE GOLDEN PRINCESS, FROM THE HANDS OF THE SINSTER TIGER MEN WHO DOMINATED THAT PLANET.
COPYRIGHT JOHN F. DILLE CO.

FIRST, WILMA NAMED OUR ROCKET SHIP—
I CHRISTEN THEE SATELLITE!

WE RECEIVED A SPECIAL COMMISSION FROM THE PRESIDENT HIMSELF.
– –AND WHATEVER BEFALLS, MAY YOU UNFALTERINGLY UPHOLD THE HONOR OF EARTH!

THEN WE SHOT SKYWARD, ON OUR FORTY SEVEN MILLION MILE JOURNEY THROUGH SPACE, TOWARD MARS – AND WE KNEW NOT WHAT!
382
LT. DICK CALKINS
TO BE CONTINUED

IMPORTANT Dates IN SPACE

from *The Day We Walked on the Moon*

by George Sullivan

1957

October 4 — *Sputnik 1*, the first artificial satellite is launched by the Soviet Union.

1958

January 31 — The United States launches its first satellite, *Explorer 1*.

July 28 — The National Aeronautics and Space Administration (NASA) is founded.

1961

April 12 — With the launching of *Vostok 1* by the Soviet Union, Yuri Gagarin becomes the first human in space; Gagarin orbits the earth.

May 5 — Cmdr. Alan B. Shepard, Jr., launched in a *Mercury 3* spacecraft, becomes the first American in space.

1968

December 21–27 — *Apollo 8*, orbits the moon 10 times.

1969

July 16–24 — *Apollo 11* makes the first lunar landing. Neil Armstrong becomes the first human to walk on the moon.

"All the News That's Fit to Print"

The New York Times

LATE CITY EDITION

VOL. CXVIII..No. 40,721

NEW YORK, MONDAY, JULY 21, 1969

10 CENTS

MEN WALK ON MOON

ASTRONAUTS LAND ON PLAIN; COLLECT ROCKS, PLANT FLAG

Voice From Moon: 'Eagle Has Landed'

A Powdery Surface Is Closely Explored

By JOHN NOBLE WILFORD

1981

April 12–14 — First flight of space shuttle *Columbia*.

1983

June 18 — Launching of *Challenger* carrying Sally Ride, the first American woman in space.

1986

January 28 — Shuttle *Challenger* explodes 74 seconds after lift-off, killing all seven crew members.

1988

September 29 — United States space program resumes with launching of shuttle *Discovery*.

1991

April 25 — NASA takes delivery of space shuttle *Endeavour*, built as the replacement for *Challenger*.

Blast-off and Re-entry

from *TO SPACE & BACK*

by Sally Ride with Susan Okie

ALA Notable Book
SLJ Best Books of the Year

My first space flight was in June 1983, with four other astronauts: Bob Crippen, Rick Hauck, John Fabian, and Norm Thagard. We went up in the space shuttle, the world's first spaceplane, which carries all of today's astronauts into space. We blasted off from a launch pad in Florida; then we circled the Earth for seven days. As we went around and around the planet, we launched two satellites, studied the Earth, and learned about weightlessness. After a week in orbit we returned to Earth. Our adventure ended as the space shuttle glided back through the atmosphere to a smooth landing in California.

Crip, Rick, John, Norm, and I have each had a chance to visit space again. We have found time on every trip to relax, enjoy weightlessness, and admire the view of the Earth and the stars. And, like all astronauts, we have found time to take pictures. The pictures help us to capture the excitement of our trip into space and share the adventure with our friends when we get back.

Most of the photographs in this book were taken by astronauts on board the space shuttle. Some were taken on my flights, some on other space shuttle flights. They will show you what it's like to eat from a spoon floating in midair, to put on a spacesuit for a walk in space, and to gaze at the Earth's oceans far below.

When I was growing up, I was always fascinated by the planets, stars, and galaxies, but I never thought about becoming an astronaut. I studied math and science in high school, and then I spent my years in college learning physics—the study of the laws of nature and the universe. Just as I was finishing my education, NASA, the United States space agency, began looking for scientists who wanted to become astronauts. Suddenly I knew that I wanted a chance to see the Earth and the stars from outer space. I sent my application to NASA, and after a series of tests and interviews, I was chosen to be an astronaut.

On January 28, 1986, this book was almost ready to go to the printer, when the unthinkable happened. The space shuttle *Challenger* exploded one minute after lift-off. After the accident I thought a lot about the book, and whether or not I wanted to change any part of it. I decided that nothing except the dedication and the words I write here should be changed.

I wrote this book because I wanted to answer some of the questions that young people ask of astronauts. Many of the questions are about feelings, and one that now may have added meaning is, "Is it scary?"

All adventures—especially into new territory—are scary, and there has always been an element of danger in space flight. I wanted to be an astronaut because I thought it would be a challenging opportunity. It was; it was also an experience that I shall never forget. *—Sally Ride*

LAUNCH MORNING.

6 . . . 5 . . . 4 . . .

The alarm clock counts down.

3 . . . 2 . . . 1 . . .

Rrring! 3:15 A.M. *Launch minus four hours.* Time to get up.

It's pitch black outside. In four hours a space shuttle launch will light up the sky.

Nine miles from the launch pad, in the astronaut crew quarters, we put on our flight suits, get some last-minute information, and eat a light breakfast.

Launch minus three hours. It's still dark. We leave the crew quarters, climb into the astronaut van, and head for the launch pad.

The space shuttle stands with its nose pointed toward the sky, attached to the big orange fuel tank and two white rockets that will lift it—and us—into space.

The spotlights shining on the space shuttle light the last part of our route. Although we're alone, we know that thousands of people are watching us now, during the final part of the countdown.

When we step out onto the pad, we're dwarfed by the thirty-story-high space shuttle. Our spaceplane looked peaceful from the road, but now we can hear it hissing and gurgling as though it's alive.

The long elevator ride up the launch tower takes us to a level near the nose of the space shuttle, 195 feet above the ground. Trying hard not to look down at the pad far below, we walk out onto an access arm and into the "white room." The white room, a small white chamber at the end of the movable walkway, fits right next to the space shuttle's hatch. The only other people on the launch pad—in fact, the only other people for miles—are the six technicians waiting for us in the white room. They help us put on our escape harnesses and launch helmets and help us climb through the hatch. Then they strap us into our seats.

Because the space shuttle is standing on its tail, we are lying on our backs as we face the nose. It's awkward to twist around to look out the windows. The commander has a good view of the launch tower, and the pilot has a good view of the Atlantic Ocean, but no one else can see much outside.

Launch minus one hour. We check to make sure that we are strapped in properly, that oxygen will flow into our helmets, that our radio communication with Mission Control is working, and that our pencils and our books—the procedure manuals and checklists we'll need during lift-off—are attached to something to keep them from shaking loose. Then we wait.

The technicians close the hatch and then head for safety three miles away. We're all alone on the launch pad.

Launch minus seven minutes. The walkway with the white room at the end slowly pulls away. Far below us the power units start whirring, sending a shudder through the shuttle. We close the visors on our helmets and begin to breathe from the oxygen supply. Then the space shuttle quivers again as its launch engines slowly move into position for blast-off.

Discovery
USA

Launch minus 10 seconds . . . 9 . . . 8 . . . 7 . . . The three launch engines light. The shuttle shakes and strains at the bolts holding it to the launch pad. The computers check the engines. It isn't up to us anymore—the computers will decide whether we launch.

3 . . . 2 . . . 1 . . . The rockets light! The shuttle leaps off the launch pad in a cloud of steam and a trail of fire. Inside, the ride is rough and loud. Our heads are rattling around inside our helmets. We can barely hear the voices from Mission Control in our headsets above the thunder of the rockets and engines. For an instant I wonder if everything is working right. But there's no more time to wonder, and no time to be scared.

In only a few seconds we zoom past the clouds. Two minutes later the rockets burn out, and with a brilliant whitish-orange flash, they fall away from the shuttle as it streaks on toward space. Suddenly the ride becomes very, very smooth and quiet. The shuttle is still attached to the big tank, and the launch engines are pushing us out of Earth's atmosphere. The sky is black. All we can see of the trail of fire behind us is a faint, pulsating glow through the top window.

Launch plus six minutes. The force pushing us against the backs of our seats steadily increases. We can barely move because we're being held in place by a force of 3 g's—three times the force of gravity we feel on Earth. At first we don't mind it—we've all felt much more than that when we've done acrobatics in our jet training airplanes. But that lasted only a few seconds, and this seems to go on forever. After a couple of minutes of 3 g's, we're uncomfortable, straining to hold our books on our laps and craning our necks against the force to read the instruments. I find myself wishing we'd hurry up and get into orbit.

Launch plus eight and one-half minutes. The launch engines cut off. Suddenly the force is gone, and we lurch forward in our seats. During the next few minutes the empty fuel tank drops away and falls to Earth, and we are very busy getting the shuttle ready to enter orbit. But we're not too busy to notice that our books and pencils are floating in midair. We're in space!

The atmosphere thins gradually as we travel farther from Earth. At fifty miles up, we're above most of the air, and we're officially "in space." We aren't in orbit yet, though, and without additional push the shuttle would come crashing back to Earth.

We use the shuttle's smaller space engines to get us into our final, safe orbit about two hundred miles above Earth. In that orbit we are much higher than airplanes, which fly about six miles up, but much lower than weather satellites, which circle Earth more than twenty-two thousand miles up.

Once we are in orbit, our ride is very peaceful. The engines have shut down, and the only noise we hear is the hum of the fans that circulate our air. We are traveling at five miles a second, going around the Earth once every ninety minutes, but we don't feel the motion. We can't even tell we're moving unless we look out the window at Earth.

We stay much closer to home than the astronauts who flew space capsules to the moon in 1969. When those astronauts stood on the moon, they described the distant Earth as a big blue-and-white marble suspended in space. We are a long way from the moon, and we never get far enough from Earth to see the whole planet at once.

We still have a magnificent view. The sparkling blue oceans and bright orange deserts are glorious against the blackness of space. Even if we can't see the whole planet, we can see quite a distance. When we are over Los Angeles we can see as far as Oregon; when we are over Florida we can see New York.

We see mountain ranges reaching up to us and canyons falling away. We see huge dust storms blowing over deserts in Africa and smoke spewing from the craters of active volcanoes in Hawaii. We see enormous chunks of ice floating in the Antarctic Ocean and electrical storms raging over the Atlantic.

Sunrises and sunsets are spectacular from orbit. Since we see one sunrise and one sunset each time we go around the Earth, we can watch sixteen sunrises and sixteen sunsets every twenty-four hours. Our sightseeing doesn't stop while we are over the dark

side of the planet. We can see twinkling city lights, the reflection of the moon in the sea, and flashes of lightning from thunderstorms.

These natural features are not the only things we can see. We can also spot cities, airport runways, bridges, and other signs of civilization. When our orbit takes us over Florida, we are even able to see the launch pad at Cape Canaveral, where we crawled into the space shuttle just hours earlier.

Astronauts are sent into space to launch new satellites into orbit, to return orbiting satellites to Earth, to fix broken satellites, and to perform many different types of scientific experiments.

The space shuttle carries satellites into orbit in its cargo bay. Satellites may be as small as a basketball or as large as a bus. Most are designed to be released from the spaceplane; a few are retrieved before the shuttle returns to Earth, but generally they are left in orbit to do their jobs. Some relay television signals across the country, some point telescopes at distant stars, and some aim weather cameras back at Earth.

It is not an easy job to launch a satellite. Before a flight, astronauts practice every step over and over so that they will be able to release the satellite at exactly the right time, at exactly the right spot over the Earth, and with the shuttle pointing in exactly the right direction. During the countdown to the satellite launch, the crew works as a team—a very well trained team working very closely together. Each astronaut "plays a position" on the flight deck: two are seated (wearing seatbelts to avoid floating away from the computers at a critical moment), one is near the windows, and one is floating behind the seats near the satellite switches.

What kind of scientific experiments do we conduct in space? We observe the stars and the Earth from our position two hundred miles up. On some flights we carry telescopes outside in the cargo bay. Because our orbit is above the atmosphere, these telescopes get a clearer view of the sun, stars, planets, and galaxies than any telescope on Earth. On some flights we carry sensitive cameras to take pictures of the land, sea, and weather back on Earth. Information gathered at shuttle height can help scientists study storms, air pollution, and volcanic eruptions and learn more about the planet we live on.

Inside the space shuttle, astronauts perform experiments exploring ways to make new substances—medicines, metals, or crystals—in weightlessness. We also record data about our own bodies to help scientists understand the effects of weightlessness. Before astronauts can set out on a two-year trip to Mars, scientists must be able to predict what will happen to people who stay in space that long.

THE DAY BEFORE THE SHUTTLE RETURNS TO EARTH, astronauts have to put away all loose equipment. Cameras, food trays, and books will stay attached to the ceiling or walls with Velcro as long as they are weightless, but they would come crashing to the floor if we left them out during re-entry. We drift around collecting things and stowing them in drawers. An amazing number of lost pencils and books turn up floating behind wall and ceiling panels.

Immediately after launch we folded and put away all but two of our seats to give us more room inside. Now we have to reattach them to the floor so we can sit in them during re-entry. We must also find the suits, boots, helmets, and life vests that we haven't worn since launch and put them on again for landing. It is often hard to remember where we stored everything. Once I almost had to come back to Earth barefoot because I had forgotten where I had put my boots!

Four or five hours before landing, we begin to drink liquid—four or more big glasses each—and take salt pills to keep the liquid in our bodies. We have to do this because our bodies have gotten rid of some water during the flight to adjust to weightlessness. Now we are about to feel Earth's gravity again, and if we do not replace the lost fluid ahead of time, we will feel very thirsty and lightheaded—and maybe even pass out—as gravity pulls the fluid in our bodies toward our legs.

We also put on "g-suits," pants that can be inflated to keep the blood from pooling in our legs. If we begin to feel lightheaded as we re-enter the atmosphere, a sign that not enough blood is reaching the brain, we can inflate our g-suits.

Finally we strap ourselves into our seats, connect our helmets to the oxygen supply, and fire the shuttle's small space engines. This "de-orbit burn" slows the shuttle down and brings us back into Earth's atmosphere. Once the engines are fired to start re-entry, there is no turning back.

The space shuttle re-enters the atmosphere about thirty minutes later. It is moving very fast, and as it collides with molecules of gas in the air it becomes very hot—in places, over twenty-five hundred degrees Fahrenheit. Only the special heat tiles glued on the outside of the spaceplane keep it from melting. The tiles protect the shuttle so well that inside we do not even feel the heat. But we can tell that it is very hot outside, because all we can see through the windows is a bright, flickering orange glow from the hot air around us.

After we have traveled a short distance down into the atmosphere, we begin to hear the rushing of wind as we shoot through the thin air. We feel a little vibration, like what passengers might feel on a slightly bumpy airplane ride. Gravity slowly begins pulling us into our seats, and we start to feel heavier and heavier. Since we are used to weightless books, pencils, arms, and heads, all these things now seem very heavy to us. It's an effort even to lift a hand.

As the shuttle falls farther down into the atmosphere, it flies less and less like a spacecraft and more and more like an airplane. It gradually stops using its small space jets to maneuver and starts using the control surfaces on its tail and wings instead. These surfaces were useless in the vacuum of space, but they become more effective as the air thickens. When the shuttle is about as low as most airplanes fly, it is only a few miles from the runway and is traveling below the speed of sound. At this point it is flying like a glider—an airplane with no engines.

Until this stage of re-entry the computers have been flying the spaceplane, but now the commander takes control. We approach the runway much more steeply than we would in an ordinary airplane, and we feel almost as if we're flying straight down. We slide forward in our seats, held back only by our shoulder harnesses, as the shuttle dives toward the ground. The pilot lowers the landing gear when the spaceplane is only a few hundred feet above the ground. The landing gear slows us down, but we still land at about two hundred miles per hour—quite a bit faster than most airplanes. The rear wheels touch the runway first, so gently that inside we can't even be sure we've landed. Then the nose wheel comes down with a hard thump, and we know we're back on Earth.

The space shuttle rolls to a stop. As I unstrap myself from my seat and try to stand up, I am amazed at how heavy my whole body feels. My arms, my head, my neck—each part of me seems to be made of lead. It is hard to stand straight, it is hard to lift my legs to walk, and it is hard to carry my helmet and books. I start down the ladder from the flight deck to the mid-deck—the same ladder that was unnecessary just an hour ago—and I have to concentrate just to place my feet on the rungs. My muscles are nearly as strong as they were before the one-week space flight, but my brain expects everything to be light and easy to lift.

My heart, too, has gotten used to weightlessness. For several days, it has not had to pump blood up from my legs against gravity. Now it is working harder again, and for several minutes after we land it beats much faster than normal.

My sense of balance also needs to adjust to gravity. For a few minutes I feel dizzy every time I move my head. I have trouble keeping my balance or walking in a straight line for about fifteen minutes after landing.

We stay inside the spaceplane for a little while to give ourselves a chance to get over these strange sensations. We do knee bends and practice walking while the ground crew moves a boarding platform over to the shuttle and opens the hatch. Then a doctor comes on board to make sure everyone is in shape to get off. We are all still a little wobbly, but about thirty minutes after landing we are ready to climb out of the space shuttle and walk down the stairs to the runway.

Once my feet are on the ground, I look back and admire the space shuttle. I take a few moments to get used to being back on Earth and to say goodbye to the plane that took us to space and back.

Think It Over

1. *When, do you think, are the most dangerous times for astronauts during shuttle flights?*
2. *At what point are the astronauts officially "in space"?*
3. *How many sunrises do the shuttle astronauts see during a twenty-four-hour day?*
4. *Why can't the shuttle astronauts ever see the entire Earth at once?*
5. *Describe the changes that the astronauts' bodies go through upon their return to Earth.*

Write

Would you want to blast off in the space shuttle? Write a paragraph explaining why you would or would not.

THEME WRAP-UP

SPACE FLIGHTS

Think about how the selections provide contrast to one another. How does what we really know about space and space travel differ from what we enjoy imagining about them?

Space travel can be dangerous as well as exciting. Based on what you've read in these selections, do you think the risks are worth taking? Explain your answer.

WRITER'S WORKSHOP There are many noteworthy events in space exploration in addition to the space shuttle program. Satellites, rockets, telescopes, and deep-space probes are only a few of the exciting developments in space exploration. Research the history of the American space program, as well as the space programs of other countries, and prepare a two- or three-paragraph report entitled "Additional Important Dates in Space."

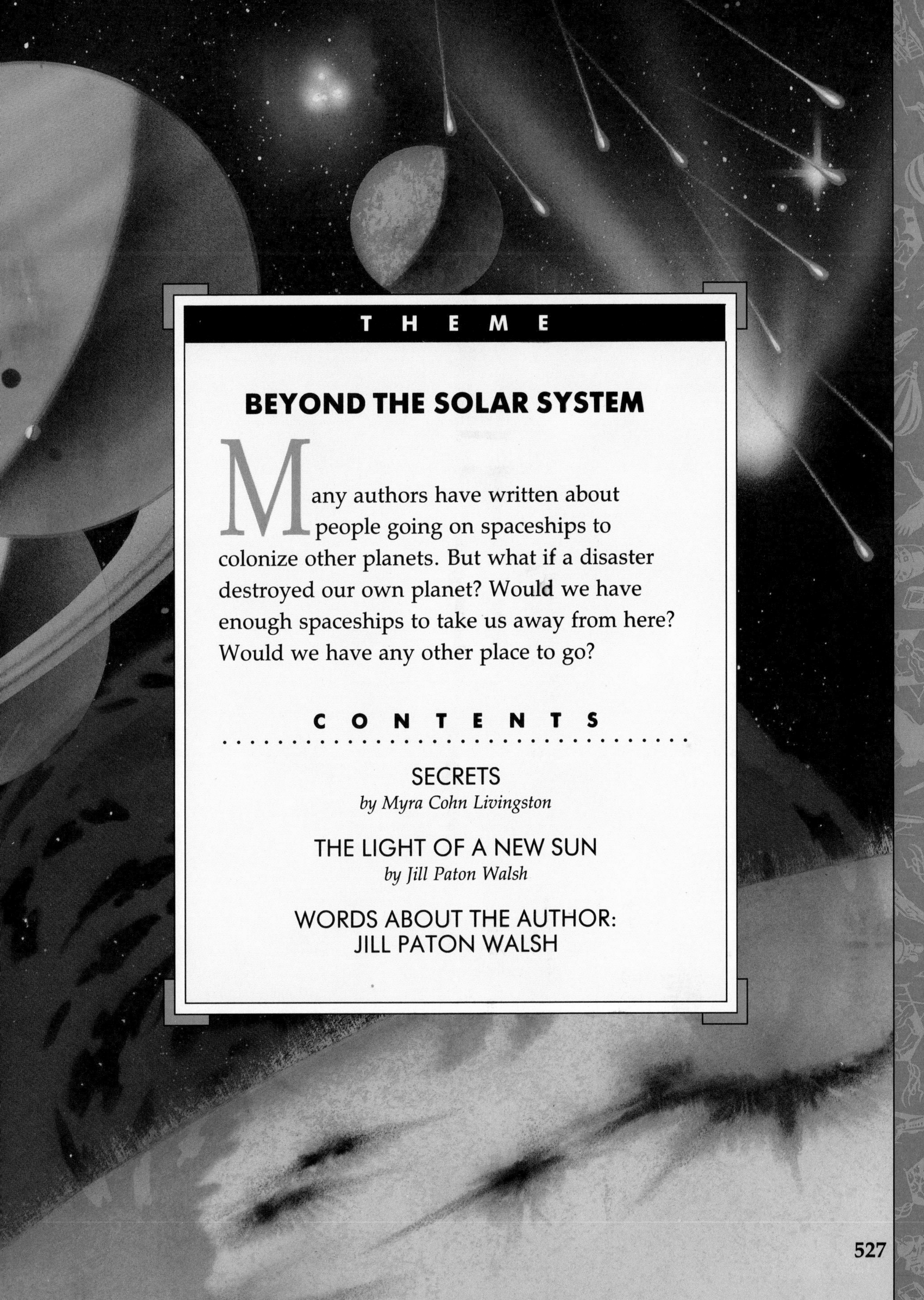

THEME

BEYOND THE SOLAR SYSTEM

Many authors have written about people going on spaceships to colonize other planets. But what if a disaster destroyed our own planet? Would we have enough spaceships to take us away from here? Would we have any other place to go?

CONTENTS

SECRETS

from
Space Songs
by Myra Cohn Livingston

Space keeps its secrets
hidden.

It does not tell.

Are black holes time machines?
Where do lost comets go?

Is Pluto moon or planet?

How many, how vast
unknown galaxies beyond us?

Do other creatures
dwell on distant spheres?

Will we ever know?

Space is silent.

It seldom answers.

But we ask.

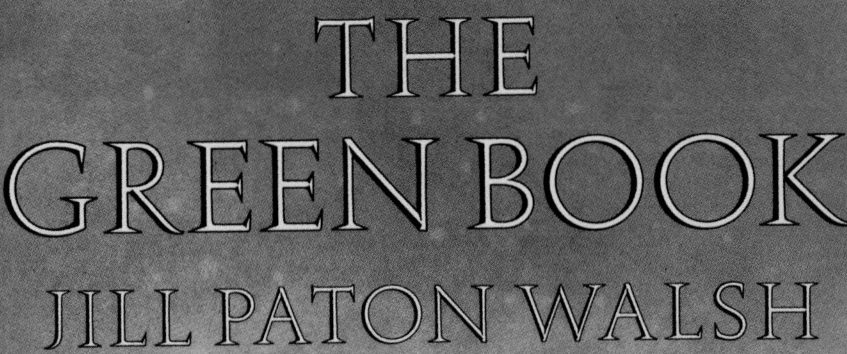

SLJ Best Books of the Year

Will Pattie and her family survive on the planet Shine?

The Light of a New Sun

from *The Green Book*

by Jill Paton Walsh

illustrated by Jay Leach

Father said, "We can take very little with us." The list was in his hand. "Spade, saw, file, ax, for each family. Seeds, etc., will be provided. Iron rations will be provided. For each voyager a change of clothing, a pair of boots, one or two personal items only; e.g., a favorite cooking pan, a musical instrument (small and light), a picture (unframed). Nothing under this heading will be taken if it is bulky or heavy, fragile or perishable. One book per voyager."

It was easy to pack. We were allowed so little, and we didn't have to bother about leaving anything tidy behind us. Only the books caused a little delay. Father said, "I must take this." He showed us an ugly big volume called *A Dictionary of Intermediate Technology.* "But you must choose for yourselves," he said. "It wouldn't be fair of me to choose for you. Think carefully."

We didn't think. We were excited, disturbed, and we hadn't really understood that everything else would be left behind. Father looked wistfully at the shelves. He picked up *The Oxford Complete Shakespeare.* "Have you all chosen your books?" he asked. "Yes," we told him. He put the Shakespeare back.

We had time to waste at the end. We ate everything we could find.

"I don't want to eat iron," Pattie said, but nobody knew what she meant.

Then Father got out the slide projector, and showed us pictures of holidays we had once had. We didn't think much of them.

"Have they all gone brownish with age, Dad?" said Joe, our brother, the eldest of us.

"No," said Father. "The pictures are all right. It's the light that has changed. It's been getting colder and bluer now for years . . . but when I was young it was this lovely golden color, just like this—look."

But what he showed us—a beach, with a blue sea, and the mother we couldn't remember lying on a towel, reading a book—looked a funny hue, as though someone had brushed it over with a layer of treacle.

Pattie was glad that Father wasn't going to be able to take the slide projector. It made him sad.

And the next day we all went away, Father and Joe, and Sarah, and Pattie, and lots of other families, and left the Earth far behind.

When this happened, we were all quite young, and Pattie was so young that later she couldn't remember being on the Earth at all, except those few last hours, and even the journey was mostly forgotten. She could remember the beginning of the journey, because it was so exciting. When we could undo our seat belts, and look out of the windows, the world looked like a Chinese paper lantern, with painted lands upon it, and all the people on the ship looked at it, and some of the grownups cried. Father didn't cry; he didn't look, either.

Joe went and talked to Father by and by, but Sarah and Pattie stood at a porthole all day long, and saw the world shrink and shrink and diminish down till it looked like a round cloudy glass marble that you could have rolled on the palm of your hand. Pattie was looking forward to going past the moon, but that was no fun at all, for the ship passed by the dark side and we saw nothing of it. And then we were flying in a wide black starry sky, where none of the stars had names.

At first there were voices from the world below, but not for long. The Disaster from which we were escaping happened much sooner than they had thought it would, and after two days the ship was flying in radio silence, alone, and navigating with a calculator program on the computer, and a map of magnetic fields.

The journey was very boring. It was so long. The spaceship was big enough to frighten us when we thought of it flying through the void. Joe kept telling Pattie not to worry. "Heavy things *don't* fall down in space," he told her. "There's nowhere for them to fall; no gravity."

"When I knock things over, they fall down, just like at home," Pattie said, doubtfully.

"That's just the ship's gravity machine, making it happen inside the ship," said Joe. "To make us feel normal."

But the ship was *small* enough to frighten us too, when we thought of spending years inside it. "We will still be here when I'm fourteen!" said Joe, as though he found that as hard to believe as Pattie found the lack of gravity.

"Better get used to it, then," said Sarah. We had pills to make us sleep a lot of the time, but the rules said everyone had to be awake some of each forty-eight hours. When people were awake, they played games, which were all on the ship's computer and could be played with the video screens. And one of the grownups had even brought along as his special luxury a funny hand set for playing chess which let you play it with another person instead of with the computer. When we weren't playing games, we could read the books we had brought. Joe asked Father why there were no books to read on the computer screens.

Father told us that all the new, well-equipped spaceships belonged to big wealthy countries. They had flown off to find distant, promising-looking planets. "We were the bottom of the barrel," he said, "the last few to go from an old and poorer country, and only an old ship available, and no time to outfit it properly. Our computer was intended for exploration journeys, not for colonization. It has no spare memory; it can barely manage our minimum needs. And there was so little fuel we couldn't get lift-off with anything extra on board—no useful livestock, like sheep or cows; just ourselves, and what the organizers thought we needed for survival. But we are lucky to be away at all, remember, and they allocated us a much nearer destination so that our old ship could get us somewhere."

There were some chickens in cages on the ship, with two very noisy cocks who had lost their sense of timing in the flight through darkness and crowed at all the wrong times when we were trying to sleep. And there were rabbits too; we could let them out and play with them. Rabbits are fun when you are very small and like furry things, but they aren't much fun, really. You can't teach them tricks. All they ever think about is munching. And when we got bored with rabbits, all we had was that one book each to go back to. Of course, we tried to read slowly. "Read each sentence at least twice, before you read another," the rule books said, under "Helpful Suggestions." But Sarah couldn't read that slowly. At home she read four or five books every week. She finished her book quickly and then wanted to borrow Pattie's.

Pattie wouldn't let her. So she swapped with Joe, and read his. He had brought *Robinson Crusoe.* Sarah didn't much like *Robinson Crusoe.*

"You'd better think about him, old girl," Joe said to her. "That island is just like where we're going, and we have to scratch a living on it, just like Crusoe."

Joe didn't like Sarah's book any better than she liked his. Hers was called *The Pony Club Rides Again.* Joe didn't like horses, and he couldn't resist telling Sarah that, after all, she would never see a horse again as long as she lived.

So then they both wanted to borrow Pattie's book. Pattie wouldn't lend it. "I haven't finished it myself yet," she kept saying. "It's not fair. You finished yours before you had to lend it."

In the end, Father made her give it to them. It was thin and neat, with dark green silky boards covered with gold tooling. The edges of the pages were gilded and shiny. It had a creamy silk ribbon to mark the place, and pretty brown and white flowered endpapers. And it was quite empty.

"There's nothing in it!" cried Sarah, staring.

"It's a commonplace book," said Joe.

"What's that?" asked Sarah.

"A sort of jotter, notebook thing, for thoughts you want to keep."

"And she's been pretending to read it for months!" said Sarah, beginning to giggle. They both laughed and laughed. Other people came by and asked what the joke was. Everyone laughed.

"Oh, Pattie, dear child," said Father when he heard about it. He didn't laugh, he looked a mixture between sad and cross.

"It was my choose," said Pattie very fiercely, taking her book back and holding it tight.

Father said, "She was too young. I should have chosen for her. But no use crying over spilt milk."

We did get used to being on the ship, in the end. A funny thing happened to the way people felt about it. At first, everyone had hated it, grumbled all the time about tiny cubicles, about no exercise, about nothing to do. They had quarreled a lot. Grownup quarreling isn't very nice. We were luckier than most families; we didn't seem to quarrel, though we got very cross and scratchy about things, just like other people. But time went by, and people settled down to playing games, and sleeping, and talking a little, and got used to it, and so when at last everyone had had four birthdays on the ship, and the journey had been going on for what seemed like forever and ever, and the Guide told us all there were only months to go now, people were worried instead of glad.

"We shall be lucky if we can walk more than three steps, we're so flabby," said Father, and people began to do pushups in their cabins, and line up for a turn on the cycle machine for exercising legs.

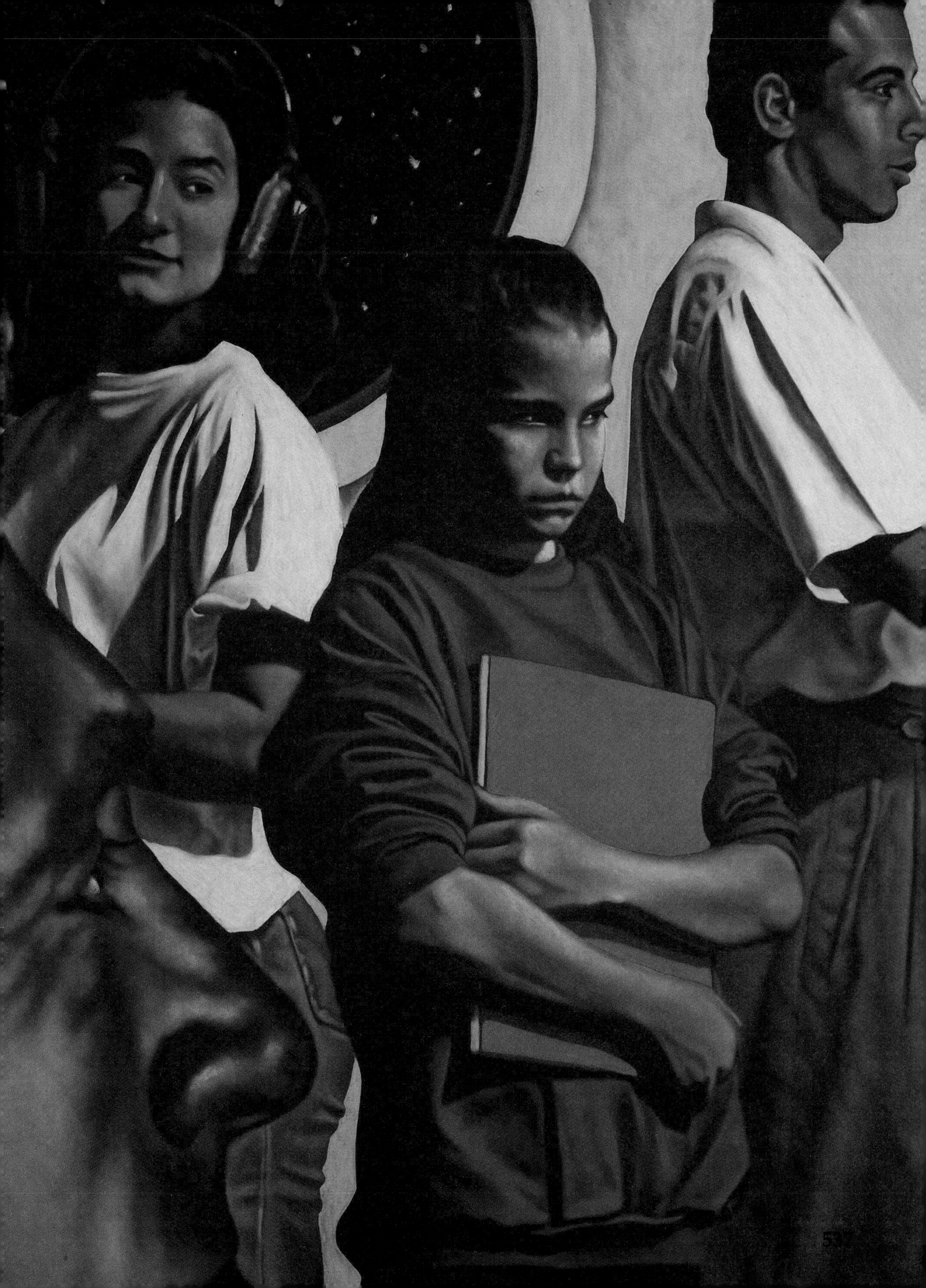

Joe began to ask a lot of questions. He didn't like the answers he got and he talked to Pattie and Sarah about it after lights-out in sleeping times. "They just don't know what this place is going to be like," he told them. "They *think* it should support life; they know there is plant growth on it, and they suppose that means we could grow wheat. But there may be wild animals, or any kind of monster people on it already, they don't know."

"Couldn't there possibly be wild ponies, Joe?" said Sarah.

"No, sis, I don't think so," said Joe, very kindly. "And if this place isn't any good, we can't go anywhere else. The fuel won't last."

* * * * *

A time came when we reached the light of a new sun. Bright golden light filled the spaceship from the starboard portholes. The cocks woke up and crowed as if for all the missing mornings on the whole long trip. The sun warmed the ship, and made it hard to sleep at sleeping time. And then the new planet loomed up on the starboard side. It looked unlike the Earth, said the grownups, who could remember what the Earth had looked like. It was redder and shinier; it had no cloud drifts around it. When it got near, it looked like maps in bright colors. It didn't look green. People spent all day looking anxiously through the portholes at it, trying to guess the meaning of what they could see. Just before touchdown, we could all see a land with mountains, craggy and rocky, and large lakes lying on the land surface everywhere; but as the ship came in to land, nightfall was racing us across the ground—a big black shadow, engulfing everything, moving faster than we were ourselves, its crescent edge going at a dizzy speed, and leaving us behind, so that we landed in total darkness. It was an auto-control landing anyway. It happened smoothly. The ship landed at a steep angle, but immediately straightened up by leveling its podlike legs. Then it switched off its own gravity and hummed quietly into run-down cycles.

When the gravity machine switched off, everyone felt lightheaded, and, indeed, light. The planet's own gravity was less than the ship had got us used to. Pattie found she could jump up and touch her cabin roof, and land without thudding enough to make anyone cross. Everyone felt full of energy, and eagerness to get out. But the Guide said the ship must be kept locked till daylight. So little was known, it would be dangerous to go out.

Arthur, the head of one of the families, said he would go and have a look, at his own risk, and then the Guide spoke to us very sternly.

"It's natural to feel excited," he said. "But this is not a holiday. We are a handpicked group; we are the minimum number that can possibly survive and multiply. Between us we have the skills we require. But the loss of a single member of our party will endanger the survival of us all. There is no such thing, Arthur, as 'your own risk.' Not any more. And may we all remember that."

We sat around, fidgeting, restless, talking together in lowered voices, waiting for dawn. None of the games interested us now. Pattie couldn't sleep, though Father made her lie down on her bunk. The feeling of suspense, the unfamiliar rhythm of the machines running themselves toward shutdown, the altered pitch of the voices around her kept her awake so late, so long, that when dawn broke at last she was fast asleep and did not see it.

But Sarah told her it had come like a dark curtain being swept aside in a single rapid movement; for a few minutes there was a deep indigo light, and after that, brilliance.

The Guide walked around the ship, looking out of each porthole in turn. All that he could see was rocks, white and gray, rather glittery crags, all very near the ship, blocking any distant view. They gave Arthur a breathing mask and put him through the inner door to the ship's main hatch, closing it behind him before he opened the outer door. He came back very quickly. "Come out," he said. "The air is good."

So we trooped down the ramp and found ourselves in the shadow of the ship, in a narrow gully between one rock face and another. It seemed to be a sort of hanging valley in a hill. A tiny runnel of flowing clear liquid threaded between rocks in the bottom of the dip, over a bed of silver-white sand and pebbles. Malcolm, the party's chemist, took a sample of the stream in a little specimen bottle, to test it.

Pattie was so sleepy after the night before that she could hardly walk, and Father picked her up and carried her, nodding with drowsiness, rather than leave her alone in the ship. She went in his arms, up the slope toward a gentle saddle between one side of the valley and the other, where all the others were walking. It was easy to walk, even up the slope; Pattie felt light and easy to carry. So up we all went to the rim of the hollow, and looked over.

Before us lay a wide and gentle plain sloping to the shores of a round wide lake some miles across. Beyond the lake, a very high mountain with perfectly symmetrical slopes rose into the sky, topped with snow. A mirror image of the lovely mountain hung inverted in the lake, quite still, for the surface was like glass, perfectly unruffled by even the slightest impulse of the air. The surface of the plain was gray and silver, shining like marcasite in places, in others with a pewter sheen. To the left and right of the plain, on gentle hills, were wide sweeps of woodland, with quite recognizable and normal trees, except that the leaves upon them were not green but shades of red, and shining, like the blaze of an amazing autumn. It was very beautiful, and perfectly silent, and perfectly still.

The children ran forward onto the open expanse of land before them, shouting. And at once we were limping, crying, and hopping back. We were still wearing the soft ship slippers we had been given to keep down the noise in the corridors of the spacecraft, and the pretty gray grass and flowers had cut through the thin leather at once, and cut our feet. The Guide ordered the crate of boots to be brought from the store and unpacked. Someone fetched ointment and bandages. Meanwhile, we stooped and picked the sharp plants, which broke easily in our fingers when gathered; they seemed to be made of glass, sharp and shining like jewels. But as soon as we all had boots on, we could walk over them safely, for the growth was crushed beneath the soles, as fragile and as crunchy to walk on as the frost-stiffened grass of winter on Earth.

We all walked over the crisp and sparkling frost plain, down toward the shores of the lake. It took an hour to reach it. The lake shore was a wide silver beach, made of soft bright sand, like grains of worn-down glass. And all the time we walked toward the lake, it did not move, or ruffle, even enough to shake the curtains of reflected mountain and reflected sky that hung in it. And though the air smelled good and sweet to breathe, it was windless, and as still as the air in a deep cave underground. Only the little rivulet that followed us across to the lake from the crag valley where the ship had lodged moved; it chuckled gently from stone to stone, and sparkled as brightly as the glass leaves and grass. When we got to the beach, Pattie went to look where it joined the lake, to see if it would make some splash or ripples for just a little way, but it seemed to slide beneath the surface at once and made only the faintest ripple ring, quickly dying in the brilliant mirror of the lake.

"I think we may be lucky," said the Guide. "I think this place is good."

People laughed, and some of the grownups kissed each other. The children ran to the edge of the lake and made it splash. Jason's mother ran along the beach, calling to the wading children not to drink from the lake until Malcolm had made sure it was water. Everyone was thirsty from walking, and the lake looked clear and good, but we all obediently drank from the flagons of recycled water from the ship.

"Right," said the Guide. "We shall begin the settlement program. And first we need to name the place we are about to build. The instructions suggest that the youngest person present should give the name. That can't include the real babies, obviously; Pattie or Jason—which is the youngest?"

Jason's mother and Pattie's father spoke together.

"It is Pattie, by a few days," said Father. "Well, Pattie, where are we?"

"We are at Shine, on the first day," said Pattie, solemnly.

"Good girl," said the Guide. "This place, then, is Shine. And now we must all work, and fast, for we do not know how long the days are here, or what dangers there may be." And he began to hand out jobs to each one in turn.

So people went back to the ship to unload the land truck, fill it with tents and food and sleeping bags, and bring them to the shore. Malcolm went to complete his tests for water. A work party was formed to unload the land hopper and put it together. The land hopper would glide or fly just above the ground, and let us explore quickly, and then it would run out of fuel and be of no more use. And the Guide had two men standing with guns ready, one each side of the camping ground, in case of wild beasts, or enemies.

"In science fiction, bullets go right through things and they come right on anyway, roaring, *urrrrrr*!" said Jason. "And we're in science fiction now, aren't we, so what good are guns?"

"We are in Shine," said Pattie. "And no monsters will come." Jason hadn't talked to her much on the flight; he was much shorter than she, and he thought she was older. But now he had found that, although she was taller, she was younger, and he got friendlier.

There was no job for either, so they watched Joe setting up a tally stick. It was a huge plastic post with rows and rows of holes in it, and black pegs to move in the holes.

"What's it for, Joe?" they asked.

"It's a calendar," said Joe. "We have to count the days here, or we'll lose track. All the things on the ship will run down and stop working—clocks, calculators, everything. So this thing just keeps a count—you move one hole for each day. You move the peg, and you remember when you are."

"A tree of days," said Pattie.

The grownups brought a stove from the ship, and a can of fuel, and set it up to cook supper on the beach, for the sand was soft and easy to sit and walk on, unlike the gray glass grass. A ring of tents went up around the stove. Malcolm decided that the little stream and the huge lake were both good water, fit to drink—and after the stale recycled water we had been drinking for so long, how fresh and clean and cool the lake water tasted! Everyone laughed again, and passed the cups from hand to hand, exclaiming.

The Guide said they must set a guard over the camp all night. "Any kind of living thing, harmless or savage, may be here," he said. The wilderness seemed so beautiful and so still it was hard to believe that, but they chose five of the men to take turns on watch.

And only just in time, for soon after the watch was chosen, the night came upon us. A curtain of deep lilac light swept across the lake, obscuring the sight of the mountain, and sinking almost at once to a deepening purple, then inky darkness. It got dark much quicker that it would have done on Earth—in less than half an hour. The darkness was complete for a moment or two; and then as our eyes got used to it, it was pierced by hundreds of bright and unknown stars—nameless constellations shining overhead. People began to spread their bedding in the tents, and to settle to sleep, and as they did so, a gust of air shook the tent walls, and there was a sighing sound of wind in the woods, and a lapping of water on the shore close by, unseen in the dark. And then the air was quite still again, and it began to rain, heavily and steadily, though the stars were still bright and clear above. When Pattie fell asleep she could hear Father and Malcolm talking together in low voices at the other end of the tent.

"There must be no dust at all in this atmosphere," said Malcolm. "That would scatter light and delay the dark. No wonder it feels so invigorating to breathe."

Father took his turn on watch, but nothing stirred all night, he said. The rain stopped in an hour or so, and not so much as a gust of air moved anywhere around. At the sudden return of daylight, all was well.

Think It Over

1. *What is the reason for the space voyage in this story?*
2. *Why won't Pattie trade books with the other children?*
3. *What are the most important tasks facing the travelers once they land on their new planet?*
4. *Why does the Guide choose Pattie to name the new planet?*
5. *Would you want to set out on a four-year voyage to an unknown planet? Explain your answer.*

Write

The children are allowed to take only one book apiece on the journey. Write a paragraph explaining what book you would take and why.

Words About the AUTHOR: Jill Paton Walsh

AWARD-WINNING AUTHOR

Jill Paton Walsh grew up in London, England, during World War II. It was a time of danger, upset, and change for the whole world—especially for children.

Ms. Walsh was born with Erb's palsy, which causes her right hand to be weak. When she was little, people thought she could not do many things and that she would have trouble learning easily in school. But young Jill found out she could do most things if she tried. In fact, when people thought she couldn't do something, it made her want to do that thing even more. Over the years, Ms. Walsh has learned there are only a few things she cannot do. She cannot lift heavy things from high shelves or be a bell-ringer or put curlers in her hair. But these things are not important to her. What are important are all the things she is able to do despite her weak hand.

Ms. Walsh graduated from Great Britain's famous Oxford University. Then she got married and became a teacher. She quit teaching when her first baby was born, but soon she was bored. She got an old typewriter and began to write children's books. Why children's books? She says, "It never occurred to me to write any other kind." Even when she was a busy mother of three, she continued to write them because "you always have the time for what you really want to do."

THEME WRAP-UP

BEYOND THE SOLAR SYSTEM

Myra Cohn Livingston asks several questions in her poem "Secrets." Which questions might space travelers be able to answer someday?

How did you picture outer space as described by Jill Paton Walsh in "The Light of a New Sun"? Compare your mental picture to the artist's illustration of outer space in "Secrets."

WRITER'S WORKSHOP Pretend that you are the organizer of a trip to the planet Shine. Think of several reasons why people would benefit from going on this trip. Organize your reasons in a letter that might persuade someone to accompany you to the new planet.

CONNECTIONS

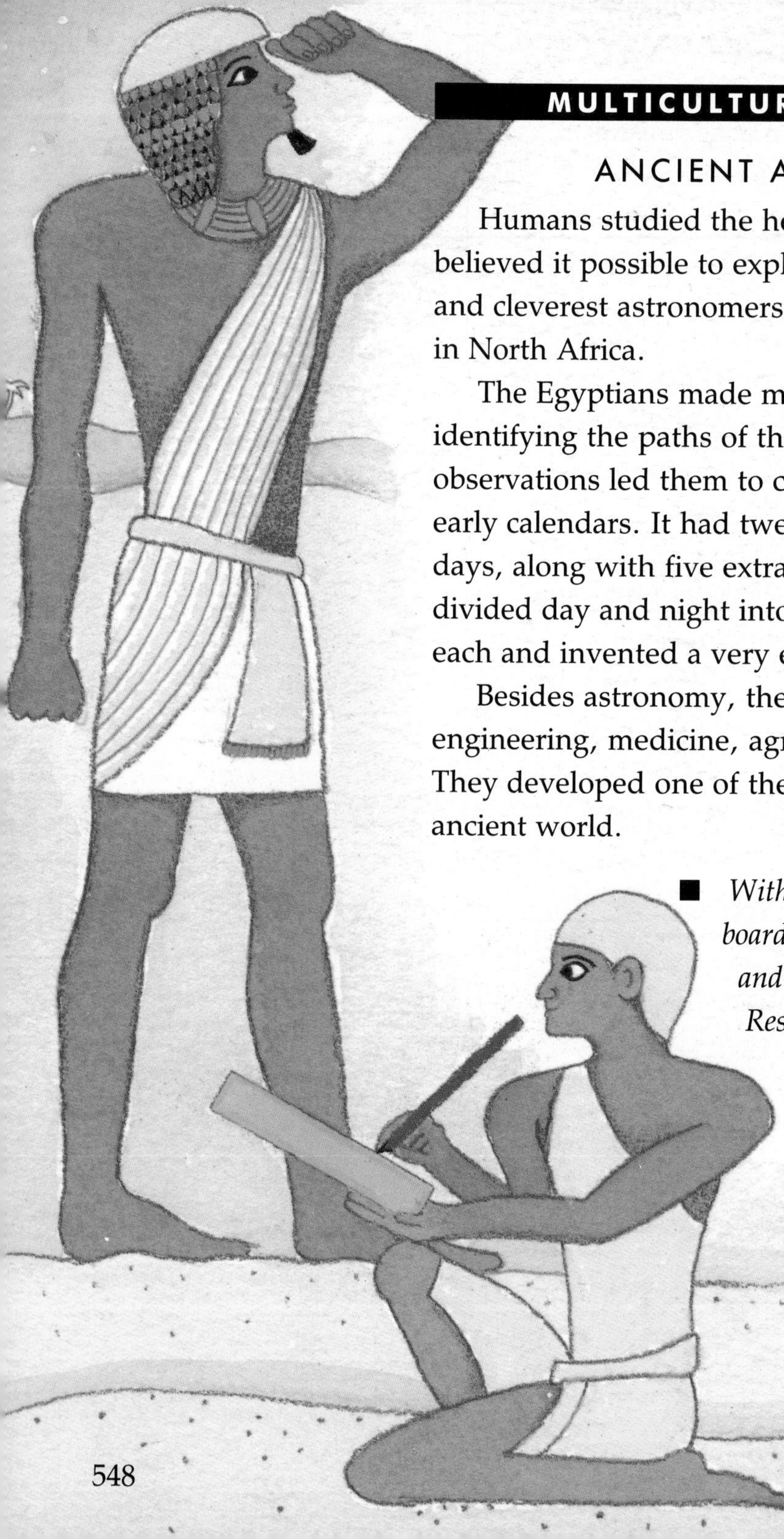

MULTICULTURAL CONNECTION

ANCIENT ASTRONOMERS

Humans studied the heavens long before they believed it possible to explore them. Among the earliest and cleverest astronomers were those of ancient Egypt, in North Africa.

The Egyptians made maps of the night sky, identifying the paths of the moving stars. Their observations led them to create the most accurate of the early calendars. It had twelve months, each with thirty days, along with five extra days in each year. They also divided day and night into twelve equal parts of time each and invented a very exact water clock.

Besides astronomy, the Egyptians excelled in engineering, medicine, agriculture, and many arts. They developed one of the greatest civilizations of the ancient world.

- *With your classmates, create a bulletin board display that shows the knowledge and the methods of early astronomers. Research such groups as the Anasazi, Aztec, Maya, Olmec, Pawnee, Tairona, Arabs, Babylonians, Chinese, Greeks, Romans, (east) Indians, and Khmer of Cambodia.*

SOCIAL STUDIES CONNECTION

SPACE EXPLORERS

Since people first studied the sky long ago, we have gradually learned more about it. Research an astronomer, a pilot, an inventor, or an astronaut who helped add to our knowledge of the heavens. Share what you learn by writing a news story about that person.

You can use a drawing like this one to help you record the facts you find.

Astronaut Guy Bluford

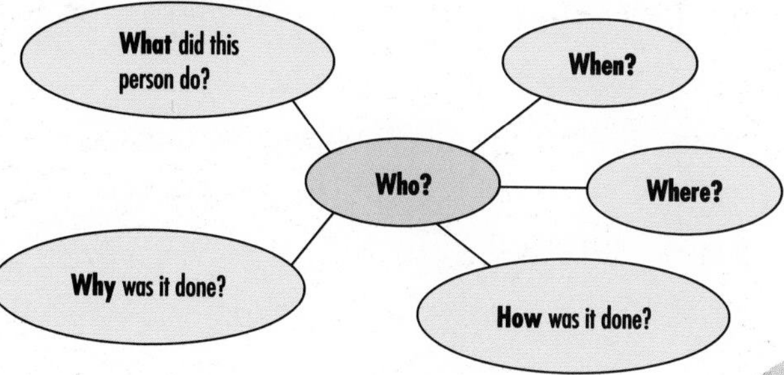

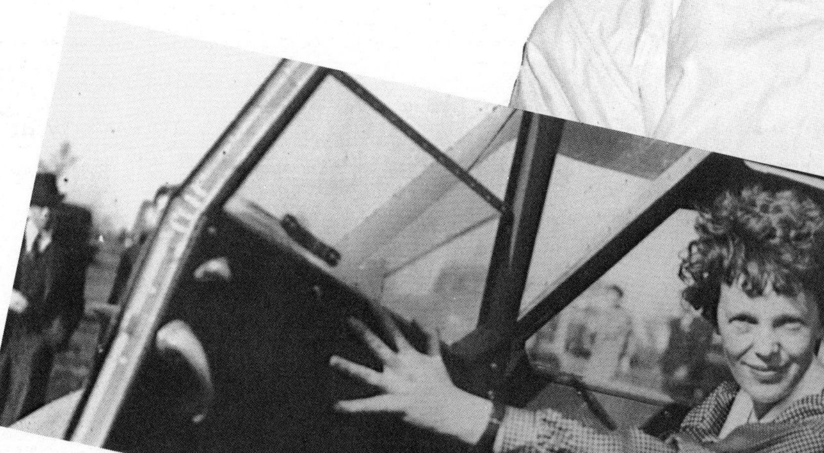

Aviator Amelia Earhart

SCIENCE CONNECTION

YOUR OWN SKY CHART

The winter nighttime sky is different from the summer nighttime sky. Find out how and why star positions change over a year. Look for interesting and unusual facts. In an oral report to your classmates, share what you learn.

Handbook for Readers and Writers

Active Reading Strategies

Think about the last time you read a story in your reading textbook or a comic strip in a newspaper. Did you understand everything you read? Everybody sometimes has trouble understanding what they read. Fortunately, there are reading strategies that can help. Strategies are plans for doing things. Look at the strategies these fifth-graders use.

Juan knows that good readers do certain things before, during, and after reading.

Before reading, Juan

- ✓ **previews** the material by reading the title and any subtitles, looking at illustrations, maps, or diagrams, and reading quickly through the first few paragraphs to find clues
- ✓ **thinks about the topic** and considers what he already knows about it
- ✓ **predicts** what will happen or what he will learn from his reading
- ✓ **sets a purpose** for reading

During reading, Juan

- ✓ **checks his predictions** once in a while to decide whether they are confirmed in the selection
- ✓ **changes his predictions** when he reads something that doesn't match what he expected

After reading, Juan

- ✓ **thinks about what he read** and decides whether he liked it
- ✓ **compares what he learned** with what he already knew about the topic
- ✓ **summarizes** what he learned from his reading to help himself remember it

Torah monitors her understanding during reading. When she discovers that she does not understand what she is reading, she uses these strategies. Torah

- ✓ rereads some of the paragraphs to **clarify** information
- ✓ **asks herself questions** that she hopes to answer as she reads
- ✓ **visualizes,** or tries to picture in her mind, the things she is reading
- ✓ slows her **rate of reading** to make sure she is focusing on the facts necessary for understanding
- ✓ notices when unfamiliar words are keeping her from understanding and then decides whether to reread, to read on, or **to find the meaning of the words**
- ✓ tries to make connections between what she is reading and **her own experiences**

If you combine the strategies that Juan and Torah use, you will discover that you are a more active reader. You will be able to get more out of whatever you are reading.

READING FICTION

What do you think about when you read fiction? Do you predict what might happen? Do you confirm your predictions? Do you put yourself in the place of a character? Do you draw conclusions about characters or events? Let's follow Ray's thoughts as he reads the beginning of "Tornado Alert!" He uses many good strategies both before and during his reading.

Before he reads, Ray previews. He predicts what will happen from information in illustrations, the title, and the introduction.

The title is a strong warning of danger. The introduction helps me predict that a tornado will strike these boys.

He recalls what he already knows about the subject and sets a purpose for reading.

From my science project I know about tornadoes. I'd like to read an exciting story about one!

During reading, Ray confirms his first prediction and makes a new one.

It's definitely a tornado. Now I know that Dan's mom, dad, and grandma won't be able to help.

Tornado Alert!
from *Night of the Twisters*
by Ivy Ruckman

The night of June 4, 1980, is a dark and stormy one in Grand Island, Nebraska. Some people are even predicting a tornado. Dan is at home baby-sitting his brother Ryan. Unafraid of the gathering storm, his friend Arthur has come over to watch a comedy on TV.

Sometime in there, in the middle of all that comedy on the screen, the siren began. Now, *that* is a very sobering sound. It's unlike anything else, having its own built-in chill factor.

I thought of Mom first. She'd hear it and come back, I told myself.

Then I thought of Dad and how far the farm was from town. They wouldn't even hear the siren out there.

In half a second, I was at the phone, dialing 555-2379.

Four rings. Then I heard Grandma's voice.

"Grandma!" I shouted into the phone. "Where have you been? There's a tornado just north of G.I. The siren's going, can you hear it?"

A voice said something, but it sounded so far away.

"Talk louder, Grandma! I can't hear you."

The voice faded away entirely. I wasn't even sure it was Grandma's now.

"There's a tornado coming! Can you hear me?"

Finally, there wasn't anything on the line but the sound of another phone ringing very faintly, as if it were in New York or someplace far away. I couldn't figure it out.

By then, Arthur was standing next to me. I was just about to hand him the phone when, abruptly, the siren stopped. It didn't taper off, it just quit, as if someone snipped it with scissors. Except for the TV, everything around us suddenly seemed very still.

"Hey," he said, raising his eyebrows, "they changed their minds."

I hung up the phone. I didn't know what was happening.

"Maybe they got their weather signals crossed," he suggested happily. "They could, you know. I read a book once about that happening, where this whole fleet of fishing boats put out to sea . . ." he rattled on.

I ran to the door, thinking I might see Mom pulling into the driveway, but no luck.

"It's quit blowing," I called over my shoulder to Arthur.

Sure enough, the wind had died down. Maybe the storm wouldn't amount to anything after all.

That nice comforting thought had hardly entered my mind when the siren blared forth again. With a jolt, I remembered what Mom had told us to do.

"We always turn on the radio," Arthur said, already on his way to the kitchen. "You want me to? I'll get the weather station."

I was hardly listening. I hurried down the bedroom hallway to Ryan's room at the end. I hated like everything to get him up. He'd cry. I knew he'd wake up and cry. Without Mom, Arthur and I would have him screaming in our ears the whole time.

When I saw him in his crib, peacefully sleeping on the side of his face, his rear end in the air, I just didn't have the heart to wake him up. I'd wait a minute or two. Mom would be back. Anyway, it's blowing over, I told myself, it won't last.

Quietly, I closed the door behind me.

That's when the lights started flickering.

In the hallway, I practically had a head-on with Arthur, who was coming at me real fast. The look on his face scared me.

"There's no . . . there's no . . ."

"*What?*"

"There's no radio reception anymore. It just went dead! This guy . . . He kept saying, 'Tornado alert, tornado alert!' Then it went dead."

He draws a conclusion about Arthur's character and makes another prediction.

Arthur doesn't sense the danger the way Dan does. I predict that Dan will have to take charge.

Ray confirms a prediction and draws a conclusion from Dan's actions.

Dan is starting to take charge. But I think he is still trying to convince himself that the storm will blow over.

He visualizes the scene and puts himself in Dan's place.

This is really getting scary. I wonder what I'd do if I were Dan, trapped in that house.

(See pages 126–135 for the entire selection "Tornado Alert!")

READING NONFICTION

Nonfiction is different from fiction and requires different reading strategies. One strategy especially useful for textbooks is known as **SQ3R**. Terri has used SQ3R to read this information-filled selection from *The Kids' World Almanac of Baseball.* Look at the explanation of SQ3R and at Terri's responses.

SURVEY: Look over the entire selection. How is it put together? Look at the title, the headings, and the pictures. What is the general topic? What do you already know about it?

Because the title mentions foreign leagues and baseball, and the headings talk about Latin America and Japan, I see that the general topic is baseball outside the United States.

QUESTION: Turn the selection title and headings into questions. Your purpose for reading is to find the answers.

1. *What are foreign leagues like?*
2. *What is the Latin American connection?*
3. *Why is Japan crazy over baseball?*

Foreign Leagues
from *The Kids' World Almanac of Baseball*
by Thomas G. Aylesworth

Baseball was born in the United States, but it has become popular in other countries over the years. Part of this popularity stems from the fact that Americans have carried the game with them wherever they have gone, both in peace and in war. American servicemen, for example, have been playing the game among themselves for many years now, and in so doing have introduced the game to many people around the world. The American-based Little League has also spread the game among young people in many countries.

It seems natural that baseball would be played widely and well in our neighboring countries, Canada and Mexico. After all, their minor league teams have long fed players to the major leagues.

The Latin American Connection

Baseball has been extremely popular throughout Latin America and the Caribbean Islands, and not only in places where the United States has had direct contacts, such as in Puerto Rico, Panama, and the Virgin Islands. Baseball is popular in Venezuela, Nicaragua, and the Dominican Republic, and there is a lengthening list of players from those countries who have moved up to become prominent players in the major leagues.

READ: Read the selection to achieve your purpose and to prove or disprove your predictions.

Cuba is a special case. Baseball was played there as early as 1878, and eventually Cuba supported a team, the Havana Cubans, which belonged to the Triple A International League. After Fidel Castro (who was good enough to have had a minor league contract offer to play baseball in the U.S.) took over as president, the United States severed diplomatic relations with Cuba in 1961, and thus cut off movement between the two countries. Now there are two independent leagues in Cuba, and baseball remains as popular as ever.

Japan Crazy over Baseball

Baseball was introduced to Japan by Horace Wilson, an American teacher in Tokyo, in 1873. The sport caught on quickly and was supported by schools and universities, spurred on by occasional tours by American collegiate teams. Until the 1930s, baseball in Japan was an amateur sport, with the strongest teams coming out of the Japanese universities. To this day, the university teams remain as the "farm teams" for the professional leagues.

Then came the visit of an "all-star" team of American professionals in 1931 and the visit of Babe Ruth in 1934. Since then, the Japanese have embraced baseball. They now support two major leagues, the Pacific and the Central, each with six clubs that play 130-game seasons and play their own Japan Series.

Baseball has yet to catch on elsewhere around the world as it has in Japan and in Latin America, but it is played by semiprofessional teams in Italy, France, the Netherlands, Belgium, Spain, England, South Africa, Australia, Taiwan, and Tunisia. Baseball has truly become international.

("Foreign Leagues" appears on pages 68–69.)

RECITE: Say in your own words what you learned from each section. This is what Terri said:

Americans have taken baseball with them to other countries, where the people like it. A lot of famous players come from Latin America. Cuba doesn't have ties to the United States now, but it still has baseball. Baseball became very popular in Japan in the 1930s, when Babe Ruth and others toured there. Baseball is played semiprofessionally in other countries, too.

REVIEW: Look back over the selection. Answer your questions from memory.

1. *Some foreign leagues are like our amateur leagues, and some are like our professional ones.*
2. *Baseball is very popular in Latin America. Players from there often play in the major leagues in the United States.*
3. *In Japan, Babe Ruth and other stars started a baseball craze in the 1930s that continues today.*

VOCABULARY STRATEGIES

An unabridged, or complete, dictionary of the English language may contain 600,000 words! No reader, no matter how experienced, could possibly recognize all these words. That is why good readers use a number of strategies when they come upon unfamiliar words.

When your reading is interrupted by an unfamiliar word, ask yourself, "Do I need to know this word to understand what I am reading?" If you cannot understand the selection without knowing the word, try using **context clues** and **structural analysis.**

CONTEXT CLUES: There may be clues around an unfamiliar word that tip you off to its meaning. Here are some kinds of context clues you may find. A word's **definition** may be part of its context. An **appositive** is a word or a phrase placed after a word to explain it. A **synonym,** or a word with a similar meaning, may also provide a clue. Occasionally, an **antonym,** or a word that has the opposite meaning, will appear. Tamara uses these context clues to figure out unfamiliar words in the passage below.

I haven't seen this word galaxy *before. Oh, great! The **definition** comes right after it.*

A galaxy, such as our own Milky Way, is a group of many millions of stars. Nebulas, or galaxies outside the Milky Way, take their name from the Latin word for *cloud*. This is because they appear somewhat hazy and indistinct, rather than clear.

What about nebulas? *That's easy. An **appositive** set off by commas follows it.*

I'm not sure about indistinct. *Wait.* Hazy *looks like a **synonym** for it. And* rather than *shows that* clear *is an **antonym** of both words.*

STRUCTURAL ANALYSIS: The structure, or composition, of a word can be a clue to its meaning. A word is often made up of several parts. The **root** is the main part. A **prefix** comes before the root and changes its meaning. A **suffix** is a word ending. It usually changes the way the word is used. Sometimes it adds something to the meaning. Here is how Tamara uses structure to figure out two words.

It is doubtful that we will ever be able to transport ourselves across the huge distances of intergalactic space.

Trans *and* port *are from Latin.* Trans *means "across" and* port *is "carry."* Transport *means "carry across."*

I know inter- *is a prefix that means "between." The root* galact *must have something to do with the word* galaxy *I just learned. I think the suffix* -ic *shows the word is an adjective.* Intergalactic space *must be the space between galaxies.*

OTHER STRATEGIES: If these strategies don't help you with an unknown word, try looking it up in a dictionary or a glossary. Or talk with someone who knows about the meaning and uses of the word.

One way to remember new words is to write them in a vocabulary notebook. Label a page for each letter of the alphabet. Under the appropriate letter, list the word with its meaning, and write a sentence using it. Add a hint to help you remember the word. You might try to find something interesting about its history. Below is Tamara's notebook entry for the word *galaxy*.

galaxy A group of many millions of stars. We can see the stars of a distant galaxy with a telescope. Galaxy comes from the ancient Greek word for <u>milk</u>. The Greeks first called our galaxy the Milky Way because it looked to them like milk spilled across the night sky.

SPEAKING

Do you feel nervous when you have to speak in front of people? You're not alone. Many people of all ages feel nervous about speaking. The best way to become a confident speaker is to identify your purpose, and then prepare and practice.

PURPOSE: Common purposes for speaking are sharing information, giving directions, entertaining, and persuading.

PREPARE: Good speakers prepare well ahead of time. They write key facts and quotations on cards to refer to as they speak.

PRACTICE: Good speakers speak clearly, slowly, and loudly enough to be understood. They use an interesting variety of words and speak with enthusiasm and expression. Julie and Marco are helping each other practice speeches they will make to their class.

- Julie's purpose is to share information. She will announce a local appearance of a famous Chinese kite maker. Julie will tell her classmates what to do to enroll in a kite-making workshop.

- Marco's purpose is to entertain. He will describe the funny experiences he had on his first day at school. As he practices, he tries to include emotion and humor in his speech.

LISTENING

If you have ever had to speak in front of a group, you probably realize how important it is to have an audience of good listeners. Like reading, writing, and speaking, listening is an important skill that takes practice.

PURPOSE: Good listeners begin by identifying their purpose for listening. There are three general purposes for listening:

- **Listening for appreciation** includes listening to poetry, drama, comedy, singing, and so on. Marco's listeners will enjoy his story of his terrible day!

- **Listening for information** includes listening to announcements, lectures, news stories, and historical accounts. Julie's listeners will find out about the Chinese kite maker.

- **Listening for directions** includes listening to learn how to do something, how to make something, or how to get somewhere.

BEHAVIOR: How you listen to a speaker depends on **the speaker, the type of speech,** and **the size of the audience.** For example, when you listen to a serious speaker, your behavior will probably be more formal than when you listen to a comical speaker. When listening in a small group, you can interact with the speaker by offering feedback and by cooperating. In a large group, you show your appreciation and respect by listening attentively and offering comments or questions only when asked to do so.

THE WRITING PROCESS

Do you ever get stuck when you are starting a writing assignment? All writers do. But don't worry—there is a cure! The best way to avoid getting stuck is to approach your task one step at a time. The writing process helps you do this.

Before you start the process, ask yourself three questions.

1. What is my **task**? Is it to write a descriptive paragraph? A business letter? A book report?
2. What is my **purpose** for writing? Is it to entertain? To persuade? To inform?
3. Who is the **audience** for my writing? Is it my classmates? The president of a company? The editor of a newspaper?

Carmen chooses to write a descriptive paragraph as her task, with her classmates as her audience, and to entertain as her purpose.

PREWRITING

Carmen starts by thinking about possible topics. She recalls scenes from her reading that were described so vividly that she can still remember the details. She makes a list of topics.

1. the tornado strike in "Tornado Alert!"
2. animals caught in the flash flood in "One Day in the Desert"
3. the new planet Shine in "The Light of a New Sun"

When Carmen considers this list, she decides that the first two topics might be better for a story than for a description. The third seems perfect for a descriptive paragraph. She decides to imagine and write about a beautiful new planet named Carmen.

Her next job is to organize her ideas. She could make a list, an outline, or even a web, but a drawing of the planet with descriptive words and phrases written on it seems best to her.

Drafting

With the ideas and the details for her description in order, Carmen begins drafting. She knows that she just wants to get her ideas on paper. She can change details and make corrections later. First, she writes a sentence announcing her topic.

```
The planet Carmen is one of the most
beautiful places in all of the universe.
```

Next, she chooses the best features from her picture and describes them in colorful sentences. After she finishes her draft, she rereads it to see whether she likes it well enough to go on to the next stage. At any point in the writing process, she knows she can go back and rewrite anything she doesn't like.

Responding and Revising

Now, Carmen shows her draft to her writing partner. Travis suggests some better words and a more lively ending. Carmen decides which suggestions she likes and uses editor's marks to make the changes in the last part of her description.

```
crash  wild                         sparkling
       The purple waves of the Saphire Sea
against
~~touch~~ the blue beaches.  From the
                       spectacular
quiet green valley to the golden plain
           bright rainbow
Carmen is a ~~very special place~~ in
Space.
```

EDITOR'S MARKS

- ∧ Add something.
- Cut something.
- Move something.
- Replace something.

PROOFREADING

Carmen's next step is to check for and correct her mistakes. To do so, she uses more editor's marks.

EDITOR'S MARKS	
≡ Capitalize.	∿ tr Transpose.
⊙ Add a period.	◯ Spell correctly.
∧, Add a comma.	¶ Indent paragraph.
∨∨ Add quotation marks.	/ Make a lowercase letter.

Carmen checks to see whether she has indented the paragraph. She has not, so she uses this mark: ¶ .

She checks to make sure she has begun each sentence with a capital letter and has ended it with a period. She uses these symbols: ≡ and ⊙.

¶ The planet Carmen is one of the most beautiful places in the universe. Two suns shine all the time on the cold, clear snow of the Crystal Mountains ⊙ it is never dark on Carmen, except down in the Great Quarts (Quartz) Caves. The wild purple waves of the Saphire (Sapphire) Sea crash against the sparkling blue beaches. From the quiet green valley to the spectacular golden plain ∧, Carmen is a bright rainbow in Space.

Carmen checks for capitalization errors. This word should be lowercase. She changes it with this mark: / .

Carmen checks for mistakes in grammar and punctuation. She uses this symbol to add a comma: ∧, .

She looks for spelling errors and circles the words she is not sure of. She checks each one in the dictionary and writes the correct spelling above it.

Publishing

Carmen's final step is to make a clean copy of her descriptive paragraph and to decide how to publish it. First, she makes all the corrections. She may want to publish her paragraph just by letting her classmates read it. She decides to brainstorm with her writing partner to come up with some additional ideas.

She could make a poster-size map of the planet Carmen, attach her paragraph to it, and hang the poster on the wall.

Carmen might create some unusual plants, animals, and people for the planet. She could brainstorm with her classmates for ideas, then draw the plants and inhabitants. She could attach the paragraph to the bulletin board and surround it with the drawings.

Carmen might pretend to be a travel agent and record a radio or television commercial for tours to the planet Carmen. She could place the audiocassette or videotape in the classroom library.

RESEARCHING INFORMATION

Learning how to do research can be helpful to you in many ways. Whether you are studying for a test on the American Revolution, learning how to build your own Chinese kite at home, or writing a report on the solar system, research is the first step. Frequently, research can seem overwhelming because of the large amount of information to sort through. **Skimming, scanning,** and **taking notes** are three strategies that can help you do research more quickly and efficiently.

SKIMMING: Skimming means looking over a book or a reference source quickly to find out its subject, divisions, and headings.

SCANNING: Scanning means looking quickly through a passage to find certain key words or phrases.

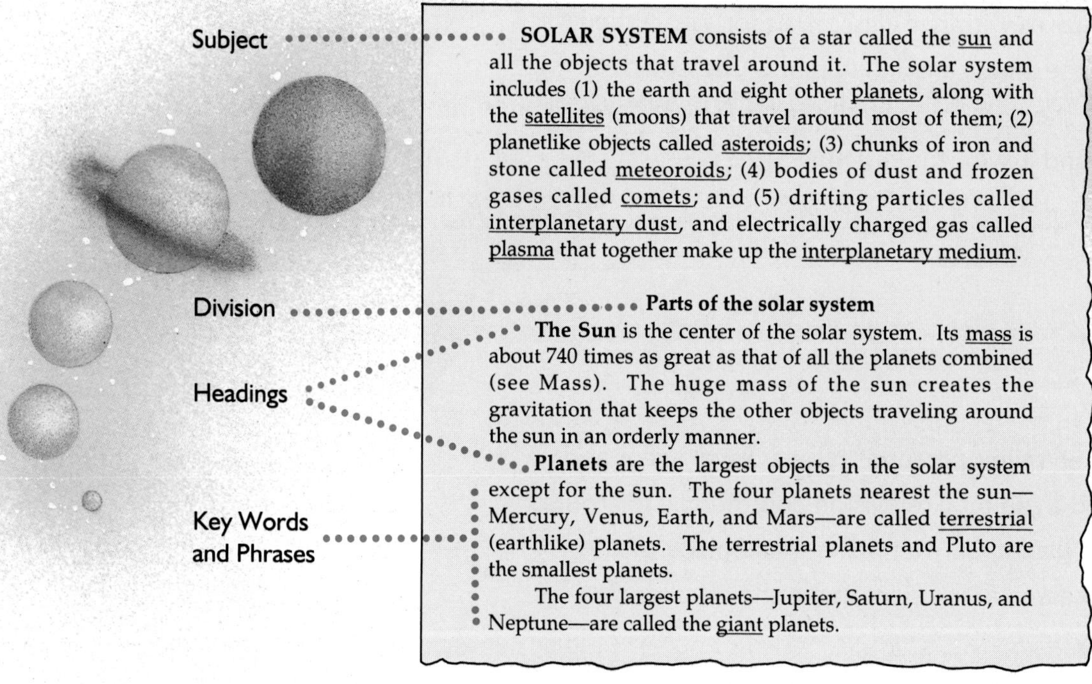

SOLAR SYSTEM consists of a star called the sun and all the objects that travel around it. The solar system includes (1) the earth and eight other planets, along with the satellites (moons) that travel around most of them; (2) planetlike objects called asteroids; (3) chunks of iron and stone called meteoroids; (4) bodies of dust and frozen gases called comets; and (5) drifting particles called interplanetary dust, and electrically charged gas called plasma that together make up the interplanetary medium.

Parts of the solar system

The Sun is the center of the solar system. Its mass is about 740 times as great as that of all the planets combined (see Mass). The huge mass of the sun creates the gravitation that keeps the other objects traveling around the sun in an orderly manner.

Planets are the largest objects in the solar system except for the sun. The four planets nearest the sun—Mercury, Venus, Earth, and Mars—are called terrestrial (earthlike) planets. The terrestrial planets and Pluto are the smallest planets.

The four largest planets—Jupiter, Saturn, Uranus, and Neptune—are called the giant planets.

TAKING NOTES: Taking notes can help you store the information from your research until you are ready to use it on a test or in a writing project. One very useful method for taking notes is known as Cornell Notetaking.

To use the Cornell Notetaking method, set up a notebook page so that you have a wide column for **Sentences** on the right and a narrow column for **Clues** on the left.

While you are reading your research material, use the right column to record each **main idea** in the form of a **complete sentence.** You will use this column to *store* information.

Clues	Sentences
	Mercury, Venus, Earth, Mars, and Pluto are the smallest planets.
	Jupiter, Saturn, Uranus, and Neptune are the largest planets.

After you have finished reading, use the left column to record the **most important words or phrases** from each sentence. You will use this column to quickly locate information.

Clues	Sentences
smallest planets	Mercury, Venus, Earth, Mars, and Pluto are the smallest planets.
largest planets	Jupiter, Saturn, Uranus, and Neptune are the largest planets.

The Library

The amount of information and ideas stored in an average library would probably surprise you! Libraries hold books; magazines and newspapers; reference materials such as atlases, encyclopedias, and almanacs; and audiovisual materials.

Libraries are organized in a way that makes it easy for you to find the materials you need. The **card catalog** lists every book in the library in alphabetical order. Each book is listed on three different cards by **title, author,** and **subject.**

The author card lists the author's last name first.

J
629.4
Branley, Franklyn M.
Rockets and Satellites / Franklyn M. Branley ;

The subject card lists the subject of the book first.

ROCKETS
Branley, Franklyn M.
J
629.4
Rockets and Satellites / Franklyn M. Branley ;

The title card lists the title of the book first.

Rockets and Satellites.
Branley, Franklyn M.
J
629.4
Rockets and Satellites / Franklyn M. Branley ;
Illustrated by Giulio Maestro.
New York : Thomas Y. Crowell, c1987.

Although the cards are often filed in drawers, many libraries now store card catalog information on computer data bases or on microfilm. Computerized catalogs are also organized by title, author, and subject. Suppose you want to use a computerized catalog to find information on rockets. First, you type the subject command and the word *rockets* on the computer keyboard. Printed instructions will appear on the screen to explain the steps as you go along. The instructions may tell you to type a command such as *R=rockets*. The computer will then give you a list of names and call numbers of books on the subject *Rockets*.

CALL NUMBERS: Each nonfiction book has a **call number** that appears on its three cards, on a computer screen, or on microfilm. *Rockets and Satellites* has a call number of 629.4. You will also find call numbers listed on the library shelves and on the spines of the books. Books of fiction are identified and alphabetized by letters of the author's last name. They do not have call numbers.

DEWEY DECIMAL SYSTEM: Call numbers are taken from the **Dewey Decimal System.** Most school and local libraries use the Dewey Decimal System to arrange nonfiction books by subject area. The subject areas are shown in the chart below. Next to each subject are topics that are typically found within it. The numbers on the left are the range of call numbers for the books located in each subject area.

000—099	General works (encyclopedias, atlases, newspapers)
100—199	Philosophy (ideas about the meaning of life)
200—299	Religion (world religions, myths)
300—399	Social Science (government, law, business, education)
400—499	Language (dictionaries, grammar books)
500—599	Pure Science (mathematics, chemistry, plants, animals)
600—699	Applied Science (how-to books, engineering, radio)
700—799	Arts and Recreation (music, art, sports, hobbies)
800—899	Literature (poems, plays, essays)
900—999	History (travel, geography, biography)

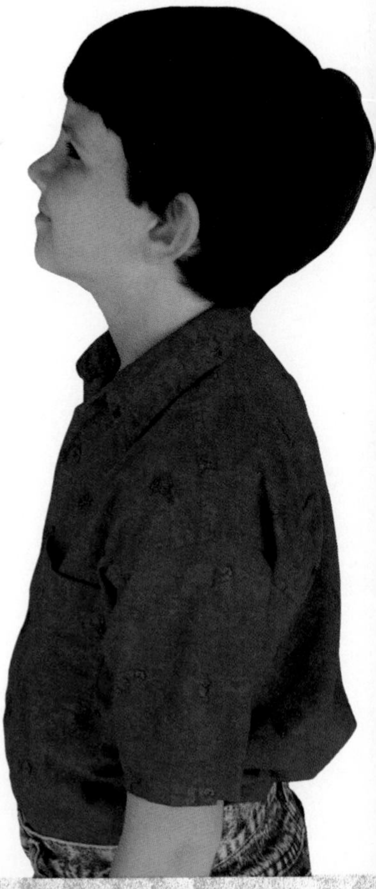

Rockets and Satellites is in the category of Applied Science, as you can tell from its call number.

GLOSSARY

The **pronunciation** of each word in this glossary is shown by a phonetic respelling in brackets; for example, [ak′rə•bat′iks]. An accent mark (′) follows the syllable with the most stress: [dis•krēt′]. A secondary, or lighter, accent mark (′) follows a syllable with less stress: [i•vap′ə•rā′shən]. The key to other pronunciation symbols is below. You will find a shortened version of this key on alternate pages of the glossary.

Pronunciation Key*

a	add, map	m	move, seem	u	up, done
ā	ace, rate	n	nice, tin	û(r)	burn, term
â(r)	care, air	ng	ring, song	yōō	fuse, few
ä	palm, father	o	odd, hot	v	vain, eve
b	bat, rub	ō	open, so	w	win, away
ch	check, catch	ô	order, jaw	y	yet, yearn
d	dog, rod	oi	oil, boy	z	zest, muse
e	end, pet	ou	pout, now	zh	vision, pleasure
ē	equal, tree	o͝o	took, full	ə	the schwa,
f	fit, half	ōō	pool, food		an unstressed
g	go, log	p	pit, stop		vowel representing
h	hope, hate	r	run, poor		the sound spelled
i	it, give	s	see, pass		a in *above*
ī	ice, write	sh	sure, rush		e in *sicken*
j	joy, ledge	t	talk, sit		i in *possible*
k	cool, take	th	thin, both		o in *melon*
l	look, rule	t͟h	this, bathe		u in *circus*

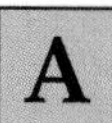

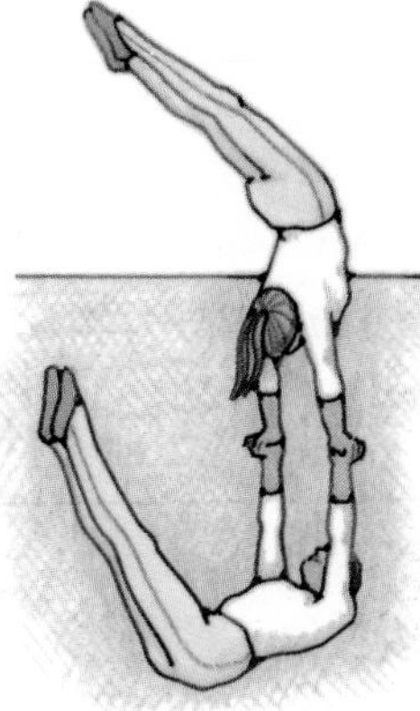
acrobatics

amateur

amateur Athletes who are paid for playing are called *professionals.* Those who take part in sports without payment for the sheer love of it are known as *amateurs.* Indeed, this word means "lover." It came into English by way of French from the Latin word *amare,* meaning "to love."

a·bate [ə·bāt′] *v.* **a·bat·ed, a·bat·ing** To gradually become less.

ab·o·li·tion·ist [ab′ə·lish′ə·nist] *n.* A person who believed there should not be any slavery in the United States: **In school we read a story about the *abolitionist* Sojourner Truth, who worked to end slavery.**

a·brupt·ly [ə·brupt′lē] *adv.* Suddenly: **Felix *abruptly* stopped singing when he forgot the words.**

a·bun·dant [ə·bun′dənt] *adj.* Very plentiful: **Tomatoes from the garden were so *abundant* this year that we couldn't eat them all.** *syn.* ample

ac·cu·sa·tion [ak′yo͞o·zā′shən] *n.* A statement from one person saying another person has committed a crime or a bad deed: **Aurelio's *accusation* that Jeff stole his story idea turned out to be correct.** *syn.* charge

ac·ro·bat·ics [ak′rə·bat′iks] *n.* Showy, skillful, and difficult movements: **The monkeys were swinging from branch to branch and doing *acrobatics* in the treetops.** *syn.* gymnastics

a·dapt [ə·dapt′] *v.* **a·dapt·ed, a·dapt·ing** To change to fit certain conditions. *syns.* adjust, conform

ad·just [ə·just′] *v.* **ad·just·ed, ad·just·ing** To reposition or reset something. *syns.* rearrange, regulate

al·le·giance [ə·lē′jəns] *n.* A strong belief in something: **On some national holidays, we sing patriotic songs to show our pride in and *allegiance* to our country.** *syns.* devotion, loyalty

al·lo·cate [al′ə·kāt′] *v.* **al·lo·cat·ed, al·lo·cat·ing** To set something apart for a special reason: **Mr. Flores *allocated* a part of his garden for beans and a part for peppers and tomatoes.**

am·a·teur [am′ə·cho͝or *or* am′ə·t(y)o͝or] *adj.* For enjoyment rather than money; not professional: **Joyce plays in an *amateur* soccer league on weekends.**

am·ble [am′bəl] *v.* **am·bled, am·bling** To walk very slowly: **The young puppy scurried rapidly across the room, but its mother merely *ambled.*** *syn.* stroll

a·nat·o·my [ə·nat′ə·mē] *n.* The structure of a person, a plant, or an animal: **Doctors must understand human *anatomy* thoroughly.**

a·non·y·mous [ə·non′ə·məs] *adj.* Not known: **Jean wanted to remain *anonymous,* so she left her name off the letter she sent to the editor.**

ap·pro·pri·ate [ə·prō′prē·it] *adj.* Right or proper; right to do at a certain time: **It is *appropriate* to send flowers when someone is sick.** *syn.* suitable

ar·thri·tis [är·thrī′tis] *n.* A disease that makes one's joints hurt.

ar·ti·fi·cial [är′tə·fish′əl] *adj.* Not made from nature: **Mr. Fernandez bought an *artificial* Christmas tree for his family last year.**

as·bes·tos [as·bes′təs] *n.* A mineral that will not burn or let heat pass through it: **Before it was found to be harmful to our lungs, *asbestos* was used to keep heat from escaping from homes.**

as·sure [ə·shŏŏr′] *v.* **as·sured, as·sur·ing** To make someone feel certain or convinced. *syn.* guarantee

a·stray [ə·strā′] *adv.* Off the correct path; away from the mark.

at·mo·sphere [at′məs·fir] *n.* The air around the earth.

au·thor·ize [ô′thə·rīz′] *v.* **au·thor·ized, au·thor·izing** To give the right or permission to do something: **Mr. Wilson *authorized* Carmello to take attendance before every meeting.**

au·to·mat·i·cal·ly [ô′tə·mat′ik·lē] *adv.* Like a machine; without trying or thinking first: **Lindell *automatically* washes his face every morning before getting dressed.**

B

beam [bēm] *v.* **beamed, beam·ing** To smile happily: **When the teacher praised his poem, Cesar *beamed* with pride.** *syn.* grin

beck·on [bek′ən] *v.* **beck·oned, beck·on·ing** To call by silent motions or by sending a signal.

bond·age [bon′dij] *n.* Slavery: **A person who is a slave is in *bondage.***

C

cam·ou·flage [kam′ə·fläzh′] *v.* **cam·ou·flaged, cam·ou·flag·ing** To hide by changing one's looks to blend in with the surroundings: **The soldier *camouflaged* herself in the woods by putting green, leafy tree branches on her helmet.**

camouflage

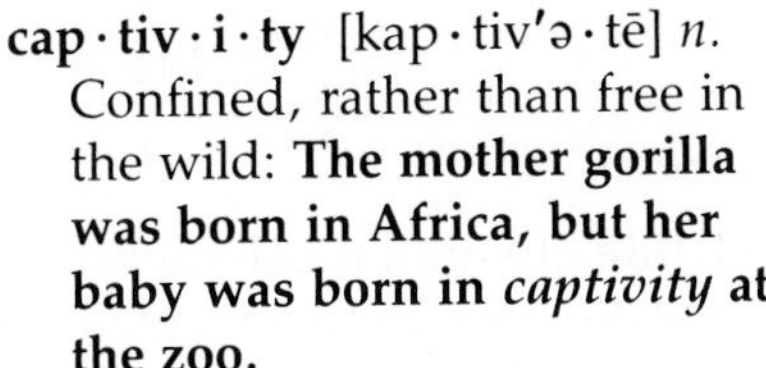

cap·tiv·i·ty [kap·tiv′ə·tē] *n.* Confined, rather than free in the wild: **The mother gorilla was born in Africa, but her baby was born in *captivity* at the zoo.**

car·a·van [kar′ə·van′] *n.* A group of people traveling together.

car·bo·hy·drate [kär′bō·hī′drāt′] *n.* An important class of foods, supplying energy to the body: **People all over the world eat bread, which provides them with *carbohydrates.***

ca·reen [kə·rēn′] *v.* **ca·reened, ca·reen·ing** To sway or lean over to one side: **The speeding car hit a curb and then *careened* on two wheels, throwing the passenger across the seat.**

a	add	**ŏŏ**	took
ā	ace	**ōō**	pool
â	care	**u**	up
ä	palm	**û**	burn
e	end	**yōō**	fuse
ē	equal	**oi**	oil
i	it	**ou**	pout
ī	ice	**ng**	ring
o	odd	**th**	thin
ō	open	**th̶**	this
ô	order	**zh**	vision

ə = a in *above*, e in *sicken*, i in *possible*, o in *melon*, u in *circus*

cartwheel

chortle Sometimes writers like to coin, or invent, words. Once in a while, these words catch on with readers and become an everyday part of the language. In 1872, Lewis Carroll, the author of *Alice's Adventures in Wonderland,* coined the word *chortle.* Actually he took two words, *chuckle* and *snort,* and, as linguists say, "blended" them.

conceal

cart·wheel [kärt′(h)wēl′] *n.* A sideways flip that is done by springing the body onto one hand and then the other, followed by the feet: **The gymnast turned three *cartwheels* and landed perfectly on his feet.**

chor·tle [chôr′təl] *v.* To make a chuckling or snorting noise. *syn.* chuckle

cir·cu·late [sûr′kyə·lāt′] *v.* To move about or around: **I opened the window to let the air *circulate.***

cit·i·zen [sit′ə·zən] *n.* A person whose legal home is in a certain place: **Elena and Ramon became U.S. *citizens* six years after they moved from Mexico.**

civ·il de·fense [siv′əl di·fens′] *n.* Program for protecting the public from attack or disaster, such as a flood or tornado.

col·lide [kə·līd′] *v.* **col·lid·ed, col·lid·ing** To come together with great force: **The car raced through a red stoplight and *collided* with a truck.** *syns.* crash, smash

col·o·ni·za·tion [kol′ə·nə·zā′·shən] *n.* The act of setting up homes in a new place with the purpose of staying and living a long time: **Some people believe we should consider *colonization* of the moon.**

com·mis·sion [kə·mish′ən] *n.* Pay that is a percentage of the price of an item that is sold: **Juana earned ten percent *commission* for selling the statue.** *syn.* percentage

com·mo·tion [kə·mō′shən] *n.* Noisy confusion: **The *commotion* was caused by raccoons trying to get into the garbage cans.** *syns.* disturbance, uproar, agitation

com·pli·ment [kom′plə·mənt] *n.* Praise; nice words said about someone: **Lucia gave her brother a *compliment* for the careful way he had planned the party.** *syn.* flattery

com·pound [kom·pound′] *v.* **com·pound·ed, com·pound·ing** To make by mixing together.

com·pute [kəm·pyo͞ot′] *v.* **com·put·ed, com·put·ing** To figure mathematically. *syns.* calculate, reckon

con·ceal [kən·sēl′] *v.* To hide something.

con·jure [kon′jər *or* kun′jər] *v.* **con·jured, con·jur·ing** To seem to create by magic.

con·ser·va·tion [kon′sər·vā′shən] *n.* The saving or protecting of something.

con·tam·i·nate [kən·tam′ə·nāt′] *v.* **con·tam·i·nat·ed, con·tam·i·nat·ing** To poison or to make dirty: **The campers did not drink from the river because pollution *contaminated* the water.** *syn.* pollute

con·ti·nen·tal [kon′tə·nen′təl] *adj.* Having to do with a certain continent, such as North America or Europe: **The rivers that flow into the Pacific Ocean all begin west of the invisible line called the *Continental* Divide that runs through North America.**

con·trap·tion [kən·trap′shən] *n. informal* An invention, such as a machine, that is odd and unusual: **Miguel built a *contraption* for watering his lawn from some wood, a hose, and a power lawn mower.**

cre·a·tiv·i·ty [krē′ā·tiv′ə·tē] *n.* The ability to make or invent things: ***Creativity* is a quality shared not only by artists and scientists but by anyone who is good at solving problems.** *syns.* originality, inventiveness

crim·i·nal [krim′ə·nəl] *adj.* Having to do with crime or those involved in crime.

crit·i·cal [krit′i·kəl] *adj.* Very important: **Completing every assignment is *critical* to your success.** *syns.* crucial, decisive

cu·ri·os·i·ty [kyo͝or′ē·os′ə·tē] *n.* The feeling of wanting to know about something: **Emiko's great *curiosity* about our school led her to ask many questions about our courses and teachers.**

cur·ric·u·lum [kə·rik′yə·ləm] *n.* The classes that a school requires or offers: **Math, reading, and science are part of the fifth-grade *curriculum* in our school.**

de·but [dā′byo͞o′ *or* dā·byo͞o′] *n.* A first appearance or performance before an audience.

de·cline [di·klīn′] *v.* **de·clined, de·clin·ing** To steadily become less: **Attendance at the football games has *declined* in the past year because the admission prices have risen.** *syn.* shrink

ded·i·ca·tion [ded′ə·kā′shən] *n.* **1** Devotion to something: **The doctor received an award for her *dedication* to her patients.** **2** A personal note in a book in which the author thanks or remembers someone: **The author's *dedication* to her father was on the third page of her new book.**

des·per·ate [des′pər·it] *adj.* With great need; very anxious: **Marie was *desperate* to get home because she was afraid she had left the iron plugged in.** *syn.* frantic

de·ter·mined [di·tûr′mind] *adj.* Feeling very strongly about making sure that something is done: **Allison was *determined* to finish building the model, even if it meant she had to work all night.** *syns.* committed, resolute

dig·ni·ty [dig′nə·tē] *n.* The quality of being respected and respecting oneself: **The winners of the trophies received the applause with pride and *dignity*.** *syns.* worth, pride

dil·em·ma [di·lem′ə] *n.* A situation in which a person must make a difficult choice: **The boys' difficult *dilemma* was whether to tell what they saw and risk punishment or to keep quiet and let a crime go unpunished.**

debut When a rookie baseball player steps up to the plate for the first time in the major leagues, we say that he is making his *debut*. This is an especially appropriate use of *debut* because the word first appeared in the world of sports. It came from an Old French word, *desbuter*, meaning "to play first" in a game or sports match.

dedication

a	add	**o͝o**	took
ā	ace	**o͞o**	pool
â	care	**u**	up
ä	palm	**û**	burn
e	end	**yo͞o**	fuse
ē	equal	**oi**	oil
i	it	**ou**	pout
ī	ice	**ng**	ring
o	odd	**th**	thin
ō	open	**t͟h**	this
ô	order	**zh**	vision

ə = a in *above*, e in *sicken*, i in *possible*, o in *melon*, u in *circus*

drape

eccentric If you try to spin a circular top on a spindle that is off-center, the top will move and behave in a strange way. Similarly, people whose behavior seems odd compared to the rest of us may be called *eccentric*, or "off-center." *Eccentric* comes from the ancient Greek *ek-*, meaning "out of," and *kentros*, "center."

engulf

di·min·ish [di·min′ish] *v.* To become smaller or look smaller: **We watched the kite *diminish* as it went higher.**

dis·charge [dis′chärj *or* dis·chärj′] *n.* Something that is released or sent out from its source.

dis·crete [dis·krēt′] *adj.* Set apart from others: **A huge job can seem easier when you break it down into separate, *discrete* tasks.**

dis·trac·tion [dis·trak′shən] *n.* Interruption in attention.

dra·mat·i·cal·ly [drə·mat′ik·lē] *adv.* In a sudden and sometimes scary way: **The principal's voice boomed *dramatically* from the public address system.**

drape [drāp] *v.* **draped, drap·ing** To cover with a piece of cloth: **The statue was *draped* so that no one would see it before the party.**

dread·ful [dred′fəl] *adj.* Awful, terrible: **We were scared to drive on that *dreadful* road because it had many sharp turns and no street lights.**

drear·y [drir′ē] *adj.* Causing sadness: **The house with its sagging roof and broken porch was a *dreary* sight in the rain.** *syn.* gloomy

dumb·found [dum′found′] *v.* **dumb·found·ed, dumb·found·ing** To make silent from surprise; to shock.

dwarf [dwôrf] *v.* **dwarfed, dwarf·ing** To make something look small by comparison: **My baby sister is *dwarfed* by the trees she is playing under.**

E

ec·cen·tric [ik·sen′trik] *adj.* Being odd or different from most people. *syns.* peculiar, weird

e·lab·o·rate [i·lab′ər·it] *adj.* Complicated; carefully planned out; detailed: **The suspect told an *elaborate* story about where he was and what he was doing at the time of the crime.** *syn.* complex

e·lec·tri·cal [i·lek′tri·kəl] *adj.* Having to do with electricity, which is a form of energy that is used for light and heat. *syn.* electric

em·bank·ment [im·bangk′mənt] *n.* A wall used to hold back water: **Mr. Payo walked down the steep *embankment* toward the river.**

em·brace [im·brās′] *v.* **em·braced, em·brac·ing** To hug; to accept something completely: **Carlos *embraced* his stepfather's way of doing things because it was usually better.**

en·er·get·ic [en′ər·jet′ik] *adj.* Lively; not easily tired: **The most *energetic* dancer was Stephanie, who didn't stop once.**

en·gulf [in·gulf′] *v.* **en·gulfed, en·gulf·ing** To cover completely; to close over.

en·light·en·ing [in·līt′(ə)n·ing] *adj.* Educating, informative: **After Ms. Estrella's *enlightening* talk, we felt we had learned a great deal about whales.** *syn.* instructive

e·nor·mous [i·nôr′məs] *adj.* Extremely large: **The donkey almost disappeared under the *enormous* load of straw on its back.** *syns.* huge, immense

en·to·mol·o·gist [en′tə·mol′ə·jist] *n.* A scientist who studies insects: **The *entomologist* identified the insect as an earwig.**

et·i·quette [et′ə·kət] *n.* Rules that one should follow for polite behavior: ***Etiquette* requires that you write a thank-you note to someone who sends you a gift.** *syn.* manners

e·vap·o·ra·tion [i·vap′ə·rā′shən] *n.* The loss of water into the air: **In science class we compared the rate of *evaporation* from pans of water during humid and dry days.**

e·ven·tu·al·ly [i·ven′cho͞o·əl·ē] *adv.* After the passing of some time: **The drive home from Grandmother's was very long, but we knew that we would *eventually* get there.** *syn.* ultimately

ev·i·dence [ev′ə·dəns] *n.* One or more facts or items that can be used as proof.

e·volve [i·volv′] *v.* **e·volved, e·volv·ing** To come into being: **Over the years, the quiet little town *evolved* into a big, busy city.** *syn.* develop

ex·hib·it [ig·zib′it] *n.* An item on display: **The museum has *exhibits* of Civil War uniforms.**

ex·pan·sion [ik·span′shən] *n.* The increase in the size of something: **The *expansion* of his business meant that he had to hire more employees.**

ex·pec·tant [ik·spek′tənt] *adj.* Waiting for something or someone: **The *expectant* children were awake early on the day of the trip.**

ex·pose [ik·spōz′] *v.* **ex·posed, ex·pos·ing** To make something easy to see: **The boy lifted up the heavy rock, *exposing* an active colony of ants underneath.** *syns.* reveal, uncover

ex·tinct [ik·stingkt′] *adj.* No longer existing or living: **If dinosaurs were not *extinct*, we would be able to study them in the wild and perhaps keep some in zoos.**

entomologist You may already know that the word ending *-logist* means "a person who studies." You probably don't know that the ancient Greek word for "insect" was *entomon.* If you put the parts together, you now know that an *entomologist* is someone who studies insects.

F

fa·nat·ic [fə·nat′ik] *n.* A person whose interest in something is greater than normal: **Bonita loved baseball so much that she was not just a fan, but a *fanatic.***

fas·ci·nate [fas′ə·nāt′] *v.* **fas·ci·nat·ed, fas·ci·nat·ing** To attract and hold interest: **She was so *fascinated* by the bird building its nest that she couldn't stop watching it.**

feist·y [fī′stē] *adj. informal* Very active or jittery.

flail [flāl] *v.* **flailed, flail·ing** To move wildly as if beating something: **Charles was *flailing* around in the water so violently that the people on the beach thought he was drowning.** *syn.* thrash

exhibits

a	add	**o͝o**	took
ā	ace	**o͞o**	pool
â	care	**u**	up
ä	palm	**û**	burn
e	end	**yo͞o**	fuse
ē	equal	**oi**	oil
i	it	**ou**	pout
ī	ice	**ng**	ring
o	odd	**th**	thin
ō	open	**th**	this
ô	order	**zh**	vision

ə = a in *above*, e in *sicken*, i in *possible*, o in *melon*, u in *circus*

funnel

gnarled

gunnysack When you say *gunnysack,* you are repeating yourself. *Goni* is the word for "sack" in Hindi, a language of northern India. So a *gunnysack* is really a "sack-sack."

flax [flaks] *n.* A slender plant with blue flowers, used to make linen cloth: **Whenever we visit the farm, we see *flax* growing in the meadow.**

flick·er [flik′ər] *v.* **flick·ered, flick·er·ing** To change unsteadily from bright to dim light: **The light was *flickering* during the thunderstorm.**

free·style [frē′stīl′] *n.* A contest in which any style of swimming may be used: **Gus's parents were proud because he won a medal for the *freestyle* race at the swimming meet.**

fret·ful [fret′fəl] *adj.* Restless and unhappy or seeming to be: **The music sounded *fretful,* like screeching birds.** *syn.* irritable

fruit·less [fro͞ot′lis] *adj.* Without any success; useless: **Teresa knew it would be *fruitless* to try pushing the fallen tree, so she took a different path.**

frus·tra·tion [frus·trā′shən] *n.* A feeling of anger or disappointment at not being able or allowed to do something: **Antonia's *frustration* increased when she could not finish the test.**

ful·crum [fo͝ol′krəm] *n.* What a lever leans against when it is being used to raise an object: **Hiroko used a board as a lever and a rock as a *fulcrum* when she pried open the heavy garage door.**

fun·nel [fun′əl] *n.* An open cone, wide at the top with a smaller end: **Mrs. Francisco used a *funnel* to pour cereal into a jar.**

G

gasp [gasp] *v.* **gasped, gasp·ing** To pant breathlessly. *syns.* puff, wheeze

gen·u·ine [jen′yo͞o·in] *adj.* Real; not fake.

gnarled [närld] *adj.* Twisted or knotted. *syn.* tangled

goad [gōd] *v.* **goad·ed, goad·ing** To use some object to make an animal move: **Luz was *goading* the horse with a small stick so that it would run faster.**

graf·fi·ti [grə·fē′tē] *n. pl.* Words illegally written or painted in public places: **The *graffiti* on the buildings and fences made the city look very ugly.**

grap·ple [grap′əl] *v.* **grap·pled, grap·pling** To grab and struggle. *syns.* wrestle, contend

grove [grōv] *n.* A group of trees.

guile [gīl] *n.* Cleverness; the ability to trick others: **The spy used *guile* to win the trust of the official and trick her into giving him the plans.** *syn.* slyness

gun·ny·sack [gun′ē·sak′] *n.* A sack made out of heavy cloth.

H

hab·i·tat [hab′ə·tat′] *n.* The place in nature where an animal lives. *syn.* home

hail·stone [hāl′stōn′] *n.* A small, round pellet of frozen rain.

hoarse [hôrs] *adj.* Sounding husky or rough.

home·ly [hōm′lē] *adj.* Plain looking: **His *homely* face suddenly looked beautiful as he rocked the child to sleep.**

home·stead [hōm′sted′] *v.* To make a place one's home: **Pioneers of the west had to *homestead* land to earn the right to own it.** *syn.* occupy

hor·i·zon·tal [hôr′ə·zon′təl] *adj.* Level from side to side, the way the horizon looks: **Book shelves are *horizontal* to the ground.**

hor·ri·fy [hôr′ə·fī′] *v.* **hor·ri·fied, hor·ri·fy·ing** To make someone very scared or upset: **We were *horrified* when we learned that someone had fallen through the ice.**

hy·giene [hī′jēn′] *n.* Practices that keep people clean and healthy: **Good dental *hygiene,* like toothbrushing, helps prevent cavities.**

I

ig·no·rant [ig′nər·ənt] *adj.* Not knowing something: **The students were *ignorant* of the history of their state until they studied it in school.** *syn.* unaware

il·lu·mi·nate [i·lo͞o′mə·nāt′] *v.* **il·lu·mi·nat·ed, il·lu·mi·nat·ing** To fill with light: **We lit several candles which *illuminated* the room.**

im·mac·u·late [i·mak′yə·lit] *adj.* Spotlessly clean; pure: **Matsue wore her *immaculate* new shoes to the party.**

in·con·ven·ience [in′kən·vēn′yəns] *v.* To annoy or make trouble: **I hope it will not *inconvenience* you to let me go ahead of you in line.**

in·crim·i·nat·ing [in·krim′ə·nāt′ing] *adj.* Showing proof of guilt: **The burglary tools found in the trunk of his car were considered *incriminating* evidence by the jury.**

in·di·cate [in′də·kāt′] *v.* To show or describe: **The directions *indicate* which way we should turn.**

in·flu·en·tial [in′flo͞o·en′shəl] *adj.* Important; able to change people's thoughts on something: **Albert Einstein was an *influential* scientist because his work changed the way people think about the universe.**

in·her·it [in·her′it] *v.* To receive something, usually from a parent or relative, after that person dies: **When his aunt dies, Sergio will *inherit* her house.**

in·i·ti·a·tive [in·ish′(ē)ə·tiv] *n.* The ability to start something or take the first step: **Mr. Díaz has the *initiative* necessary to become a good salesman.**

in·suf·fi·cient [in′sə·fish′ənt] *adj.* Not enough: **We could not make tacos because we had *insufficient* amounts of tomatoes and cheese.** *syn.* inadequate

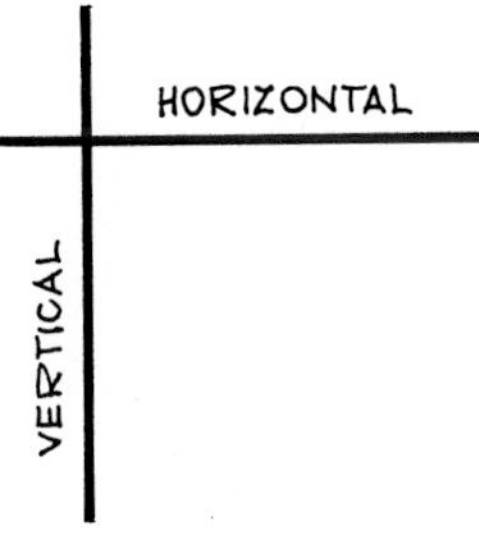

horrified Have you ever been so scared that your hair stood on end, or bristled? Our word *horrified* goes back to the Latin word *horrere,* meaning "to bristle." This word was used most often for the bristling that takes place when people or animals are frightened. Think about what happens when your cat meets a dog!

a	add	**o͝o**	took
ā	ace	**o͞o**	pool
â	care	**u**	up
ä	palm	**û**	burn
e	end	**yo͞o**	fuse
ē	equal	**oi**	oil
i	it	**ou**	pout
ī	ice	**ng**	ring
o	odd	**th**	thin
ō	open	**th**	this
ô	order	**zh**	vision

ə = a in *above*, e in *sicken*, i in *possible*, o in *melon*, u in *circus*

javelin

limelight The chemical calcium oxide was discovered in 1808. This material, often called lime, shone with a bright white light when heated. This quality made it useful for lighting plays and shows in dark theaters. Even in the age of electrical lighting, people who are the center of public attention are "in the limelight."

lopsided

in·tel·lec·tu·al·ly [in′tə·lek′cho͞o·əl·ē] *adv.* In a way that uses or shows the reasoning powers of the mind: **Computer programming can be *intellectually* satisfying work.**

in·tim·i·date [in·tim′ə·dāt′] *v.* To make someone afraid: **Lorenzo looks tough, but he is too nice to *intimidate* anyone.**

in·ven·tive·ness [in·ven′tiv·nis] *n.* Skill at creating things: **Luisa's *inventiveness* helped her win first prize in her class's Build-a-Better-Mousetrap contest.** *syns.* creativity, originality

ir·re·sis·ti·bly [ir′i·zis′tə·blē] *adv.* In a way that cannot be overcome or opposed: **Although I was unsure of what might be in the room, my curiosity drew me *irresistibly* toward the door.** *syn.* magnetically

ir·ri·ta·tion [ir′ə·tā′shən] *n.* Something that makes a person mildly angry: **At the picnic, the bee buzzing around our food was an *irritation.*** *syn.* annoyance

i·so·lat·ed [ī′sə·lāt′əd] *adj.* Set apart from everything else; out of the way: **The *isolated* cabin was at the end of the trail, deep in the woods.**

J

jave·lin [jav′(ə)·lin] *n.* A spear that is thrown for distance as an athletic event: **My father won an athletic scholarship for throwing the *javelin.***

K

keen·ing [kēn′ing] *adj.* Sharp; strong: **The *keening* howl of the coyote made shivers run down my spine.**

L

lab·y·rinth [lab′ə·rinth] *n.* A place that has a complicated layout, like a maze: **The princess in the fairy tale could not find her way out of the forest because it was a *labyrinth* of many paths.**

lime·light [līm′līt′] *n.* The attention or notice of other people. *syn.* spotlight

lop·sid·ed [lop′sī′did] *adj.* Hanging over to one side; uneven: **The cake was lower on one side, so it looked *lopsided.***

lux·u·ry [luk′shər·ē] *n.* An item that adds to pleasure and comfort but is not necessary: **The Dillman family decided to cut back on buying *luxuries,* so they decided not to get a video camera.**

M

ma·chet·e [mə·shet′ē *or* mə·shet′] *n.* A long, curved knife used for cutting tall vegetation.

man·do·lin [man′də·lin *or* man′də·lin′] *n.* A musical string instrument with eight to ten strings.

ma·neu·ver [mə·n(y)o͞o′vər] *v.* **ma·neu·vered, ma·neu·ver·ing** To move in a skillful way: **Elbowing her way through the crowd, the photographer *maneuvered* herself to a position near the stage.**

man·gle [mang′gəl] *v.* **man·gled, man·gling** To break apart; ruin: **The washing machine *mangled* Sandy's lace collar.**

mar·i·o·nette [mar′ē·ə·net′] *n.* A puppet that is moved by pulling the strings attached to its arms and legs.

mar·vel [mär′vəl] *n.* Something that is remarkable or exciting: **The white tiger was a *marvel* to the patrons of the circus.** *syns.* sensation, wonder

mas·sive·ly [mas′iv·lē] *adv.* Hugely; with much size and weight: **The house, *massively* enlarged by the two new wings, now seemed to sprawl across the whole hilltop.**

me·chan·i·cal [mə·kan′i·kəl] *adj.* Having to do with machines.

meg·a·phone [meg′ə·fōn′] *n.* A cone or electric device that makes the voice sound louder when it is spoken into.

me·te·or·ol·o·gist [mē′tē·ə·rol′ə·jist] *n.* A person who studies the weather.

me·thod·i·cal·ly [mə·thod′i·klē] *adv.* As if with a purpose; steadily without stopping: **The project will get done if we stick to it and work *methodically.***

mi·gra·tion [mī·grā′shən] *n.* The movement of an animal, such as a bird, from one place to another place when the season changes.

min·gle [ming′gəl] *v.* **min·gled, min·gling** To join or mix together: **At the party Oscar *mingled* with the other guests, but he still felt out of place.** *syn.* associate

mis·er·a·ble [miz′ər·ə·bəl] *adj.* 1 Causing unhappiness. 2 Shameful: **The *miserable* conditions at the jail caused problems among the prisoners.**

mis·giv·ing [mis·giv′ing] *n.* A feeling of worry: **Michael had *misgivings* about the picnic because dark storm clouds were gathering.** *syn.* qualm

mo·bile [mō′bēl] *n.* A sculpture with objects attached that moves lightly as air passes it: **Rosa made a *mobile* out of wood and paper and hung it over her sister's crib.**

mol·e·cule [mol′ə·kyo͞ol′] *n.* A tiny particle: **Scientists tell us that *molecules* and atoms are the basic building blocks of everything in the world.**

mor·sel [môr′səl] *n.* A little piece of food: **Kay loved the cake, and she ate every tiny *morsel* on her plate.** *syn.* bit

mo·tive [mō′tiv] *n.* A reason for doing something: **What was your *motive* for not telling your friends that it was your birthday?**

mourn·ful·ly [môrn′fəl·lē] *adv.* In a sad manner. *syn.* sorrowfully

mandolin

mechanical

migration

a	add	**o͝o**	took
ā	ace	**o͞o**	pool
â	care	**u**	up
ä	palm	**û**	burn
e	end	**yo͞o**	fuse
ē	equal	**oi**	oil
i	it	**ou**	pout
ī	ice	**ng**	ring
o	odd	**th**	thin
ō	open	**th**	this
ô	order	**zh**	vision

ə = a in *above*, e in *sicken*, i in *possible*, o in *melon*, u in *circus*

musket

nauseous Have you ever been seasick? If so, you really know what *nauseous* means! The ancient Greeks associated this feeling with sea voyages and named it *nausia* from *naus,* their word for "ship."

navigate

parlor The room in your house called the *living room* was once known as the *parlor.* This word is related to the French word *parler,* meaning "to speak." A *parlor,* then, was a room in which people gathered to talk with each other.

mus·ket [mus′kit] *n.* An old type of gun with a long barrel, similar to a rifle: **Each soldier in the volunteer army brought his own *musket.***

mys·ti·fied [mis′tə·fīd] *adj.* Puzzled or not able to figure something out: **Rick was *mystified* by the strange sound and decided to find out exactly where it was coming from.**

nau·seous [nô′shəs *or* nô′zē·əs] *adj.* Sick to the stomach.

nav·i·gate [nav′ə·gāt′] *v.* **nav·i·gat·ed, nav·i·gat·ing** To control or decide in which direction something will go: **Bernardo was *navigating* the boat, and I was rowing.**

near·sight·ed [nir′sī′tid] *adj.* Able to see only things close by: ***Nearsighted* people often need glasses so they can see what is written on signs.** *syn.* myopic

nes·tle [nes′əl] *v.* **nes·tled, nes·tling** To sit very close to someone else: **All five children *nestled* together on the small couch.** *syns.* cuddle, snuggle

neu·tral [n(y)o͞o′trəl] *n.* Someone who is not on either side during a war: **During the American Revolution the *neutrals* refused to take the sides of either the colonists or the British.**

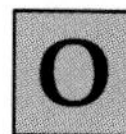

ob·vi·ous [ob′vē·əs] *adj.* Easily noticed or understood: **The rainstorm makes it *obvious* that we can't play outside today.**

off·hand·ed [ôf′han′did] *adj.* Without a lot of care or planning: **Because Tom told us about the play in an *offhanded* way, we didn't think he cared if we came.** *syn.* casual

op·po·nent [ə·pō′nənt] *n.* A person or group that takes the opposite position, as in sports. *syn.* rival

or·i·gin [ôr′ə·jin] *n.* The first use or the beginning: **Our class learned about the *origin* of the use of silver by Native American artists.**

pan·to·mime [pan′tə·mīm′] *n.* A play in which actors use only gestures with no speech. *v.* Express in gestures alone.

parch·ment [pärch′mənt] *n.* A scraped and dried piece of animal skin used to write or paint upon.

par·lor [pär′lər] *n.* A room that is usually used for talking or entertaining.

par·tic·i·pa·tion [pär·tis′ə·pā′shən] *n.* The act of getting involved with others: ***Participation* in team sports can be fun.**

pen·du·lum [pen′jo͝o·ləm *or* pen′də·ləm] *n.* A weight that hangs down and swings evenly from side to side: **A large clock with a *pendulum* is usually called a grandfather clock.**

per·ish·a·ble [per′ish·ə·bəl] *adj.* Likely to spoil.

per·ma·nent [pûr′mən·ənt] *adj.* Meant to last without changing: **This time, Robert's cure was *permanent* and the illness did not come back.** *syn.* enduring

per·mis·sion [pər·mish′ən] *n.* An act by one person that allows someone else to do something: **Ashley went to ask for her mother's *permission* to go to the dance.** *syns.* approval, consent

per·sist [pər·sist′] *v.* **per·sist·ed, per·sist·ing** To keep doing something; insist: **Lome *persisted* in bouncing the ball on the floor even after I asked him not to.** *syn.* continue

pes·ky [pes′kē] *adj. informal* Annoying; being like a pest.

pes·ti·cide [pes′tə·sīd′] *n.* A chemical used to kill unwanted animals or plants: **Mr. Chin sprayed *pesticides* on the weeds in his yard to kill them.** *syn.* poison

phy·si·cian [fi·zish′ən] *n.* A medical doctor: **Our family *physician* prescribed penicillin when I had a sore throat and a fever.**

plum·met [plum′it] *v.* **plum·met·ed, plum·met·ing** To fall quickly: **The heavy rock *plummeted* to the bottom of the pond.**

plun·der [plun′dər] *v.* **plun·dered, plun·der·ing** To steal things by using force. *syn.* loot

pol·lu·tion [pə·lo͞o′shən] *n.* Trash or other things that make air, water, or land dirty.

pounce [pouns] *v.* **pounced, pounc·ing** To jump onto something: **The cat *pounced* happily on the ball of yarn.** *syn.* leap

pre·fer [pri·fûr′] *v.* **pre·ferred, pre·fer·ring** To like one thing better than another: **Mrs. McCormick *preferred* working in her vegetable garden to seeing a movie.**

pre·his·tor·ic [prē′his·tôr′ik] *adj.* From the time before historical records were kept: **Since they left no written records, the only way to learn about *prehistoric* humans is to study their drawings and the things they made.** *syn.* ancient

pre·lim·i·nary [pri·lim′ə·ner′ē] *n.* A contest whose winner takes part in the main contest: **Lisa swam well in two out of three *preliminaries*.**

pre·miere [pri·mir′] *n.* The first showing or display: **We're going to the *premiere* of Ellen's new play.**

prick·le [prik′əl] *v.* **prick·led, prick·ling** To tingle or sting. *syn.* tingle

pro·ce·dure [prə·sē′jər] *n.* The certain way in which something is done: **To learn how to work this machine, you have to follow the *procedure* described in the booklet.**

pendulum

pollution

a	add	**o͝o**	took
ā	ace	**o͞o**	pool
â	care	**u**	up
ä	palm	**û**	burn
e	end	**yo͞o**	fuse
ē	equal	**oi**	oil
i	it	**ou**	pout
ī	ice	**ng**	ring
o	odd	**th**	thin
ō	open	**th**	this
ô	order	**zh**	vision

ə = a in *above*, e in *sicken*, i in *possible*, o in *melon*, u in *circus*

pyramid

rankle When someone's insulting remark *rankles* inside you, you might imagine that a little dragon is gnawing at you. The Latin word for "dragon" was *draco.* A "little dragon" was called *dracunculus.*

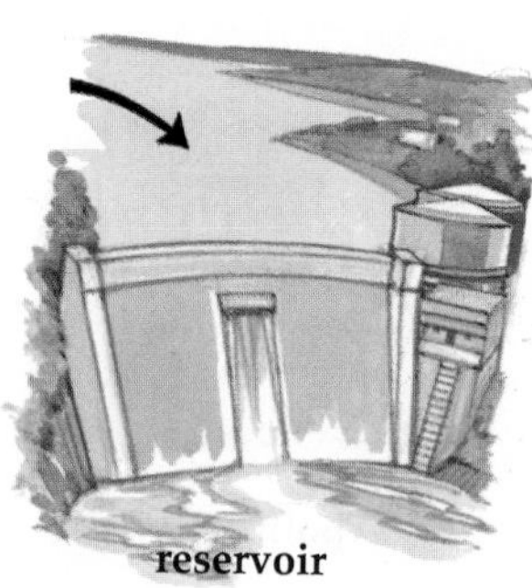
reservoir

residence

prom·i·nent [prom′ə·nənt] *adj.* Important; well-known: **The mayor is the most *prominent* woman in our town.**

pros·per·ous [pros′pər·əs] *adj.* Doing well: **The Joneses are a happy, *prosperous* family with good jobs, healthy children, and a big garden full of vegetables.** *syn.* successful

pro·tein [prō′tēn′ *or* prō′tē·ən] *n.* One of several substances that are a necessary part of our diet: **Meat, fish, dairy products, nuts, and beans can supply needed *protein* in our diet.**

pyr·a·mid [pir′ə·mid] *n.* A huge structure in which ancient Egyptian rulers were buried: **Each side of a *pyramid* looks like a triangle.**

Q

qual·i·fy [kwol′ə·fī′] *v.* **qual·i·fied, qual·i·fy·ing** To win the right to take part in an event: **Our soccer team won the game, thus *qualifying* for the playoffs.**

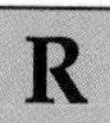

R

ran·kle [rang′kəl] *v.* To make someone annoyed and mad: **Losing the game by forfeit still *rankles* Yoshio and makes him feel angry whenever he thinks about it.**

re·con·struct [rē′kən·strukt′] *v.* To put something together or make it again: **After the barn blew down in the storm, we worked to *reconstruct* it.** *syn.* rebuild

re-en·act [rē′in·akt′] *v.* To act out again; to perform as if for the first time: **Mr. Jackson's seventh-grade class will *reenact* several scenes from American history for the school assembly.**

ref·uge [ref′yo͞oj] *n.* A place to hide: **When the bears came into the camp, the family ran to the car because it was a safe *refuge.***

re·ha·bil·i·ta·tion [rē′hə·bil′ə·tā′shən] *n.* Helping a person or animal have good health or skills again: **After she broke her wrist, Miss Meyers went to a *rehabilitation* center to relearn how to type.**

rel·ic [rel′ik] *n.* A very old object.

re·lieve [ri·lēv′] *v.* **re·lieved, re·liev·ing** To free from worry, pain, or unhappiness. *syn.* ease

rep·re·sent [rep′ri·zent′] *v.* To act or speak for someone or something; to stand for something.

res·er·voir [rez′ər·vwär′ *or* rez′ər·vwôr′] *n.* A place where water is stored.

res·i·dence [rez′ə·dəns] *n.* The place where a person legally lives: **My *residence* is 123 Main Street, Minneapolis, Minnesota.**

rest·less [rest′lis] *adj.* Not relaxed; eager to do something else: **Anna felt bored and *restless* having to sit still during the long movie.**

re·strain [ri·strān′] *v.* To hold back: **Please *restrain* your dog by putting it on a leash.**

re·sume [ri·zo͞om′] *v.* To start again after stopping: **My father's cooking class *resumes* after two weeks of vacation.**

re·treat [ri·trēt′] *v.* To turn around and go back to where one came from. *syn.* withdraw

rhyth·m [rit͟h′əm] *n.* A motion or sound that is repeated after regular pauses; a steady beat: **My sister taps the *rhythm* with her foot when she plays the piano.**

rit·u·al [rich′o͞o·əl] *n.* A set action or series of actions: **Andy went through a *ritual* of pulling up his socks and tugging on his shirt every time he shot a free throw.**

rook·ie [ro͝ok′ē] *n.* A first-year player in sports; a beginner.

S

sa·van·nah [sə·van′ə] *n.* A grassy plain that has very few trees.

scoot [sko͞ot] *v. informal* **scoot·ed, scoot·ing 1** To move quickly. **2** To slide something, especially while seated.

scur·ry [skûr′ē] *v.* To move about quickly. *syn.* scamper

sem·i·cir·cu·lar [sem′ē·sûr′kyə·lər] *adj.* Shaped like a half-circle: **Tiffany draws *semicircular* lines that look like smiles.**

set·tle·ment [set′(ə)l·mənt] *n.* A new place for people to live: **When the pioneers first reached the valley, they built a *settlement*.**

shin·dig [shin′dig′] *n. slang* A party with noise and dancing.

shud·der [shud′ər] *n.* A quick, light shaking motion; shiver: **The cold air made a *shudder* run through my body.**

slan·der [slan′dər] *n.* A cruel, false, and sometimes illegal spoken public statement made about a person: **Anyone who publicly says something untrue about another person is guilty of *slander*.**

sleigh [slā] *n.* A carriage with runners instead of wheels that is pulled by a horse over ice or snow: **After the last snowfall, Mr. Cowley let us hitch up the horses and ride in both *sleighs*.**

so·ber·ing [sō′bər·ing] *adj.* Serious; causing to be suddenly aware and able to think clearly.

sol·emn·ly [sol′əm·lē] *adv.* Quietly and seriously: **Mr. Jenkins *solemnly* read the names of the people who had been injured.**

spon·sor [spon′sər] **1** *n.* Someone who helps animals or people by caring for them, being responsible for their welfare, or giving them money. **2** *v.* To be a sponsor, sometimes by paying for something.

star·board [stär′bərd] *adj.* The right-hand side of a ship: **We looked for sharks and whales over the *starboard* railing.**

shindig The only thing word experts agree on is that *shindig* comes from Ireland. The word may have come from a game called *shindy,* a wild kind of hockey played on a field with balls and curved sticks. Or *shindig* may go back to the Irish word *sinteag,* which means "a skip" or "a jump."

sleigh

a	add	**o͝o**	took
ā	ace	**o͞o**	pool
â	care	**u**	up
ä	palm	**û**	burn
e	end	**yo͞o**	fuse
ē	equal	**oi**	oil
i	it	**ou**	pout
ī	ice	**ng**	ring
o	odd	**th**	thin
ō	open	**t͟h**	this
ô	order	**zh**	vision

ə = a in *above*, e in *sicken*, i in *possible*, o in *melon*, u in *circus*

summit

suspicious When we see *suspicious* characters, we are likely to *suspect* them of wrongdoing. *Suspect* and *suspicious* go back to two Latin words. *Sub* had the sense "from below," and *specere* meant "to look at." Looking up at people may have meant secretly watching them and perhaps catching them behaving suspiciously.

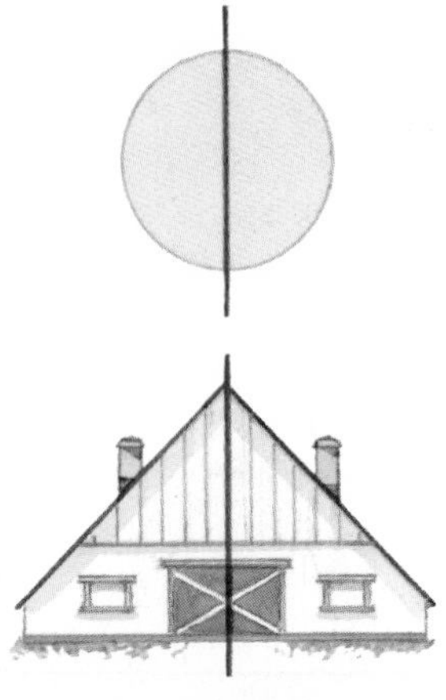

symmetrical

technology

stat·ic [stat′ik] *n.* A rough sound that comes from a radio or television set that is not receiving properly.

stern·ness [stûrn′nis] *n.* The quality of being serious and tough. *syn.* harshness

stow [stō] *v.* **stowed, stow·ing** To store; put away.

stu·pen·dous [st(y)o͞o·pen′dəs] *adj.* Wonderful. *syn.* fabulous

sub·dued [sub·d(y)o͞od′] *adj.* Calmed down; not excited; quiet.

sub·mit [səb·mit′] *v.* To say or to put something forward for someone else's reaction; to suggest in a formal way.

sue [so͞o] *v.* To legally ask a court to solve a problem.

suf·fra·gist [suf′rə·jist] *n.* A person who thinks that the right to vote should be extended to others.

sum·mit [sum′it] *n.* The top of a mountain. *syn.* peak

sum·mon [sum′ən] *v.* **sum·moned, sum·mon·ing** To send a signal to someone to do something.

sup·port [sə·pôrt′] *v.* To provide food and clothing and other necessities: **Mrs. Swoboda will *support* the family while her husband looks for a new job.**

sur·feit [sûr′fit] *n.* Too much of something. *syn.* overabundance

sus·pi·cious [sə·spish′əs] *adj.* Not fully trusting or believing: **My teacher was *suspicious* when I told her the dog ate my homework.**

swag·ger [swag′ər] *v.* **swag·gered, swag·ger·ing** To walk in a boastful and proud way. *syn.* strut

sym·met·ri·cal [si·met′ri·kəl] *adj.* Alike on both sides.

ta·per [tā′pər] *v.* To fade; decrease in amount or size.

tech·nol·o·gy [tek·nol′ə·jē] *n.* A way to use science to produce useful things: **Computers and cars both make use of modern *technology*.**

temp·ta·tion [tem·tā′shən] *n.* An instant urge or desire: **The *temptation* to eat the cookies may be too much to resist.**

ter·rain [tə·rān′] *n.* The features of an area of land: **The race was run on rough *terrain* of steep hills and rocky valleys.**

tes·ti·mo·ny [tes′tə·mō′nē] *n.* The answers to a lawyer's questions in court that must be the truth.

tour·na·ment [to͝or′nə·mənt *or* tûr′nə·mənt] *n.* A set number of contests that includes many teams or players and produces one winner overall.

trai·tor [trā′tər] *n.* A person who goes against his or her family, friends, or country to join the opposite side during a war. *syn.* betrayer

trans·mis·sion [trans·mish′ən] *n.* The sending of pictures or sounds through the air, as by radio or television.

tum·ble [tum′bəl] *v.* **tum·bled, tum·bling** To turn over and over: **The puppies were rolling and *tumbling* on the carpet.**

tur·bu·lence [tûr′byə·ləns] *n.* Wind currents that move very quickly.

ul·ti·mate·ly [ul′tə·mit·lē] *adv.* Finally; at the end: **We will *ultimately* arrive in California after we stop in Arizona for a rest.**

u·nan·i·mous·ly [yo͞o·nan′ə·məs·lē] *adv.* With all voters voting the same way: **Sasheen was *unanimously* elected class president when all the students voted for her.**

un·rav·el [un·rav′əl] *v.* **un·rav·eled, un·rav·el·ing** To take apart the threads of material.

un·stead·i·ly [un·sted′ə·lē] *adv.* In a shaky way.

vague [vāg] *adj.* Not clearly understood.

ver·ti·cal [vûr′ti·kəl] *adj.* Straight up and down.

vig·or·ous·ly [vig′ər·əs·lē] *adv.* Very fast or with great energy: **The chief *vigorously* waved his arms to get our attention.** *syns.* energetically, rapidly

vi·o·lent·ly [vī′ə·lənt·lē] *adv.* Harshly; with destructive force.

vis·u·al·ize [vizh′o͞o·əl·īz′] *v.* To imagine; to see something in the mind.

volt [vōlt] *n.* A measure of electricity.

wal·low [wol′ō] *v.* To tumble or roll with slow and lazy movements: **My cat likes to *wallow* in the warm sand.**

weight·less·ness [wāt′lis·nəs] *n.* Having little or no weight: **A helium-filled balloon's *weightlessness* will allow it to float away if you do not hold it.**

whit·tle [(h)wit′(ə)l] *v.* To shape wood with a knife. *syn.* carve

wind·break [wind′brāk′] *n.* Anything that blocks the force of the wind, such as a wall or a line of trees.

wist·ful·ly [wist′fəl·ē] *adv.* Wishing for something.

wretch·ed [rech′id] *adj.* Very unhappy: **My ankle ached so badly that I had a *wretched* day at school.** *syns.* miserable, poor

tumble

vague If the details of that story you just read are *vague,* maybe your mind was wandering as you turned the pages. *Vague,* in fact, is closely connected to the Latin word *vagari,* meaning "to wander." We call people who wander around aimlessly *vagabonds* and *vagrants.*

windbreak

a	add	**o͝o**	took
ā	ace	**o͞o**	pool
â	care	**u**	up
ä	palm	**û**	burn
e	end	**yo͞o**	fuse
ē	equal	**oi**	oil
i	it	**ou**	pout
ī	ice	**ng**	ring
o	odd	**th**	thin
ō	open	**th**	this
ô	order	**zh**	vision

ə = a in *above*, e in *sicken*, i in *possible*, o in *melon*, u in *circus*

INDEX OF
TITLES AND AUTHORS

Page numbers in light type refer to biographical information.

Acknowledgments continued
Clemente (Retitled: "The Way of the Jíbaro") by Paul Robert Walker. Text copyright © 1988 by Harcourt Brace Jovanovich, Inc. Pronunciation Key from *HBJ School Dictionary*, Third Edition. Text copyright © 1990 by Harcourt Brace Jovanovich, Inc.

HarperCollins Publishers: "The Growin' of Paul Bunyan" from *A Telling of the Tales* by William J. Brooke. Text copyright © 1990 by William J. Brooke. From *The Sense of Wonder* by Rachel Carson, cover photograph by Charles Pratt. Text copyright © 1956 by Rachel Carson; copyright © renewed 1984 by Roger Christie. Cover photograph copyright © 1965 by Charles Pratt. "Fireflies" from *Joyful Noise* by Paul Fleischman, illustrated by Eric Beddows. Text copyright © 1988 by Paul Fleischman; illustrations copyright © 1988 by Eric Beddows. *One Day in the Desert* by Jean Craighead George. Text copyright © 1983 by Jean Craighead George. Published by Thomas Y. Crowell. From *Hector Lives in the United States Now: The Story of a Mexican-American Child* (Retitled: "We Are a Nation of Immigrants") by Joan Hewett, photographs by Richard Hewett. Text copyright © 1990 by Joan Hewett; photographs copyright © 1990 by Richard R. Hewett. Published by J. B. Lippincott. From pp. 79-93 in *In the Year of the Boar and Jackie Robinson* (Retitled: "The Chinese Rookie") by Bette Bao Lord. Text copyright © 1984 by Bette Bao Lord. From pp. 3-27 in *Sarah, Plain and Tall* (Retitled: "Tell Them I Sing") by Patricia MacLachlan. Text copyright © 1985 by Patricia McLachlan. Cover illustration by Ruth Sanderson from *The Facts and Fictions of Minna Pratt* by Patricia MacLachlan. Illustration © 1988 by Ruth Sanderson. From *Flower Moon Snow: A Book of Haiku* by Kazue Mizumura. Copyright © 1977 by Kazue Mizumura. Published by Thomas Y. Crowell. From pp. 46-56 in *Night of the Twisters* (Retitled: "Tornado Alert!") by Ivy Ruckman. Text copyright © 1984 by Ivy Ruckman. Cover illustration by Wendell Minor from *Mojave* by Diane Siebert. Illustration copyright © 1988 by Wendell Minor. Published by Thomas Y. Crowell.

Holiday House: Cover illustration from *Ferret In the Bedroom, Lizards In the Fridge* by Bill Wallace. Copyright © 1986 by Bill Wallace.

Houghton Mifflin Company: From *The Edge of the Sea* by Rachel Carson. Text copyright © 1955 by Rachel L. Carson; copyright © renewed 1983 by Roger Christie. From *Silent Spring* by Rachel Carson. Text copyright © 1962 by Rachel Carson.

Richard Kennedy: "Oliver Hyde's Dishcloth Concert" from *Richard Kennedy: Collected Stories* by Richard Kennedy. Text copyright © 1987 by Richard Kennedy.

Alfred A. Knopf, Inc.: "In Time of Silver Rain" from *Selected Poems* by Langston Hughes. Text copyright 1938, renewed 1966 by Langston Hughes. *Like Jake and Me* by Mavis Jukes, illustrated by Lloyd Bloom. Text copyright © 1984 by Mavis Jukes; illustrations copyright © 1984 by Lloyd Bloom. Cover illustration by Lloyd Bloom from *No One Is Going to Nashville* by Mavis Jukes. Illustration copyright © 1983 by Lloyd Bloom. From pp. 61-72 in *The Kid in the Red Jacket* (Retitled: "The Second Day at School") by Barbara Park, cover illustration by Rob Stauber. Text copyright © 1987 by Barbara Park; cover illustration copyright © 1987 by Rob Stauber.

Lerner Publications Company: Cover illustration from *Before the Wright Brothers* by Don Berliner. Copyright © 1990 by Lerner Publications Company.

Little, Brown and Company: Cover illustration from *The Wonderful Flight to the Mushroom Planet* by Eleanor Cameron. Copyright © 1954 by Eleanor Cameron. From *And Then There Was One: The Mysteries of Extinction* by Margery Facklam, illustrated by Pamela Johnson. Text copyright © 1990 by Margery Facklam; illustrations copyright © 1990 by Pamela Johnson. From *Self-Portrait with Wings* (Retitled: "Flying") by Susan Green. Text and cover illustration copyright © 1989 by Susan Green.

Little, Brown and Company, in conjunction with Sierra Club Books: From *Tree of Life: The World of the African Baobab* (Retitled: "Tree of Life") by Barbara Bash. Copyright © 1989 by Barbara Bash.

Lothrop, Lee & Shepard Books, a division of William Morrow & Company, Inc.: From *To Space and Back* (Retitled: "Blast-off and Re-entry") by Sally Ride with Susan Okie. Text copyright © 1986 by Sally Ride and Susan Okie. Cover illustration by Carole Byard from *Have a Happy . . .* by Mildred Pitts Walker. Illustration copyright © 1989 by Carole Byard.

Macmillan Publishing Company: From *The House of Dies Drear* (Retitled: "A New Home in Ohio") by Virginia Hamilton, cover illustration by Eros Keith. Text copyright © 1968 by Virginia Hamilton; cover illustration copyright © 1968 by Macmillan Publishing Company. Cover photograph by Christopher Knight from *Sugaring Time* by Kathryn Lasky. Photograph copyright © 1983 by Christopher G. Knight.

Morrow Junior Books, a division of William Morrow & Company, Inc.: Cover photograph by Margaret Miller from *Ramona: Behind the Scenes of a Television Show* by Elaine Scott, photographs by Margaret Miller. Photograph copyright © 1988 by Margaret Miller.

William Morrow & Company, Inc.: From *Storms* (Retitled: "Thunderstorms") by Seymour Simon. Text copyright © 1989 by Seymour Simon.

Margery G. Nichelason: "A Matter of Taste" by Margery G. Nichelason. © 1989 by Margery G. Nichelason.

Philomel Books, a division of The Putnam & Grosset Group: Cover illustration by Mitsumasa Anno from *Anno's Hat Tricks* by Akihiro Nozaki. Illustration copyright © 1984 by Kuso-Kubo and Akihiro Nozaki.

Jerry Pinkney: Cover illustration by Jerry Pinkney from *Pride of Puerto Rico: The Life of Roberto Clemente* by Paul Robert Walker.

Plays, Inc.: The Case of the Punjabi Ruby by Frank Willment from *Plays: The Drama Magazine for Young People*. Text copyright © 1989 by Plays, Inc.

Pocket Books, a division of Simon & Schuster, Inc.: Cover illustration by Robert Tanenbaum from *Do Bananas Chew Gum?* by Jamie Gilson. Illustration copyright © 1989 by Robert Tanenbaum.

Positive Images: Cover photographs by Jerry Howard from *The Edge of the Sea* and *Silent Spring* by Rachel Carson.

G. P. Putnam's Sons: Cover illustration by Tomie dePaola from *Shh! We're Writing the Constitution* by Jean Fritz. Illustration copyright © 1987 by Tomie dePaola. Cover illustration by Stephen Gammell from *Thunder at Gettysburg* by Patricia Lee Gauch. Illustration copyright © 1975 by Stephen Gammell. Cover illustration by Ted Lewin from *The Search for Grissi* by Mary Francis Shura. Illustration copyright © 1985 by Mary Francis Shura.

Marian Reiner, on behalf of Myra Cohn Livingston: "Secrets" from *Space Songs* by Myra Cohn Livingston. Text copyright © 1988 by Myra Cohn Livingston.

Marian Reiner, on behalf of Eve Merriam: "Elizabeth Blackwell" from *Independent Voices* by Eve Merriam. Text copyright © 1968 by Eve Merriam.

Kenneth Rosen: "My Friend the Wind" by King D. Kuka and "Wishes" by Ya-Ka-Nes from *Voices of the Rainbow: Contemporary Poetry by American Indians*, edited by Kenneth Rosen. Text copyright © 1975 by Kenneth Rosen.

Scholastic Inc.: From *You Be the Jury* (Retitled: "Order in the Court") by Marvin Miller. Text copyright © 1987 by Marvin Miller. From "Important Dates in Space" in *The Day We Walked on the Moon: A Photo History of Space Exploration* by George Sullivan. Text copyright © 1990 by George Sullivan.

Charles Scribner's Sons, an imprint of Macmillan Publishing Company: "Jackrabbit" from *Desert Voices* by Byrd Baylor, illustrated by Peter Parnall. Text copyright © 1981 by Byrd Baylor; illustrations copyright © 1981 by Peter Parnall. Cover illustration by Gail Owens from *Stinker from Space* by Pamela F. Service. Copyright © 1988 by Gail Owens.

Songs Music, Inc: Melody and lyrics from "Arkansas Traveler" in *Treasury of Songs for Children* by Tom Glazer. Copyright © 1964 by Tom Glazer.

Rosemary A. Thurber: Many Moons by James Thurber. Text copyright 1943 by James Thurber; text copyright renewed 1970 by Rosemary Thurber.

Charles E. Tuttle Co., Inc.: From *Chinese Kites: How to Make and Fly Them* (Retitled: "An Array of Chinese Kites") by David F. Jue. Copyright 1967 by Charles E. Tuttle Company, Inc.

Viking Penguin, a division of Penguin Books USA Inc.: From *Rachel Carson: Pioneer of Ecology* (Retitled: "Somebody Had to Warn the World") by Kathleen V. Kudlinski. Text copyright © 1988 by Kathleen V. Kudlinski. Cover illustration from *Lentil* by Robert McCloskey. Copyright 1940 by Robert McCloskey, renewed © 1968 by Robert McCloskey. From *A Long Way to Go* (Retitled: "The Speech") by Zibby Oneal. Text copyright © 1990

by Zibby Oneal. Cover illustration by Bert Dodson from *Hannah's Fancy Notions* by Pat Ross. Illustration copyright © 1988 by Bert Dodson. Cover illustration from *The Secret Language of the SB* by Elizabeth Scarboro. Copyright © 1990 by Elizabeth Scarboro.
World Almanac Books, an imprint of Pharos Books: From "Foreign Leagues" in *The Kids' World Almanac of Baseball* by Thomas G. Aylesworth. Text copyright © 1990 by Thomas G. Aylesworth.

Handwriting models in this program have been used with permission of the publisher, Zaner-Bloser, Inc., Columbus, OH.

Photograph Credits

Key: (t) top, (b) bottom, (l) left, (c) center, (r) right.

Pages 17, HBJ/Britt Runion; 18(t), HBJ Photo; 18(b), HBJ Photo; 19(t), HBJ Photo; 19(cr), HBJ Photo; 19(b), HBJ Photo; 20–21, HBJ/Debi Harbin; 22–23, HBJ Photo; 24, HBJ Photo; 34–35, HBJ Photo; 46–47(background), HBJ Photo; 46, Irina Faskianos; 47, Myrleen Ferguson/PhotoEdit; 48–49, HBJ Photo; 70, HBJ Photo; 72, National Baseball Library; 74, Archive Photos; 76, Walter Iooss Jr./*Sports Illustrated;* 78, Pittsburgh Pirates; 80, UPI/Bettmann; 81, UPI/Bettmann; 84–85, HBJ/Britt Runion; 86, HBJ Photo; 103 (background), HBJ/Britt Runion; 103(inset), Arthur Tilley/FPG; 103(foreground), HBJ/Rick Friedman, Black Star; 104(background), HBJ/Britt Runion; 104(inset), Arthur Tilley/FPG; 106(l), Brylak/Gamma Liaison; 106(r), Brylak/Gamma Liaison; 107(t), HBJ/Dan Peha; 107(b), HBJ Photo; 109, HBJ/Britt Runion; 110(t), HBJ Photo; 110(b), HBJ Photo; 111(t), HBJ Photo; 111(cr), HBJ Photo; 111(b), HBJ Photo; 117, HBJ/Alan S. Orling, Black Star; 118–119 (background), A. & J. Verkaik/The Stock Market; 118(inset), reprinted with permission from the University Corporation for Atmospheric Research, National Center for Atmospheric Research/National Science Foundation (HBJ Photo); 120(t), Ralph Wetmore, TSW/Chicago; 120–121, Tom Ives/The Stock Market; 121(c), Ralph Wetmore, TSW/Chicago; 121(r), Ralph Wetmore, TSW/Chicago; 122, A. & J. Verkaik/The Stock Market; 123(background), Everett C. Johnson/Leo de Wys, Inc.; 123(t), Roger M. Wakimoto; 123(ct), Roger M. Wakimoto; 123(c), Roger M. Wakimoto; 123(b), Roger M. Wakimoto; 124–125, A. & J. Verkaik/The Stock Market; 125, NOAA; 126–127, HBJ Photo; 142–143, HBJ/Britt Runion; 176, HBJ/Britt Runion; 196, HBJ/Larry Mayer, Black Star; 198, Allen Russell/ProFiles West; 199(t), Deborah Davis/PhotoEdit; 199(ct), Arthur Sirdofsky; 199(c), Allen Russell/ProFiles West; 199(b), Rubin Klass; 201, HBJ/Maria Paraskevas; 202(t), HBJ Photo; 202(b), HBJ Photo; 203(t), HBJ Photo; 203(cr), HBJ Photo; 203(b), HBJ Photo; 204, HBJ/Britt Runion; 246(l), Library of Congress; 246(r), Library of Congress; 247(tl), UPI Photo; 247(cl), copyright © 1990 *The Saturday Evening Post*/Indianapolis; 247(cr), photograph courtesy of The Supreme Court Historical Society, copyright The National Geographic Society; 247(br), Government of the District of Columbia; 262–263, HBJ/Maria Paraskevas; 264–265(c), Carlo Ontal; 264–265(b), HBJ/Britt Runion; 266, HBJ Photo; 274, HBJ Photo; 292(t), Harry Langdon Photography/Office of March Fong Eu; 292(b), State Bar of Arizona; 293(t), "Bread and Roses," traditional song from *Here's to the Women* by Hilda E. Wenner & Elizabeth Freilicher, copyright © 1987 Syracuse University Press; 293(b), Brown Brothers; 295(t), HBJ/Maria Paraskevas; 295(b), HBJ/Maria Paraskevas; 296(t), HBJ Photo; 296(b), HBJ Photo; 297(t), HBJ Photo; 297(cr), HBJ Photo; 297(b), HBJ Photo; 298–299, HBJ/Maria Paraskevas; 300, HBJ Photo; 302–303(background), HBJ Photo; 302–303, HBJ Photo; 332, HBJ Photo; 352(t), HBJ Photo; 352(b), Alec Frost; 354–355, HBJ/Maria Paraskevas; 356, HBJ Photo; 382, CBS; 383(t), HBJ Photo; 383(bl), HBJ/Erik Arnesen; 383(br), TRW, Inc.; 385, HBJ/Britt Runion; 386(t), HBJ Photo; 386(b), HBJ Photo; 387(t), HBJ Photo; 387(cr), HBJ Photo; 387(b), HBJ Photo; 388, HBJ/Maria Paraskevas; 408(background), Dick Dietrich/FPG; 408(inset), Jean Craighead George; 414–415, HBJ/Britt Runion; 417, Erich Hartmann/Magnum; 418, HBJ Photo; 422, HBJ Photo; 424, HBJ Photo; 428–429, HBJ Photo; 439, courtesy, Museum of Fine Arts, Boston; 440, Superstock; 444, HBJ Photo; 472, The Goldman Environmental Foundation; 473(t), HBJ/Mike Matthews; 473(bl), NASA; 473(br), HBJ Photo; 475, HBJ/Debi Harbin; 476(t), HBJ Photo; 476(b), HBJ Photo; 477(t), HBJ Photo; 477(cr), HBJ Photo; 477(b), HBJ Photo; 482–483, HBJ Photo; 486, HBJ Photo; 502, HBJ/Debi Harbin; 506(tl), TASS/Sovfoto; 506(tr), L. Howe/Photri; 506(cr), NASA/Photri; 506–507(b), NASA; 507(tl), Robert Brenner/PhotoEdit; 507(tr), NASA/Photri; 507(cl), NASA/Photri; 507(cr), NASA; 508–509, NASA; 509(inset), Ben Weaver; 510, NASA; 513, NASA; 514, NASA; 517, NASA; 518–519, NASA; 520, NASA; 523(background), NASA; 523(inset), NASA; 526, HBJ/Debi Harbin; 528–529, copyright © 1959 California Institute of Technology; 530, HBJ Photo; 546, Jill Paton Walsh; 549(t), NASA; 549(b), Historical Pictures Service; 552, HBJ/Maria Paraskevas; 553, HBJ/Maria Paraskevas; 555, HBJ/Maria Paraskevas; 556–557, HBJ/Debi Harbin; 560, HBJ/Maria Paraskevas; 561, HBJ/Maria Paraskevas; 565, HBJ/Maria Paraskevas; 569, HBJ/Maria Paraskevas; 572, Gail Denham from PP/FA; 581(t), Gail Denham from PP/FA; 581(b), Frank Whitney/The Image Bank; 585, Gail Denham from PP/FA; 586, Jay Freis/The Image Bank.

Illustration Credits

Key: (t) top, (b) bottom, (l) left, (c) center, (r) right.

Table of Contents Art

Abby Carter, 4 (tl), 6 (bl), 9 (tr), 12–13 (c); Regan Dunnick, 5 (br), 6–7 (c), 10 (tl), 12 (bl), 15 (tr); Cameron Eagle, 5 (tr), 7 (br), 8–9 (c), 12 (tl), 14 (bl); Jennifer Hewitson, 4 (bl), 7 (tr), 9 (br), 10–11 (c), 14 (tl); Tracy Sabin, 4–5 (c), 8 (tl), 10 (bl), 13 (tr), 15 (br); Rhonda Voo, 6 (tr), 8 (bl) 11 (tr), 13 (br), 14–15 (c).

Unit Opening Patterns

Tracy Sabin

Bookshelf Art

Alex Boies, 386–387; Gerry Bustamante, 110–111; Callie Butler, 18–19; David Diaz, 202–203; Armen Kojoyian, 296–297; Randy Verougstraete, 476–477.

Theme Opening Art

Alex Boies, 298–299, 478–479; Michael Bull, 204–205; Gerald Bustamante, 442–443; David Davis, 526–527; Todd Doney, 112–113; John Alfred Dorn, 20–21; Nathan Jarvis, 58–59; Dave Jonason, 328–329; Margaret Kasahara, 142–143; Mercedes McDonald, 388–389; Susan Nees, 228–229; Kenton Nelson, 502–503; Nancy Stahl, 176–177.

Theme Closing Art

Seymour Chwast, 197, 291; David Davis, 141, 353, 547; Regan Dunnick, 83, 413; Mark Frueh, 57, 441, 471; Tuko Fujisaki, 175, 327; Peter Horjus, 525; Edward Martinez, 261; Paul Meisel, 227; Walter Stuart; Lynn Tanaka, 105, 381; Roxana Villa, 501.

Connections Art

HBJ, 548–549.

Selection Art

Natalie Babbitt, 426–427; Barbara Bash, 444–455; Debra Becker (Computer Illustration), 117, 352, 546; Eric Beddows, 300, 301; Lloyd Bloom, 302–313; Dick Calkins, 504–505; Harvey Chan, 70–82, 166–174; Robert Chronister, 22–33; Floyd Cooper, 34–45; Normand Cousineau, 324–326; Lambert Davis, 274–290; David Diaz, 370–380; Marcel Durocher, 150–165; Katy Farmer, 314–323; Sheldon Greenberg, 248–260; Ronald Himler, 136–140; Pamela Johnson, 428–438; David F. Jue, 482–485; Oleana Kassian, 390–407; Jay Leach, 530–545; Gary Lippincott, 208–226; Jack Molloy, 266–273; Wendell Minor, 480–481; Kazue Mizumura, 330–331; Alex Murawski, 458–470; Michelle Nidenoff (Map), 208–209; Tomio Nitto, 178–195; Buster O'Connor (Backgrounds), 426–427; Peter Parnall, 409–412; Jerry Pinkney, 114–116; Goro Sasaki, 416–425; Gordon Sauve, 486–500; Marcia Sewall, 86–102, 356–367; Marc Simont, 332–351; Peter Sis, 144–149; Douglas Smith, 230–241; Michael Stiernagel, 68–69; Jeffrey Terreson, 126–135; Ian Watts, 60–67; Janet Wilson, 456–457.